The Civil War on
Pensacola Bay, 1861–1862

ALSO BY JOHN K. DRISCOLL
AND FROM MCFARLAND

*Rogue: A Biography of Civil War
General Justus McKinstry* (2006)

The Civil War on Pensacola Bay, 1861–1862

JOHN K. DRISCOLL

McFarland & Company, Inc., Publishers
Jefferson, North Carolina, and London

The present work is a reprint of the illustrated case bound edition of The Civil War on Pensacola Bay, 1861–1862, *first published in 2007 by McFarland.*

LIBRARY OF CONGRESS CATALOGUING-IN-PUBLICATION DATA

Driscoll, John K., 1935–
The Civil War on Pensacola Bay, 1861–1862 / John K. Driscoll.
p. cm.
Includes bibliographical references and index.
ISBN 9978-0-7864-7512-4
softcover : acid free paper ∞

1. Pensacola (Fla.)— History— Civil War, 1861–1865 — Naval operations.
2. Pensacola (Fla.)— History— Civil War, 1861–1865 — Campaigns.
3. Pensacola Bay (Fla.)— History, Naval —19th century.
4. Pensacola Bay (Fla.)— History, Military —19th century.
5. Fort Pickens (Fla.)— History —19th century.
6. United States. Navy — History — Civil War, 1861–1865.
7. United States. Army — History — Civil War, 1861–1865.
8. United States — History — Civil War, 1861–1865 — Naval operations.
9. United States — History — Civil War, 1861–1865 — Campaigns.
I. Title.
F319.P4D75   2013   973.7'59 — dc22   2007025262

BRITISH LIBRARY CATALOGUING DATA ARE AVAILABLE

© 2007 John K. Driscoll. All rights reserved

No part of this book may be reproduced or transmitted in any form or by any means, electronic or mechanical, including photocopying or recording, or by any information storage and retrieval system, without permission in writing from the publisher.

On the cover: *from top* Map of Pensacola Bay, 1862; USS *Powhatan*

Manufactured in the United States of America

*McFarland & Company, Inc., Publishers
Box 611, Jefferson, North Carolina 28640
www.mcfarlandpub.com*

Table of Contents

Preface 1

1. The Bay, the Yard, and the Forts 3
2. "To Use Whatever Means He Had" 20
3. "If Blood Is Shed, You Are Responsible" 33
4. "Pickens Is Not Worth One Drop of Blood" 50
5. "Too Much Dallying and Curtseying" 79
6. "Give the *Powhatan* to Captain Mercer" 106
7. "When the Arrow has Fled from the Bow" 125
8. "Fort Pickens Now Stood Alone" 137
9. "A More Innocent War Was Never Carried On" 159
10. "The Enemy Failed in All Objectives" 179
11. "A Signal Gun Fired at 10:00 A.M." 197
12. "Fort Pickens Stands to This Day" 206

Notes 213
Bibliography 223
Index 229

Preface

Pensacola Bay is formed off the coast of western Florida by Santa Rosa Island, a strip of barren white sand reaching forty miles off toward the east and lying up to a mile from the mainland. The bay forms a magnificent harbor offering protection to vessels from the storms of the Gulf of Mexico. Pensacola, on the shore of the bay, was one of the earliest settlements founded by Europeans in North America and by the 1860s was the largest community in the state. Florida, however, was the second least populated state in the Union, and Pensacola's growth never paralleled that of its two major neighbors to the west, Mobile and New Orleans. Pensacola did not have navigable rivers for access to the commerce of the interior and its railroad contact at the time with the outer world was barely functioning. As a result, Pensacola tended to be seen as a backwater far from the exciting events that were taking place throughout the rest of the nation.

Pensacola did have, though, that magnificent harbor. The Federal government had constructed four major fortifications to protect the bay against foreign incursion, and the United States Navy had constructed the only navy yard south of Norfolk for the support and supply of its squadrons operating in the Caribbean Sea, the Gulf of Mexico, and the southern Atlantic Ocean. It was upon this remote location far from everything in the North and South that the attention of the nation was focused in the months before the inauguration of Abraham Lincoln on March 4, 1861. It was at this remote location that the American Civil War might have started.

This work is not intended to be a history of everything that happened in Florida or on Pensacola Bay in the years between 1861 and 1865. It is the story of the events that took place before and early into the opening months of that conflict. It is the story of the people involved and how their personalities and attributes came into play as unforeseen and extraordinary events began to unfold before them.

Most of history is written about events that have taken place, and so these events are described afterward as if they were the logical result of a procession of certain events and actions. But that is not how history happens. History is a series of occurrences that are usually not foreseen, that take place without plan or oversight, and that have consequences that are impossible to predict while they are happening. That is how I have tried to approach the events that began on Pensacola Bay during the months before and early into the American Civil War. I have tried to contain my narrative to what the people involved saw and thought as it was happening, not as they reported it afterward. And that was hard to do at times when the only record is the written report of the event. But I have tried.

There is a wealth of information available to a writer willing to do the hard work involved in digging it out, but there is a critical lack of important information regarding life within the town of Pensacola and the villages of Warrington and Woolsey during the events described herein. Both villages were almost destroyed during the bombardments late in 1861, and the town of Pensacola was abandoned upon the withdrawal of the last of the Confederate forces early in 1862, so there is a void in the record of life within the civilian population.

It is impossible to approach or complete a work of any scope alone. There are many people and institutions to whom I want to offer my gratitude. The excellent institutions and repositories at the National Archives, the Library of Congress, the United States Army Military History Institute, the Department of the Navy, Naval Historical Center, the Pensacola Historical Society, the Gulf Islands National Seashore of the National Park Service, the Historical Society of Montgomery County, PA, and the staff at the John C. Pace Library, University of West Florida, were extremely helpful, as were the staff and resources of that jewel in the crown of my state, the State Historical Society of Wisconsin. My good friend, advisor, traveling companion, and research helper, Gaizka Usabel, took part in the long trip from Wisconsin to Pensacola Bay, and my editor, Sharon E. Heuer, worked diligently to make me look much better than I am. For special help with illustrations and doing research at the National Archives, I want to thank Ethan Bishop of Hanover, PA, and Martin Baldessari, of Washington, DC. And, throughout, my family has been supportive, enthusiastic, and there.

1

The Bay, the Yard, and the Forts

Rivers in the lower Appalachian Mountains flow across southern Alabama and western Florida to the Gulf of Mexico. Their waters carry rocks and stones which tumble and scrape together, grinding themselves into gravel and then into fine white sand. Where the rivers meet the gulf, that sand is churned and thrown back by wave action and tidal rhythm into barrier islands. Off the mouth of the Escambia River, one of these is Santa Rosa Island, a barren strip of sand up to a mile wide and some forty miles long. The waters of the Escambia River flow out to the gulf through a narrow passage between the western point of Santa Rosa Island and the eastern tip of Perdido Key. Santa Rosa Island forms an immense harbor at its western end and stretches eastward off the coast of the mainland as far as Chocktawhatchee Bay.

Early in time nomadic people had wandered into the region. They found a haven rich with sustenance from land and sea. In 1516 their descendants, Panzacola Indians, hid in the undergrowth on the mainland and watched in awe as a Spanish expedition under Don Diego Miruelo, and his nephew of the same name, sailed a galleon into the channel between the western point of Santa Rosa Island and the eastern tip of Perdido Key. The Miruelos entered the bay and mapped it but left nothing behind on their departure. Almost half a century later in 1559, a Spanish flotilla of thirteen vessels from Vera Cruz, Mexico, under the command of Tristan de Luna arrived in the region that de Luna named Bahia Santa Maria de Filipina. These first Europeans built a settlement on Santa Rosa Island which perished in a hurricane two years later. Spanish influence returned in 1598 under Admiral Andrés de Arriola who resettled the western point of Santa Rosa Island and, for defense against French raids from the west, constructed a small fort, San Carlos de Austria, atop the clay banks — *barrancas* in Spanish — that rose on the mainland forty feet above the entrance to the bay. From this elevated position, its few iron guns could bring under fire hostile vessels attempting to force an entrance to the bay through the channel between the western point of Santa Rosa Island and the eastern tip of Perdido Key. In 1722 a hurricane again devastated this small settlement on Santa Rosa Island which caused the survivors to relocate to a protected cove on the mainland at the mouth of a fresh water bayou eight miles to the east of the entrance channel. They named this new site Pensacola after the earlier people who had inhabited the region. The flags of Spain, France, and England flew over the hamlet and the bay until 1821 when Spain ceded the region to the United States. By then, with Andrew Jackson in residence as provisional territorial governor, Pensacola had become an American town.[1]

Pensacola Bay was a mariner's treasure, a vast harbor with deep waters in its broad roadstead that extended for miles along the shore of the mainland. The attraction of the bay, however, far surpassed the prospects of the small settlement on its shore. The soil of western Florida was poor and the Escambia River and its tributaries were shallow for much of their length. Unable to support regional agriculture and without navigable rivers for access to the commerce of the interior, Pensacola did not evolve much beyond the limited growth that lumbering and local politics could generate. In marked contrast, fifty miles to the west where the Alabama and Tombigbee rivers formed Mobile Bay, the city of Mobile developed the population and took on the role of a thriving commercial center and, 150 miles beyond that, New Orleans, upstream from the mouth of the Mississippi River, flourished in its role as the gateway to the central regions of the North American continent. It was the importance of these two commercial centers in the overall plan for national defense that gave Pensacola Bay significance. A hostile fleet seizing the bay would conquer little of strategic value but would gain that vast harbor to use as an anchorage from which to launch campaigns against the two major seaports to the west. The United States Navy had recently demonstrated to Congress that the outlet for the flow of commerce from the great central valley of the continent lay not at the mouth of the Mississippi River nor at Mobile Bay but, in fact, further to the east at the narrow passage between Cuba and Key West. Foreign vessels blocking the Straits of Florida there would effectively close the commerce of the central regions of the nation. Pensacola Bay could provide a natural anchorage from which such a hostile fleet might operate. It was the mission of the United States Army to plan and build the fortifications and develop the strategies to prevent such a seizure of Pensacola Bay. In 1822 Lieutenant Colonel Joseph G. Totten of the United States Army Corps of Engineers wrote to Major James Kearney at Mobile describing the need for fortifications to protect Pensacola Bay from the danger of foreign incursion.[2]

Almost immediately upon the acquisition of the territory, the government at Washington began committing Federal spending for improvements at Pensacola Bay. Congress appropriated funds for the construction of a lighthouse to mark the entrance to the bay and to guide vessels into the harbor. Sited on the clay banks on the mainland where the old Spanish fort San Carlos de Austria had stood, this first lighthouse was a low wooden structure. Trees on Santa Rosa Island often shielded its lamp from vessels in the gulf. In March, 1859, Congress appropriated funds for a grand tower standing 171 feet above the clay banks with a lantern rotated by a clockwork mechanism and visible up to twenty miles at sea. With the new lighthouse, a series of navigational beacons along the shore of the mainland and of Perdido Key marked the course of the channel into the bay.[3]

While Lieutenant Colonel Totten and the Army's Corps of Engineers were planning the defenses of Pensacola Bay, the United States Navy was in the process of determining where on the gulf coast it should locate a navy yard. On November 4, 1825, a commission consisting of Captains Lewis Warrington, William Bainbridge, and James Biddle selected a site on Pensacola Bay "northward and eastward of Tartar's Point," some two miles along the shore of the mainland from the entrance to the bay. In April of the following year, Captain Warrington raised his pennant there as commodore of the West Indies Squadron and commandant of the Pensacola Navy Yard. In October of the year, Captain Melanchthon T. Woolsey began overseeing construction of the first buildings at the navy yard using slave labor hired from local masters. In an extraordinary action made necessary by the sparse population and the scarcity of skilled craftsmen in the locality, the navy recruited joiners, masons, coopers, bakers, gunsmiths, ironworkers, mechanics, sail makers, and shipwrights from cities in the North and offered to provide housing if they would relocate to Pensacola Bay. Captain Woolsey set forth the conditions he established to govern these residences in the villages of Warrington, northwest of the yard, and Woolsey, northeast of the yard, "Should any determine to build, I shall bind them to keep orderly houses and, on failure, to forfeit their privilege." The Pensacola Navy Yard became the major facility for the service and

Pensacola Bay lighthouse rises 171 feet above the clay bank on which Fort Barrancas stands (photograph by the author).

support of the squadrons of the United States Navy operating in the Gulf of Mexico, the Caribbean Sea, and the southern Atlantic Ocean. It and the navy yard at Gosport, near Norfolk, Virginia, were the only navy yards in the southern United States. A brick wall fourteen feet high closed off the yard's eighty acre tract from Warrington and Woolsey. On its southwestern and southeastern sides, the yard was open to the waters of Pensacola Bay. Thirteen brick homes two stories high with columned porticoes provided comfortable quarters for the yard's commissioned officers. By the final days of 1860 the yard's work force consisted of more than a hundred civilian employees residing in Warrington and Woolsey and eighty ordinary seamen stationed at the yard who were augmented by eighty slaves hired locally for menial work. A detachment of thirty-eight United States Marines and sixteen civilian watchmen provided security. The yard itself contained a long ship house, several storehouses, a blacksmith shop, an iron foundry capable of casting cannon balls in every standard size, a machine shop, a bakery, and four masonry cisterns each with the capacity of holding 300,000 gallons of fresh water. The marine barracks and the yard's hospital were

Sketch of Warrington, Florida, built for housing skilled tradesmen hired in the north to work at the navy yard (Pensacola Historical Society).

located close outside the walls. The pride of the yard was a massive floating dry dock that had cost the Federal government a million dollars to construct. Located more than a mile from the walls for safety was a masonry magazine containing several hundred kegs of gunpowder. The capabilities of the Pensacola Navy Yard were so extensive that during 1859 the steam sloops U.S.S. *Pensacola* and U.S.S. *Seminole* were built and launched at the yard.[4]

    The United States Army was given the responsibility for planning the defense of Pensacola Bay. In an 1825 program statement, Brigadier General Simon Bernard in his report to Major General Alexander Macomb, commanding the United States Army, identified a condition that would govern the design and construction of the fortifications to be built on the bay. "[O]wing to the nature of the sandy country surrounding Pensacola," he wrote, "the population in that quarter shall never be able to afford alone competent means to defend the navy-yard against sudden attack.... The strength of those defensive works must be calculated to allow the forces of the country the time necessary to reach Pensacola and relieve the defenders of the works." The resulting structures, therefore, would have to be large, strong, and mutually supporting. The layout and characteristics of these fortifications were dictated by land and water. The western outlet from Pensacola Bay lay in its southwestern corner. Vessels entering the bay had to pass between the western point of Santa Rosa Island and the eastern tip of Perdido Key on a northern course in the direction of the clay banks on the mainland where the fort San Carlos de Austria had once stood and where the new lighthouse would rise. The channel turned to the east as it rounded the point of

Sketch of the Pensacola Navy Yard with the floating dry dock in the lower center (Pensacola Historical Society).

Santa Rosa Island, skirting the island's bay shore before veering off in the direction of the navy yard and the town. For three miles, vessels entering or leaving Pensacola Bay would be within range of guns sited on Santa Rosa Island, Perdido Key, and the clay banks on the mainland. Army engineers drew up plans for the necessary works.[5]

Fort Pickens on Santa Rosa Island would be the focus of the program. Designed by General Bernard and named for Revolutionary War Brigadier General Andrew Pickens of South Carolina, it was a pentagonal structure with its longest face, 230 yards from corner to corner, toward the east to oppose a hostile force landing on the gulf shore of the island, out of range of its guns, and approaching from the land side. The four other faces were on the water's edge to the south, southwest, northwest, and northeast and were designed to mount heavy guns in casemates and atop the walls *en barbette*. The guns of these four faces could bring massed fire to bear on hostile vessels approaching and entering the channel from the gulf and attempting to make the close turn to the east. The fort's south and northeast faces were 155 yards in length, the southwest and northwest faces 180 yards in length, and the perimeter of the fort was 900 yards. The walls stood forty feet above the bottom of a dry moat. At each of the five corners, bastions extended from the walls from which cannon fire could be thrown into the flanks of a hostile force gathering in the moat for an assault on the walls. The parade ground was eight acres in extent, entirely within the walls, which were up to thirteen feet thick. Fort Pickens was a massive structure designed to hold more than 200 sea coast howitzers and cannon manned by a wartime garrison of 1,200 men.[6]

The guns of Fort Pickens were intended to work with those of Fort McRee, designed by Lieutenant Colonel Totten and named for Colonel William McRee of the army engineers and a hero of the War of 1812. Fort McRee would be built across the entrance channel from Fort Pickens on an extension of Perdido Key known as Foster's Bank. Fort McRee was an unusual structure, a rectangle rounded by stair towers at each end and folded back on itself at an angle so that the guns of its right face could bring under fire vessels approaching the entrance to the bay and those of its left face could join the guns of Fort Pickens in firing upon vessels attempting to pass through the entrance channel and into the bay. Fort McRee was designed to mount two tiers of heavy guns in each of its large casemates, the second tier sitting above the first on wooden platforms. The perimeter of the fort was 300 yards and its armament was to be 128 sea coast howitzers and cannon including those mounted atop the walls *en barbette*, manned by a wartime garrison of 500 men. The distance between the guns of Fort McRee and those of Fort Pickens across the channel was 2,100 yards, about a mile and a quarter.[7]

On the site of the old Spanish fort, Lieutenant Colonel Totten designed Fort Barrancas to sit atop the high clay banks on the mainland with its main armament bearing directly on the entrance channel from the gulf. This fort was a four-sided polygon with faces between 100 and 200 feet in length for a circumference of 600 feet. The walls were twenty feet high and four feet thick and separated from a fortified counterscarp by a dry moat. A drawbridge connected a sally port in the north face with the counterscarp. At the base of the height and connected to the fort by a defended tunnel a water battery constructed on the original Spanish foundations was planned to send cannon balls skimming along the surface of the entrance channel to join plunging fire from the guns on the height. Fort Barrancas would mount thirty-three cannon *en barbette* and eight heavy sea coast howitzers manned by a

The entrance channel to Pensacola Bay from Fort Barrancas. Santa Rosa Island and Fort Pickens are to the left, Perdido Key and former Fort McRee to the right (photograph by the author).

wartime garrison of 350 men. The distance from Fort Barrancas to the entrance channel between Forts Pickens and McRee was 2,800 yards, about a mile and a half. To protect Fort Barrancas against land attack from the rear and to shelter the navy yard and the villages of Warrington and Woolsey to the east, Advanced Redoubt was planned a short distance inland from Fort Barrancas. Sixteen 32-pounder cannon were intended as armament for the redoubt which was not completed due to lack of Congressional appropriations. The size of the intended wartime garrison of the redoubt was never established.[8]

The plans developed by the United States Army Corps of Engineers for the defense of Pensacola Bay were impressive. They involved the construction of extensive fortifications with interlocking fields of fire from more than 300 heavy guns which could wreak havoc against the wooden hulls of a hostile fleet of sailing vessels attempting to force the narrow entrance to Pensacola Bay. The plans were based upon several assumptions: that the threat would come from a foreign force; that the force would consist of a fleet of wooden sailing ships approaching from out in the gulf whose maneuvering would be subject to the vagaries of wind and tide; that the defenders would have the time necessary to assemble more than 2,000 trained artillerists to man the guns of the forts; and that the garrisons at Fort Pickens on Santa Rosa Island and at Fort McRee on Perdido Key could be supplied, provisioned, and reinforced by boats from the mainland in the midst of the hostilities. The strategic reasoning of the Corps of Engineers at the time was fixed on the belief that the defense of American coastal harbors could be achieved by means of large masonry forts. This had been proven resoundingly at Baltimore, Maryland, during the War of 1812 when the garrison at Fort McHenry had gallantly held out against the wooden-hulled vessels of an English sailing fleet, substantiating the corps in its thinking and incidentally giving the country its national anthem. The continuing application of this reasoning resulted in the construction of a series of large masonry forts at the principal harbors along the Atlantic seaboard and the coast of the Gulf of Mexico. Forts Pickens, McRee, and Barrancas were examples of the application of that reasoning.

Construction of the Pensacola forts began in 1829 under the supervision of Captain William H. Chase of the army's Corps of Engineers. Chase was born in Massachusetts in 1789 and had graduated from the United States Military Academy at West Point in 1815. After duty at Fort Niagara, New York, and at the forts below New Orleans, Louisiana, Captain Chase reported to Pensacola with more than a decade's experience supervising the construction of major fortifications. Because of the lack of stone in the region, Chase intended to use bricks fired from local clay for the construction of the forts. Nearby brickyards came into competition under Chase's demanding standards and supplied the masonry for the forts and for much of the navy yard. The resulting infusion of Federal money into Pensacola's economy from Chase's engineering projects brought him to prominence in the community with the result that, in addition to his duties as the supervising engineer in charge of the army's works, he became involved in banking and later in land speculation and real estate development. In 1831, Chase was one of the eight stockholders in the new Bank of Pensacola, the oldest chartered bank in Florida, and four years later he was president of the board of directors of the proposed Alabama & Florida Railroad. Fort Pickens was completed in 1834. On October 25 of that year, Company H, 2nd United States Artillery, arrived to serve as its initial garrison. Fort McRee was completed in 1837; Fort Barrancas in 1839. The forts on Pensacola Bay were not designed to provide living quarters for the troops of their garrisons during times of peace: there was no reason for soldiers to occupy the barren casemates at Fort Pickens and Fort McRee which were located several miles by water from their sources of communications, supply, and subsistence on the mainland. Wooden barracks to house the troops were built on the mainland close to Fort Barrancas but these fell into disrepair and were demolished. In 1847, ground was broken east of Fort Barrancas and construction of Barrancas Barracks was begun to provide permanent quarters for the men of the garrison. Thereafter Forts Pickens, McRee, and the partially constructed Advanced Redoubt remained unoccupied with the exception of an ordnance sergeant and some harbor pilots living in the casemates of Fort Pickens and an ordnance sergeant and his wife living in Fort McRee. Fort Barrancas hosted working parties of troops from nearby Barrancas Barracks and, on occasion, its batteries were used for gunnery practice but, to all intents, from the end of the war with Mexico in 1848, the forts on Pensacola Bay were unmanned.[9]

A Northerner by birth, Captain William H. Chase became a Pensacolan by choice. When he was ordered to West Point to take command of the United States Military Academy on April 18, 1856, Chase decided instead to resign his commission in the army and to devote himself thereafter to banking, railroad promotion, and real estate development. His future would be at his home and among his friends and his many financial endeavors on the shores of Pensacola Bay.[10]

When the year 1861 began, Florida's population was 144,000, half of which were slaves. The state had the lowest population of any of the thirty-three states in the Union with the exception of recently admitted and far distant Oregon. Only eight of Florida's cities held more than 1,600 souls and less than 15,000 of its white male population were of voting age. When admitted to the Union in 1845, Florida's population had been less that that required by Federal law for the transition from territorial status to statehood. Congress permitted Florida's admission under a program then in place through which one free territory and one slave territory were granted statehood at about the same time in order to maintain an equilibrium of representation in Congress. When Iowa Territory sought admission as a free state, having fulfilled all the requirements including achieving the necessary population, there was no other territory remaining in the South except Florida which was then admitted as a slave state although significantly lacking in population. In 1861 Pensacola was Florida's largest town with a population of 2,876 people of whom 1,789 were free whites. Lumbering was Pensacola's primary

Colonel William C. Chase, the capable engineer who built the forts on Pensacola Bay was not the soldier needed to capture them (Special Collections, John C. Pace Library, University of West Florida).

Barrancas Barracks, built to house the garrisons of the forts in peacetime (Pensacola Historical Society).

industry based on the long leaf pine and live oaks which grew in abundance along the shores of the bay. The Alabama & Florida Railroad, under William H. Chase's direction, was at Pollard, Alabama, just over the state line to the north. Connections were made there to Montgomery, north and to the east, and to Mobile, south and to the west, but the primary means of communication and commerce between Pensacola and the outer world at the time was by water. Pensacola was the region's principal port.[11]

There was tension at Pensacola as the new decade opened. On November 4, 1860, Abraham Lincoln of Illinois, the candidate of the new Republican party, had been elected and would take office as the sixteenth president of the United States on March 4. Reacting with dread to the effect "Black Republicanism" could have on the Southern way of life with its dependence on slavery, the governors of the states of the Deep South corresponded and called for commissions to convene at their state capitals for consultation on the course of action that each state should follow. Not waiting for her sister states, South Carolina seceded from the Union on December 20, 1860, and declared herself a sovereign entity. The Florida Assembly met in its regular session at Tallahassee on November 20 and proposed a state convention to consider its own course. Governor Madison S. Perry followed this with a proclamation on November 30 calling for the election of delegates to meet at the state capital on January 3. Throughout Florida, political passions were running high.[12]

Commodore James Armstrong had assumed command at the Pensacola Navy Yard on October 30, 1860, two months before. Armstrong was sixty-seven years old and had been an officer in the United States Navy since 1809. Previous to his assignment to Pensacola he had commanded the navy's East Indies Squadron in the far Pacific. Armstrong was a sick man suffering from chronic diarrhea and liver problems. He had protested the order sending him to the Florida station on his return from Hong Kong, claiming he was too old and feeble to be sent to that climate and expressing his preference that he be allowed to live out his final days at his home near Boston but his protest and his wish were ignored by the Navy Department. The elderly Armstrong easily became confused, sometimes forgetting orders he had given or decisions he had made. He relied heavily upon his two direct subordinates for guidance and support in governing the operations of the navy yard. Commander Ebenezer Farrand was the yard's executive officer. A Northerner by birth with thirty-eight years service in the navy, Farrand was Armstrong's second in command. Lieutenant Francis T. Renshaw, the yard's first lieutenant, also a Northerner by birth with thirty-two years service in the navy, directed the day-to-day work of the yard. Farrand

Commodore James Armstrong, U.S. Navy, surrendered the Pensacola Navy Yard to Southern forces in January 1861 (Naval Historical Center, Washington, D.C.).

and Renshaw were brothers-in-law, married to Southern sisters. Each considered himself, while still on active duty as a commissioned officer in the United States Navy, a Southerner first. Farrand was an outspoken advocate of secession. Renshaw favored secession and usually followed Farrand's lead. Farrand, Renshaw, and two other officers at the yard, Naval Storekeeper Samuel Z. Gonzales and Master Joiner William H. Fell, maintained close contact with each other and with secessionist groups eight miles up the shore of the mainland at Pensacola, at the state capital at Tallahassee, and at Montgomery, Alabama.[13]

As the new year opened, there was business as usual at the navy yard. The fastest steamer in the fleet, U.S.S. *Fulton*, was drawn up on the ways for repairs. *Fulton* had suffered severe damage to her bow when run aground on Santa Rosa Island the previous autumn and was undergoing a major overhaul. She had been placed out of commission, her guns taken ashore, and her officers and crew transferred while her rebuilding took place. Early in December, U.S.S. *Supply,* a sailing storeship, arrived with requisitions for coal, provisions, and munitions for the vessels of the Home Squadron operating off Vera Cruz, Mexico. The Pensacola Navy Yard was the base of supply for the squadron off Mexico which was there observing British, French, and Spanish warships threatening intervention in order to force the Juárez government of Mexico to honor its foreign debts. By the first of the year *Supply* had off-loaded several hundred tons of the sand she carried as ballast and had taken on between 300 and 400 tons of coal prior to loading provisions and munitions. Her captain was Lieutenant Commander Henry Walke, a Virginian, an officer with thirty-nine years service in the navy. Commodore Armstrong had received telegraphic instructions from the Navy Department at Washington to expedite the return of *Supply* to the Home Squadron.

Responding through Commander Farrand, Armstrong telegraphed that he would dispatch the vessel as soon as coaling was completed and provisions and munitions could be loaded aboard. At the middle of December the screw steamer U.S.S. *Crusader,* Captain Tunis A.M. Craven, hove into sight and was warped into the dry dock for repairs to her hull. The following day the screw steamer U.S.S. *Wyandotte*, Lieutenant Commanding Otway H. Berryman, arrived from her station off the southern coast of Cuba for repairs to her stack and engine. *Wyandotte* anchored off the navy yard wharf while waiting for the repairs to *Crusader* to be completed.[14]

On the day *Supply* had made fast to the navy yard wharf, Lieutenant Commander Walke granted shore leave to a portion of her 171 man crew, all of whom had been aboard ship and at sea for nearly a year. As the sailors made their way down the gangplank, there was some tension and, after a few individual exchanges, loyal seamen of the sailing vessel and secessionist members of the navy yard's work force traded angry shouts. A fight broke out and men were injured on both sides. Walke immediately canceled shore leave for the crew of *Supply.* Navy Lieutenant John Irwin, ashore with his family in Warrington, reported a high level of excitement among the civilian workers at the yard with open statements in support of Florida's secession from the Union being heard but, aside from the fight between the crew of *Supply* and the yard workers, Irwin reported no evidence of agitation or refusal to obey orders. One major reason for discontent among the workers at the yard was the fact that navy paymasters had not visited Pensacola in months. Banks at Pensacola and as far away as Mobile were refusing to extend credit on Federal vouchers and as a result the yard workers had not been paid their wages. Some who lived hand-to-mouth were actually hungry. Commodore Armstrong had telegraphed the Navy Department at Washington regarding the issue but had received no response. Eventually he took matters into his own hands and ordered the naval storekeeper to issue provisions to needy workers from the yard's stores against future payment. Captain Josiah Watson, commanding the marine detachment at the yard, telegraphed Major William B. Slack, quartermaster at Headquarters, Marine Corps, at Washington, "I send you a note that I received this morning from Mr. Knapp, the ration contractor. You will oblige me with your advice. We can get nothing on credit; cash on delivery. The government credit is very low at this point. Should you direct me to purchase, send the coin." Just as the needy civilian workers were having to do, the marines were forced to draw provisions from navy yard's stores against future appropriations. Even the loading of *Supply* was delayed by the lack of cash: slaves hired for off-loading sand and on-loading coal were withdrawn by their owners who had not been paid in two months. With his good intentions directed toward the well-being of his unpaid and needy workers, Commodore Armstrong was distracted and unable to discern that there was a serious political undertow having to do with the possibility of Florida's secession from the Union fomenting turmoil at the Pensacola Navy Yard. This was kept from his attention by his two subordinates, Farrand and Renshaw.[15]

The United States Army garrison at Pensacola Bay in January, 1861, consisted of Company G, 1st United States Artillery, under the command of Major John H. Winder. Winder had taken ill in May and was on an extended leave as was the company's second officer, First Lieutenant Asher B. Eddy. In their absence, command of Company G's forty-three artillerymen, two musicians, two artificers, and three ordnance sergeants rested with the remaining officers, First Lieutenant Adam J. Slemmer and Second Lieutenant Jeremiah H.

Left: 1st Lieutenant Adam J. Slemmer, U.S. Army, the senior officer commanding Fort Pickens on Pensacola Bay, in a *Harper's Weekly* woodcut. Right: 2nd Lieutenant Jeremiah H. Gilman, U.S. Army, the junior officer commanding Fort Pickens on Pensacola Bay, in a *Harper's Weekly* woodcut (both photographs from *Harper's Weekly*).

Gilman. Lieutenant Adam Slemmer was thirty-three years old, a native of Pennsylvania and a graduate of West Point, class of 1850. He had served with the 1st Artillery in California and in Florida and held the post of assistant professor of geology, history, and ethics at the military academy. After a year with his regiment at Fort Moultrie at Charleston, South Carolina, Slemmer had reported to Barrancas Barracks late in 1860. Slemmer was a short man; a correspondent with the *New York Herald* described him as "small and insignificant," with "narrow-rimmed spectacles, a moustache and a full beard that covered his face except a small area beneath his mouth, making him look more like a God-fearing school teacher" than a regular army artillery officer. Slemmer was married. His wife, Carrie, and their three-year-old son, Bertie, lived in the officers quarters east of Barrancas Barracks. Carrie Slemmer was a woman of twenty who considered herself quite a belle. Army gossip held that the Slemmers had requested a transfer from Fort Moultrie to Barrancas Barracks after a relationship developed between Carrie Slemmer and another officer there. Still, she and Adam, whom she called "Addy," remained close. On their fourth wedding anniversary in August, 1860, Slemmer presented her with a saddle horse to ride for entertainment. Lieutenant Jeremiah Gilman was thirty years old, a native of Maine. He had graduated from West Point, class of 1856. After service on the Texas frontier and garrison duty at Fort Adams, Rhode Island, Gilman was assigned to duty at Barrancas Barracks in 1858, preceding Slemmer by two years. Gilman was a robust man, much larger than Slemmer, with a flowing beard. He described his duties as the junior officer at Barrancas Barracks claiming "by virtue of that high rank, I was also the post treasurer, post quartermaster, post commissary, and post adjutant." Gilman and his wife, Mary, lived in the officers quarters with the Slemmers. At this time, the Gilmans did not have children.[16]

Lieutenants Slemmer and Gilman were aware of the political turmoil in the state and the nation as the new decade opened. They were in daily contact with the naval officers stationed at the yard and aboard the vessels in the harbor and with their civilian contemporaries in Warrington, Woolsey, and Pensacola. The principal topic of the day was the secession of South Carolina and the potential that the other states of the Deep South might follow her lead. The two officers had already heard rumors that citizens of Florida and Alabama might be planning moves against the forts on Pensacola Bay. The editor of the *St. Augustine Examiner* wrote on December 29 that the new year would witness "the onset of the Irrepressible Conflict" which would be a challenge, he assured his readers, that Southerners would meet "with stout hearts and nerves!" The *Examiner* reported an unusually large turnout at the mid–November regional muster of the Florida state militia brigade as evidence of the developing military ardor among the young men of Florida. Weeks earlier the *Fernandina East Floridian* carried as its masthead what its editor referred to as the popular program of the day: "The Secession of the State of Florida! The Dissolution of the Union! The Formation of a Southern Confederacy!" What brought the issue close and made it personal for the two officers was the report that their regimental brother-in-arms, Major Robert Anderson, with Companies E and H of their regiment, the 1st Artillery, at Charleston, South Carolina, had moved his command from Fort Moultrie on the mainland to unoccupied, and yet-to-be-completed, Fort Sumter on a man-made island at the mouth of Charleston Harbor. Slemmer and Gilman knew the officers and had served with the men of Anderson's command. Slemmer had been stationed at Fort Moultrie for a year and had only transferred to Pensacola Bay a few months before. He had not served under Anderson who had assumed command at Fort Moultrie about the time Slemmer left. Both officers at Barrancas Barracks understood the seriousness of Anderson's move and they followed the telegraph updates in the local press with deepening interest. Together they discussed the events taking place around them and they looked for guidance from the War Department at Washington as to what their own response should be to what was developing into a clearly unprecedented situation. Anderson's action, on the night of the day after Christmas, had brought a storm of protest from Governor Francis W. Pickens of South Carolina and a demand for explanations from Secretary of War John B. Floyd at Washington. Anderson replied he had heard rumors that state forces planned to seize his position on the mainland. Fort Moultrie was basically a barracks and a long parapet facing seaward, and open to the rear and flanks. Anderson declared he would not have surrendered the post without a fight and in order to avoid such a calamity had moved his command, with its dependents and servants, out to Fort Sumter. In his report to the War Department Anderson admitted that the issue before him had merely been deferred: he had been able to carry out to Fort Sumter no more than four months provisions for his garrison and whether further supply and provisioning from the mainland would be available to him was yet to be seen. As if to substantiate Anderson's move, the following day, Thursday, December 27, South Carolina state forces occupied Charleston's Federal Arsenal and, as Anderson reported to the adjutant general at Washington, began the construction of batteries at key points around the harbor, the guns all bearing on Fort Sumter. Slemmer and Gilman felt the political pressures rising in the nation as they came to bear on their own situation and that of Anderson. The garrisons at Pensacola Bay and at Charleston Harbor, and one company of artillery at Key West, were the only Federal forces of any significance along the Atlantic seaboard and the Gulf of Mexico. South of Fortress Monroe near Norfolk, Virginia, all other Federal forts were unoccupied or staffed by caretaker compliments of one or two ordnance sergeants. The two small garrisons at Pensacola Bay and at Charleston Harbor were about to be thrust into the focus of the attention of most of the people of the nation, North and South.[17]

At the nation's capital, President James Buchanan was serving out the final four months of his administration. A bachelor of sixty-nine, the Pennsylvanian was a conscientious politician but he was evasive and irresolute in the face of looming disunion. Buchanan had announced that he was powerless to oppose the secession of South Carolina. No state had the right under the Constitution to secede from the Union, he had declared, but were one to do so, as South Carolina had just done, he had no power under the Constitution to bring that state back by force of arms. Congress, he declared as he bypassed the responsibility of his oath of office, was the only tribunal with the power to meet the national exigency. Rather than initiate any action on his own, Buchanan suggested, "Time is a great conservative power. Let us pause at this momentous point and afford the people, both North and South, an opportunity for reflection." Senator William Seward of New York, who would carry the portfolio of secretary of state in the forthcoming Lincoln administration, said of Buchanan's reasoning at this time, "It shows conclusively that it is the duty of the President to execute the laws — unless somebody opposes him; and that no state has the right to go out of the Union — unless it wants to." Instead of addressing the unprecedented threat to the continuity of the union of the states that he was sworn to preserve and protect, Buchanan's efforts through the coming months would be devoted to avoiding a confrontation between Federal authorities and secessionist leaders in the South until he could hand the responsibility for the affairs of the nation to Abraham Lincoln on Monday, March 4, 1861, three months off. Unfortunately for the passive chief executive, Buchanan's cabinet was in turmoil as the new year commenced. Lewis Cass of Michigan, aged, revered, and feeble, had resigned as secretary of state on December 12 and had been replaced by Jeremiah Black of Pennsylvania, formerly the attorney general. Black's position was taken by Edward M.

Major Robert Anderson, U.S. Army, quiet and loyal, had to surrender Fort Sumter to Confederate forces in April 1861 (U.S. Army Military History Institute, Carlisle, Pennsylvania.).

Stanton, originally of Ohio. Howell Cobb of Georgia resigned as secretary of the treasury on December 8 and was replaced by Phillip F. Thomas of Maryland. Jacob M. Thompson of Mississippi would resign as secretary of the interior on January 9 and would not be replaced. Secretary of War John B. Floyd of Virginia resigned on December 29 and his position was taken by Judge Joseph Holt of Kentucky. Holt's former position of postmaster general would be taken by Horatio King of Maine on February 12. The one consistent portfolio through all this shuffling in the cabinet was that of Secretary of the Navy Isaac Toucey of Connecticut, a close friend of President Buchanan's. The moves within the cabinet came from several causes: age in the case of Cass, charges of misuse of Indian Trust funds in the case of Floyd, and strong secessionist positions in the cases of Cobb and Thompson. The overall effect was the replacement of a cabinet in which the majority of the members had favored secession and the South with a cabinet in which the majority of the members now favored union and the North.[18]

On December 12, General-in-Chief Winfield Scott, who had moved army headquarters from Washington to New York City to get away from presidents, secretaries of war, and other bothersome officials, was called to the capital to advise Buchanan. In spite of his self-imposed exile, Scott was smarting under what he considered neglect by the president

President James Buchanan and his cabinet. Buchanan hoped to prevent hostilities between North and South until he could turn the government over to Abraham Lincoln on March 4, 1861 (Library of Congress).

and the secretary of war but the old soldier and patriot came when his nation called. A Virginian by birth, Scott was seventy-five years old, a veteran of every war in which the nation had taken part since the War of 1812. He liked to brag that he was a year older than the Constitution he was sworn to uphold and defend. Scott was heavy, gouty, and sick when summoned from New York and had to be boosted into his railroad car for the journey south. Regardless of age and infirmity, Winfield Scott was considered the nation's foremost soldier. On December 15, Buchanan, the commander-in-chief, and Scott, the general-in-chief, met at the executive mansion at Washington to discuss the situation developing in the Deep South. Scott recommended reinforcing Fort Moultrie at Charleston, where Major Anderson was then in command, and garrisoning then-unoccupied Fort Sumter. Scott had urged Secretary of War Floyd in a meeting two days earlier to reinforce the Charleston and Pensacola forts and those at Mobile and below New Orleans on the Mississippi River. In neither session did the general-in-chief suggest to the president or the secretary of war where the troops for these reinforcements were to be found. The United States Army, as the new year was about to open, numbered 15,000 officers and men and these were almost totally committed to posts on the western frontier. To reduce garrisons at any of the western posts in order to reinforce eastern forts would imperil the inhabitants of the scattered western settlements. In the East, there were fewer than 1,000 officers and men available and these were committed to posts along the northern and southern borders and along the Atlantic coastline. President Buchanan, listening to General Scott, pondered his alternatives and confirmed his decision to pass the question of how to deal with the issue of the secession of South Carolina to Congress, and then to act only on its determinations. General Scott, however, with President Buchanan's tepid concurrence, did put in motion a series of actions to send men and provisions to Major Anderson at Fort Sumter. On January 2, 1861, he directed the army's quartermaster general to charter a commercial ocean transport at New York to make the effort. The side-wheel steamer *Star of the West* was brought under contract and made ready for the attempt. Originally, President Buchanan had asked Secretary of the Navy Toucey for the use of the navy's steam sloop of war U.S.S. *Brooklyn* for the mission but General Scott had recommended that a commercial vessel might seem less challenging to the recently-seceded leadership of South Carolina. Buchanan was most desirous that the attempt not provoke a confrontation and Scott had suggested the expedition might retain a cloak of secrecy if conducted by a commercial transport rather than a ship of war. *Star of the West* sailed from New York harbor on January 5 with 200 army recruits and a cargo of commissary provisions for Anderson's garrison.[19]

Turning his attention from Fort Sumter to Fort Pickens, Scott ordered his aide, Lieutenant Colonel George W. Lay, to write to Slemmer on January 3. Slemmer was directed to do the utmost in his power to prevent the seizure of the forts on Pensacola Bay. There was nothing in the communication to suggest that Slemmer could expect any assistance beyond what he had available within his small command. In an example of the lack of coordination that existed between the War Department and the Navy Department at the time, Lay's message suggested that Slemmer begin by "consulting with the commander of the navy yard, who will probably have received instructions to co-operate with you." That same day, Secretary of the Navy Toucey wrote to Commodore Armstrong directing him to be vigilant to protect the public property under his charge. Toucey ended his message with, "The commanding officer at the Fort has been instructed to consult with you, and you will cooperate with him." In both instances, the orders were sent overland by mail to Pensacola instead of being sent more rapidly by telegraph. On January 5, acting independently of the War Department and without informing the president, Secretary Toucey sent a telegraphic cipher ordering Captain James Glynn at Portsmouth, New Hampshire, to proceed in the sailing sloop U.S.S. *Macedonian* to Pensacola, there to report to the commodore at the navy yard and to assist in the protection of the public property under his charge.[20]

That same day at Washington Florida Senators David L. Yulee and Stephen R. Mallory requested the new secretary of war, Joseph Holt, to provide information to them on the strength of Federal garrisons in Florida and the quantities and types of munitions in the forts and arsenals within the state. Holt, who was Yulee's brother-in-law, responded that the interests of the service forbade that the information requested be made public at that time. Joseph Holt was showing himself to be quite a different secretary of war than his predecessor, John B. Floyd. That evening at Washington senators from states of the Deep South — Florida, Georgia, Alabama, Mississippi, Arkansas, and Texas — met in secret caucus and resolved that each of their states, as soon as possible, should secede from the Union and join South Carolina. Provisions were discussed for organizing a confederation of the seceded states in a convention that would meet at Montgomery, Alabama, in mid–February. And "in view of the hostile legislation that is threatened against the seceding States, and which may be consummated before the fourth day of March, we ask instructions whether the delegates are to remain in Congress until that date for the purpose of defeating such legislation." Senator Mallory telegraphed his friend and business associate, Joseph Finnegan, at Tallahassee: "The immediately important thing to be done is the occupation of the forts and arsenals in Florida. The naval station and forts at Pensacola are first in consequence." Yulee advised that the forces necessary to seize the Federal facilities would probably have to come from other states because of the sparse population of western Florida. He wrote that he had discussed this with Georgia's Senator Robert Toombs who suggested Georgia's Governor Joseph Brown might provide state troops if the Florida convention, which was scheduled to meet in February, would so request. Yulee ended his message, "Lose no time about the navy-yard and the forts at Pensacola."[21]

2

"To Use Whatever Means He Had"

At the Pensacola Navy Yard *Crusader* was towed from the dry dock on Thursday, January 3. She anchored off the wharf where she took on fresh water, provisions, and munitions from lighters and then cleared for Mobile at the end of the week. *Wyandotte* was hauled into the dock and her repairs were begun. On Friday, January 4, Paymaster Lewis Warrington mentioned to Slemmer that he had heard talk among the civilian workers at the yard about a force of undefined composition that might be preparing to march the eight miles from Pensacola to take possession of the navy yard. Nothing immediately came of this but that same day Slemmer and Gilman heard that Georgia state militia forces had seized Fort Pulaski at Savannah and that Alabama state troops had taken the United States Arsenal at Mount Vernon. This latter event directly affected the garrison at Barrancas Barracks since the Mount Vernon Arsenal was the source of ordnance for the forts on Pensacola Bay. On Saturday, January 5, they learned that Alabama state forces had occupied Forts Morgan and Gaines, 50 miles west of Pensacola on Mobile Bay. All of these facilities were unoccupied or staffed with only a few men and the seizures had taken place without violence but they had been carried out by organized forces of states that had not seceded and were still legally within the Union. On Sunday, January 6, Slemmer and Gilman learned Florida state militia had taken the arsenal at Apalachicola containing more than 5,000 pounds of gunpowder and some 173,000 musket cartridges and, on January 7, they would learn Florida state troops had seized Fort Marion at St. Augustine.[1]

On Saturday evening, January 5, Slemmer met at his quarters with Gilman and those officers from the navy yard and the vessels in the harbor whom he considered loyal. Slemmer was unfamiliar with the responsibilities he now faced and uncomfortable with what the near future might bring. He had never held a command position during his ten years in the United States Army. He had been an artillery lieutenant, usually a junior officer in a regular battery of an established regiment, and had not had to exercise personal command or control over men or events. There had always been senior officers present to give him orders defining his duties and there had been procedures in place to guide him and his fellow junior officers in carrying out these orders. Slemmer had seldom had to make a decision on his own and, through the decade of service he had behind him, he had seldom had to work very hard. The life of an army garrison officer was leisurely, if routine and somewhat boring, and, of major importance, Slemmer had never led men into battle. He had never experienced combat against an enemy and he was unsure of himself, of his strengths, of his own abilities as he talked with his guests that Saturday evening. Slemmer spoke to them about the problems they now faced as he saw them. The attitude of the people in the surrounding country had changed from the usual one of slight hostility toward the Federal government to open belligerence. Throughout the Deep South state governments had begun ordering their state forces to move against and occupy Federal facilities. During the past week Florida troops had moved against Federal installations in eastern Florida and there was every indication, Slemmer said, that this might soon be the case here in western Florida. The nearest support the Federal forces on Pensacola Bay could look for was far to the north, possibly a month distant by ship. Should the facilities on the bay come under attack, Slemmer said, then his small garrison and the detachment of marines at the navy yard could not defend all of them. He asked his guests for their opinions. Should they

The vivacious Carrie Slemmer, whom President Lincoln described as Slemmer's "pretty wife" (Library of Congress).

abandon the forts and the navy yard and take ship for the North? Should they plan to hold out until faced with overwhelming force and then surrender? Were any of them, the men sitting in his parlor this evening, prepared to make war against their neighbors and friends? Carrie Slemmer, listening in, challenged the officers, telling them if none of them were willing to fire the first gun to defend their flag, then she would do it. Her girlish enthusiasm was well-meant but it did nothing to help her husband or his guests. Slemmer concluded the meeting with the complaint that he had received nothing for his guidance from his absent superior officers nor from the War Department at Washington.[2]

Slemmer had no indication that the War Department was even aware of his situation or was at all concerned about it. The department had, however, already taken some steps regarding the security of the facilities on Pensacola Bay of which Slemmer was uninformed. After putting in motion the efforts to relieve and reinforce Fort Sumter by means of *Star of the West,* General Scott had called Major Zealous B. Tower of the United States Army Engineers to his office at Washington on the evening previous to the evening on which Slemmer had met with his colleagues at Pensacola. Zealous Tower was forty-two, a graduate of West Point, class of 1841, and an experienced engineer. Knowing that Major Winder, the commanding officer at Barrancas Barracks, was absent on leave, the general-in-chief intended to replace Winder with a senior army officer whom he knew and trusted. Scott relieved Tower of all his engineering responsibilities and placed him under his down direct command. "You will proceed without delay to the Barrancas and assume command of the troops and forts in and around Pensacola Harbor," Scott wrote. Major Tower was to call on the commander of the navy yard there and ask his "hearty cooperation in the great object of your mission, viz., to prevent the seizure of those works, or either of them, by any body of men whatsoever." Should any of the works be occupied by a hostile force when Tower arrived, "you will first summon them to surrender, and, in case of refusal, consult with the naval commander as to the sufficiency of your joint means to compel a surrender, and

First Lieutenant Adam J. Slemmer, U.S. Army, was a short, bespectacled, bearded officer who proved to be stubbornly loyal to his oath without regard to the odds against him (U.S. Army Military History Institute).

if it should appear to both on grave consideration that the means are sufficient you will exert them to a reasonable extent to effect that object." It is of interest that Winfield Scott, general-in-chief of the United States Army and the nation's foremost soldier, viewed the situation at Pensacola Bay so casually that he sent a single officer, an engineer, to assume responsibility for resolving a condition that might border on open conflict and civil war. Scott was aware of the limited strength of the garrison that Tower would find at Pensacola Bay. He would have had to have assumed that the garrison might have been expelled from the works which would then be occupied by a hostile force. Even if Tower did call upon the naval commander and receive help from that source, the reinforcement would amount only to thirty-eight marines. Scott's action well reflects the position of the Federal government at the time. Few in Washington saw the events taking place at Charleston and at Pensacola as being more than localized misbehavior on the part of some radical politicians who were known for their bombast and bluster. After all, this was not the first time authorities in South Carolina had threatened secession or something just as disruptive toward the Federal government. In the mind of the general-in-chief, sending a capable engineer, in whom he had confidence based on years of association, was an adequate and proper response. Tower apparently interpreted Scott's wording in the order from the War Department to "proceed without delay" as equally as casual as apparently the general-in-chief did because it took him forty-five days to arrive on the scene. During all that time, Lieutenant Slemmer was unaware that Tower had orders to proceed to take command at Pensacola Bay.[3]

Early on Monday morning, January 7, Slemmer and Gilman donned their dress uniforms and swords and formally called upon Commodore Armstrong in his office at the navy yard. The army lieutenants suggested in light of the events taking place in the Deep South that the two commanders should consult and develop plans for the protection of the public property under their charge. Armstrong's reply, after summoning and consulting with Farrand and Renshaw, was that, in the absence of specific orders from the Navy Department at Washington, he deemed it inexpedient to cooperate with the army. Slemmer and Gilman left but returned later in the day, hoping to find Armstrong alone but they were unsuccessful. After again conferring with Farrand and Renshaw, the elderly officer repeated that he had no instructions to cooperate with the army. By Tuesday morning, January 8, Slemmer had become alarmed at the accelerating pace of events taking place around him. He felt frustration at Armstrong's refusal to discuss cooperation between the forces on Pensacola Bay. He was concerned by the question of where the loyalties of Farrand and Renshaw might actually lie and the effect these two officers seemed to have on the commodore. Slemmer was angry that he had been left in command of Company G with absolutely no guidance from his superiors as they departed on their leaves and on the lack of any further communications from the War Department at Washington. He realized he was now facing unprecedented conditions and he was determined to use whatever means he had available to carry out his principal responsibility, that of safeguarding the public property under his charge at Barrancas Barracks and the three forts on the shores of the bay. Before daybreak, Slemmer ordered the transfer of gunpowder stored in the lower water battery at Fort Barrancas to the more secure inner magazine of the fort itself and ordered the guns of Fort Barrancas all brought into working order. Then with Gilman, and accompanied by Mr. R. H. Watts and Mr. Daniel Saint, leaders of the loyal employees at the navy yard, he went again to meet with Armstrong, Farrand, and Renshaw. In this meeting, Slemmer pressed the navy

Exterior of Fort Barrancas, 1891, with the water battery to the right (Pensacola Historical Society).

officers to come to agreement on a plan of defense in which the army and navy forces on the bay could cooperate to defend the public property under their charge. What they had learned of actions being taken by state forces throughout the Deep South, Slemmer told them, indicated to him there was a clear urgency for such cooperation and whatever was agreed upon, he insisted, had to be put into place immediately. Watts and Saint suggested raising 200 volunteers to help in the defense of the Federal installations. Farrand objected strongly to this, arguing that volunteers had not been called for elsewhere in the nation and there was no authority for them to be called for here. Slemmer told the assembled officers that he was determined to use all the means at his disposal to continue to carry out his standing orders until he was instructed otherwise by proper authority. The short, bespectacled officer insisted there was very little time. The result of the meeting was the same as the one before: without specific orders from the Navy Department at Washington, Armstrong declared, he found it inexpedient to cooperate with the army. Returning to Barrancas Barracks, Slemmer ordered a guard detail into Fort Barrancas. With darkness, he had the drawbridge over the moat raised, securing the fort from the outside. In his quarters that night, Slemmer wrote a telegram to the War Department describing the conditions on Pensacola Bay. He informed the adjutant general of the information he had received of the seizures at Mobile, Savannah, Apalachicola, and elsewhere and he reminded the adjutant general that Fort Pickens, although presently unoccupied, commanded the entrance to the harbor. Should that work be seized by state forces, his own command would be rendered useless as far as protecting the other Federal facilities on the bay. He ended his telegram with a request for instructions. Slemmer dispatched a messenger to take

Aerial view of Fort Barrancas, water battery to the left front, drawbridge and ditch in the upper right (National Park Service).

the telegram the eight miles up the shore of the mainland to Pensacola where the telegraph office was located.[4]

At the navy yard Commodore Armstrong considered the issues Slemmer had raised and ordered the marine sentries at the gates increased from one man to five with instructions that no strangers were to be admitted to the yard unless they were passed by an officer. That evening repairs to *Wyandotte's* stack and engine were completed and the steamer was hauled from the dry dock and moored at the wharf where final touches would be given to her machinery.[5]

Before midnight on Tuesday, January 8, the guards Slemmer had placed in Fort Barrancas made out figures approaching in the darkness. When the corporal of the guard challenged the party and demanded to know who they were and what their business was, the figures halted, apparently confused at finding the fort occupied. Getting no response when he challenged the party and thinking there were some twenty men beyond the drawbridge, the corporal of the guard sounded the alarm. The party ran off in the direction of Warrington. Slemmer strengthened the guard detail in Fort Barrancas with half his command but nothing further occurred during the remainder of the night.[6]

From Washington Senator Yulee wired his friend Joseph Finegan at Tallahassee that the caucus of Southern senators had agreed that should the members from the Deep South leave the Senate, "force, loan, and volunteer bills might be passed, which would put Mr. Lincoln in immediate condition for hostilities; whereas by remaining in our places until the 4th of March, it is thought we can keep the hands of Mr. Buchanan tied and disable the hands of the Republicans from effecting any legislations which will strengthen the hands of the incoming administration." For the time being the senators from the states of the Deep South intended to retain their seats and their voting powers.[7]

At Pensacola that night William H. Chase received a telegraphic order from Governor Perry appointing him a colonel and placing him in command of all Florida state forces. Chase was authorized to move on the Pensacola forts and the navy yard but only if he felt certain of success. Governor Perry also telegraphed Governor Andrew B. Moore of Alabama asking for troops from that state to aid in the seizure of the forts on Pensacola Bay. Moore communicated this to Alabama's secession convention which was meeting at Montgomery, telling its members of Governor Perry's request. The forces in western Florida available to Colonel Chase were small and not sufficient to seize and hold the forts and the navy yard, Governor Moore told the convention members. Troops from Alabama could reach Pensacola by rail before troops from middle and eastern Florida could get there by ship. With the importance of the facilities on Pensacola Bay to the interests of Alabama, Moore urged the members to grant him the authority to respond to Governor Perry's request. Further, he informed the members of the convention that he had learned from high sources that it was now the policy of the Federal government to reinforce all the forts in the states where secession was expected. "I need not suggest the danger to Florida and Alabama that must result from permitting a strong force to get possession of these forts," he told the members. In a separate telegram from Pensacola, militia captain Edward A. Perry of the Pensacola Rifles wired Moore, "Send five hundred men immediately."[8]

That same night, in spite of the efforts by General-in-Chief Scott to cloak the Fort Sumter relief expedition in secrecy, South Carolina's Senator Louis T. Wigfall telegraphed Governor Pickens, "The *Star of the West* sailed from New York on Sunday with government troops and provisions. It is said her destination is Sumter." The next morning at 6:20 off Charleston, *Star of the West's* crew ran the national flag up the mainmast and, riding the rise of the tide, brought the steamer over the bar at the mouth of the harbor. The vessel moved slowly along the shore of Morris Island and up the main ship channel with the reinforcements out of sight below decks. At 7:14 A.M., when the steamer was between Forts Moultrie and Sumter, a cannon in a battery on the north end of Morris Island fired and sent a ball flying over the vessel. First Lieutenant Charles R. Woods, in command of the troops aboard *Star of the West*, had a larger Federal flag run up the mainmast. The firing continued, the shots flying high. When the gunners ashore finally found the range, one ball struck *Star of the West's* hull just forward of her rudder and another ricocheted into the fore chains slightly above the water line and only inches below the feet of the merchant seaman throwing the lead to sound the depths. Fearing further batteries would come into play as *Star of the West* approached closer to Fort Sumter, and noticing a ship being towed down the harbor in what might have been an attempt to block the merchant steamer from returning to the open sea, Woods told *Star of the West's* master, Captain John McGowan, to turn back. Re-crossing the bar under brisk but ineffective cannon fire, the steamer touched bottom several times. Once clear, Woods told McGowan to make for New York. There had been no support from Major Anderson's guns within Fort Sumter. The situation had not yet reached the point where Anderson was willing to open fire of his own countrymen.⁹

When the mail arrived at Pensacola on Wednesday, January 9, letters addressed to the Federal facilities down the shore of the mainland were given to a courier who delivered them to Barrancas Barracks and the navy yard. The dispatches from Washington had traveled by rail for six days before they were handed to Slemmer and Armstrong. In both cases, the orders they contained were far short of what the two commanders had hoped for. Slemmer and Gilman immediately walked to the navy yard where a meeting of Armstrong, Farrand, Renshaw, Walke of *Supply,* and Berryman of *Wyandotte* was ending. Slemmer showed his orders to Armstrong who offered his own. Armstrong finally agreed on the need to discuss plans to safeguard the public property under their individual custodies with Slemmer. At this time the War Department and the Navy Department were two entirely separate branches of the Federal government with their own command structures reporting to separate cabinet secretaries. Each department had its own appropriations and priorities. There had been only a few times in the nation's history where cooperation between the two armed services had taken place. Combined operations without specific orders from either department at Washington were unusual. Slemmer made his case that, with the limited force he had, he could not attempt to hold the three forts on the bay. He would, however, attempt to hold one of them and that would be Fort Pickens which commanded the entrance channel, the other forts, the navy yard, and which could be evacuated, or reinforced and provisioned, from the gulf shore of Santa Rosa Island without the supporting vessels having to enter the bay. Surrounded by water on three sides and by the barren sand of the narrow island on the fourth, it could, of all the forts, best be defended. He would need the cooperation of the navy, Slemmer told Armstrong, to transport the men of his command and their provisions, munitions, weapons, and possessions to Santa Rosa Island. Fort Pickens, he reminded the commodore, stood empty except for its guns, many of which were not even mounted on their carriages. Armstrong agreed to send Berryman in the steamer *Wyandotte* to ferry Slemmer's command over to the island. Armstrong also agreed to Slemmer's request that he lend Slemmer all the seamen he could spare from the navy yard to help in the move and, as Slemmer reported it, Armstrong also agreed to order *Wyandotte* and *Supply,* both currently moored at the navy yard wharf, to anchor under the guns of Fort Pickens in order to add their weaponry to the defense of the land approach from the east.¹⁰

Wyandotte arrived at the Barrancas wharf at ten the following morning, Thursday, January 10, and took aboard Slemmer and a portion of the men of Company G, carrying them over to Santa Rosa Island where Slemmer began to put the massive fort into shape for defense and to mount its heavy guns, many of which had not been brought into battery in thirteen years. Gilman remained at Barrancas Barracks with the remainder of Company G packing equipment, supplies, and munitions and hauling boxes, kegs, crates, and bundles down to the wharf ready to load into *Wyandotte* when she returned. At one o'clock in the afternoon, seeing no sign of the steamer, Gilman went to the navy yard to inquire about the delay. He was informed by Armstrong that the only assistance that would be provided would be for *Wyandotte* to tow the remainder of the company of artillery over to Santa Rosa Island in a barge and for *Supply* to furnish some limited provisions to the garrison. Gilman protested, saying he would report this change to Slemmer. When he received Gilman's message, Slemmer immediately stopped all work in Fort Pickens and had the men with him return to Barrancas Barracks on the mainland in a chartered schooner. Accompanied by Gilman, he marched to the navy yard where he confronted Armstrong whom he found alone in his office. Slemmer was furious. He accused the commodore of deceit, reminding Armstrong that he had promised to provide men from the navy yard to help in the labor of putting Fort Pickens into shape for defense, and had ordered the cooperation of the two vessels of war in the harbor for the transfer of his garrison, its provisions and armaments, and for assistance in defending the eastern land approaches to the fort. Armstrong, Slemmer insisted, had it in his power to help him, and he had broken his given word. Slemmer would never have dreamed, he argued, of defending Fort Pickens with fifty men when it's wartime compliment was 1,200, without the help and cooperation of the navy. He had been at work preparing for that defense while counting on Armstrong's promise and now, with that promise broken, he had lost a whole day that could have been used in making other defensive arrangements at one of the forts on the mainland. Armstrong sent for Farrand, Renshaw, Walke, and Berryman. While waiting for them to arrive, he explained to Slemmer that he had very limited means at hand to carry out his own responsibilities. His unpaid workers were liable to turn into a hungry mob at any time. The political unrest that had become rampant at Warrington and Woolsey, just outside his gates, might cause otherwise peaceful men to take extreme actions. He could not spare any of his sailors or marines to help the army, he insisted. Taking advantage of the absence of the other naval officers, Slemmer told Armstrong he felt the commodore's executive officer and his first lieutenant were not well-affected toward the Federal government and the maintenance of the Union. He knew both men well and was aware they held strong secessionist feelings and, especially in the case of Farrand, were outspoken on the subject. Armstrong would hear none of this. His officers were under oath to support and defend the Constitution, he told Slemmer, and he counted on their allegiance. When the other officers arrived, Commander Farrand told Armstrong and Slemmer that, in his opinion, it would be useless to try to defend the facilities in the harbor. He had learned state troops were on the way to seize the installations in spite of any resistance the small army and navy garrisons might offer. Renshaw added that the forces coming were their own brethren, that resistance to them would involve spilling the blood of brothers which, he said, "was different than spilling the blood of a foreign foe." Farrand argued that the navy yard and the forts had been shamefully neglected by the Federal government and this neglect indicated the government did not intent them to be defended, given the state of affairs throughout the South. In the course of this argument, Armstrong broke down. Sitting at his desk with his head in his hands, the old man wept into his handkerchief, sobbing, "Great God, what can I do with the means I have?" Slemmer reminded the naval officers that Fort Barrancas had been approached the night before by a party of citizens who would have taken possession of it had he not stationed a guard there. He had resisted that attempt to seize Fort Barrancas, he declared, and he would resist any other attempt to take possession of the public property under his charge as best he could with the means available to him. He pressed Armstrong until the old man relented and gave the order for his original commands to be carried out. Berryman promised to have *Wyandotte* leave the navy yard for the Barrancas wharf that evening. Slemmer assured Berryman that all would be ready for the steamer's arrival. Slemmer and Gilman returned to the barracks and put all hands to work moving property to the wharf. Even Carrie Slemmer and Mary Gilman worked alongside the men struggling with barrels and bundles. Late in the afternoon a dense fog settled over the bay. There was no sign of *Wyandotte*. Slemmer kept his men at their tasks until midnight and then had them secure and turn in for the night. The dense fog, however, was not the only reason Berryman had not moved *Wyandotte* from the navy yard as promised. As the vessel was preparing to make steam, James Doyle, the yard's master machinist, dropped a critical piece of the vessel's machinery overboard. The piece was eventually replaced and *Wyandotte* was able to get up steam but this sabotage by one of the yard's key staff members delayed the vessel until the fog made movement toward the Barrancas wharf impossible. Before *Wyandotte* did cast off an hour later to anchor out in the harbor until the fog lifted, Berryman took on board thirty ordinary seamen from the yard without arms, equipment, or provisions, whom he would carry over to help with the heavy work at Fort Pickens.[11]

Commander Ebenezer Farrand maintained pressure on Armstrong even as Slemmer, Gilman, Walke, and Berryman left the commodore's office. The executive officer was in close communication with secessionist leaders at Pensacola and had learned that Alabama state troops would be joining Florida militia gathering in the town within hours. Farrand intended to keep Armstrong confused and impotent and to do all he could to prevent the transfer of Slemmer's command over to Santa Rosa Island. Farrand told Armstrong it would be an outrage and a crime to cooperate with the army officers and bring on a bloody conflict with the state troops who would be arriving shortly. Such an act would hand down the old mariner's name "in perpetual execrations throughout the land." Since Farrand could not give orders directly to the army officers, he had to try to accomplish his ends through the navy's command structure. He had little concern about his own ability to manipulate and interfere with Armstrong and he knew Renshaw would do as he was told. The officers Farrand had to try to bring under his sway were the commanders of the two vessels in the harbor, Walke of *Supply* and Berryman of *Wyandotte*. Both were Southerners, Virginians by birth. Where, Farrand had to wonder, did their true loyalties lie?[12]

That evening five companies of the 2nd Alabama Infantry Regiment under Colonel Tennent Lomax left Montgomery by rail for Pensacola. Lomax was instructed by Governor Moore before departing to act on his own discretion when he arrived and assessed the situation on Pensacola Bay.[13]

From Washington, Secretary of the Navy Toucey sent a message that evening to Commodore Garrett J. Pendergrast, commanding the Home Squadron of the United States Navy off Vera Cruz, to detach the sailing frigate U.S.S. *Sabine*, Captain Henry A. Adams, which was to proceed to Pensacola and assist the com-

Commander Ebenezer Farrand aided and abetted secessionist forces while serving as an officer in the U.S. Navy, then resigned to join the Confederacy (Naval Historical Center).

mander of the navy yard there in the protection of the public property under his charge. Also at Washington, Florida's congressional delegation, Senators Yulee and Mallory and Congressman George S. Hawkins, wired Governor Perry, "Federal troops are said to be moving, or on the move, on the Pensacola forts. Every hour is important. Georgia and Alabama, if called, will aid in the work, we think. The two seaboard forts are vacant. Chase, at Pensacola, built and knows the works."[14]

By the end of the first ten days of January, 1861, much had changed in the nation and within the Federal facilities on Pensacola Bay. South Carolina's secession in December had rocked the nation and brought long festering hatreds and alliances to the surface. The Buchanan administration was showing little appreciation for the events taking place and was publicly hoping nothing would transpire before the incumbent could hand the reins of government over to the new executive on March 4. Southern leaders were actively working among themselves, corresponding and forming conventions. They were unsure of what they were doing and how they should go about it but they were actively doing something while the Federal government seemed comfortably mired in business as usual. South Carolina authorities had already initiated action to thwart the attempt to replenish and reinforce Fort Sumter at Charleston Harbor which had been driven off by state forces firing heavy ordnance at an unarmed merchant vessel flying the national flag. Some moves on the part of the Federal government had taken place to send assistance to Pensacola Bay but, as yet, both the army and the navy commanders on the site were unaware of these. To add to the pressure of his mounting problems, Slemmer learned on the evening of Wednesday, January 9, that the state legislature meeting in Jackson had passed Mississippi's ordinance of secession. The following day he would learn by telegraph that a little before noon the convention of the people of Florida meeting at Tallahassee had done the same.[15]

From Boston, Massachusetts, Brevet Major Lewis G. Arnold reported by telegraph to the adjutant general at Washington that, pursuant to orders from the general-in-chief, he had embarked his command, Company C, 2nd Artillery, four officers and sixty-two enlisted men, on the chartered merchant steamer *Joseph Whitney* en route to garrison unoccupied Fort Jefferson, a lonely bastion eighty miles west of Key West in the Gulf of Mexico. Slemmer had no way of knowing of this but, even had he known, it is doubtful the news

The energetic Col. Tennent Lomax, C.S.A., was frustrated by being held back from making the assault on Fort Pickens.

would have made a difference in his outlook since Dry Tortugas was some 500 miles distant by sea.¹⁶

Navy Lieutenant John Irwin, ashore in Warrington to arrange the movement of his wife and children to his parents' home in Pittsburgh, Pennsylvania, had been ordered back to *Wyandotte* as executive officer by Commodore Armstrong. At 8:00 A.M. on Thursday, January 10, Irwin arrived at the Barrancas wharf in the steamer towing a large scow and all the vessel's boats. Loading and ferrying began immediately. Because he could not take the time nor did he have the means to dismount them, Slemmer ordered Gilman to take a working party and spike all of the guns of Fort Barrancas and the water battery that bore on Fort Pickens. Slemmer had himself and Gilman with the artillerymen and the ordinary seamen from the yard carried over to Santa Rosa Island. Once there, the goods, munitions, and provisions they brought were carried ashore and stowed in the casemates of the fort under the supervision of Slemmer's sergeants. Lieutenant Commander Walke had *Wyandotte* tow the sailing storeship *Supply* over to Santa Rosa Island from the navy yard. Commodore Armstrong had ordered Walke to proceed to the island and furnish stores from his vessel, taking Slemmer's receipts for the goods delivered, and to return immediately to the yard, there to complete loading the coal, provisions, and munitions for the Home Squadron with all dispatch before sailing for Vera Cruz as his original orders required. Slemmer protested to Walke that it was impossible for him to receive provisions from the storeship at that time with all the effort and confusion relating to the move of his command and its property from Barrancas Barracks. Walke sent a message by semaphore to Armstrong that the commanding officer at the fort was not prepared to take provision at that time. He anchored *Supply* off the fort, sent officers and men ashore to assist with the labor, and ordered several boats from his vessel to help with the transfer of gunpowder from the magazines of Fort Barrancas. On one of his many trips between the mainland and Santa Rosa Island, Irwin drew *Wyandotte* in to the Barrancas wharf and took Carrie and Bertie Slemmer and Mary Gilman on board. Excitement was running high on the mainland as word spread to Warrington and Woolsey that Company G was moving out to Fort Pickens and Irwin thought to the safety of the army officers' families.¹⁷

Commodore Armstrong telegraphed Secretary Toucey at Washington, "I have the honor to report to the department that, in obedience to your order contained in your letter of the 3rd instant, I have cooperated with the commanding officer at Fort Barrancas to the extent which the means at my command afford." Armstrong, most likely putting his subscript to wording composed by Farrand, was stretching the facts regarding the order from the secretary of the navy to cooperate with the army to the extent which the means at his command afforded. Were it not for Walke and Berryman, Armstrong would have allowed Farrand to prevent any cooperation at all. Were it up to Farrand, Slemmer and Gilman and their gunners would still be on the mainland at Barrancas Barracks. That evening Slemmer wrote to the adjutant general at Washington from his new headquarters in one of the casemates at the fort, "I have the honor to report that on this date I removed my command from Barrancas Barracks, Fla., to Fort Pickens, under the special instructions received the previous day from the General-in-Chief." Slemmer was also stretching the communication from Scott's aide, to do the utmost to prevent the seizure of the forts on Pensacola Bay, into special instructions permitting him to abandon Forts Barrancas and McRee and move his command out to Santa Rosa Island. With fifty regular soldiers and thirty ordinary seamen at hand, he was doing the only thing he could to prevent the seizure of the most important of the forts on the bay and thus the use of the harbor by Southern authorities. Lieutenant Adam Slemmer at Pensacola and Major Robert Anderson at Charleston were thinking alike and had taken similar actions on their own, far from Washington and in the face of the lack of any guidance from the War Department.[18]

3

"If Blood Is Shed, You Are Responsible"

Slemmer kept his men at work within Fort Pickens through the night. By morning of Friday, January 11, they had established some order as the sun rose over Pensacola Bay. Under his own supervision and that of Gilman and First Sergeant Alexander Jamieson, the men of Company G and the seamen from the navy yard had carried or dragged several tons of materials and munitions from the boats at the wharf into the fort and stowed kegs, cases, and bundles in the casemates. Even while this progress was taking place, Slemmer realized he faced a discouraging situation. Fort Pickens was a massive work. Were he required to man the walls to repel an assault, Slemmer could put only one artilleryman every twenty yards along the perimeter. Even were he to ignore the four faces on the water's edge, Slemmer could man the eastern face, the one against which a land assault would come, with a single regular artilleryman every five yards and this would have to be done without providing men for relief or without telling off men to man the guns. Most of the guns were still dismounted, their wooden carriages rotted away over time or never furnished in the first place. There were not enough shutters to close the embrasures of the casemates to prevent attackers from simply running in through the openings. Slemmer's men had been able to carry over a few shutters from Fort Barrancas but the number was hardly adequate to securely close up the embrasures of the eastern face. The casemates themselves were damp and moldy from long disuse and there were no additional structures within the walls so that officers, men, provisions, and munitions all had to share space in the casemates. The command had been able to bring over from the mainland little in the way of tackle or gear to work with in mounting guns or strengthening the fort's shortcomings so their labors depended primarily on the application of muscle power alone.[1]

Slemmer had gone without sleep the night before the move to Santa Rosa Island, being kept busy with the hundreds of details to which he and Gilman had to see. He was edgy, concerned about his wife and little son, apprehensive whether what he was doing would be approved by the War Department, worried about what was to become of himself and his small command as matters continued to worsen, and he was fatigued. He was working on mounting a gun sight on one of the sea coast howitzers when Lieutenant Commander Walke

Interior casemates of Fort Pickens with rows of cannon balls handy (Pensacola Historical Society).

approached him. The captain of *Supply* showed Slemmer written orders he had just received from Commodore Armstrong directing Walke to land the provisions Slemmer needed from his vessel with all possible dispatch and then to return immediately to the navy yard. Walke told Slemmer that Berryman had received similar orders directing him to render assistance with *Wyandotte* in the delivery of provisions and then to tow *Supply* back to the navy yard without delay. *Wyandotte* was then to prepare to steam for her station off the southern coast of Cuba. *Supply* was to complete loading coal, provisions, and munitions and sail for the Home Squadron off Vera Cruz. With this startling news, Slemmer's exhaustion and temper got the better of him. He threw down the gun sight and shouted that he would not attempt to defend Fort Pickens if Walke and Berryman deserted him in obedience to Armstrong's order. Walke calmly assured the army lieutenant that he would keep *Supply* where she was, at anchor under the guns of Fort Pickens, and would continue to support Slemmer and the army garrison to the best of his ability. Slemmer called Gilman and dictated a communication to Armstrong stating his concern upon learning the commodore's intention to withdraw the protection of the steamer *Wyandotte* and the storeship *Supply* from the fort. Without the aid of these vessels, Slemmer told Armstrong, reminding the commodore that the point had been made at their last meeting in the presence of witnesses, it would be utterly impossible for him to protect the harbor and, if the assistance of the vessels were withdrawn, he would relinquish all hope of doing so and would report the state of affairs immediately by messenger to Washington. Slemmer demanded an immediate answer. Armstrong replied, most probably signing his name to wording composed by Farrand, that *Supply* was not a vessel of war. It had been sent to Fort Pickens merely to deliver provisions to Slemmer's garrison and it had to be dispatched immediately to Vera Cruz in conformity with orders from the Navy Department. *Wyandotte* might, Armstrong allowed, be retained for purposes of cooperating with Slemmer until further orders. The threat that Slemmer would report the lack of cooperation in direct violation of the orders from the secretary of the navy contained in his January 3 letter seemed to have cut through some of the mist surrounding Armstrong's decision making. Slemmer clearly saw the hand of Farrand in the communications coming from the commodore. Unable to prevent the movement of Slemmer's command to the fort on Santa Rosa Island, the executive officer of the navy yard seemed determined to keep the small company of artillerymen helpless in the barren fort. Dispatching *Supply* to Vera Cruz was a way to prevent significant provisions that the storeship carried from being used to subsist Slemmer's garrison. However, *Supply* and *Wyandotte* remained at anchor under the guns of Fort Pickens through the day and into the following night. In the afternoon, Slemmer's and Gilman's families were transferred from *Wyandotte* to the larger *Supply*. To arm the ordinary seamen working within the fort, Berryman sent ashore thirty muskets he had taken from the navy yard over Farrand's objections and 4,800 musket cartridges which Slemmer needed. At dark, Berryman put ashore a sergeant and three marines from *Wyandotte* to stand guard while Slemmer and his men worked through the night mounting guns and blocking open casemate embrasures. During the day, boats from the navy yard under Sailing Master Pearson continued to transfer munitions, firewood, and equipment from Fort Barrancas to the Fort Pickens wharf on the bay side of Santa Rosa Island.[2]

Lieutenant Henry Erben, U.S. Navy, ready to fight, even to fisticuffs with the yard's executive officer (National Archives).

Late in the afternoon Lieutenant Henry Erben of *Supply* became concerned about the army's armaments and munitions still within Fort McRee on Foster's Bank. He mentioned this in a discussion with Slemmer and Gilman and agreed to take the resolution of the situation into his own hands at Slemmer's request since the army officers had neither the time nor the means to do anything themselves. Calling away a launch and crew, Erben had his men row down the harbor from where *Supply* was moored at the Fort Pickens wharf and up the lagoon to Fort McRee as dusk was settling over the bay. The fort was unoccupied except for an ordnance sergeant and his wife who lived there. At Erben's summons, the woman came to the gate and explained she could not let Erben enter as her husband was at Warrington. In fact, her husband was on Santa Rosa Island with Slemmer but the wife knew only that he had gone to Warrington. When Erben asked for the keys to the magazine, she refused. In minutes the crew of the launch broke the door down. Kegs containing some 22,000 pounds of gunpowder were rolled out, their heads smashed in, and the powder tumbled into the harbor. Fuses were cut and thrown into the water, ropes and harness cut and dropped over the seawall, blocks and rigging and tackle were destroyed, and all the guns facing Fort Pickens were spiked. Erben described the evening's work, "When we left Fort McRea (*sic*) it was in no condition to prevent the landing of our force of artillerymen and sailors at Fort Pickens." The ordnance sergeant's wife somehow managed to get word to Warrington. A boat of armed men set out from the village in the closing darkness, intent, in Erben's words, "to prevent the destruction or to intercept us on our way out." Full darkness covered the navy crew rowing from the lagoon, the men pulling hard for *Supply*, but they were sighted by the occupants of the boat from Warrington. The citizens hailed the launch, Erben described, "in not polite language." Pistol shots were fired and Erben shouted to his crew to "pull as I believe no other boat has ever been pulled before!" The launch reached the protection of *Supply* and the boat of armed men returned to Warrington. Erben had the launch hoisted aboard *Supply* and secured. His spirits still up, he went to Walke and asked permission to destroy the gunpowder in the magazine outside the walls at the navy yard. Walke told him to address Commodore Armstrong since that gunpowder was the property of the navy and under Armstrong's control. Erben had himself rowed to the navy yard and hurried to Armstrong's office where he told the commodore what he had accomplished at Fort McRee. He asked permission to do the same to the hundreds of kegs of gunpowder stored in the navy yard's magazine. Armstrong, in Erben's words, was completely dazed by what he heard. He showed Erben the dispatch from the secretary of the navy ordering him to be vigilant in protecting the public property at the navy yard. "Now you ask me to destroy it?" the old man wondered. Armstrong refused his permission and sent his orderly to bring Farrand. Erben later wrote, "Then I knew it was all up." Farrand rushed into Armstrong's office. He demanded Armstrong put Erben under arrest, accusing Erben of being crazy and of having been disrespectful to him earlier in the day. When Armstrong hesitated, Farrand rose, seized the chair he had been sitting on, threw it at Erben's head, and stormed from the room. Erben sat with Armstrong for a while. The old man buried his head in his hands and, Erben wrote, "He was crying like a child." Leaving, Erben stepped through the door to the veranda. Farrand jumped at him from the shadows, shaking his fist in Erben's face and shouting, "Damn you! I will teach you how to treat a superior officer!" Erben grabbed Farrand by the collar of his coat and pushed him away. Farrand came at him again. The two clinched and rolled down the steps to the ground, punching and shouting at each other. "I'll have you hanged as a traitor!" Erben promised. Farrand called out for help and Renshaw, his brother-in-law, came from behind a hedge where he had been waiting. Assistant Surgeon W. A. King of *Supply,* one of Erben's friends, came to the lieutenant's assistance. Farrand ran off toward his quarters shouting, "Erben is drunk and wants to blow up the yard!" Erben and King returned to *Supply* leaving the large magazine outside the walls of the navy yard untouched and, unknown to Erben, unguarded. Erben reported Farrand's behavior to the officers of both vessels in the harbor. A plan was put together to arrest Farrand at the first opportunity and take him aboard one of the ships. Berryman offered to take him on *Wyandotte* and keep him in the coal bunker until matters resolved themselves. Farrand learned of the scheme and avoided the waterfront where crewmen from either vessel might seize him. The plan came to nothing and Farrand remained free. "He made a narrow escape," Erben wrote, "for, had he been captured, he would never have got on shore again."³

The leading companies of the 2nd Alabama Infantry Regiment under Colonel Tennent Lomax arrived at the Pensacola railroad depot at 1 p.m. on January 10 and joined two companies of Florida militia already in the town. The Alabama companies were the Montgomery True Blues, the Wetumpka Guards, the Tuskegee Light Infantry, the Metropolitan Guards, and the Independent Rifles, all volunteer militia. When they arrived the Alabamans found the citizens of Pensacola celebrating the receipt of the news of their state's secession by firing guns and lighting bonfires. Weary and hungry from the journey, which included a long march around a section of railroad still under construction, the Alabamans were quartered in public buildings and served fried oysters, hot coffee, and rolls by the citizens of Pensacola. After eating, the Alabamans turned in for the night. At midnight they were awakened and turned out by drums beating the assembly. Colonel Lomax, mounted and obviously agitated, announced to the men that, when the expedition left Montgomery, he had understood he was to command the troops assembling at Pensacola since the majority by far were Alabamans. He had just been informed by telegraph, he announced to the men, that the force gathering in the Florida town to move on Federal forts located on Florida soil would be commanded by a Florida officer appointed by the governor of Florida, and that would be Colonel William H. Chase. The Alabamans were surprised and angered that their own colonel would be subordinate to Chase who had been born and raised a Northerner. "We came to fight!" one man shouted, "Not to be humbugged by a damned Yankee!" After grousing and threatening to return home, the men eventually followed Lomax's advice, returned to their lodgings, and went back to sleep. They had work to do in the morning.⁴

Word reached the navy yard during the early morning of Saturday, January 12, that state troops were at Pensacola. The officers of both naval vessels in the harbor and, to a man, the marine detachment under Captain Watson, wanted to defend the navy yard. Commodore Armstrong felt that a show of force would prevent any rash act on the part of the locals. He ordered sentinels to the walls of the yard and a pair of howitzers to the gates. There was no assault during the day and at dawn the following morning Farrand ordered the sentinels on the walls back to their barracks and the howitzers removed. The morning was dark and wet with showers sweeping over the bay. The marines at the gates were finding it difficult to keep the priming of their flintlock muskets dry. Armstrong met with his officers to discuss possible moves for the defense of the yard if the rumors of a pending attack proved to be valid. One plan that was discussed in detail involved anchoring *Wyandotte*, with her four 12-pounder howitzers, off the northeast gate and forming a force of armed sailors and marines in the yard. *Supply*, with her four 32-pounders, would anchor off the marine barracks beyond the northwest gate. Farrand managed to defer implementation and the plan was not implemented. No further defensive action was agreed to at the meeting which adjourned after less than an hour. At the marine barracks, the detachment was at breakfast. A messenger from Commodore Armstrong arrived with orders for Captain Watson to form his men and have them stand ready. Watson had the marines fall into formation outside the barracks with loaded muskets and fixed bayonets, standing in ranks in spite of the falling rain. He then accompanied the messenger back to Armstrong's office. The commodore told Watson he had heard a body of men was coming toward the navy yard on the Pensacola road. Armstrong admitted he did not know if the report was true but he wished Watson and his marines to be ready throughout the day.[5]

Prior to first light the Alabama and Florida volunteers formed in the streets of Pensacola. Florida's Colonel Chase gave Alabama's Colonel Lomax command of the column. The Alabaman called the troops from both states to attention and led them out of town. The distance from Pensacola to the navy yard was eight miles along the beach but by the better wagon road that Lomax chose to follow the distance was fifteen miles with twists and turns as it ran toward several bridges built at the heads of the bayous. The citizens of Warrington and Woolsey and the civilian workers at the navy yard were expecting the column when it straggled into sight, the volunteers tired, wet, and weary from marching in the rain on the muddy road. "Every man and woman and child knew these troops were coming and for what purpose," navy lieutenant Henry Erben wrote. Shortly before noon the column arrived and halted a quarter of a mile from the northeast gate of the yard after sending out a small party to take possession of the unguarded magazine. When the word spread through the yard that state troops were at the gate, Farrand immediately went there where he greeted and shook hands with Colonel Lomax and Captain Victor M. Randolph, present as the commissioner of the governor of the state of Alabama. Randolph had been an officer in the United States Navy since 1812. From 1855 to 1857 he had been the executive officer at the Pensacola Navy Yard, the position Farrand now held. Along with Lomax and Randolph were Major Samuel B. Marks, second in command of Lomax's 2nd Alabama Regiment, Mr. Richard Campbell, commissioner of the governor of the state of Florida, and a Captain Burrows, adjutant of the Alabama regiment. Leaving the volunteers standing in the road in the falling rain, Farrand hurried to Armstrong's office. It was about 1:00 P.M. when he informed the commodore that an armed force was at the gate and that commissioners of the governors of the states of Alabama and Florida were demanding an interview with him. Armstrong told Farrand to bring the commissioners to his office where he would meet them. When his executive officer left to carry out his instruction, the old sailor made his way to his house and, with the help of his wife, tore the yard's signal books to pieces and threw them into the kitchen fire. Mrs. Armstrong kept the flames working to consume the codes as Armstrong returned to his office.[6]

At some time prior to this Walke aboard *Supply* had received a written message stating Commodore Armstrong was informed that an armed force had surrounded the navy yard. Should an attack be launched against the yard, the message read, Walke was to sail immediately for Vera Cruz with just the coal and provisions he had on board. The message may have been a last effort by the aged commodore to comply with his original orders from the Navy Department but it was more likely an attempt by Farrand, over the commodore's signature, to get at least one of the two naval vessels standing by Fort Pickens out of the harbor and on its way elsewhere. As soon as Slemmer on Santa Rosa Island learned of the situation developing at the navy yard, he sent a message by semaphore, "I am informed that the navy yard is besieged. In case you determine to capitulate, please send me the marines to strengthen my command." He received no acknowledgement of the message nor any response to it.[7]

In Armstrong's office Captain Randolph and Mr. Campbell, the commissioners representing the governors of Alabama and Florida, formally notified Commodore Armstrong they were accompanied by a superior force that was at the gates and had already seized the yard's magazine. They demanded, in the names of the executives of the states they represented, that the yard be surrendered immediately with all the public property therein. Any Federal officer or other citizen of the United States, they assured Armstrong, who desired to remove from the yard would be given parole to do so. Farrand interrupted to invite Colonel Lomax, Major Marks, and Captain Burrows to join the meeting. These men crowded into the small room and surrounded the commodore who sat behind his desk, alone and confused. Armstrong said with emotion that he had served the flag of the Union in sunshine and storm for fifty years, loving it and cherishing it as he did his own heart's blood, but that he would strike that flag now rather than fire a gun or raise a sword against his own countrymen. In the present circumstances, he said, any attempt to resist would result in the useless loss of life and the destruction of the very property he was ordered to preserve. Armstrong signed the articles of surrender which were put before him about 1:30 in the afternoon. Farrand turned to Renshaw and ordered the United States flag hauled from the flagstaff. Renshaw strode into the yard. At the base of the flagstaff and watching the events taking place was an old seaman from Camden, Maine, Quartermaster William Conway. On Renshaw's order, Conway stood to the halyards. When ordered to haul down the flag, Conway refused, declaring, "I will not do it, sir! This is the flag of my country, under which I have served many years. I love it, and will not dishonor it by hauling it down now!" Conway spoke out in the midst of an excited crowd of workmen, many of whom were strong supporters of secession and who wanted to see the yard surrendered. Several men in the crowd threatened to cut Conway down where he stood at the base of the flagstaff. Conway, however, did not stand entirely alone. A worker from the yard, an Englishman named James Ivey, stood with the old quartermaster and challenged him, "Conway, you old —. Do not haul that flag down for, if you do, I hope your arm may be paralyzed!" Renshaw ordered Conway arrested and put in irons. The yard's first lieutenant had to lower the flag with his own hands.[8]

When Walke on *Supply* saw the flag at the yard come down, he ordered his quartermaster to break out and fly every United States flag and every signal pennant the ship carried. On Santa Rosa Island Slemmer and Gilman watched in sorrow and anger as the flag at the yard came down. The flagstaff at Fort Pickens had not yet been erected but Slemmer ordered the large garrison flag draped over the northeast bastion facing the yard.[9]

Earlier, Armstrong had ordered Watson to form his marines and keep them at their barracks. The captain had them standing at ease, loaded and bayoneted muskets leaning against the wall of their barracks outside the navy yard. After the meeting in Armstrong's office, Watson was ordered to have his marines stack their arms in surrender. When instructed to do so, several marines were reluctant to obey, some of them close to tears. The formation was called to attention and marched inside the barracks into one small room as events outside unfolded.[10]

Armstrong wrote a telegram to the secretary of the navy at Washington informing him that commissioners of the governors of Alabama and Florida had arrived with a regiment of armed men and had demanded the surrender of the navy yard. He had turned the facility over and struck his flag at half-past 1 o'clock. Erroneously, he added that *Supply* had sailed for Vera Cruz the moment the flag at the yard was lowered. It is probable the telegram was composed by Farrand. A courier took the message up the shore of the mainland to the telegraph office at Pensacola.[11]

Farrand took Colonel Lomax and the commissioners to his quarters where they met for half an hour. When they emerged, Lomax had his officers lead the column of troops through the yard and out the northwest gate, leaving small parties behind as sentries in the yard. The state troops occupied the marine barracks, the naval hospital, Barrancas Barracks, Fort Barrancas, and after arranging for transportation out to Foster's Bank, Fort McRee. John Porter, the naval constructor at the yard and a loyal man, counted the troops as they marched through the yard. There were seven companies, he later testified, averaging about fifty men, five of the companies from Alabama and two from Florida. Both Florida companies were from Pensacola. All but one of the companies were in uniform and armed with rifled muskets and revolvers. The exception was the one Pensacola company that had just been organized and formed. Its men wore their daily apparel and carried a collection of shotguns and pistols, and part of this company was mounted. A large crowd of civilians from Pensacola had accompanied the column, Porter reported, some of whom also were armed and many of whom had been drinking. As the Pensacola Navy Yard was changing hands, the steam whistle blew and the civilian workers who had been standing and watching what was taking place returned to work. There were some among them who were loyal to the Union and who might have been called upon by Saint and Watts to defend the yard but, lacking leadership and arms, they dared not indicate a willingness to do so. As for Saint and Watts themselves, a diligent search was launched under Farrand's order. Saint was found in the yard, bundled into a rowboat, and sent to the vessels offshore with orders not to return. Watts fled and hid in the woods for twenty days until he was tracked down. He was allowed to stay at his home in Warrington under threat of severe penalty were he to try to communicate with the force in the fort on Santa Rosa Island or with the vessels offshore. Lieutenant John Irwin, executive officer of *Wyandotte*, was still trying to arrange the movement of his wife and children to his family's home in Pittsburgh but had been delayed by the illness of a daughter. Fearing for their safety in Warrington, Irwin took them by boat out to *Supply* where Slemmer's and Gilman's families were also sheltering.[12]

Colonel Chase had returned to his home on Palafox Street in Pensacola while Lomax led the column of troops to the navy yard. Chase sent a note to Captain Randolph appointing him the commander of the navy yard and adding as a postscript the question whether Commander Ebenezer Farrand had submitted his resignation as an officer in the United States Navy. If he had, asked Chase, could he not help in putting the spiked batteries of Fort Barrancas back into working order? Later that afternoon, Chase showed his growing concern in another message to Randolph, this one referring to his home as "Headquarters, Pensacola." Would Randolph consider erecting batteries at the yard in the event of an attack by *Wyandotte*? Could *Fulton's* guns, lying ashore alongside the beached steamer, be brought into an improvised battery? If Federal vessels carrying troops arrived, Chase directed Randolph to prevent the harbor pilots from going out to guide those vessels into the harbor and, if the navy yard were attacked by Federal forces landing on the mainland, Chase wrote, Randolph and Lomax must plan together how to secure the retreat of the state troops. Chase told Randolph to advise and counsel Lomax and for the two to do the best they could. Chase was showing his apprehension. During forty-five years service in the United States Army, he had never commanded anything more than working parties of contractors engaged in construction projects. "I am overcome with fatigue," he wrote Randolph, and ended his message, "How many muskets have you in the armory?" Colonel Chase was on unfamiliar terrain now, commanding forces standing in rebellion to the nation and the Constitution he had sworn to preserve and protect. He was understandably unsettled and concerned.[13]

In the early afternoon in the midst of all the events taking place on Pensacola Bay, a sailing schooner from New Orleans carrying provisions ordered for Slemmer's command while it was still at Barrancas Barracks hove into sight. The vessel tacked back and forth until the national flag was lowered at the navy yard and then stood in for the harbor. It seemed to observers that the captain of the schooner had been expecting the navy yard to surrender and had been waiting offshore for that to happen. Erben, on *Supply,* sighted the vessel and ordered a boat lowered to intercept her. Boarding the schooner, Erben met a barrage of profanity from her skipper. One of Erben's men, Boatswain's Mate Walsh, knocked the man overboard. Erben had the schooner run up on the beach of Santa Rosa Island under the guns of Fort Pickens and three months provisions were added to Slemmer's larder. Slemmer kept his men at their work. The flanking cannon, those mounted in the bastions at each corner and positioned to fire along the face of the walls against attackers forming for an assault in the ditch, were loaded with grape or canister and made ready for use. Casemate embrasures still open on the land face were blocked as well as could be done with the scant materials at hand. Slemmer and Gilman were certain an assault would not be long delayed. Now that Southern troops had possession of everything on the mainland, Fort Pickens, commanding the entrance to the bay, could not be permitted to deny the use of the great harbor and access to the navy yard to the Southern authorities. The two Federal officers did not know the strength of the force ashore but they knew it had to be well in excess of their fifty artillerymen and thirty ordinary seamen. The two lieutenants were determined to hold the fort as best they could but they did not have a lot of faith that it would be for

Sunset on Pensacola Bay, January 10, 1861, with Fort Pickens, a vessel standing in to the harbor from the Gulf, Fort McRee, Fort Barrancas, U.S.S. *Supply,* **and the navy yard (Naval Historical Society).**

long. Toward evening, Slemmer had the command called into formation for retreat, the military ceremony involving lowering the flag at the end of the work day although Fort Pickens did not yet have a flagstaff from which to lower its flag and the men would continue to work through the night. The army garrison at Fort Pickens was a command of United States Army regulars and Slemmer intended to maintain as much order, discipline, and routine as the circumstances permitted.[14]

Shortly after the ceremony, Slemmer was called to the gate by the corporal of the guard. Four men had crossed from the mainland in a small boat and were demanding entry to the fort. Accompanied by Gilman, Slemmer met Mr. S. Thayer Abert, the civil engineer at the navy yard and a man known to the army officers. Abert had been the weekly riding companion of Carrie Slemmer after Adam gave her the saddle horse on their wedding anniversary. Abert introduced the men with him: Captain Victor Randolph, Major Samuel Marks, and Lieutenant John Randolph. "We have been sent by the governors of Florida and Alabama to demand the peaceful surrender of this fort," Captain Randolph said. Slemmer, short, bearded, bespectacled, stubborn, and exhausted from days without sleep, faced up to the four men. He told them, "I am here by the authority of the president of the United States, and I do not recognize the authority of any governor to demand the surrender of United States property. A governor is nobody here." "Do you mean the governor of Florida is nobody?" Randolph demanded. "The governor of Alabama is nobody?" "I know neither of them," Slemmer replied, "and they are nothing to me." As the rebuffed visitors turned to leave, Abert mentioned to Gilman that he had heard rumors Fort Sumter at Charleston had been given up to South Carolina authorities. He told the Federal officers he had come over from the mainland in no official capacity but merely as an individual to make the introductions. He added there was already a large force of Alabama and Florida state troops at the navy yard and more troops were expected daily. Slemmer thanked Abert for his courteous gesture in doing the introductions and sent the four men on their way. On the way back to the mainland, the commissioners showed a flag of truce and had themselves rowed to *Supply* and *Wyandotte,* demanding in the names of the two governors the immediate return of both vessels to the navy yard as part of the naval contingent that Armstrong had surrendered. Walke and Berryman sent the commissioners on their way. Slemmer kept his gunners and seamen at work until midnight when they were told off to the batteries they would man through the night. They stood to the guns, lanyards in hand, ready to repel the assault that was expected momentarily. The night was dark, cold, and with steadily falling rain. Nothing untoward happened.[15]

Colonel Lomax had his volunteers settle into buildings at the navy yard and the army facilities on the mainland and had his officers put the men to work building sand and log batteries to ward off what Colonel Chase was certain would be an imminent attack by Federal troops from a fleet of ships suddenly appearing over the horizon. Lomax also put his men to work assembling scaling ladders. The Alabaman had every intention of moving to the assault on Fort Pickens as soon as he could get his inexperienced and undisciplined volunteers organized and recovered from the disruption their quick conquest had caused within their ranks. Very few of his officers and practically none of his men had any military experience other than what the social side of civilian militia musters had given them. As an example of the inexperience of the fledgling Southern military effort, Lomax received a telegram from Colonel John Seibels, aide to Alabama's Governor Morris, asking him to have a correct role made of the men in the Alabama companies under his command, those already at Pensacola and those on the way to him. In the rush to leave Montgomery, no one had thought to make a list of the names of the men in the hastily organized units.[16]

Tennent Lomax was dissatisfied with the command structure at Pensacola. He complained about it in a telegram to Governor Moore. In response he received a letter from Colonel Seibels stressing the importance to the Southern cause of having possession of all the fortifications on Pensacola Bay and urging immediate moves to take Fort Pickens. Seibels assured Lomax of the governor's confidence in him and, while cautioning him not to unnecessarily expose the lives of his volunteers, he allowed that some sacrifice might be necessary to fulfill the mission of taking possession of Fort Pickens. Lomax would have to conform to the orders of a Florida officer, "if one were appointed over him," as Seibels knew Chase already had been. But he urged Lomax to press upon the Floridian the importance of immediate action. Seibels passed on information, which was partially incorrect, that the telegraph operator at Augusta, Georgia, had copied messages passing on the line indicating that the Home Squadron had been ordered to concentrate at Pensacola. On the positive side, Seibels continued, 300 reinforcements from Mississippi would leave Mobile for Pensacola that day and three companies of Alabama troops had just been ordered to join Lomax there. Six additional companies were at Montgomery in readiness to march at a moment's notice. Ending, Seibels passed on Governor Moore's satisfaction with the report of Lomax's troops "gallant behavior since their arrival at Pensacola." With this advice that additional troops were on the way to him, there was now no doubt in Lomax's mind that the sole purpose of the buildup was the immediate occupation of Fort Pickens, even assuming that a direct assault upon its walls might involved considerable loss of life. When a company of sixty men, well-uniformed and armed, arrived by rail from Montgomery later in the day, Lomax became even more confirmed in his conviction. Colonel Chase, however, was content to consolidate the facilities already taken and to organize the volunteers on Pensacola Bay and those due to arrive in the coming days. He saw the arrival of reinforcements as justification for his position that overwhelming odds would soon convince Slemmer that resistance was futile and surrender was inevitable. Chase emphatically did not want to launch an assault on Fort Pickens. He ordered new flags raised over the navy yard, the forts, barracks, and hospital and, further, the first hoisting at each location was to be accompanied by the firing of a thirteen gun salute. Eldridge Lawton, the engineer in charge of the machinery of the beached *Fulton*, a loyal Unionist, described Chase's flag as "a dingy, white flag; looked like an old signal flag with a star put upon it."[17]

At mid-day on Sunday, January 13, *Wyandotte* came to the navy yard wharf under a flag of truce carrying as a passenger a Lieutenant Daniels, first lieutenant of *Supply*. When the screw steamer made fast, Daniels stepped ashore and held a conversation with Captain Randolph, Colonel Chase, and Colonel Lomax. After several minutes, Daniels was permitted to pass and walked to Commodore Armstrong's house. The commodore returned with Daniels and the two naval officers met with the three Southern officers on the wharf. Daniels announced that *Supply* would take on board all who wanted to leave for the North. Ninety-nine people boarded *Wyandotte* for transfer to *Supply* where they would join Slemmer's, Gilman's, and Irwin's families. The new passengers included James M. Cooper, gunner of the yard, his wife and five children; Robert Dixon, boatswain of the yard, his wife and two children; four warrant officers from the yard; nine sick sailors from the hospital; twenty-seven ordinary seamen from the yard including the gallant quartermaster William Conway; and the thirty-eight marines. Commodore Armstrong and Captain Watson opted to take a steamer to Mobile and then to travel north by rail.[18]

From his quarters on officers row, Commander Ebenezer Farrand wrote out and mailed his resignation from the United States Navy. His brother-in-law, Lieutenant Francis T. Renshaw, would submit his resignation three days later.[19]

Slemmer kept his men at work on Santa Rosa Island in spite of their fatigue and the steadily falling rain which had begun the day the command moved over to the island and had kept on without letup. The expected attack the night before by forces crossing over from the mainland in the darkness and assaulting the fort on its land side from the east had not materialized but Slemmer was convinced this would happen as soon as the commanders ashore could organize it. Sunday night was extremely dark. Slemmer put out sentries east of the fort. About midnight they saw in a flash of lightning a party of men moving in the darkness in the direction of the fort. The sentries fired in their direction and the intruders hurried away in the darkness. One of the sentries, a seaman from the navy yard, came in to report to Gilman who was officer of the guard. The man had tried to fire his own musket at the intruders but he was not familiar with weapons and his musket had not gone off. Gilman sent a regular artilleryman to replace the seaman with orders for the sergeant of the guard to send forward a small patrol. Two soldiers carefully made their way eastward on the island and came back to report seeing a party of eight or ten men about a mile from the fort. Sent back out, they encountered the party of armed men nearer the fort on the bay side of the island. The soldiers fired shots at the party which returned their fire before fading away. Slemmer now had to face a serious choice. He did not have enough men to send out a large patrol to find and encounter whomever was moving around east of the fort in the darkness and rain and he could not risk sending out a small patrol that might get cut off if a large force were out there forming for an attack. He recalled his sentries and had the men stand to the guns throughout the night, waiting for an assault that did not come.[20]

On Monday morning, January 14, Brevet Second Lieutenant John S. Saunders of the United States Army's Ordnance Department stepped out of his hotel at Pensacola and walked to the town wharf. Saunders had graduated from West Point the previous July and was waiting the availability of a permanent billet in one of the department's offices. While filling in temporarily at headquarters at Washington, Saunders had been called to the office of the general-in-chief and given an assignment. The War Department was aware of the defenseless condition of Fort Jefferson on Dry Tortugas, a barren reef eighty miles west of Key West in the Gulf of Mexico holding the masonry fort still under construction and occupied by an engineering officer and a small party of civilian workers and hired slaves. General-in-Chief Scott had asked Secretary of the Navy Toucey to provide protection to Fort Jefferson until army reinforcements under Brevet Major Lewis G. Arnold, en route aboard the chartered merchant steamer *Joseph Whitney* from Boston, could arrive. Toucey's order was for *Crusader* to steam from Pensacola to Dry Tortugas to protect the public property there and to prevent the landing of unauthorized persons. Toucey was unaware *Crusader* had cleared the Pensacola Navy Yard for Mobile the previous weekend. Toucey was hesitant to commit the information involved in the order to the casual observation of every telegraph operator on the line between Washington and Pensacola, nor did he wish to commit it to the slow overland mail or even slower transit by sea. In a rare example of cooperation between the services, Toucey asked Scott if he could make use of the War Department's scheduled overland courier to carry the dispatch to Armstrong at Pensacola. Scott agreed and Saunders left Washington by rail on January 8. When he arrived at Pensacola six days later, he suddenly became aware he was heading into a conflict. While on the cars some twenty miles from Pensacola the previous evening, he learned the navy yard had surrendered to state forces but the two naval vessels in the harbor were still flying the national flag. Saunders heard Commodore Armstrong was no longer in command and that *Wyandotte* was serving as a truce boat plying between the state forces on the mainland and the Federal forces within Fort Pickens. Saunders decided that, if he could not deliver his dispatches to Commodore Armstrong, to whom they were addressed, he would place the dispatches he carried into the hands of the captain of *Wyandotte*. On his first attempt, he was unable to find a way to get to the steamer which was off the navy yard eight miles from the Pensacola town wharf. Saunders returned to his hotel and no sooner had he stepped up to the porch than he was arrested by two men who claimed to have orders from Colonel Chase to take him into custody. Taken to Chase's home on Palafox Street, Saunders faced the colonel and six or eight of his officers. His dispatches were demanded. He refused to give them up, claiming they were addressed to Commodore Armstrong and he would deliver them to him alone. To avoid a confrontation, Chase agreed to let him place the dispatches in Armstrong's hands but only in the presence of Captain Randolph who now commanded at the yard. Saunders was taken down the shore by three mounted troopers and escorted to the navy yard. Armstrong was at his desk copying letters and documents he wished to carry north with him. Saunders handed the packages of sealed dispatches to Armstrong. Randolph demanded the packages, received them from the commodore, opened them, read them, and ordered a messenger to take them to Colonel Chase back at Pensacola. The most important of the dispatches, the one to Armstrong telling him to order *Crusader* to Fort Jefferson, had been written the day the steamer sailed for Mobile and was of no import other than to alert the Southern authorities at Pensacola that the Federal government was aware of the defenseless condition of Fort Jefferson which it was attempting to rectify. Saunders was given a safe conduct pass to return through the states of the South to Washington and he departed the following day by rail.[21]

Rain continued to fall as it had since Slemmer's command moved to Fort Pickens and Slemmer's artillerymen and seamen were approaching the limit of their endurance. They had been mounting guns, transferring provisions and supplies, and improving the fortifications for the past six days and then standing to the guns in anticipation of an assault each night. Slemmer asked Walke if navy officers from *Supply* would volunteer to come into the fort to relieve himself and Gilman from duty in order for the two of them to get some sleep. Walker passed the request to his officers but they declared they were unwilling to serve under army officers. In the case of *Wyandotte*, Berryman and Irwin were the only officers aboard the steamer and neither could be spared. That night, with the heavily falling rain, Slemmer had the men take their places at the guns as usual but he allowed them to sleep while he and Gilman made the rounds to see that all was in readiness and that the few sentries were alert.[22]

At Key West, Florida, Captain John Brannan moved his command, forty-four men of Company B, 1st Artillery, across the small island from their barracks on the opposite shore and occupied Fort Taylor which, prior to the move, had been occupied by a single officer,

Above: Current image of the main gate at Fort Pickens (photograph by the author). *Left:* Lieutenant Commander Henry Walke, U.S. Navy, loyal and dependable in spite of a court-martial for doing what he thought was right (Library of Congress).

Captain Edwin B. Hunt, the engineer in charge of completing its construction. This movement by Brannan put the three forts in Florida still in Federal hands well along the way toward being secure. Fort Pickens at Pensacola was held by Slemmer's command, Fort Jefferson on Dry Tortugas was about to be occupied by Major Arnold's command, and now Fort Taylor at Key West was firmly in the hands of Brannan's men.[23]

On Tuesday, January 15, Colonel Chase and Commander Farrand crossed over to Santa Rosa Island in a small boat and landed at the Fort Pickens wharf. Slemmer and Gilman were waiting. "I have come on business which may occupy some time," Chase told the Federal officers, indicating that the four men were standing in the steadily falling rain. "If you have no objection, we had better go inside your quarters." Slemmer told the former engineering officer that he had strong objections. He could hardly be expected to take the pair of Southern officers into the fort. "As I built the fort and know all its weak and strong points," Chase told him, "I would learn nothing new by going in and had no such object in proposing it." Slemmer said he understood but it would be improper to take the two men inside and, further, Chase had no idea what Slemmer had done during the previous week to improve conditions. Chase concurred and said he would state his business standing there before the gate in spite of the falling rain. It was a most distressing duty, he told Slemmer. He had come to ask the two Federal officers to surrender the fort. He would not be asking if he did not think it right and necessary to avoid the shedding of blood. Fearing he might not be able to speak his message and in order for the Federal officers to have it in proper form, he had put it in writing and would read it. Before he could read more than a few lines, however, his voice broke and his eyes filled with tears. He handed the document to Farrand saying, "Here, Farrand, you read it." Farrand took the paper but remarked he had not brought his spectacles and his eyes were poor, so he handed the document to Gilman to read, putting the Federal officer in the ironic position of having to read out the demand for the surrender of his own position. The document stated that Chase had full power from the governor of Florida to take possession of the forts and the navy yard in the harbor and that he desired to do this without sacrificing the honor of the two Federal officers and their gallant men. The fort and the public property within would be surrendered into his hands to be held subject to any agreement that might be entered into between commissioners of the state of Florida and the Federal government at Washington. "If the Union now broken should be reconstructed, Fort Pickens and all the property passes peacefully under the Federal authority," Chase's message read. "If a Southern Confederacy separates from the Union, would it not be worse then folly to attempt the maintenance of Fort Pickens, or any other fortified place within its limits?" Listen to him, Chase pleaded when Gilman folded the document and placed it in his pocket. Surrender the fort, Chase urged. The officers and men of the command could reoccupy their barracks at Barrancas on their simple parole to remain there quietly until ordered away, or to resume command of the forts in the harbor should an adjustment of the present difficulties in the Union be arrived at. "Consider this well," Chase told them, "and take care that you will so act as to have no fearful recollections of a tragedy that you might have averted, but rather to make the present moment one of the most glorious, because Christian-like, of your life." Slemmer considered Chase's message for several moments. He knew Chase well, having dealt with him socially in Pensacola during the months Slemmer had been here. Chase had the reputation of being an honorable man but Slemmer had to see him in the position of an officer who had sworn to defend the Constitution of the United States and who now had forsworn that oath. "How many men have you?" Slemmer asked. By night, Chase told him, he would have between 800 and 900. "Do you imagine you could take this fort with that number?" Slemmer asked. He did, Chase replied; he could carry it by storm. He knew every inch of the fort and its condition. "With your knowledge of the fort and your troops, what portion of them do you imagine will be killed in such an attack?" Slemmer asked. Chase thought and answered, supposing that Slemmer had made the best possible preparations to defend the place, he might lose half his men in the assault. "At least," Slemmer assured him, "and I don't think you are prepared to sacrifice that many men for such a purpose." Slemmer must understand, Chase countered, that he could not be expected to hold the fort with the small force he had and, further, Florida could not permit him to do so. The troops assembling on the mainland were determined to have the fort and, if not surrendered peacefully, an attack and the inauguration of civil war could not be prevented. If it were a questions of numbers and 800 were not enough, Chase assured Slemmer, he could easily bring in thousands more. Slemmer walked and talked with Gilman for several minutes and then returned to stand before Chase and Farrand. He would consider the contents of Chase's letter and give him an answer the following morning, he told the two men. He wished to consult with the captains of the Federal vessels lying off the fort. Chase agreed, adding he would make arrangements for the captains of the vessels to come to the fort as he passed them on his return to the mainland.[24]

Slemmer had several good reasons for delaying his response. He was certain Chase would not launch an assault while awaiting the possible peaceful surrender of Fort Pickens and that would allow Slemmer to give his men the first full night's sleep they had had in more than a week. Also, he wanted to consult with Walke and Berryman with regard to what could affect their common cause. Neither captain came to the fort, however. Slemmer learned later Chase had offered permission to visit in a form that neither Walke nor Berryman would accept. The offer allowed them to visit the fort on condition of disclosing nothing that could be injurious to the state of Florida. Both naval officers held that they needed no permission from state authorities to go anywhere or consult with anyone on Federal business. Toward evening of the day Slemmer called out the garrison to man the guns facing the main ship channel as the merchant steamer *Oregon* passed between Fort McRee and Fort Pickens and rounded the point of Santa Rosa Island on its way to Pensacola. Rain was still falling steadily and winds and heavy seas had battered the steamer all the way from Mobile. The 300 reinforcements aboard, Mississippians, were part of a contingent that by morning would bring Chase's numbers to more than a thousand men. For the moment the Mississippians, many of them seasick, were worried whether the big guns of Fort Pickens were about to blow them out of the water. Slemmer could not give the order to fire. As yet, he had no reason to interfere with lawful commerce coming into and leaving the port of Pensacola. After the steamer passed, Slemmer had the men secure from their stations and turn in for their first full night's sleep since leaving Barrancas Barracks.[25]

Early in the morning of Wednesday, January 16, the sentries on the walls of Fort Pickens called Slemmer and Gilman to the parapet. *Supply* and *Wyandotte*, both of which had been anchored in the harbor the previous evening, were under way for the gulf, the steamer towing the sailing storeship. Slemmer sent Gilman in a small boat to learn the reason for the departure. When Gilman's craft closed with *Supply*, Walke told him to go aboard *Wyandotte* where he would join him and Berryman. There Walke told Gilman he had decided to clear for New York with the dependents and paroled men he had taken aboard *Supply*, and had ordered Berryman to tow him out through the channel to where he could take advantage of favorable winds that had risen with dawn. As the senior naval officer now on station after Armstrong's surrender, Walke directed Berryman to remain and lend all possible assistance to the army garrison while he took his own overcrowded sailing vessel back to her home port of New York. Within the hour *Supply* sailed with Carrie and Bertie Slemmer, Mary Gilman, Lieutenant John Irwin and his family, and the paroled officers and men from the navy yard. *Wyandotte* turned shoreward and entered the harbor, anchoring under the guns of Fort Pickens. On his return Slemmer had Gilman compose his response to Chase. Under the orders he had from the War Department, Slemmer had decided, after consulting with the officers of the United States Navy vessels in the harbor, that it was his duty to hold his position until such force might be brought against it so as to render it impossible for him to defend it, or until the political situation in the nation became such as to induce him to surrender the public property under his care to such authorities as might legally be delegated to receive it. He deprecated as much as Chase, Slemmer dictated, the present condition of affairs or the possible shedding of blood but, he closed, "In regard to this matter, however, we must consider you the aggressors, and if blood is shed that you are responsible therefore." Berryman carried Slemmer's letter to the navy yard wharf and then ran *Wyandotte* out of the harbor and out of sight. The weather had worsened with strong winds out of the northeast and heavy rains falling all afternoon and evening. Berryman considered it safer for the steamer to ride out the oncoming storm in the open gulf than to try to do so anchored close in to Santa Rosa Island in the bay.[26]

4

"Pickens Is Not Worth One Drop of Blood"

Commissioners from South Carolina had arrived at Washington on December 28 to meet with President Buchanan. These were distinguished gentlemen from that state and were known to the president: former Senator Robert W. Barnwell, former Governor James A. Hopkins, and former Congressman and Governor James L. Orr. President Buchanan, clinging to the hope that no further secessions beyond that of South Carolina would take place, at least before the inauguration of Abraham Lincoln, had offered to meet with the commissioners as private citizens but had declined to hold official communication with them. After five days the commissioners gave up hope that negotiations on their part with the Federal government could take place in a timely manner or to their advantage. They put their frustrations in a letter to the president on January 2 and left the city. Buchanan read the letter to his cabinet the following morning. He wrote on the document that it was worded in such a style that he declined to receive it. The letter was returned and the breach widened between the authorities of South Carolina and the president of the United States who was trying to avoid a direct confrontation while not abdicating his authority and responsibilities of office completely. Buchanan's attempt at diplomatic propriety was taken by the other states of the Deep South as a rejection of South Carolina's claim to independence and further secessions, of course, did follow. Further on this line, on Wednesday, January 16, Isaac W. Hayne, attorney general of the state of South Carolina, arrived at Washington as the personal emissary of Governor Pickens to President Buchanan, this time with a demand for the immediate surrender of Fort Sumter. The demand included the pledge "that the valuation of such property will be accounted for by this state upon the adjustment of its relations with the United States." Hayne returned to Columbia with Secretary of War Holt's letter informing Governor Pickens that the sale of Fort Sumter would not be considered. Florida Senators Yulee and Mallory advised Governor Perry by telegraph that they had ceased to participate in legislative proceedings in Congress and awaited only an authenticated copy of Florida's ordinance of secession before leaving for home. Mallory sent a telegram to Colonel Chase advising him that the stores, munitions, and armaments seized at the Pensacola Navy Yard were valued by the Navy Department in the neighborhood of $117,000.[1]

Then, suddenly, a change in strategy took place among the Southern leaders at Washington. Senator Mallory wired Governor Perry that the caucus of representatives from the Southern states had met and agreed that no blood should be shed before the Southern Confederacy could be organized and brought into being, "Jeff. Davis tells me to say that in the present condition of affairs Pensacola forts not worth one drop of blood." To Chase, Mallory wired, "Southern men are unanimous that no blood must be shed in present state of affairs; that we must first organize a Southern Confederacy. Jeff. Davis tells me to say that he hopes none will be shed and that Pickens is not worth one drop of blood." To his friend and neighbor at Pensacola, Judge Augustus E. Maxwell, Mallory wired, "Bloodshed at present will ruin our cause. Of this we are all unanimous here. Jeff. Davis says Fort Pickens is not worth one drop of blood. See to this, and avoid a collision at all hazards." Mallory was describing the reaction of the Southern Congressional membership to a telegram from Colonel Chase warning that an assault on Fort Pickens would involved heavy casualties. This, combined with the realization suddenly dawning upon the Southern leaders that their impetuous secessions were one thing but the organization and establishment of a political and military entity capable of standing against the might of the United States was another, and this caused them to pause and ponder. The seceded states of the Deep South were not organized politically or militarily. There was no indication which way each of the states of the Upper South might move, or when. The Border States, so important to the stability of both North and South, had not made clear their intentions. The situation at Charleston Harbor, where Anderson's command still faced South Carolina troops, was a stalemate that suddenly could move one way or the other. Bloodshed on Pensacola Bay might lead to a situation the Southern leaders were as yet unprepared for and unable to address. Two days later the caucus of senators from the states of the Deep South met at Washington and again discussed the situation at Pensacola Bay. All but one signed a telegram to Governor Perry pressing their views against an attack on Fort Pickens and advising they were sending the same message to Colonel Chase. The one senator who did not sign the telegram was Florida's Senator Yulee but his concurrence with the content of the message can be assumed.[2]

All of this was unknown to Adam Slemmer and his command at Pensacola Bay. On Thursday morning, January 17, the weather continued miserable and cold. Winds out of the northeast blew strongly all morning and rain fell through the afternoon. Slemmer had his men involved in mounting a 12-pounder gun and an 8-inch sea coast howitzer on the northeast bastion facing the land approach from the east. The 24-pounder flank defense howitzers had been mounted within the bastion casemates and sited to fire along the eastern face into the ranks of attackers gathering in the ditch for an assault. Company G's field battery of four brass 12-pounder howitzers stood in place atop the eastern rampart.[3]

On the mainland, also unaware of the telegraphed advices from Washington, Colonel Tennent Lomax was still determined to launch the assault on Fort Pickens. Governor Moore had expressed his approval in writing of the manner in which Lomax was conducting affairs and had indicated his willingness to accept justifiable losses if the fort were taken. The men, especially his Alabamans, were willing to attempt the assault. They had come to Pensacola fully intending to make the attack and they wanted to get on with it or they wanted to return to their homes. They did not want to continue doing what they had been doing so far, drilling and filling sand bags. One soldier predicted a revolt against the commanders on the mainland if nothing happened in the coming week. Chase received much of the blame for what the men considered unjustifiable delays. Many wondered if the former engineer who had built the fort was awed by the strength of his handiwork, or if he feared an assault against it might show it to be vulnerable. The volunteers from Alabama and Mississippi also questioned Chase's right to command them. He was sixty-three, an old man in their minds, in poor health, a Northerner by birth and an engineer by profession who had never led troops in battle. Tennent Lomax, on the other hand, was one of their own, a younger man at forty-two and a major landowner in Alabama, a wealthy man who owned more than a hundred slaves and $200,000 in property. A newspaper editor in Georgia before settling in Alabama, Lomax was a veteran of the Mexican War and had commanded troops in battle there. The men in the volunteer companies on the mainland looked to Tennent Lomax for leadership, not to William Chase. Lomax worried that the delays Chase was allowing might give time for the arrival of naval reinforcements from the Home Squadron off Vera Cruz. Beyond that, he did not know what the Federal government might be planning and he did not want to wait any longer than necessary before launching his volunteers against the walls of Fort Pickens. He called a council of war that evening. Colonels Lomax and Chase attended as well as Captain Randolph, commanding the navy yard; William H. J. Kelly, Chase's adjutant; Colonel Charles H. Abert, commanding the Alabama/Tennessee Regiment; and Major Samuel Marks, second in command of Lomax's 2nd Alabama Regiment. After discussions that at times grew heated and personal, Lomax called for a vote. Surprisingly, only he and Major Marks voted for an immediate assault on Fort Pickens. The other members of the council voted to wait for reinforcements that would bring the Southern forces on the mainland to such overwhelming numbers that Slemmer would have no choice but to submit and surrender. Lomax put his frustrations in a letter to Governor Moore that evening. He had, he reminded the state's executive, agreed to accept his post at Pensacola on the understanding that he would launch the assault on Fort Pickens immediately upon the arrival of 1,500 men. "The policy of Col. Chase is to remain on the defensive. He will not attack Fort Pickens unless he can concentrate 4 to 5,000 men here. If the Gulf Squadron appears here before the forces are concentrated, all is lost," he wrote. "This ends the matter for the present," Lomax conceded, although maintaining that he thought Slemmer would surrender to a smaller force if threatened at once.[4]

From Washington Secretary Toucey sent a telegram to Commodore Armstrong acknowledging receipt of his message announcing the surrender of the navy yard and advising Armstrong he was relieved of command, effective with the date of the surrender document, and to consider himself awaiting further orders. The telegram ended, "Of course, all work at the yard will be considered suspended from that date."[5]

On Friday morning, much to the relief of Slemmer and Gilman, *Wyandotte* hove back into sight, having weathered the worst of the storm in open water. The steamer anchored in the gulf two miles from the fort. At noon, Commander Farrand arrived at the Fort Pickens wharf with a letter for Slemmer from Colonel Chase. Significant reinforcements had arrived by sea, the colonel wrote, and he was therefore again requesting the surrender of the fort. Slemmer told Farrand that it was necessary for him to communicate with Berryman who had been away running before the storm that still continued to blow. He would advise Farrand the result of that communication the following morning. Slemmer was aware reinforcements had arrived on the mainland and he had heard that the total approached 1,300 or 1,400 men. He ordered a gun fired and a signal hoisted and Berryman sent a boat to pick up Slemmer and Gilman. Once aboard *Wyandotte,* the officers discussed the situa-

The screw steamer U.S.S. *Wyandotte*, under Lieutenant Commander Otway H. Berryman, stood alone to defend Santa Rosa Island with Slemmer (Naval Historical Center).

tion facing them. With *Wyandotte* lying off the fort in the waters of the gulf, there was nothing to prevent Southern troops from crossing from the mainland to Santa Rosa Island on a dark night and landing on the bay shore several miles to the east, out of sight and out of range of the guns of the fort. A sudden dash on the eastern wall, coming without warning out of the dark, would overrun Slemmer's small garrison in a matter of minutes. Such an attack by a horde of enthusiastic volunteers against the disciplined regulars of the garrison would be terrible in its cost. There was no hope Slemmer's men could withstand the fury of close fighting in the darkness against overwhelming numbers. Berryman would not be able to get boats to the shore to carry Slemmer's men off in time to prevent their slaughter. Slemmer told Berryman he was determined to hold out as long as he could, that every day his flag flew from the recently erected flagstaff at Fort Pickens was one more day Southern authorities were denied full use of the great harbor and one day closer to the arrival of help or, at least, advice from the War Department at Washington. As far as he had been able to learn, hostilities between the Federal forces and those of the seceded states of the Deep South had not broken out anywhere in the nation and Slemmer was beginning to doubt whether the leaders of the seceded states would want to open those hostilities with a massacre on Pensacola Bay. When darkness fell Berryman sent ashore six marines from *Wyandotte*, all volunteers, to relieve the garrison from sentry duty so the soldiers could work into the hours of the night and then get some sleep. That night, as had been the case for the last ten, was dark, wet, misty, and cold. Slemmer and Gilman saw what appeared to be a number of lights passing over the bay from the navy yard in the direction of the middle reaches of Santa Rosa Island. Even though they hoped Chase would hold back from launching an assault pending the response due to Farrand in the morning, the officers had to consider the attack they had been anticipating might be mounted. Slemmer had the long roll beaten. The soldiers and seamen turned out. Cannon were primed. The garrison stood to arms through the night but, other than the sound of some gunfire from the mainland which

Slemmer took to be sentinels discharging their muskets as they came off watch, the night passed quietly. From Dry Tortugas Major Arnold wrote the adjutant general at Washington that his company had arrived on the steamer *Joseph Whitney* and now occupied Fort Jefferson, relieving Captain Montgomery C. Meigs, the engineer who had been there with a small party of civilian workmen and hired slaves completing the construction of the fort. Fort Jefferson, Arnold reported, held no armament.[6]

On Saturday morning, January 19, Slemmer dictated his response to Chase's most recent demand for surrender, having Gilman write the older officer that, in response to his letter of the day before, Slemmer knew of no reason why his reply to Chase's original demand of the 16th should be changed and he respectfully referred Chase to that. By this time, Slemmer could see that the volunteers on the mainland had extended their encampments from the navy yard on the east to Fort Barrancas and the lighthouse on the west. From the ramparts of Fort Pickens, he could see men working to construct an arc of sand batteries that stretched from the navy yard to Fort McRee, a distance of just under four miles. Slemmer was anxious about the threat to his command that was visible on the mainland but he was trying to remain patient, aware that every day that passed was one more day toward some point in the future when the government at Washington might tell him what more to do. The morning of Sunday, January 20, a northeast gale whipped the waters off Pensacola. Drenching rain fell on Fort Pickens. Berryman sent a shore party from *Wyandotte* to help Slemmer's men mount a 10-inch columbiad. The huge gun had to be moved a distance in the fort with imperfect tackle and simple appliances, relying almost entirely on muscle power. The job was not finished until the following day. Off Vera Cruz with the Home Squadron, Commodore Pendergrast wrote Secretary of the Navy Toucey acknowledging receipt of orders directing him to send the sailing frigates *Sabine* and U.S.S. *St. Louis* to Pensacola. They would sail in a day or two, Pendergrast responded, "or as soon as money can be obtained to pay their bills." The United States Navy's Home Squadron was experiencing the same difficulties with absent paymasters as the Pensacola Navy Yard had. This, and the unwillingness of Mexican bankers to honor United States Treasury drafts for political reasons, would delay the dispatch of naval reinforcements to Pensacola Bay. On the mainland, however, Tennent Lomax was chafing under the unsettling result of the council of war on Thursday. The situation was simple, the Alabaman thought, He wanted to fight and Chase did not. Lomax complained to Governor Moore in a letter and heard back from Colonel Seibels that the governor fully appreciated the colonel's frustration and that of his troops. The importance of Pensacola Bay to the state of Alabama was the reason Lomax and his command were there, Seibels wrote. In order to accomplish their objective, the capture of Fort Pickens and the defense of the navy yard and the forts on the bay, it was necessary, since the forts were in Florida, that the governor of Florida command the operation and appoint the officer in charge. As it was, Lomax would have to learn to live with Chase. Seibels had considered Lomax's request that he and his men be ordered elsewhere but, for that to happen, Florida would have to assume the responsibility for the defense of the bay and Florida simply did not have the manpower base from which to raise the troops to do that. Seibels ended his letter with, "The governor feels sure that you and the brave men under your command will endure whatever privations and danger the exigencies of the service may call for with the same alacrity, gallantry, and self-sacrificing devotion that has already characterized your conduct."[7]

At Richmond, Virginia, one of the Southern states which had not yet decided its place in the issue of union or secession, the legislature adopted a resolution inviting delegates from all the states interested in promoting peace to assemble at Washington on Thursday, February 14. The legislature appointed former President John Tyler, of Virginia, to serve as commissioner to President Buchanan and Supreme Court Justice John Robertson, of Alabama, to serve as commissioner to the governors of the seceded states. President Tyler and Justice Robertson were charged with obtaining from both parties pledges to refrain from hostile acts until the commission completed its work. This would provide a means for the authorities commanding the forces concentrating against each other at Charleston Harbor and Pensacola Bay time to consider alternatives.[8]

At Washington Secretary Toucey handed orders to Captain Samuel Barron, fifty-two years of age, a Virginian by birth with forty-one years service in the navy, directing him to carry a secret dispatch to Captain William Walker, commanding the steam sloop U.S.S. *Brooklyn* at Old Point Comfort near Norfolk, Virginia. Barron was to deliver the orders to Walker and then proceed immediately overland to Pensacola and there put himself in contact with Lieutenant Slemmer and the naval commanders in the harbor. Barron was to direct Slemmer to communicate with the captains of any vessels of the United States Navy approaching the harbor the order of the secretary of the navy that forbade their entering the port until receipt of further orders. The secret dispatch to Captain Walker directed him to proceed with *Brooklyn* to Fort Monroe, Virginia, and there take on such United States Army troops as the War Department would designate and convey them to Fort Pickens. Walker, on his arrival off Pensacola, was not to enter the harbor but was to land the troops on the gulf shore of Santa Rosa Island as near the fort as possible and then remain in the vicinity to cooperate in the defense of the army force in case of an attack. Secretary Toucey's orders to Captain Walker ended with, "You will remain off Pensacola Harbor until otherwise instructed by this department, and will act strictly on the defensive." At the War Department at Washington Assistant Adjutant General Lorenzo Thomas issued orders for Colonel Justin Dimick, commanding at Fort Monroe, to embark one company of the 1st Artillery with at least three officers, arms, munitions, and as much subsistence not to exceed three month's supply as the captain of *Brooklyn* was willing to take on board. Dimick was to write the name of the officer selected to command the company in the blank space next to the salutation of the letter and then seal the orders which were not to be opened until *Brooklyn* was at sea. The officer so selected by Dimick was Captain Israel Vogdes, West Point class of 1837, a Pennsylvanian of fifty-nine. Vogdes had spent twelve years at the military academy as professor of mathematics after service in Florida during the Second Seminole War. He had the reputation at West Point of being a skillful chess player and was said to be the best read officer in the United States Army on the military history and the campaigns of Napoleon Bonaparte. Vogdes was amiable but irritable with a highly pitched voice. His command was Company A, 1st United States Artillery, the same regiment to which Slemmer's Company G, on Pensacola Bay, and Anderson's Companies E and H, at Charleston Harbor, belonged. Vogdes's orders read that he was to embark his company on *Brooklyn* to reinforce Fort Pickens, of which he would become commander, as well as any of the forts and barracks which were in his power to occupy and defend, in cooperation with the commander of the naval forces laying off the bay. The adjutant general cautioned Vogdes in the orders, "You are to understand that you are not to attempt any reoccupation or recapture involving hostile collision, but that you are to confine yourself strictly to the defensive." *Brooklyn,* Vogdes was informed, would touch at Key West and Dry Tortugas where he was to make contact with the army commanders there, Captain Brannan at Fort Taylor and Major Arnold at Fort Jefferson. The following Wednesday, January 23, Colonel Dimick advised the adjutant general that Company A, 1st Artillery, had embarked on *Brooklyn* the day before under Captain Vogdes. The command had been filled to the maximum standard of eighty-three by transferring enlisted men from other commands at Fort Monroe. Three months' provisions went on *Brooklyn,* that being the limit the vessel could carry. Fifteen hundred musket cartridges, four mountain howitzers, and two 12-pounder field howitzers, each with 100 rounds of ammunition, were taken. First Lieutenants Loomis Langdon and Abner Snead went as Vogdes's junior officers and Brevet Second Lieutenant James Wittemore, temporarily assigned from the 2nd Artillery, was ordered along as the third subaltern.[9]

At the Navy Department on Monday, January 21, Commander Farrand's letter of resignation, dated and mailed from Pensacola on January 13, was received and was immediately accepted by Secretary Toucey without question or comment. Renshaw's letter of resignation, dated January 16, was received the following day and again, without question or comment, was accepted by Toucey. From Washington that same day, now former Senator Stephen R. Mallory wired Chase at Pensacola that an order had been sent keeping all ships of the navy out of the harbor at Pensacola and ordering the nation's naval forces there to act strictly on the defensive. "I leave tomorrow," he added. "Send future communications to Slidell here."[10]

Captain Samuel Barron was a senior officer in the United States Navy and was known for his strong secessionist associates and feelings; he resigned to join the Confederacy (Chicago Historical Society).

On Tuesday, January 22, the weather at Pensacola continued foul with hard rain and wind sweeping the waters of the bay so severely that Slemmer gave permission for half his men to spend the night sheltered and sleeping in the casemates, judging that conditions were too severe for the Southern commanders on the mainland to attempt a crossing. The northeaster pounded the bay well into the following day. Rain had fallen steadily since the 12th, the day the navy yard had been surrendered. Gilman wrote, "Our men were having extremely hard duty, being wet to the skin most of the time, and many of them without a change of clothes, having left their extra clothing at the barracks or the navy yard." *Wyandotte* was not in sight, Berryman having run her out into the gulf to ride out the storm far from shore. Late in the night a small steamer came down the bay from Pensacola and tied up at the navy yard wharf. Slemmer ordered his men to the guns, thinking the vessel might

The screw steamer U.S.S. *Brooklyn* transported Israel Vogdes and his command to Fort Pickens and ended up housing them offshore for three months (Naval Historical Society).

be intended to tow barges of troops over to the island in the darkness. Nothing came of that. At Fort Jefferson on Dry Tortugas Major Arnold wrote the adjutant general he had sent the steamer *Joseph Whitney,* with Captain Meigs of the engineers on board, to Fort Taylor at Key West for armaments. The steamer had returned well-laden and Meigs reported he would have the guns mounted and ready by nightfall. No longer would the bastion on Garden Key be unarmed and open to attack. Meigs's action was timely. Less than a week later the steamer *Galveston* out of New Orleans approached Fort Jefferson carrying an armed force intent on landing and taking possession of the unoccupied fort. Surprised to find a Federal garrison present with heavy ordnance mounted and ready to be brought into action. *Galveston* turned about and steamed away.[11]

In response to another letter venting his frustration at being held back from attacking Fort Pickens, Tennent Lomax received a telegram from Colonel Seibels telling him that the political considerations growing from the advice of the senators at Washington rendered the defensive posture on Pensacola Bay imperative. It would be impractical and unnecessary, Seibels wrote, to enter into explanations as to the propriety of the course since the governor of Alabama was confident Lomax, his officers, and his men would cheerfully obey the orders of their superiors without explanation. The governor appreciated the many trials, difficulties, and privations to which Lomax and his men were being subjected and he promised to alleviate them when he could. In essence, Seibels told Lomax to quit complaining and do what he was told.[12]

The storm continued to batter Pensacola Bay. The ditches before the walls of Fort Pickens, normally dry, by now held twelve to fourteen inches of water. Slemmer wrote to Chase that mail for the garrison had been held up at the Warrington post office since his command moved to Santa Rosa Island. He asked if he could arrange for *Wyandotte* to come to the navy yard to receive the mail. Chase responded two days later saying he had just returned from meetings at Montgomery. He would look into the matter of the mail and, he further informed Slemmer, the garrison on Santa Rosa Island would be supplied with fresh provisions daily if Slemmer so desired. Slemmer sent Gilman to the mainland to consult with Chase and work out a procedure for receiving mail and obtaining fresh meat and vegetables. In a separate letter Chase advised Slemmer he had issued orders that no citizens were to be permitted to pass over from the mainland or to land on Santa Rosa Island. He had just been informed, he wrote, that a party of four or five men had started on a fishing expedition to the island and he requested, if they had landed, they be sent back. "Any collision growing out of persons going over to the island," he wrote, "would be most unfortunate in the present state of affairs, and I would request that you join me in preventing it; and to this effect I would also request that persons in boats be warned off, and if any should land, they should be ordered to re-embark. This should be done in a way to prevent angry feelings between the parties." Slemmer responded he had already apprehended the fishermen and returned them to the navy yard. Later in the day, Chase sent over the accumulated mail with assurances it would be made available in the future without delay. Slemmer was still unaware that the decision to defer the attack on Fort Pickens had been made by Southern authorities at Washington and was pleased to take advantage of every accommodation Chase was willing to make.[13]

At the nation's capital, on Friday, January 25, acting in his role as commissioner to President Buchanan, former President John Tyler met with Secretary of State Jeremiah Black and Attorney General Edwin M. Stanton. Tyler had learned *Brooklyn* had sailed from Fort Monroe with reinforcements for Fort Pickens. The previous day in an interview with President Buchanan there had been no mention that such an act was in process. Black and Stanton deferred making any comment when asked if they knew of the move. Tyler went and saw Buchanan at midnight. The president would only say regarding *Brooklyn's* sailing that she went "on an errand of mercy and relief," and her departure was in no way connected with events taking place at Charleston Harbor. Tyler passed this information by telegraph to his co-commissioner, Justice John Robertson, who was at this time at Charleston.[14]

That same day at Washington Commodore James Armstrong arrived from Pensacola and wrote his report on the surrender of the navy yard to the secretary of the navy. The following morning he wrote, "I now have to request that a court of inquiry may be instituted to enquire into all the facts and circumstances of said capture, and the opinion of the court." The resulting court of inquiry found sufficient grounds for further proceedings and within days Secretary Toucey appointed Captains George W. Storer, Elie A. F. Lavalette, and Levin M. Powell as members of a court-martial "for the purpose of inquiring into the circumstances connected with the surrender by Captain James Armstrong, of the navy, on or about the 12th day of January, 1861, of his command and the public property under his charge at the navy yard near Pensacola, Fla." James M. Carlisle, Esq., was directed to serve as judge advocate.[15]

On Monday morning, January 28, *Wyandotte* carried Gilman over to the navy yard to pick up the mail and deliver correspondence from Slemmer for Chase. Gilman asked for and was granted permission to visit Barrancas Barracks. There he found Company G's former home occupied by Alabama troops with whom he chatted, encountering no hostility. He was told of the peace efforts being put forward by Virginia in an attempt to resolve the crisis between the Southern states and the Federal government and that, if these were successful, there would be no need for a confrontation between the two sides. Gilman went to the officers quarters and gathered up the personal belongings of Major Winder and Lieutenant Eddy. He carried their belongings with him back to Fort Pickens on his return. Hearing of Gilman's visit and becoming concerned at the possibility of socializing between the officers on both sides taking place, Colonel Chase at Pensacola wrote to Captain Randolph at the navy yard expressing concern about security and ordering all further intercourse between officers and men at Fort Pickens and on the mainland to be confined to the Federals sending a boat for mail and fresh provisions to the central wharf at the navy yard and then only one person, an officer or non-commissioned officer, was to be allowed ashore where he was to remain only long enough to complete his business and then leave.[16]

At Montgomery Governor Moore received a query from the state convention on the propriety of withdrawing, or continuing in service, the Alabama troops at Pensacola. Moore wrote back that he had met with former Senators Mallory of Florida and Fitzpatrick of Alabama. They, along with Senator Slidell of Louisiana, had conferred at Washington the previous week with President Buchanan and Secretary Toucey and had been assured that no offensive operations were contemplated regarding Fort Sumter and Fort Pickens. There was to be no excuse, they were emphatically told by the Federal officials, for the shedding of blood during the remainder of the Buchanan administration. The president and the secretary deemed it of major importance that no attack be made at either location by Southern forces for this very reason. Further, Moore informed the members of the convention that he had learned it was the policy of the in-coming Republican party to try to force an early conflict between Federal forces and those of the seceded states before the inauguration of Abraham Lincoln so that responsibility for commencing a war would rest with the out-going Democratic administration of James Buchanan. The withdrawal of Alabama troops from Pensacola, therefore, "might induce the belief among the Black Republicans that resistance was not intended if coercion were attempted on their part and thus give encouragement to them"[17]

Stephen Mallory's home was at Pensacola. The recently resigned senator left Washington

Stephen R. Mallory, Confederate secretary of the navy. The former senator was determined to prevent the reinforcement of Fort Pickens (Library of Congress).

by rail, traveling in company with Captain Samuel Barron who carried the secret orders for *Brooklyn* to embark troops at Fort Monroe and the order to Slemmer to prohibit naval vessels from entering Pensacola Harbor. While in the Senate, Mallory had chaired the Committee on Naval Affairs. He and Barron were acquainted and both men, the former senator and the still-serving naval captain, were ardent secessionists. On Sunday, January 27, the two arrived at the Pensacola railroad depot. Barron had himself rowed out to Fort Pickens and met with Slemmer. He informed the lieutenant that *Brooklyn* was on the way with reinforcements and provisions, and the sailing vessels *Macedonian*, *St. Louis*, and *Sabine* could be expected. None of these vessels were to cross the bar nor enter the harbor lest they draw fire from Forts McRee and Barrancas and from the many batteries lining the shore of the mainland. *Brooklyn*, however, was to land the reinforcements and the provisions she carried. Barron told Slemmer the Southern authorities had decided to defer an attack on both Fort Pickens at Pensacola and Fort Sumter at Charleston for the time being. Although greatly relieved at the news Barron brought, Slemmer was determine not to relax his watchfulness, understanding he most probably would have no notice of a change in Southern policy other than an attack on his walls without warning. At 11:00 A.M., Captain Barron called on Colonel Chase at his home in Pensacola and informed him of the orders he carried from Washington, that United States vessels were not to enter Pensacola Harbor and were to avoid any act that might lead to hostilities. Barron also informed Chase of the secret orders he had carried to Fort Monroe for reinforcements and provisions to sail on *Brooklyn*. Stephen Mallory sat in on this meeting. The former senator was not satisfied with what he heard. He wanted more than just an order preventing Federal vessels from entering the harbor; he wanted to stop the troops aboard *Brooklyn* from coming ashore and reinforcing the garrison at Fort Pickens. He telegraphed Senator Slidell, still at Washington, of the news Barron brought. Mallory knew the personalities and characters of the people in the Buchanan administration. The language in his telegram to Slidell regarding Fort Pickens was clear: "No attack on its garrison is contemplated but, on the contrary, we desire to keep the peace and, if the present status be preserved, we will guarantee that no attack will be made upon it but, if reinforcement be attempted, resistance and a bloody conflict seem inevitable. Should the government thus attempt to augment its force, assault may be made upon the fort at a moment's warning. All preparations made. Our whole force — 1,700 strong — will regard it as a hostile act. Impress this upon the President and urge that the inevitable consequence of

Isaac Toucey, President Buchanan's Secretary of the Navy, co-authored the Pensacola truce agreement. Toucey left office under the censure of Congress (The Connecticut Historical Society).

reinforcement under present circumstances is instant war." Slidell, with Virginia's Senator R. M. T. Hunter and Pennsylvania's Senator William Bigler, took Mallory's telegram to the executive mansion where they laid it before Buchanan. The president read the document carefully. He had to consider, he later wrote, that *Brooklyn* might not arrive in time to land the reinforcements and preserve the fort. Also, the peace convention being brought together under the auspices of Virginia was about to assemble and a collision between the forces on Pensacola Bay might prove to be fatal to that effort. In addition, Buchanan knew that a major portion of the United States fleet had been ordered to Pensacola and, once there, could react powerfully and quickly were an attack against the fort launched. He would consider the proposition, he told his three visitors, and talk with them in the morning. Buchanan later insisted that every member of his cabinet had reviewed and approved his final decision. At Pensacola Stephen Mallory hardly left the telegraph office after sending his telegram. The following morning, Tuesday, January 29, he received the response he had been awaiting and immediately sent Chase a copy of the instructions that had been issued jointly by Secretary of War Holt and Secretary of the Navy Toucey. Addressed to James Glynn, commanding *Macedonian,* William S. Walker, commanding *Brooklyn,* to other naval officers in command, and to Lieutenant Adam J. Slemmer, commanding Fort Pickens, this document described what became known as the truce of Fort Pickens, and it read:

> In consequence of the assurances received from Mr. Mallory in a telegram of yesterday ... you are instructed not to land the company on board the *Brooklyn* unless said fort shall be attacked or preparations shall be made for its attack. The provisions necessary for the supply of the fort you will land. The *Brooklyn* and other vessels of war on the station will remain and you will exercise the utmost vigilance and be prepared at a moment's warning to land the company at Fort Pickens, and you and they will instantly repel an attack on the fort.... Your right and that of the other officers in command at Pensacola freely to communicate with the government by special messenger, and its right in the same manner to communicate with yourself and them, will remain intact as the basis on which the present instruction is given.[18]

That same day Secretary Holt called Lieutenant Saunders to his office and dispatched the young officer on another trip to Pensacola, this time with Holt's letter of instructions to Slemmer regarding the implementation of the truce order. Holt wanted to make certain Slemmer received the original order with no alteration being made to it along the way. In his letter Holt commended Slemmer's move to Santa Rosa Island and expressed the gratification of the War Department at its success. Slemmer was to act only on the defensive, Holt directed, and as far as possible avoid collision with hostile troops. If attacked, he was to make the best defense his position and resources were capable of. Slemmer was to take advantage of Saunders's return to Washington by sending with him details of the transfer of his command, the force now available to him for service, the

Judge Joseph Holt, secretary of war in the Buchanan cabinet, co-authored the Pensacola truce agreement (Library of Congress).

character of the preparations for defense he had made, and any other matters in any way bearing on his own and his command's ultimate safety. Saunders departed Washington that evening on the next train of cars.[19]

Elsewhere, *Macedonian* arrived at Fort Jefferson on Dry Tortugas on Thursday, January 31, twenty-six days out of Portsmouth. Naval paymasters had been avoiding *Macedonian* also. Because of a lack of cash, Captain Glynn reported he had been prepared to pay the harbor pilot by bartering with provisions from the ship's stores were it not for an advance of army engineering funds from Captain Montgomery Meigs. Glynn reported he would sail for Pensacola the following morning. From Fort Taylor at Key West, Captain Brannan reported that *Brooklyn,* with Captain Vogdes's command aboard, had arrived that morning and would sail for Dry Tortugas the following day. Vogdes sent his first report since departing Fort Monroe to the adjutant general which included the fact he had not been able to lay in a supply of desiccated vegetables prior to sailing and asked the adjutant general to have a supply sent to him. A schooner reaching Key West five days from Pensacola brought word that all the forts except Fort Pickens were in the hands of the seceders, Vogdes wrote, adding that all had been quiet on Pensacola Bay when the schooner sailed. From Fort Sumter in Charleston Harbor, Major Anderson reported a lighter had arrived to take aboard the families and dependents of his garrison for transfer to a steamer waiting off the bar that

Fort Pickens, interior view, with the demolished bastion from the 1899 fire and explosion. The concrete structure within the fort is a later addition (National Park Service).

would carry them to New York. And off Vera Cruz Commodore Pendergrast received orders to send the side-wheel steamer U.S.S. *Powhatan,* Captain Samuel Mercer, to New York for decommissioning and a badly needed overhaul.[20]

By Friday, February 1, Slemmer had been able to mount a total of fifty-four guns with the labor of the men of his command, the seamen from the navy yard, and the help that had been furnished by Berryman from the crew of *Wyandotte*. His provisions, with care, would last the garrison at least five months. Much to his surprise and greatly to his satisfaction, Slemmer and his small force had been able to delay the assault on their position by a force from the mainland that, by now, outnumbered them almost twenty to one. Slemmer knew better than to credit this astonishing fact to anything other than confusion and lack of direction on the part of the leadership ashore and to further confusion and disorganization among the leaders of the seceded states. He had no expectation that the experienced politicians in charge of the developing Southern effort would permit these conditions to last and he wondered how long the willingness of the Federal authorities at Washington to give in to Southern demands would continue. Regardless, Slemmer saw some hope for the success of his efforts, even if measured in terms of days rather than in longer periods of time. Suddenly, however, Slemmer's cautious optimism with his handling of the threats from the mainland was upset. He and Gilman now faced a problem from a totally unexpected quarter. The seamen from the navy yard had been drafted for duty with Slemmer. None of them had volunteered for their service with the army within the fort. None had expected this additional duty to extend much beyond the end of the first day of ferrying men and supplies over to Santa Rosa Island but, by now, they had been pressed into service as soldiers and laborers for three weeks, living in dank casemates, working extended hours at hard manual labor, and subjected to rain, cold, and sleeplessness. There had been some growling and dissatisfaction about being confined in the fort, the harsh living conditions, and especially about being stranded on Santa Rosa Island while the remainder of the naval contingent at the navy yard sailed away aboard *Supply* for that greatest of all liberty ports, New York City. Slemmer and Gilman had discounted the displeasure as mere grouching until First Sergeant Jamieson came to Slemmer at five o'clock in the evening to report that some of the seamen were refusing to march to supper, claiming they had not been issued adequate rations of fresh bread. Slemmer told Jamieson to lock the troublemakers in the guardhouse. Jamieson told Slemmer that the protesters outnumbered his guards and they had already refused to obey his orders. Slemmer and Gilman hurried to the parade and found the seamen milling about, determined to have their way. Gilman later wrote, "In fact, they were in open mutiny." Slemmer ordered his full command to form under arms, parading his regulars with loaded muskets and fixed bayonets in front of the seamen. Slemmer asked those he identified as the leaders whether they would obey orders. Whatever the reply, Slemmer deemed it unacceptable and ordered First Sergeant Jamieson and the other sergeants to "buck" the leaders while the rest of the company held bayoneted muskets level and ready to use. With the leaders seated in line on the sand, securely and painfully trussed, several of the remaining seamen shouted and demanded the same treatment as their mates were receiving. Slemmer ordered them lashed to the posts of the piazza around the parade. Realizing the short, bearded, bespectacled officer was not going to give in, these men retracted their words and were untied. They promised to obey orders without further trouble. Of the bucked seamen, some gave in after two hours and most of the remainder during the night. Only two men held out until morning. "We had no further trouble with them," Gilman wrote, "but at no time, either before or after, did we have the same confidence in them as in our own men."

That day Colonel Chase reported to the War Department at Montgomery that he now had 1,500 men from Florida, Alabama, and Mississippi encamped on the shore of Pensacola Bay. He still believed overwhelming numbers would bring Slemmer to realize the impossible situation he faced and to surrender the fort.[21]

On Saturday, February 2, sentinels patrolling the gulf coast east of Fort Pickens brought in six wet and disheveled sailors they had found on the beach. When questioned, the men claimed to be from the schooner *Marie Norton* out of Powderhorn, Texas, bound for Pensacola and wrecked several miles to the east. Slemmer held the men in close confinement until the weather cleared enough to send them to the mainland several days later. That same day, Private Patrick Travers, discharged from Company G in December upon the expiration of his five year enlistment, had been doing some celebrating at New Orleans while waiting to book passage back home to Ireland. Hearing of the circumstances of his former comrades at Fort Pickens, Travers made his way to Pensacola, slipped over to Santa Rosa Island in a stolen rowboat, and signed on for another five year enlistment. Travers had been Gilman's clerk at Barrancas Barracks. On his re-enlistment, he resumed his former duties and served in Gilman's office until retiring from the army in 1875.[22]

On Monday, February 4, the convention met at Montgomery, Alabama, to organize a confederation of the seceded states. Six states of the Deep South were represented: South

Fort Pickens, ditch and casemate embrasures for flanking howitzers (photograph by the author).

Carolina, Georgia, Alabama, Mississippi, Florida, and Louisiana. On the same day the peace convention hosted by Virginia met at Washington with delegates from twenty-one states sent to try to find a way to avoid the rendering of the Federal Union. None of the six seceded states sent delegates.[23]

At New York, *Supply,* nineteen days out of Pensacola, arrived with the officers, men, dependents, and marines from the navy yard. Walke immediately wrote a report to the secretary of the navy explaining what had taken place at Pensacola and why he had sailed to New York instead of Vera Cruz as originally ordered. "I reported the sailing of this vessel and the circumstances by letter to you from Warrington, but the mails not being reliable, I respectfully repeat the same in this report." Walke stated he trusted his actions would meet with the approbation of the secretary. In spite of the fact that obeying orders long out of date and no longer relevant, with most of the Home Squadron having been ordered away from Vera Cruz, and carrying only a portion of the coal and none of the provisions and munitions requisitioned by the vessels of the squadron, and with a hundred helpless parolees and dependents crowded on board, Walke was charged with leaving his station before being regularly relieved and with disobeying the orders of Commodores Armstrong and Pendergrast. He was court-martialed and found guilty. The court sentenced him to be admonished in writing by the secretary of the navy.[24]

On Tuesday, February 5, Brevet Second Lieutenant Saunders arrived again at Pensacola bearing Slemmer's official copy of the truce order. Other than the brief note from Colonel Lay instructing him to communicate with Commodore Armstrong in safeguarding the public property under his charge, this was the first direct correspondence Slemmer had received from the War Department and he was greatly relieved by the secretary of war's approbation of his actions. He was able to compose his own report of everything that had taken place since January 7, knowing he could send the report to the adjutant general in safety by Saunders's hand on his return trip overland. As to his present circumstances, he wrote, his garrison consisted of eighty men, fifty regular artillerymen of Company G and thirty ordinary seamen from the navy yard. Of these, seventy-seven were fit for duty, the others sick. He had organized the men into two reliefs which stood guard duty every other day. All the casemate flank guns were in good order, those intended to fire along the faces of the fort's walls in case of an attack. On the walls, he had nearly all the guns that were available mounted and ready. He admitted, "I now have more guns shotted than with my entire command in case of an attack I could use." As far as he was able to determine, there were no preparations taking place on the mainland for an impending assault. The Southern forces were busy erecting sand batteries opposite Fort Pickens but Slemmer thought this might be intended more at keeping the volunteers on the mainland busy than for eventual use against Fort Pickens. The distance from the batteries on the mainland to the walls of the fort was too great for breaching batteries to take the walls under fire with telling effect without heavy rifled cannon which Slemmer was sure the Southern forces did not yet possess. Shells, however, could be fired from the mainland to burst inside the fort with deadly effect. His primary concern, however, was not the effect of artillery fire on his position. The principal danger to the fort was from storming parties crossing from the mainland in small boats, approaching the eastern land face under cover of darkness, and then making a concerted rush over the wall. Even with the disciplined troops under his command, Slemmer wrote, it would be impossible to prevent the attacking force from capturing the fort in a matter of minutes. Further, naval vessels ordered to stand off Fort Pickens and support his garrison in the event of an attack could render him little assistance. Before they could land their detachments of sailors and marines, the fate of the fort and the garrison would have been determined. Slemmer summarized, "I cannot close this report without saying a few words with reference to my command. From the first to this day, they have nobly vindicated the honor of the American army. Through all the toil and excessive labor by day and standing by the guns at night, for ten days wet to the skin, without adequate sleep or rest, not one word of complaint had been uttered but the most cheerful obedience readily given to all commands. Had we been attacked during those days dreadful would have been the havoc, and we were menaced every day and night, from the 12th to the 26th, by the increasing number opposite us, numbering at one time over 2,000 men. All that prevented, I am confident (for such was the pitch to which their mad folly had carried them) was Colonel Chase's knowledge of the strength and the means of resistance within the fort, and our steady and firm adherence to the course determined from the beginning, not to allow ourselves for one moment to think of surrendering unless absolutely overpowered by numbers. I would recommend especially to the favorable notice of the General-in-Chief First Sergeant Alexander Jamieson, Sergeant Boyd, Corporals Caldwell and O'Donnell, of Company G, 1st Artillery, for especial coolness and activity in their several stations." Of Gillman Slemmer wrote, "I have only to say that during the whole affair we have stood side by side and if any credit is due for the course pursued, he is entitled equally to myself."[25]

At Baton Rouge, the Louisiana convention created a state army on Wednesday, February 6. Governor Thomas O. Moore appointed Braxton Bragg to its command with the rank of major general in the Louisiana forces. Bragg was fifty-four, a graduate of West Point, class of 1837. He had served in the artillery in garrisons and in the field during the Second Seminole War in Florida and had earned fame during the war with Mexico at the battle of Buena Vista on February 23, 1847. Army commander Zachary Taylor had told the battery commander standing in the face of charging Mexican infantry either "Give them a little more grape, Mr. Bragg," or "Double-shot your guns and give them hell!" Winning three brevets for gallantry, Bragg had resigned from the army in 1856 to devote his time to managing his wife's Louisiana plantation. He had developed and maintained a close personal relationship with the colonel commanding the Mississippi volunteers at Buena Vista, Jefferson Davis.[26]

Major Israel Vogdes, U.S. Army, was held aboard *Brooklyn* for seventy-seven days while Captain Adams refused to land his company. Vogdes finally commanded Fort Pickens for only seventy-two hours (Library of Congress).

Brooklyn arrived off Santa Rosa Island and dropped anchor that same day. Captain Vogdes learned to his dismay of the order prohibiting his company from landing and himself from taking command of the fort and its garrison.

Vogdes did go ashore where he met with Slemmer and, in his own words, assumed command even though he would have to return to and remain aboard *Brooklyn*. He found the fort, he wrote in his report to the adjutant general, in a very inefficient state for defense. At the time of Slemmer's occupation, only forty guns had been mounted and since his arrival Slemmer had been able to mount only another fourteen. Slemmer had forty-eight regulars for duty, the seamen from the yard being, in Vogdes's words, "entirely untrained, insubordinate, and of but little use in case of an attack." Fifty-seven of the embrasures were empty of cannon and most of these had only wooden shutters to close them from the outside. The bottom of the ditch, he wrote, was seven feet below the sill of the casemates presenting only a slight obstacle to a storming party that gained the base of the walls. There was no ammunition for the heavy columbiads and no cartridge bags nor any flannel from which to make them. There was no medical officer. The men had no bunks and there was no bedding for the sick.

Should an enemy attack, Vogdes continued, it was probable the assaulting columns would penetrate the fort before his own command could be landed from *Brooklyn* or help could be sent from the other vessels offshore. He had asked that the ships offshore be moved one and a half miles further to the east of Fort Pickens, off the gulf shore of Santa Rosa Island, to where they could bring an enemy force attempting to approach the fort from the east under fire by shelling the columns as they moved westward. This would provide some time for the garrison to look to its defense and for troops to begin landing from the vessels. Otherwise, Vogdes wrote, "We may have the mortification and disgrace of seeing the fort taken by an armed body of untrained troops under our very noses." Slemmer, he reported, had been obliged to employ his command in putting guns into position and barricading embrasures. He had kept half his men under arms every night and they were by now nearly exhausted with fatigue. Vogdes concluded, "Lieutenant Slemmer had done all that it has been possible to do with the small force under his command. His resolution to defend his post at all hazards evinces the highest moral courage on his part, but at the same time, I must state that with any amount of vigor on the part of the assaulters, his defense would have been hopeless. His resolution has probably been the means of preserving Fort Pickens from the seceders." Vogdes asked Captain Walker of *Brooklyn* for boat crews to land the provisions and ordnance he had brought with him. Slemmer's men would have to see to moving these across the beach and into the fort since none of the reinforcements were permitted by the terms of the truce to come ashore.

The attitudes of the two officers now claiming to be in command at Fort Pickens made an interesting comparison. Slemmer had been in the fort for three weeks and had worked with everything he had available to prevent the fort from falling into enemy hands while Vogdes had only just arrived and, although he had orders from the War Department to assume command, he was now restrained by orders from a higher authority to remain aboard *Brooklyn*. Slemmer's correspondence with the adjutant general reflects a determination to hold out against overwhelming odds and a gratitude for every opportunity or advantage that came his way without regard to scope or import. Vogdes's correspondence with the adjutant general describes all that was wrong within Fort Pickens and what he considered as the hopelessness of the situation. Slemmer's optimism reflects his determined attitude hoping for the best. Vogdes's negativism reflects his attitude based on justifying possible future failure. That same day the sailing frigate *Sabine*, Captain Henry Adams, dropped anchor off Santa Rosa Island, arriving from her former station at Vera Cruz. Adams was now the senior naval officer on station, outranking Walker of *Brooklyn* and Berryman of *Wyandotte*. Adams was sixty-one years of age with forty-seven years in the navy. He was said to resemble in many ways the old fashioned sailing vessel he commanded. Adams had developed a reputation for strict obedience to orders.[27]

At Washington on Thursday, February 7 General Scott asked former naval officer Gustavus V. Fox to accompany him to see President Buchanan. Fox had resigned his commission in the navy and was presently managing the Bay State Woolen Company's knitting mill at Lawrence, Massachusetts. Fox earlier had brought Scott a plan to relieve Fort Sumter that was simple. Troops and provisions would embark on a large ocean steamer which would carry extra sailors and enough armed launches to land all the troops in one night. Two light-draft tugboats would accompany the steamer, their exposed engines protected by bales of straw or cotton. The tugs would tow the launches carrying the troops and provisions over the bar at Charleston Harbor. If the waters were calm, the tugs would release the launches which the navy crews would row to the fort. If the waters were rough, the tugs would tow the launches all the way. The screw sloop U.S.S. *Pawnee*, drawing only twelve feet of water and able to cross the bar and enter the harbor, would provide cover for the tugs and launches with her eight guns as they ran past the batteries on the shore at night. Fox counted on the guns of Fort Sumter to provide further protection by driving off any hostile vessels while the operation was under way. The keys to Fox's plan were speed and secrecy. As long as the plan for the project could be kept from South Carolina authorities and as long as it could be executed swiftly under cover of darkness, Fox was certain of success. Buchanan listened as the former navy officer laid out the details. The president considered the potential benefits of Fox's proposal. If the Federal government could reinforce and provision Anderson's garrison within Fort Sumter successfully, the South Carolina authorities would face an accomplished fact. The Buchanan administration would have exercised its Federal prerogative to supply and support one of its garrisons within one of its installations. Anderson's command would gain several months provisions and the government several months of time. As it was, Anderson reported he had less than sixty days provender with which to feed his men. Buchanan approved the plan and Secretary of War Holt ordered the expedition to prepare to put to sea. The following day, however, news

Bvt. Lieutenant General Winfield Scott, U.S. Army, the nation's foremost soldier, was older than the Constitution he was sworn to uphold (U.S. Army Military History Institute).

The sailing frigate U.S.S. *Sabine*, commanded by Captain Henry Adams, both of whom were relics of an earlier time (Naval Historical Center).

that the convention at Montgomery had formed a provisional government of the seceded states reached Washington. Buchanan pondered the effect this might have on pending events and ordered the Fort Sumter relief expedition canceled. He did not want to initiate any action that might lead to a confrontation between the opposing sides this close to the inauguration of Abraham Lincoln on March 4, in less than a month.[28]

On Friday morning, February 8, off Santa Rosa Island, Captain Vogdes on *Brooklyn* wrote to Captain Adams on *Sabine* introducing himself and stating he had been ordered to seek the cooperation of the naval forces off the harbor in the defense of Fort Pickens. Vogdes sent his letter by the hand of his second-in-command, Lieutenant Loomis Langdon, who also carried a copy of the order placing Vogdes in command of the army forces on the bay. Mentioning the poor state of the defenses of Fort Pickens, Vogdes asked that *Brooklyn* with his company of troops be positioned as near the fort as possible in the event he had to land and reinforce it against an assault. Adams agreed to Vogdes's request and ordered Captain Walker to move the steamer accordingly. The following day *Macedonian*, Captain Glynn, arrived off Santa Rosa Island and joined *St. Louis*, Captain Charles H. Poor, *Sabine*, *Brooklyn*, and *Wyandotte*. By now a major portion of the United States Navy's Home Squadron was concentrated at the offing of Pensacola Bay. Within Fort Pickens, Gilman packed his valise to travel overland to Washington. Captain Vogdes was anxious for his version of events to be on the record and had selected Gilman to carry his initial dispatch to the War Department. Vogdes wanted eye-witness testimony to the events that had taken place from the beginning. Since no reinforcement of the garrison was allowed under the terms of the truce, Gilman's absence over an extended period of time would leave Slemmer as the only officer on duty at the fort. Correspondence with Colonel Chase led to his concurrence that Lieutenant Langdon could take Gilman's place in the fort during his absence without violating the terms of the agreement.[29]

Off Vera Cruz, Commodore Pendergrast reported to the secretary of the navy he had transferred his flag from the side-wheel steamer *Powhatan,* which had been ordered to the Brooklyn Navy Yard at New York for decommissioning and extensive repairs, to the sailing sloop U.S.S. *Cumberland*. Pendergrast wrote he would order *Cumberland* and the screw steamer U.S.S. *Pocahontas* to Hampton Roads in response to instructions "as soon as the ships' bills can be settled on shore." The few remaining vessels of Pendergrast's Home Squadron at Vera Cruz were still suffering the effects of the United States Navy's apparently universal shortage of cash.[30]

On Sunday, February 10, Slemmer and his command had been within Fort Pickens for a month. On that day a severe storm whipped the gulf and Captain Adams signaled the squadron at the offing to disperse. Some of the vessels were driven before the winds as far as Mobile, fifty miles to the west. Adams was concerned that Chase might take advantage of the frequent gales that swept the gulf at that season and launch an attack on Fort Pickens while the squadron was scattered and before it could return and reassemble to support the fort or to land reinforcements. Such an attack would be a violation of the terms of the truce agreement but Adams understood that any apology from the Southern authorities for having done so would probably be sent from within the captured fort. After his return and a meeting with Vogdes, Adams drew up a contingency plan to land, in the event of an attack, in addition to Vogdes's command, 200 armed sailors and marines from *Sabine,* 140 from *Brooklyn,* and fifty from *St. Louis*. Adams did not plan to keep *Macedonian* on station for long and *Wyandotte* was now stationed inside the bay serving as the flag of truce boat between the opposing forces. The following day Adams ordered *Macedonian* to sail for Vera Cruz, unaware that Commodore Pendergrast was moving the remainder of the Home Squadron to Hampton Roads. Adams was becoming concerned whether he could supply his remaining vessels with provisions, coal, and fresh water. *Macedonian* was a sailing vessel and, like *Sabine* and *St. Louis,* was awkward and difficult to maneuver close in to shore. The benefit of her heavy armament was

Captain Henry Adams, U.S. Navy, had earned the reputation for strict adherence to orders (Naval Historical Center).

more than offset by the demands that her large crew made for provisions and water. Adams found himself in the ironic position of blockading his squadron's access to its regular base of supply, the Pensacola Navy Yard.[31]

On the mainland the first of the state units that had enlisted for twelve months service, the 1st Regiment of Alabama Volunteer Infantry, arrived at Pensacola by rail and began relieving the early volunteer commands, the men of which were considering whether to sign on for twelve months themselves or go back to their homes. The 1st Alabama moved into Barrancas Barracks and was assigned to man several of the sand batteries its predecessors had constructed along the shore.[32]

On Santa Rosa Island, while Captain Vogdes considered that he commanded all army forces on Pensacola Bay, Slemmer was firm in his position that he had not relinquished command of Fort Pickens nor its garrison. Without reference to Vogdes, Slemer wrote to Colonel Chase, "I observe you are erecting and arming a battery west of the lighthouse. I deem it my duty to protest against its further continuance, and also of all batteries which may bear on Fort Pickens." Chase replied he had received Slemmer's letter and was determined to make good all assurances he had given that no attack would be made on Fort Pickens. He did not consider the erection of batteries on the mainland as being a preparation for such an attack on the fort but, desiring to avoid any actual or implied preparations for an attack, he would give orders for the work to cease. Neither of the officers in command at Pensacola Bay were experienced combat commanders but it was obvious they were knowledgeable and well-versed in the protocols of military correspondence.[33]

At Montgomery, the Provisional Congress of the Confederate States of America elected Jefferson Davis of Mississippi as president of the new nation. Davis would take office the following Monday, February 18. The next day the Congress resolved to take under its charge all questions and difficulties between the several states of the Confederacy and the government of the United States relating to the occupation of forts, arsenals, navy yards, and other public establishments. The Congress ordered Braxton Bragg, now a brigadier general in the Confederate States Army, from Baton Rouge to Pensacola, there to assume command of all Confederate forces on the bay.[34]

On Wednesday, February 13, the merchant steamer *Tortugas* docked at Fort Jefferson on Dry Tortugas carrying orders for Captain Montgomery Meigs to turn over his engineering responsibilities at the fort to First Lieutenant Chauncey B. Reese who had arrived from New Orleans the preceding day. Meigs was ordered to report to Washington. Meigs was forty-five, a graduate of West Point, class of 1836. As an engineer he had worked on a series of major projects prior to being assigned to Washington where he was given responsibility to design and oversee the construction of the aqueduct that was to provide Washington and Georgetown with fresh water to replace the springs and wells on which the communities had depended heretofore. Meigs subsequently was assigned responsibility for completion of the dome of the national Capitol and the addition to the Central Post Office. By the end of the administration of President Franklyn Pierce in 1856, Meigs was well known in the capital city. Among his patrons and supporters were then-Secretary of War Jefferson Davis and New York Senator William H. Seward. With the inauguration of President James Buchanan in 1857, John B. Floyd had become secretary of war. Floyd was an ambitious politician "with a capacity to win influential friends by demonstrating what pleasant consequences could ensue if so obliging a gentleman as John B. Floyd were in a position to dispense public patronage and government contracts." No sooner had Floyd taken office than he and Meigs clashed over the secretary's attempt to confer contracts for work on the aqueduct on a syndicate of supporters of the Buchanan administration. Meigs successfully turned back this first foray into the contracting efforts of the Corps of Engineers but at a significant cost to himself. Floyd concluded the engineer was "too damned honest!" The army captain of engineers and the president's secretary of war were on a collision course. There were further conflicts over the submission of payroll records and the hiring and dismissal of certain civilian employees. Finally, exasperated and unwilling to submit to the will of a man he considered a dishonest politician, Meigs stormed into the executive mansion one afternoon during President Buchanan's reception hour. The president, even then, would do his best to avoid any kind of conflict. He asked Meigs to return at another time when the halls leading to his office would be less crowded with supplicants and seekers. Meigs insisted he would not and demanded there and then that the president of the United States decide whether his administration would support him in his struggle with the secretary of war. The president had Meigs shown out, promising to consider the issue and to provide a response. On August 4, 1860, by-passing the army's chain of command, Meigs wrote out his complaints against Floyd and his demands for support, and sent these directly to Buchanan. The commander-in-chief could not permit insubordination, regardless of either party's claim. He returned Meigs's letter. He had read only the first paragraph, Buchanan wrote, "from which it appears to be a renewal, on your part, of the discussion of the Washington Aqueduct. This is done in no unfriendly spirit but from a sense of duty which I owe to my position." Meigs's appeal from the instructions of the secretary of war, Buchanan advised, was sanctioned neither by law nor by practice and, even had it been otherwise, the appeal should have reached the president through Meigs's superior officer according to army regulations. In kind but firm words, Buchanan informed Meigs that the president's response was to be understood to be an explicit order from the commander-in-chief of the army and navy to a captain of engineers that ended all direct correspondence between them on the matter. On September 18, 1860, while working at his desk in his office, Meigs received an order from the secretary of war removing him from all responsibilities at Washington and ordering him to Dry Tortugas, there to take charge of completing the construction of Fort Jefferson. Now, shortly after the resignation of Secretary Floyd, Meigs was on his way back from exile to Washington to resume his previous position and responsibilities.[35]

At Washington Gilman arrived and reported to the general-in-chief. He had a long interview with Scott in which he explained the sequence of events that had taken place on Pensacola Bay. Scott approved the course of action the two officers had taken, telling Gilman as he rose to leave, "Young man, you have both done nobly. You have been true to your country at a time when she had been false to herself. You shall not be forgotten. God bless you."[36]

On Thursday, February 14, Colonel Chase considered the strategic situation facing him and put his thoughts in a letter to Governor Moore of Alabama. In a confrontation the navy yard, Fort Barrancas, and Fort McRee, he wrote, would be untenable under the fire of the guns at Fort Pickens and those of the ships of war offshore. Although no attack by the Federal forces should be expected during the remainder of the administration of President Buchanan, that would all change in eighteen days upon the inauguration of President

Lincoln. A considerable force could be landed from the ships now off Pensacola Bay and those elsewhere in the Gulf of Mexico which might, combined with the garrison within Fort Pickens, total a thousand men, and "we should not forget that this force may be greatly increased by and after the 4th of March next." In previous communications he had urged that 5,000 men be available on the mainland by March 1, a force which should be capable of preventing Federal forces from retaking and fortifying the navy yard and the approaches to Fort Barrancas until Confederate troops on the mainland could obtain guns of sufficient weight, caliber, and numbers to allow them to batter the walls of Fort Pickens as a prelude to an assault that would have a chance of carrying the fort. "It would be better to withdraw our forces all together than to expose them to an attack which they could not resist by reasons of inadequate numbers," Chase concluded. The former engineer was firmly committed to the persuasive power that he believed overwhelming numbers would give him.[37]

On Friday, February 15, the newly organized Congress of the Confederate States of America resolved, now that its command and support capabilities were coming into place, that immediate steps should be taken to obtain possession of Forts Sumter and Pickens as early as possible, either by negotiations or by force. The Congress authorized President Jefferson Davis to make all necessary diplomatic or military preparations for carrying that resolution into effect. Forts Sumter and Pickens at this time were of major importance in the minds of the political leaders on either side of the issue of secession. Historian Frederick Bancroft wrote, "If the Confederacy had gained possession of all the forts within its territory, as it did of all the post-offices and custom-houses, probably there would have been no war for the Union. But Fort Sumter, in Charleston harbor ... was still held by United States troops. They also retained possession of Fort Pickens, off Pensacola, Florida, which was the chief stronghold on the Gulf.... Neither Fort Sumter nor Fort Pickens could be voluntarily surrendered or evacuated by the United States without national humiliation and a confession of inability or fear to resist disunion. Nor could the Confederacy consent to the retention of these forts by the Federal government without inviting the reproach that it dared not assert the sovereignty it claimed. Hence, thoughtful men on each side calculated that if there was to be a war, it would begin at one of these points."[38]

Indicating concern on the part of the Federal government at Washington, on February 16 Secretary Toucey telegraphed Captains Adams, Walker, and Poor orders to maintain such positions off Pensacola Harbor as could be done consistently with the safety of the vessels under their command, "that you may readily throw in reinforcements and cooperate with the army troops in resisting any attack on Fort Pickens." This telegram was probably sent in response to a request from Secretary of War Holt based on information General Scott had received and passed on during his interview with Gilman at Washington. Toucey was making the point that the navy intended to cooperate fully with the army at Fort Pickens while maintaining caution and concern regarding the safety of its vessels, especially the sailing vessels which could not maneuver close in to shore with any degree of safety, being subject to the erratic whims of wind, current, and tide. By now the steamer *Wyandotte* was permanently stationed inside the harbor, serving as the flag of truce boat and communicating between Santa Rosa Island and the navy yard. She was still making regular but barely adequate deliveries of fresh provisions, water, and coal from the navy yard to the vessels of the squadron. Offshore, *Sabine* and *St. Louis*, both sailing vessels, were able to maneuver close to shore only by hauling by their crews in boats or by being towed by the steamer *Brooklyn*.[39]

On Monday, February 8, Brevet Major General David E. Twiggs had surrendered all United States Army posts and garrisons in the Department of Texas to state authorities. Until this time, state forces throughout the Deep South had been seizing Federal facilities but these had been unoccupied or manned with token caretaker staffs. Twigg's action for the first time put large numbers of United States regulars under the control of Southern authorities. The Federal garrisons were not taken prisoner but were ordered to march to port cities for evacuation to the North.[40]

Also on Monday, Major Zealous B. Tower arrived off Pensacola in a sailing schooner from Havana. He had been ordered there by the general-in-chief on January 4, a month and a half earlier. There is no indication of the reason for Tower's slow response other than for the fact that Tower was an officer in the peacetime army of the United States and that army was working at a pace established by and fitting for a peacetime organization. In comparison, Brevet Second Lieutenant Saunders, fresh out of West Point, had managed to make the journey overland from Washington carrying Slemmer's letter of instructions on the truce agreement in just seven days. On his arrival Major Tower met with Captain Vogdes in his quarters aboard *Brooklyn*. Vogdes informed Tower that, under the terms of the truce agreement, he could not enter the fort and, further, Tower's orders to assume command of the facilities were superseded by Vogdes's more recent orders. Also, Vogdes was an artillery officer, Tower was an engineering officer, and command of Fort Pickens properly rested with an artillery officer, thus with Vogdes. Finally, both Tower and Vogdes were prohibited by the terms of the truce agreement from setting foot on Santa Rosa Island or within Fort Pickens. Even were Tower permitted to move into and reside at the fort in his role as an engineer, being there without civilian workers to perform labor, he would accomplish little. Tower reluctantly accepted Vogdes's rather tightly wrapped version of facts and remained aboard *Brooklyn* with no duties. Slemmer remained within Fort Pickens, commanding in fact, while his brother officers aboard *Brooklyn* disagreed about who really should command in name. From his flagship offshore, Captain Adams sent a detailed report to the Navy Department, writing that he had ordered *Macedonian* to Vera Cruz. The vessel would have been a major drain on his supplies without adding to his tactical capability off the island. Were his sources of provision, water, and coal interrupted or stopped completely, none could be obtained nearer then Key West or Havana, eight or ten days sail away. Adams reported to the Navy Department that if he were unable to obtain a reliable source of fresh water by the 15th of March, he planned to send one of his vessels in search of it. "We are now on an allowance," he wrote. In addition to his anxiety about provisions, water, and coal, there was the further worry about his ability to keep his vessels on station. They could remain at anchor or under way, and near enough to the entrance of the harbor to communicate with *Wyandotte* inside the harbor and with Fort Pickens by signal flags, but a storm could force the vessels of the squadron to have to disperse and run out into the gulf. The gale of the 10th had scattered the squadron for several days. Were the ships of Adams's squadron again driven away by weather, an expedition could leave the navy yard under cover of night and in a few hours the fate of Fort Pickens would be decided. Adams reported *Macedonian* added little to his strength compared to her consumption of resources so he had ordered her to Vera Cruz. Unknown to Adams, the Navy Department was, in fact, concerned about provisioning the squadron off Pensacola. Secretary Toucey telegraphed Commander Alexander Gibson, now commanding *Supply* in place of Walke at New York,

"The moment the U.S. Storeship *Supply*, under your command, shall be ready for sea, you will proceed with her with the utmost dispatch to the offing at Pensacola and report your arrival to the senior commanding officer of the U.S. Navy present. After furnishing the vessels of the U.S. Navy at Pensacola with such provisions, etc., as they may require, you will return with the *Supply* to New York. Should your cargo be insufficient to meet the requirements of the vessels, you will, before proceeding to New York, repair to Key West for additional stores and return with them to the vessels off Pensacola." *Supply*, however, would require more than three weeks to make the long voyage by sail from New York.[41]

On Wednesday, February 20, Captain Montgomery Meigs arrived at Washington late in the evening from Fort Jefferson, four months to the day after his departure into exile. On Thursday, he called on the general-in-chief, on the secretary of war, and on Brigadier General Joseph G. Totten, the Army's chief engineer and his immediate superior. Meigs was warmly welcomed in every instance. Secretary of War Holt immediately reassigned him to his former responsibilities, the completion of the dome of the Capitol and the aqueduct project. With his reinstatement, Montgomery Meigs came to understood that his unprecedented stand against Secretary of War John Floyd had been vindicated. He had perceived the secretary as an incompetent and corrupt civilian holding an appointed office who, for political advantage, was interfering with the army's and his own authority. Meigs had confronted that situation and had paid a severe penalty for his righteous indignation. Now, however, he had been brought back from his lonely exile to what, in his mind, was complete exoneration. This helped Montgomery Meigs confirm in his own mind that his instincts and his abilities were above those of the other men with whom he served, regardless of their rank or station.[42]

At Montgomery on Friday, February 22, the Congress of the Confederate States of America passed an act that created the Confederate States Navy. President Davis named his friend and former Senator Stephen R. Mallory, now at his home at Pensacola, to head the department. On the same day Davis wrote to Governor Perry at Tallahassee regarding the resolution the Congress had adopted on February 15 which empowered him to take steps to obtain possession of Forts Sumter and Pickens. Davis asked Perry to keep the resolution and the correspondence regarding it confidential. It was not intended that progress toward one means should retard or effect the other, Davis wrote. While negotiations were taking place, he promised Florida's executive that earnest efforts were also being made to procure men of military science and experience and the necessary munitions and machinery of war to support the alternative. President Davis fully intended that Fort Pickens would rightly come under the control of the newly established government one way or the other.[43]

On Monday, February 25, Gilman arrived back at Fort Pickens from Washington, having made his return journey by steamer to Havana and thence by sailing schooner to Pensacola. He brought Slemmer and the beleaguered garrison nothing of significance other than their general-in-chief's approbation and blessing. Reporting first to Captain Vogdes aboard *Brooklyn*, he repeated the concern of the administration that there be no collision before the inauguration of President Lincoln on the coming Monday. Later in the day another storm, a norther, blew the vessels of the Federal squadron out into the gulf. While the Federal army and navy forces at Pensacola Bay were constrained by specific orders to avoid collision under almost any conditions, Captain Adams had no way of knowing whether similar constraints had been imposed on the Confederate forces ashore or whether there had been any change. If so, the anticipated assault on Fort Pickens could be launched over the period of days it would take his vessels to run before the fury of the storm and then return and reposition themselves off the fort. Were the forces ashore prepared to launch the assault, they would have all the time they needed to await opportune weather conditions which, at this season of the year, came frequently. Neither Adams nor Slemmer would have any forewarning. During this time, Berryman, riding out the storm on *Wyandotte* inside the harbor, had been working to maintain the flow of provisions, water, and coal from the mainland to Adams's squadron. Captain Randolph at the navy yard under Colonel Chase's command had been cooperating but Randolph was ordered to Montgomery and was replaced by Commander Farrand. Berryman wrote to Adams, "I feel the peculiar feelings of Farrand disturb my diplomatic influences, not from any especial talent of his own, but from downright prejudice. The indications are that you can not get water, and that I can get neither water or coal. I have some resources left, which I will tell you of at a proper time. I shall try again today what may be done." Ever positive in the face of great odds, Berryman, the only officer on board *Wyandotte* at the time, added, "Things look — if not brighter — at least we have some scintillations of light." On Wednesday, February 28, he reported to the squadron commander, "I have been quietly endeavoring to get what you want. The peculiarities of these authorities (new) makes it important and, indeed, cautious. Already I have overcome the indisposition for furnishing you with water, and I shall probably bring out a tank tomorrow if it is smooth. What next I cannot say." Berryman was taking *Wyandotte* out to the squadron off Santa Rosa Island almost daily and returning to his station inside the harbor. In so doing, he passed under the guns of Fort McRee going and coming. He received a note on Friday from Captain Theodore O'Hara, commanding the fort, "With great respect, allow me to suggest to you that in the present very critical attitude of affairs, it is not exactly the thing (especially for a Virginian) to be moving up and down, and in a very excited manner, with respect to this fortress. I ask you, sir, not again, if you please, to pass this fort (either in or out) as you did this morning and evening, without an explanation." Berryman forwarded the note to Farrand at the navy yard, commenting on the apparent lack of coordination between the Confederate forces ashore. He ended his cover letter with tongue in cheek, "I am sure you understand my perfect determination not to do anything to offend the feelings of the assembled forces near this locality." Farrand apparently explained the facts to O'Hara because there was no further correspondence from the commander of Fort McRee.[44]

At Tallahassee on Tuesday, February 28, Florida's legislature formally brought the state into the Southern Confederacy by ratifying the Constitution of the Confederate States of America. To Slemmer and Gilman and the men of the garrison at Fort Pickens, to the officers and men of the Federal vessels off Pensacola, this action made a major change in the events that had taken place since the first days of the new year. Prior to the ratification of the Confederate Constitution there had been political and editorial bombast and commotion and even the seizures of the navy yard and the forts and Federal facilities throughout the states of the Deep South. In spite of that, however, there still had been the remote chance of reconciliation. Colonel Chase, in his surrender demands, had allowed for such a possible resolution, a return to what had been before. The ratification of the Confederate Constitution, the act by the legislature of Florida on behalf of its people, made the break of those states now joined into a confederation a reality. To Slemmer and Gilman, the officers and men of the United States army and navy at Pensacola, the past was gone with no hope of restoration and the future was uncertain. At Fort Pickens as the month of February ended, Slemmer, Gilman, fifty artillerymen, and thirty ordinary seamen had held out for seven weeks against forces on the mainland that at any time could have come over to Santa Rosa Island and rushed into Fort Pickens. Slemmer's stubborn courage had, thus far, won out over the inability of the authorities on the mainland to apply and follow a specific policy. For all the hard talk and bluster, even including the seizure of the facilities ashore, the leadership of the seceded states was still somewhat in awe of the power and the resources of the Federal government, at least for the time being. However, from this point forward, Slemmer and the men with him realized the scattered policies and pronouncements of the seceded states would now have a common origin.[45]

From Montgomery on Friday, March 1, the new secretary of war of the Confederate States of America, Leroy Pope Walker, wrote to Governor Pickens of South Carolina that President Davis shared the governor's belief that Fort Sumter should now be in the possession of the Confederate States and at the earliest possible moment. That feeling, Walker wrote, though natural and just, still had to yield to the realities of the actual situation. Thorough preparation had to be made, he cautioned, because the first blow by the forces of the new nation must be successful for both moral and physical reasons, or the result might be disastrous. A failure would demoralize the people and make them and their government appear in the opinion of the people of the world to be reckless and precipitate. Walker's words applied as much to the situation at Pensacola regarding Fort Pickens as they did to Charleston regarding Fort Sumter. As evidence of his concern, Walker wrote to the governor, Brigadier General Pierre G. T. Beauregard had been named to command the Confederate forces on Charleston Harbor. At Pensacola, Colonel William Chase resigned as the officer in command of Southern forces on Pensacola Bay in order to accept a commission as major general of Florida State Troops. Colonel John H. Forney of Alabama temporarily assumed command in place of Chase pending the arrival of Brigadier General Braxton Bragg who was en route to assume the permanent command.[46]

At Washington, Captain Montgomery Meigs read in the papers that the side-wheel steamer *Powhatan* had been ordered to New York from duty with the Home Squadron off Vera Cruz. *Powhatan* was to go into the Brooklyn Navy Yard for decommissioning and a severely needed rebuilding and engine overhaul. Side-stepping army channels of communication completely, Meigs wrote to his patron, Senator William Seward, that his next-door neighbor, Navy Lieutenant David Dixon Porter, should be ordered to command *Powhatan* and sail her from New York to Pensacola Harbor at once, there to prevent Southern forces from crossing over

Dour and unimaginative Leroy Pope Walker, first secretary of war of the Confederacy (Library of Congress).

from the mainland and assaulting Fort Pickens. Meigs was unaware *Powhatan's* hull was rotten and her boilers worn out.[47]

Also at Washington as the end of the Buchanan administration drew near, the anger of several members of Congress at Secretary of the Navy Isaac Toucey's immediate and unquestioned acceptance of the resignations of naval officers who were leaving the service to join the secession forces erupted. The House Select Committee resolved, "The Secretary of the Navy, in accepting without delay or inquiry, the resignations of officers of the navy, who were in arms against the government while tending the same, and those who sought to resign that they might be relieved from the restraint imposed by their commissions upon engaging in hostility to the constitutional authorities of the nation, has committed a grave error, highly prejudicial to the discipline of the service, and injurious to the honor and efficiency of the navy, for which he deserves the censure of the House." The members were especially incensed at the acceptance of the resignations of Commander Farrand and his brother-in-law, Lieutenant Renshaw. In a final act before its scheduled adjournment, Congress voted as a body on Saturday, March 2, to confirm the motion of the Select Committee. The final report included charges against Toucey for leaving the coasts undefended while sending the active elements of the navy off to foreign stations, for omitting to put into service the twenty-eight vessels presently dismantled and unfit for service while an appropriation of over $600,000 for their repair and maintenance lay unspent, and for failing to safeguard the property and the rights of the citizens of the nation. Most of the anger of Congress was focused on Toucey's immediate and unquestioned acceptance of the resignations of Farrand and Renshaw, officers who, while on duty at Pensacola, had been openly engaged in the treasonous conspiracy that resulted in the surrender of the navy yard.[48]

5

"Too Much Dallying and Curtseying"

On Monday, March 4, at Washington Supreme Court Chief Justice Roger B. Taney administered the presidential oath of office to Abraham Lincoln. This was the seventh time the eighty-four-year-old jurist had done so to a chief executive beginning with President John Tyler in 1841. The ceremony took place in front of the Capitol, its dome sheathed in scaffolding as the temporary copper and wood structure was being replaced with a cast iron dome under the direction of Captain Montgomery Meigs. To provide security for the event, General-in-Chief Scott had been able to bring to the city an army contingent of only 653 rank and file under Colonel Harvey Brown which included the demonstration company of sappers and miners from West Point, several hundred untrained recruits from Fort Hamilton in New York Harbor and from the cavalry school at Carlisle Barracks, Pennsylvania, and five regular artillery and infantry companies.[1]

President-elect Abraham Lincoln had arrived at Washington on Sunday, February 24, after a circuitous journey that carried him through many of the important states of the North. He was welcomed at the national capital by New York Senator William H. Seward. one of the founders of the Republican party, and Congressman Elihu B. Washburne, a representative from Lincoln's home state of Illinois and a close friend. Senator Seward had intended to come away from the Chicago convention as the candidate of the Republican party instead of Abraham Lincoln and he could barely contain his disappointment that the honor had gone to a man he held in low esteem. Seward considered himself the focus of the Republican party and, with this first election that brought the party to power at Washington, the foremost Republican in the nation. Nonetheless, he was polite and respectful of the president-elect when they met. He offered to edit a draft of Lincoln's inaugural address and he returned the document with the notation, "I have suggested many changes of little importance severally but in their general effect tending to soothe the public mind." Seward was telling the president-elect that his own years of experience and his high stature among the elected leaders of the nation were available. In his soul, Seward knew it was himself who should be giving the inaugural address, not editing it. Seward was an experienced politician. He had learned to accept political life with its high expectations and its sometimes disappointing realities. He had decided that, with Lincoln having won the nomination and then the election, if he could not be president, he would be premier. Seward was well known throughout the nation, especially in the Southern states where he was feared more than most other Northern politicians. The *New Orleans Bee* recognized this in an editorial on January 3, "Though not seated on the throne, he is the power behind the throne, greater perhaps than the occupant himself."[2]

In his inaugural address, President Lincoln wanted to reach out to and calm the emotions that were boiling throughout the states of the South but he also made it clear he was assuming certain responsibilities in taking the oath of office. He declared he would ensure "as the Constitution itself expressly enjoins upon me," that the laws of the Union should be faithfully executed in all the states. He continued, promising,

> In doing this, there needs be no bloodshed or violence, and there shall be none unless it be forced upon the national authority. The power confided in me will be used to hold, occupy, and possess the property and places belonging to the government and to collect the duties and imposts, but beyond what may be necessary for these objects, there will be no invasion, no using of force against or among the people anywhere.[3]

North and south, those who heard or read Lincoln's address inferred that the reference to the property and places belonging to the government included specifically the facilities and garrisons at Fort Sumter and Fort Pickens. Of the other forts remaining in the possession of the Federal government located in the Southern states, Forts Taylor and Jefferson, at Key West and Dry Tortugas, were not threatened, and Fort Monroe, at Hampton Roads, Virginia, was not an issue since Virginia had not seceded. The focus of the nation was on those properties and places located at Charleston Harbor and at Pensacola Bay.[4]

The new president was an experienced trial lawyer, debater, and public speaker but he was inexperienced in dealing with members of Congress although he had been elected to and had served one term as a junior member in the House of Representatives in 1847. He was not yet acquainted with all the members of his own cabinet nor were they familiar with him. As the head of the Republican party only recently come to power for the first time in the land, he did not have available to him experienced administrators from within his own party to whom he could look for support and guidance. Lincoln, therefore, felt he had to rely heavily on his newly appointed secretary of state, Senator William Seward. The secretary was eight years older than Lincoln and far more experienced and able. Seward had led the New York

Lincoln's secretary of state William H. Seward. If he could not be president, Seward decided he would be premier (Military History Institute).

state senate and had been governor of that state. Seward had served in Congress with stalwarts Clay, Webster, and Calhoun during the years Lincoln was keeping store, sitting in the Illinois legislature, and serving his one term in Congress. As he assumed the office of the chief executive of the nation, the most pressing issue on Lincoln's agenda was the decision he had to make on whether to adopt an aggressive policy toward the seceded states and thereby risk losing the support of the large peace movement in the North, while possibly driving the border states into secession, or to delay decisive action, hoping for some resolution to develop but thereby risk alienating the radical wing of his own party which was already showing impatience at the lack of firm standing during the Buchanan administration's final months. Abraham Lincoln was confident that he could look to William Seward for guidance through this difficult time.[5]

On the morning of the day of Lincoln's inauguration, Connecticut lawyer, journalist, and editor Gideon Welles learned, having been summoned to Washington, that he would be asked to serve in President Lincoln's cabinet as secretary of the navy. Welles was not sure whether he should take the position. Secretary of the navy was considered one of the least desirable portfolios and was often the last one filled. Welles accepted, knowing his predecessor, Isaac Toucey, was leaving town under censure of the House of Representatives. Chief Justice Taney found time on that busy day to administer the oath of office to the new Secretary of the Navy Welles.[6]

Entering his office the following morning, Tuesday, March 5, Abraham Lincoln was handed a letter by Judge Joseph Holt who had agreed to remain as acting secretary of war until Simon Cameron of Pennsylvania would be able to assume the role several days later. At this early hour on the first day of the Lincoln administration, the other cabinet members were not in their offices. Some had not yet assumed their roles. The letter Holt handed the new executive was a communication just received from Major Robert Anderson at Fort Sumter informing the secretary of war that new batteries had been erected by South Carolina forces on the mainland which commanded Anderson's position, that the channels into the harbor had been obstructed, and that patrol boats were constantly observing him and his garrison. In Anderson's opinion, the commander at Fort Sumter opined, it would take an army of 20,000 men to relieve him and hold the fort thereafter. Anderson added that he had rations for his garrison for only about twenty-eight more days. After that time, if not provisioned, he would be starved into having to evacuate the fort. Holt explained to the new president that Anderson's declaration had taken the War Department by surprise. None of his previous communications had intimated such a critical state of conditions. The president sent for General Scott and asked his advice. Lincoln was shocked when the general told him Fort Sumter should be given up as untenable. Lincoln asked about the other threatened Federal facility in the Deep South, Fort Pickens. Holt then added to his concerns by informing the president of the order he and Secretary of the Navy Toucey had sent on January 29 establishing the truce at Pensacola Bay and prohibiting Captain Vogdes from landing his command and reinforcing Fort Pickens. Lincoln considered the news for several minutes and told General Scott it was his intention to maintain all the forts still in the government's possession and for the general to make whatever arrangements were necessary to reinforce them. He handed Major Anderson's letter to General Scott, telling him to read it and prepare comments on it.[7]

Diplomats John Forsythe, Martin J. Crawford, and Andrew B. Roman arrived at Washington from Montgomery, "duly accredited by the Government of the Confederate States of America as commissioners to the Government of the United States." Secretary of State Seward met privately and unofficially with Crawford who only recently had withdrawn as congressman from Georgia on January 23. Seward and Crawford had known each other during their years in government and considered themselves more adept at diplomacy and governance than the present occupant of the executive mansion. Seward advised Crawford that Lincoln would not acknowledge the commissioners from a government he could not recognize. During their lengthy discussion, Seward led Crawford to believe that the reference in Lincoln's inaugural address pledging the protection of public property to the fullest extent of the national power was merely a general expression that should not be taken seriously. Seward assured the commissioner of his own good intentions and promised to maintain communications with these three men.[8]

From within the nation's capital city newspaperman Littleton Quinton Dennis Washington wrote to Confederate Secretary of War Walker at Montgomery on that same day. Washington was a Southern sympathizer, connected with Southern figures in both branches of Congress and in the bureaucracy, and a close associate of Virginia's Senator Robert M. T. Hunter. L. Q. Washington wrote that he had been asked by Alabama's Senator Clement C. Clay, prior to Clay's departure for home, to telegraph or write to Governor Moore of Alabama on any matters of importance. This having taken place before the establishment of the Confederate government at Montgomery, Washington now thought he should communicate directly with the Confederate secretary of war there. It was being discussed in Federal army circles, he wrote, that Fort Sumter would be reinforced. Simultaneously, or prior to this, there was to be a change at Pensacola which, of the two, the Federal government considered the point of greater importance. Washington suggested the Confederate authorities prevent anything in the form of dispatches, letters, or messages going through to Lieutenant Slemmer. He ended his letter with the promise to "endeavor to get hold of movements as soon as possible, and advise you."[9]

The following day, Wednesday, March 6, General Beauregard wrote to Secretary Walker from Charleston that, in his opinion, if Fort Sumter were properly garrisoned and armed, it would be a perfect Gibraltar to anything but constant shelling night and day from the four points of the compass. As it was, the Creole general declared, the weakness of its garrison constituted the greatest advantage to the Confederacy and "we must for the present turn our attentions to preventing it from being reinforced." At Montgomery, the Confederate Congress passed legislation authorizing the creation of the Confederate States Army.[10]

At the nation's capital, Commodore Armstrong's court-martial convened at the Navy Department. Secretary of the Navy Welles, new to the office and somewhat overwhelmed by events, took advantage of the officers assembled for the court who were, in his mind, some of the most intelligent and experienced in the naval service. They were Captains Charles Steward, Francis H. Gregory, Silas H. Stringham, and Hiram Paulding. Welles availed himself of the opportunity to obtain their views and opinions on the subjects of Forts Sumter and Pickens, among other matters. The secretary weighed their suggestions against the fact that each of them was a veteran of the War of 1812 and, while the possessors of long careers and loyal reputations, they were all very old men. Welles had known Captain Stringham for years and selected him to serve as the chief of the Navy Department's detailing office, the position responsible for the selection and placement of officers throughout the navy. Welles would rely heavily on Captain Stringham in the months to come.[11]

Secretary Holt called at the Navy Department and asked Secretary Welles to accompany him to the War Department. Arriving, Holt and Welles met Generals Scott and Totten and soon-to-be Secretary of War Simon Cameron. Scott opened the discussion by announcing that the agenda, at the direction of the president, was the dispatch received from Major Anderson the day before and the new and alarming time element it had introduced. Anderson and his garrison would be starved out of Fort Sumter within four weeks unless they were re-supplied immediately or removed. To Secretary Welles, the information was "unexpected and astounding, and there was, on the part of such of us as had no previous intimation of the condition of things at Sumter, an earnest determination to take immediate and efficient measures to relieve and reinforce the garrison." General Scott, without opposing that idea, related the fate of the attempt that had already been made by *Star of the West* in January and the difficulties that now could be expected from the numerous Southern batteries newly erected around Charleston Harbor. One attempt had been made and that had failed, Scott declared, and another attempt was impractical. It was a matter, Scott declared, for the naval authorities to decide because the army could do nothing further. The general-in-chief did not, he told his audience, expect any conclusions to be reached during this hurriedly called meeting. He had brought them together at the direction of the president to communicate the information that had just been received from Major Anderson. General Scott asked them to consider the issues overnight and be prepared to meet with the president the following day. Scott suggested to Secretary Welles that Commander James H. Ward, who had been involved in planning the earlier attempt to relieve Fort Sumter, be called to Washington from his current station, commanding the receiving ship U.S.S. *North Carolina* at the Brooklyn Navy Yard.[12]

From Greenville, Alabama, some ninety miles north of Pensacola, the editor of the *Southern Messenger*, reacting to the Southern command's decision to allow the supply of fresh provisions, coal, and water to the garrison of Fort Pickens and to the Federal vessels offshore, wrote to the authorities on the bay, "There had been too much dallying and curtseying to Lieutenant Slemmer and his men — make them in the future keep their places, for you need expect no return for your kindness." From Montgomery on Thursday, March 7, Acting Adjutant General Deas telegraphed Brigadier General Braxton Bragg at Baton Rouge confirming his appointment to the command of all Confederate troops at or near Pensacola, to which station he was to repair without delay. Also from Montgomery, newly-confirmed Secretary of the Navy Stephen Mallory wired Florida's Governor Perry that the gunpowder stored in the exterior magazine at the Pensacola Navy Yard was insecure and asked if the governor had any objection to its removal to the Mount Vernon, Alabama, arsenal for safekeeping. The governor had no objection and the powder was moved.[13]

At Washington, President Lincoln was entering into his third day in office. He met with his military advisers and asked Secretary of State Seward to read the message Major Anderson had sent, the message that General Scott had used as the agenda for the meeting the day before. Lincoln had not yet heard the opinions of those who had been in attendance at that meeting and who had since had the opportunity to consider the contents of Anderson's message. With him this morning were Secretary of State Seward, Secretary of the Navy Welles, Simon Cameron who had just been sworn in as secretary of war, Generals Scott and Totten. Secretary Welles had asked Captain Silas Stringham to accompany him. Welles began by insisting that Fort Sumter could and should be provisioned and reinforced by tugs moving in under cover of night, closely following the plan developed and put forward by Commander Ward several months previously during the Buchanan administration. Secretary of State Seward, however, strongly opposed an attempt to reinforce the garrison. Both he and the president were anxious to avoid any measure that might disturb public opinion in those Southern states which had not yet seceded. The meeting ended and the members went their separate ways but, Welles realized, without any one of them understanding with whom the responsibility for further action rested.[14]

Senator Simon Cameron, Lincoln's first secretary of war, was inept and ill-suited for his position (U.S. Army Military History Institute).

At Pensacola on Friday, March 8, Mr. C. P. Knapp, the ration contractor on the mainland, wrote Captain Walker on *Brooklyn* that there was no potable water tank available locally in which to transport fresh water out to his vessel and not enough wooden casks to hold the quantity of fresh water Walker's quartermaster had ordered. Knapp offered to send out about 1,000 gallons at a time in a small boat if the Confederate authorities ashore permitted, "but it would be very expensive." Access to fresh water for the crews of all his vessels was becoming a major concern to Captain Adams. *Brooklyn* carried an apparatus for distilling fresh water from sea water but the equipment had broken down. Walker advised Adams that his mechanic, Mr. Joshua Follansbee, was working to repair the device but Walker admitted he had little hope of success soon. Provision also were growing short. On *Brooklyn*, Walker had agreed with Vogdes that the army officer would replace the provisions his men were consuming during their extended and unexpected presence on the warship. This replacement, however, could only be done after Vogdes's company had entered Fort Pickens since the provisions Vogdes had brought had already been landed and were stored in the casemates within the fort. Until such time, Vogdes's men were consuming ship's provisions and adding to the strain on *Brooklyn's* larder and supply of fresh water.[15]

At Washington, Secretary Seward assured the editors of the *National Intelligencer* that Fort Sumter would be evacuated in due time. He had not discussed this assurances with the president beforehand. He then met with the Confederate commissioners, Forsythe, Crawford, and Roman, and left them believing that he intended to delay any action directed toward provisioning or reinforcing Fort Sumter.[16]

On Saturday, March 9, the Confederate War Department called on the governors of the seceded states for 11,700 volunteers, 5,000 of whom were to go to Pensacola. Alabama, Georgia, and Louisiana were each to furnish 1,000; Mississippi, 1,500, and Florida 500.

Secretary Walker asked the governors of the states to keep the movements of these troops concealed from the government of the United States.[17]

At Washington, President Lincoln chaired his first full cabinet meeting. The topic of Major Anderson and the garrison at Fort Sumter was laid before the members, some of whom questioned how such a condition had been allowed to arise. Without exception, the members rejected General Scott's recommendation that Fort Sumter be evacuated. Secretary Seward was not in attendance at this initial cabinet meeting; he was at Harrisburg, Pennsylvania, on political business. Lincoln learned that his verbal order to Scott for the general to make whatever arrangements were necessary to reinforce the forts, given on Tuesday, had not been carried out. The commander-in-chief had assumed the situation on Pensacola Bay, where Vogdes's command sat offshore on *Brooklyn,* had been resolved by that order. At the president's specific direction, Secretary of War Cameron now put the order in writing. Simon Cameron was a Pennsylvania politician with little administrative ability and no experience whatsoever with his duties and responsibilities as chief of the War Department. The department itself consisted of some ninety employees, many appointed during the term of Secretary of War John Floyd from the states of the South, perhaps a third of whom could not be relied upon to uphold the Lincoln administration in a civil conflict. Cameron did not know to make use of the department's resources and thus his written order to Scott was far from peremptory: "I am directed by the president to say that he desires you to exercise all possible vigilance for the maintenance of all places within the military department of the United States, and to promptly call upon all departments of the government for the means to that end." Assuming that the situation at Pensacola had thus been resolved, Lincoln turned to the issue of Fort Sumter. He directed the general-in-chief to answer three questions in writing: How long could Fort Sumter hold out? Could it be reinforced or resupplied during that period with the existing means available to the government? If not, what additional forces would be required? The new president had determined to learn more before he would seriously consider the aged general's advice to give up the fort.[18]

Brigadier General Braxton Bragg, C.S. Army, commanded the forces at Pensacola facing those on Santa Rosa Island. A stern disciplinarian and drill master, he could not win the loyalty of his officers and men (Chicago Historical Society).

On Sunday, March 10, Braxton Bragg was en route to his new command at Pensacola. The Confederate government at Montgomery telegraphed ahead for him to report his needs in terms of artillery and munitions of war with the view of achieving the reduction of Fort Pickens soon after his arrival. Also from Montgomery, Captain Randolph wired Commander Farrand at Pensacola that Secretary of the Navy Mallory desired a statement on the condition of the steamer *Fulton* now hauled up on the ways at the navy yard. Mallory wanted a detailed report on her condition and an estimate of the time that might be involved in preparing her for launching and being placed back in commissioned for service at sea. Mallory was wasting no time in trying to bring together the few resources he had at hand to build a navy for the Confederacy.[19]

On this day, the second Sunday of March, 1861, Slemmer and his command of fifty gunners and thirty seamen had been within Fort Pickens for two months and were still effectively preventing the Confederate authorities from occupying the fort or making full use of the facilities on Pensacola Bay.

On Monday, March 11, Secretary of State Robert Coombs wired the three Confederate commissioners at Washington that his government would not let the Federal government bind its hands for even a day without agreeing to the evacuation of both Fort Pickens and Fort Sumter. It was idle to talk of peace negotiations, he wrote, and instructed the commissioners to "pertinaciously demand" the withdrawal of the Federal vessels and troops off Pensacola. The commissioners called upon Virginia's Senator Robert M. T. Hunter and asked him to intercede with Secretary Seward in an attempt to achieve even an informal interview. Seward replied the following morning to Hunter that it was not within his power to receive "the gentlemen of whom we conversed yesterday." The Lincoln administration was not going to grant an iota of legitimacy, even informally, to the existence of a rebellious government.[20]

After a stage ride of forty-eight miles from Mobile over what he described as "a bad road," Braxton Bragg arrived at and assumed command over the Confederate forces on Pensacola Bay where he established his headquarters at Barrancas Barracks. Offshore, aboard *Brooklyn*, Captain Israel Vogdes was somewhat amused when he learned of the change of command that had taken place on the mainland. He and Bragg had been classmates at West Point, graduating fifth and eleventh respectively in the class of 1837. The historian Bruce Catton described Braxton Bragg as being "as baffling a mixture of high ability and sheer incompetence as the Confederacy could produce." Braxton Bragg had the reputation from his days as a cadet at West Point of priding himself on being the ugliest man in the corps. Bragg had also developed a reputation at the Military Academy as being "a reckless and daring fellow, who was always ready for any sort of a racket. He was one of the few who were addicted to nocturnal excursions to Benny Havens' ranch, and many were the hair-breadth escapes he and the other frisky ones had on getting back to quarters after a jolly time at 'Benny Havens, Oh!'" Later in his career, however, General Jones M. Whithers described Bragg as "a good officer, a man of fair capacity, [but] self-willed, arrogant, and dictatorial." At this time no one within the Confederacy questioned Bragg's fitness for the important task that the government at Montgomery had called upon him to assume. Confederate Congressman James L. Pugh wrote to Bragg that no general in the army had more of the public's confidence. His praise was on the lips of every man, Pugh wrote, and one official described Bragg as the only general within the Confederacy who earned the reputation of having accomplished all he undertook. Grady McWhiney, Bragg's biographer, described Bragg as "Too ambitious to be satisfied with himself or with others; he sought perfection, and was disappointed when he failed to find it or achieve it. Authoritarian himself, he nevertheless resented his superiors' authority." His demanding manner drove him to extremes that often had fellow officers in the peacetime army wondering about his stability. McWhiney mentions Ulysses S. Grant remembering Bragg as "a remarkably intelligent and well-informed man, professionally and otherwise," who had an "irascible temper and was naturally disputatious.... As a subordinate he was always on the lookout to catch his commanding officer infringing his prerogatives; as a post commander he was equally vigilant to detect the slightest neglect, even of the most trivial order." Grant recounted a story about Bragg at a western post when he was serving as both a company commander and the post quartermaster. "As commander of the company he made a requisition upon the quartermaster — himself— for something he wanted. As quartermaster he declined to fill the requisition, and endorsed on the back of it his reasons for so doing. As company commander, he responded to this, insisting that his requisition called for nothing but what he was entitled to, and that it was the duty of the quartermaster to fill it. As quartermaster he still persisted that he was right." Unable to resolve the dilemma, Bragg referred the whole matter to the post commander, who exclaimed, "My God, Mr. Bragg, you have quarreled with every officer in the army and now you are quarreling with yourself!" Bragg was later described as "dull, sour, pedantic — seemed unable to inspire his officers. Even his letters home to his wife resemble battle reports and lacked any semblance of affection. He had little social life in the army, and his personal mannerisms, which his own chief of staff later termed as repulsive, failed to incite enthusiasm or warmth. The men respected his abilities as a drillmaster and disciplinarian, but little else." Part of Bragg's interpersonal problems might have stemmed from his chronic ill health. Bragg suffered from migraine headaches, boils, dyspepsia, and rheumatism and the symptoms tended to increase with either despondency or frustration, or both. Bragg's assumption of command, however, was well received at Pensacola. His presence was seen as bringing authority and control to the bay area instead of having it exercised from Montgomery as had been the case in the past. One newspaper reported, "On his arrival at the yard, the officers and soldiers manifested their gratification at his presence by the most vociferous demonstrations of applause. We mingle our congratulations with those of the citizens generally upon the accession of one to the command here who has the unlimited confidence of all friends and the respect of those opposed to him."[21]

From Washington, former Texas Senator Louis Wigfall wired General Beauregard at Charleston, basing his communication on interpretations of statements made by Secretary Seward over the past several days and on information gathered and passed on to him by L. Q. Washington, "Believe here that Anderson will be ordered to evacuate Sumter in five days. Was certainly informally agreed on in Cabinet Saturday night. May have been done as a ruse to throw you off your guard and enable them to reinforce."[22]

President Lincoln reacted to Secretary Cameron's vaguely worded order to General Scott of Friday by personally sending another order in writing through the War Department specifically directing Scott to order the landing of Vogdes's company to reinforce Fort Pickens. Lincoln kindly assumed Scott's neglect of his earlier order had been due to the old soldier's preoccupation with events taking place at Fort Sumter. By now, however, the commander-in-chief was slowly learning the ways of government. He sent his order through the office of the adjutant general at the War Department to insure there was a record of it and that the proper persons and channels would be involved.[23]

On Tuesday, March 12, at Fort Pickens Slemmer's sentinels brought in four runaway slaves seeking freedom. The men had stolen a small boat and rowed to Santa Rosa Island determined to plead for their liberty. This brought Slemmer to a serious conflict between his official duty and his personal feelings. While he and his command were at Fort Pickens to protect the public property under their charge, they were also there to uphold and carry out the laws of the land which, at the time, required that they return fugitive slaves to their masters. Slemmer had to overlook the existence of a government in rebellion claiming to represent the seceded states, and he had to put aside his own personal feelings with regard to human bondage. Slemmer had the four men sent to the mainland and turned over to the town marshal at Pensacola. That evening four more black men appeared with the same intent and were sent back to the same disposition, this time Slemmer accompanying the escort in person.[24]

At Washington General Scott finally had the order issued that should have been given at the president's direction on March 5, the day after the inauguration. Addressing Captain Vogdes, Assistant Adjutant General Lieutenant Colonel Edward D. Townsend wrote, "At the first favorable moment, you will land with your company, reinforce Fort Pickens, and hold the same until further orders. Report frequently, as opportunities present themselves, on the condition of the fort and the circumstances around you." General Scott asked Secretary Welles to provide a naval vessel to carry the order to Vogdes. Welles telegraphed Commander Andrew H. Foote, temporarily commanding the Brooklyn Navy Yard, to dispatch the screw steamers *Crusader,* Lieutenant Commanding Tunis A.M. Craven, and U.S.S. *Mohawk,* Lieutenant Commanding James Strong. Both vessels were immediately to put to sea, one to convoy the merchant steamer *Empire City* en route to Texas to take on board the army detachments that had been surrendered there by General Twiggs. The other was to make for Pensacola with Scott's order to Vogdes. Welles left it to Foote to determined which vessel was to do what; both would carry copies of the order. *Mohawk,* Foote decided, would deliver the dispatch. He did not realize that would take nineteen days after an unusually rough passage down the Atlantic coast and around the long Florida Peninsula. With the order finally on the way, the president and his cabinet were once again sure the matter on Pensacola Bay was resolved and they turned their attention and resources toward what they now considered the more volatile problem, that at Charleston Harbor. From Washington, Postmaster General Montgomery Blair telegraphed for his brother-in-law, Gustavus Fox, to come to the capitol. Blair wanted Fox to meet the president and to review with him the plan developed the previous winter by Commander Ward to relieve Fort Sumter.[25]

Capable Gustavus Vasa Fox put in place and led the almost successful expedition to relieve Fort Sumter in April 1861 (Naval Historical Center).

On Wednesday, March 13, immediately upon assuming command on the mainland, General

Bragg wrote to Slemmer. He sent his adjutant, Captain Roger C. Wood, to carry the letter and to communicate Bragg's views. Bragg asked Slemmer for "information necessary to enable me to understand our relative positions." Slemmer had gone by boat to Pensacola to oversee the return of the escaped slaves to the city marshal and did not get to meet Wood. He wrote to Bragg upon his return to Fort Pickens, sending Bragg a copy of the truce agreement and asking whether Bragg considered the agreement binding on his part. Bragg replied that his intention was to conform strictly to the spirit of the truce agreement and, demonstrating his contentious nature at the outset, indicated to Slemmer that the erection of a battery on Santa Rosa Island bearing on the navy yard was, in his view, in direct violation with the agreement. Construction of defensive works on the mainland, however, Bragg reported, was fully justified, "especially so under the threats of the new administration." Slemmer replied the battery mentioned in Bragg's letter did not exist. Two days later, after conferring with Captain Adams himself and not through Captain Vogdes regarding the intentions of the naval squadron off Santa Rosa Island, Slemmer wrote to Bragg that the assurances given in his previous note were satisfactory. "Of the question of batteries on either side," Slemmer wrote, "I have only to say that our views on that point are directly opposite."[26]

Captain Walker on *Brooklyn* wrote Adams regarding the offer of Knapp, the purveyor ashore, to supply fresh water. Walker thought the squadron should take on several thousand gallons even though Knapp had not yet named his price nor indicated his having permission from the authorities on the mainland to deliver it. Walker also mentioned that Berryman now was certain he could get coal from the mainland but at $15 a ton, "a high price unless in a case of great emergency." Neither of the options provided a permanent resolution of his provisioning requirements to Captain Adams.[27]

At Washington, Postmaster General Blair took Gustavus Fox to meet the president. Fox, recently retired from the navy and now a successful businessman, had volunteered to take the relief expedition into Charleston Harbor under the Buchanan administration and he repeated his willingness to do so again, asking only that he be permitted to visit Charleston Harbor and Fort Sumter before committing entirely to the project. After the interview, Blair and Fox went to General Scott's office and discussed the proposition with him. Scott held firm to his position that the Confederate batteries recently erected on both sides of the channel into Charleston Harbor made the plan to reinforce Fort Sumter from the ocean impossible. Fox argued that naval vessels, propelled by steam, could pass any number of guns because their course would be at right angles to the fire of the batteries and the distance, about thirteen hundred yards, was too great for accurate shooting in the dark. Also, he stated, there was no certainty that Southern batteries would actually open on vessels bringing provisions to the beleaguered garrison of Fort Sumter; whether they would fire on vessels carrying bread was the question. Scott did not concur but did agree to consider Fox's plan.[28]

On Thursday, March 14, Assistant Adjutant General George Deas wrote from Montgomery to General Bragg at Pensacola that it was necessary to establish a single command over the Confederate forces on Pensacola Bay. The government had decided the navy yard and all matters connected with it were to be included in the order assigning to Bragg to the command of the forces there. "Will you please convey this information to Commander Farrand as the orders of the government?" he asked. On another matter, Deas advised that requisitions had been made on Alabama, Mississippi, Louisiana, Georgia, and Florida for 5,000 troops for Bragg's command and a large portion of this force should begin reporting to him in the next ten days. Also from Montgomery, based on information forwarded to him by L. Q. Washington at the nation's capital, Secretary Walker wired General Beauregard at Charleston, "Steamers *Star of the West, Harriet Lane, Crusader, Mohawk,* and *Empire City* ordered to sail from New York last night. Said to carry arms, provisions, and men. Destinations not known." Copies of the telegram were forwarded to Bragg at Pensacola and to the Confederate commanders at Fort Morgan, below Mobile, and Forts Jackson and St. Philip, below New Orleans.[29]

On Friday, March 15, General Bragg wrote to Captain Adams acknowledging receipt of Slemmer's communication on Wednesday. He called Adams's attention to his correspondence with Slemmer regarding the erection of batteries on Santa Rosa Island and on the mainland. "The works which have been thrown up on this side bearing on the channel were the necessary consequence of the threatening position assumed by your government, and can no more be regarded as menacing Fort Pickens than the mounting of guns in Fort Pickens could be considered as menacing us. Both should be looked on as precautions against threatened attack." Bragg had referred the whole matter to his government, he told Adams, and its decision would be made known to the naval officer when received. "In the meantime, you may rest assured that I shall make no disposition for the attack on Fort Pickens."[30]

At Washington, President Lincoln brought Gustavus Fox and his plan to reinforce and provision Fort Sumter before the cabinet. Fox would embark the men and material involved on a large ocean steamer and, convoyed by light draft New York Harbor tugs, would sail for Charleston in company with two warships he had selected, the revenue service sidewheeler U.S.S. *Harriet Lane* and the navy steam sloop U.S.S. *Pawnee,* both light-draft vessels which could cross the bar and enter Charleston Harbor. When he first arrived off the Charleston bar, Fox planned that he would observe conditions closely day to day. Were the Confederate authorities to show indications of opposing his attempt to relieve the fort, the two armed warships would enter the harbor and destroy or drive ashore any vessels coming out against them, supported by the heavy guns of Fort Sumter. Having so disposed of Southern opposition afloat, Fox proposed that, starting two hours before high tide at night, to run the reinforcements and provisions over the bar and to the fort in launches towed by the tugs. After reviewing Fox's presentation, President Lincoln wrote to every member of the cabinet asking each to respond in writing to the question, "Assuming it to be possible to now provision Fort Sumter, under the circumstances, is it wise to attempt it?" On this day only two members of the cabinet were in favor of attempting the relief, Postmaster General Montgomery Blair and, somewhat hesitantly, Secretary of the Treasury Salmon P. Chase. Secretary of State Seward argued that any relief would be temporary in that the general situation would not change and efforts to relieve and provision the garrison would be again called for later on. The majority of the members cautioned Lincoln, were the attempt to result in disaster and the loss of the fort, the political ramifications would be disastrous. The way out of the problem, they suggested led by Seward, was to give up the fort under the imperative of present military necessity which already existed because of the Buchanan administration's inept handling of the crisis for which the Lincoln administration was in no way responsible. Lincoln considered his cabinet's advice and decided, for the moment, to defer a decision. Neither Lincoln nor his cabinet members had any experience in matters such as those they faced at this time, a week and a half into their new roles at the helm of government. After the meeting, Seward met informally with Supreme Court Justice Samuel Nelson, his neighbor and fellow New Yorker. Seward told the justice he was working to find a way to maintain the peace. Nelson mentioned this conversation to Supreme Court Justice John A. Campbell of Alabama who was serving in the role of confidante and sponsor to the three commissioners of the Confederate government. Nelson and Campbell returned to Seward's office and discussed with him the possibility of his officially receiving the commissioners of the Confederate government. Seward demurred to an open acknowledgement of the existence of a government of the seceded states, which such an official meeting would involve, but he told Nelson and Campbell that the evacuation of Fort Sumter was pending, although that was all the Lincoln administration could bear politically at this time. Judge Campbell offered to write this to President Davis as a safeguard against any hostile action. "Tell him," Seward said, "that before the letter reaches him"— interrupting himself to ask how far it was to Montgomery—"the telegraph would have informed him that Fort Sumter was to be evacuated." As to the forts in the Gulf of Mexico, Fort Pickens, Fort Taylor, and Fort Jefferson, Seward assured the two men, "We contemplate no action there. We are satisfied with the position of things there." Judge Campbell sent a note to Commissioner Crawford telling the former Congressman he had been assured by Seward through Judge Nelson that Fort Sumter would be evacuated within the next five days— that being the time involve for mail to travel from Washington to Montgomery. Further, Campbell wrote that no measures that might change the existing status regarding the Southern Confederacy in a prejudicial manner were being contemplated by the Federal authorities. He cautioned, however, that pursuing the demand for an answer to the commissioners earlier request for official recognition should not be pressed at this time. Judge Campbell furnished a copy of his note to Seward that same evening so there is no doubt that the secretary of state of the United States knew what the Southern commissioners and their supporters were thinking. Seward was acting on his own, fully aware that his words and actions would be reported to the authorities at Montgomery. He was conducting diplomacy from the State Department without informing the president and without reflecting Lincoln's policies. Seward had determined on his own that Fort Sumter would be surrendered, its loss blamed on the inaction of the Buchanan administration. Seward's concentration in the coming weeks would be aimed at achieving the evacuation of Fort Sumter by thwarting its provisioning and reinforcement. Postmaster General Montgomery Blair would write in later years that Seward was pledged to the surrender of Fort Sumter, and had determined to be the central element in the salvation of Fort Pickens, which would demonstration concession on the one hand, and forceful determination on the other. This, he felt, would put Seward well in front of his detractors within the Republican party on all sides.[31]

On Saturday, March 16, Paymaster Thomas Looker on *Brooklyn*, reported to Captain Adams on *Sabine* that there were now twenty-one days provisions on hand for the officers, crew, and embarked troops except for flour, butter, sugar, and beans which had given out entirely. The shortage of provisions was tied to, among other things, the continuing shortage of hard currency with which to pay the squadron's bills. Without cash, merchants and purveyors on the mainland who were not yet politically opposed to doing business with the Federal forces offshore would not consider commerce. Adams had contacted the Bank of

Mobile trying to obtain funds with a draft against the United States Treasury; the officers of the bank informed Adams they declined to make any arrangement respecting the matter. The banking firm of St. John, Power & Co. of Mobile advised it would advance gold against treasury drafts but at an exorbitant discount of seventeen percent; their experience with drafts against the Federal Treasury under the previous administration, they wrote Adams, had not been satisfactory and they were understandably more particular now than at ordinary times regarding the purchase of such drafts.[32]

From Montgomery, Assistant Adjutant General Deas ordered Captain John C. Booth, commanding the recently seized Baton Rouge Arsenal, to transfer with all possible dispatch to Pensacola an extensive list of shot and shell, spherical case, grape, cartridge bags, priming tubes, matches, friction tubes, and musket cartridges. And from the navy yard at Pensacola, John Hoodless, acting master carpenter, wrote to Commander Farrand, in response to his query the previous Sunday, sending his estimate of the labor and materials needed to complete the work on *Fulton*. With the facilities at hand, Hoodless advised, the steamer could be launched by June 1 and be ready for sea by August 1.[33]

On Sunday, March 17, Captain Vogdes wrote his monthly report to the adjutant general from his stateroom on *Brooklyn*. He described in detail the departure from Fort Monroe under sealed orders that assigned him to command the forts on Pensacola Bay. Arriving, he had been shown telegraphic orders from the secretary of war preventing the commanding officer of *Brooklyn* from landing his company. Then, a few days since, Vogdes complained, he had requested a copy of the post return for the Fort Pickens garrison from Lieutenant Slemmer in order to make the monthly return for his entire command. Slemmer had declined to give it as he considered that the more recently issued truce order superseded Vogdes's earlier written order and thus deprived Vogdes of the right to command the fort itself or its garrison. Vogdes did not construe the telegraphic order in any such way, he wrote, nor did he consider it binding upon himself since it was not addressed to him nor had he ever received a copy of it. Should he have to land his company in the event of an attack on the fort, he warned, arrangements should be made beforehand which could not be made by Slemmer alone nor would Vogdes consent to Slemmer's making dispositions of himself or his command. All ambiguity as to his right to command should be removed at once, he insisted. He ended by asking that the commissary and quartermaster officers of his command be supplied with money as it was impossible to obtain supplies or provisions without it. On Monday, March 18, the day after Vogdes wrote his report to the adjutant general, Slemmer composed his own. Nothing significant had taken place since his previous report to disturb the relationship that existed between his command and the Confederate forces on the mainland. He was continuing the efforts to put the fort in better condition for defense as far as the means and the men at his disposal permitted. Echoing what appeared to be a common problem with payments by the Federal government, he wrote that the provisions purveyor on the mainland now refused to furnish fresh beef and vegetables to his garrison. The man claimed he was without funds with which to purchase cattle. The United States had not paid the purveyor for more than three months. Significantly, Slemmer made no mention in his report of the arrival of *Brooklyn* bearing Vogdes and his company nor of the conflicting command arrangements this had brought to the scene. Slemmer was no more willing to surrender his command to a Federal senior officer bearing questionable credentials than he was to surrender it to the hostile forces under Bragg on the mainland.[34]

At New York the British merchant steamer *Arabia* made port from Liverpool carrying among its first-class passengers William Howard Russell, a correspondent sent by the editors of the *London Times* to report to its readers on what was taking place in the former colonies. Russell had only recently returned to England after an extensive and successful journalism tour with British forces in the Crimea. He found in America, he wrote in one of his first dispatches, the public interest was centered on two Federal forts, Pickens at Pensacola Harbor and Sumter at Charleston Harbor. "As Alabama (*sic*) and South Carolina had gone out, they now demanded the possession of these forts as on the soil of their several states and attached to their sovereignty. On the other hand, the government of Mr. Lincoln considered it had no right to give up anything belonging to the Federal government, but evidently desires to temporize and evade any decision which might precipitate an attack on the forts by the batteries and forces preparing to act against them. There is not sufficient garrison in either fort for an adequate defense, and the difficulty of procuring supplies is very great. Under the circumstances every one is asking what the government is going to do? The Southern people have declared they will resist any attempt to supply and reinforce the garrisons, and in Charleston, at least, have shown they mean to keep their word. It is a strange situation."[35]

The orders to Captain Vogdes to land his command that had been issued by Assistant Adjutant General Townsend the previous Tuesday, March 12, were telegraphed ahead to Key West while their copies were under way aboard *Mohawk*. A revenue cutter from Key West arrived at the squadron off Pensacola Bay carrying two army officers who asked to see Captain Vogdes on *Brooklyn*. Captain Adams had the three officers brought to *Sabine* where he graciously turned over to them the use of his own stateroom. Adams waited on deck with his executive officer, Lieutenant William Murdaugh. The three army officers soon joined the two navy officers, Vogdes holding a document in his hand. He told Adams it was the order to land his company at Fort Pickens immediately. Adams asked from whom the order came. From General Scott, Vogdes replied. "I do not know General Scott in this matter," Adams told him, "and you cannot land your men until I get proper orders to that effect." Vogdes was stunned. "Do you mean to say that your boats cannot land my men?" he asked. Adams assured him that was the case. Vogdes declared he would charter one or more of the local fishing sloops that continued to work in and out of the bay in order to land his men. "No," Adams stated, "you do not leave this ship until I get proper orders to that effect." Adams was firm in his decision not to make a move without specific orders from the Navy Department but he was uncomfortable with the continuing lack of communication from Washington. He did not doubt he was correct in ignoring orders from General Scott which were addressed to Captain Vogdes. Adams was not going to violate an order from the secretary of the navy addressed to the commanding officers of the naval vessels off Pensacola by following the dictates of the War Department which were not addressed to him. As far as he was concerned, the matter was an issue between elements of the army and was none of the concern of the navy. Adams did immediately write a lengthy report to the secretary of the navy in which he detailed the problems he had faced since his arrival off Santa Rosa Island on February 6. He described the difficulties he was having obtaining supplies of water and provisions for the officers and men of the squadron and the troops aboard *Brooklyn*. He had been able to obtain some small quantities of stores from ashore, he wrote, but his means for purchasing were now exhausted. "There is not one dollar of public money in the squadron. I have been using my private funds to pay bills, and Lieutenant Belknap and Paymaster Price of *St. Louis,* Lieutenant Cash of the Marine Corps of this ship, and Lieutenant Washington Gwathmey have tendered me what money they have for the same purpose." He had been obliged to purchase water at extravagant prices, he wrote. The apparatus for distilling fresh water from sea water on *Brooklyn* had finally been repaired so the vessels of his squadron might soon face the unusual situation of having supplies of fresh water in excess of their stores of provisions. Adams added he had seen in a New York newspaper obtained from a passing merchant vessel that *Supply* would sail for the squadron about the 1st of April by which time the vessels of his command would be out of food. Should *Supply* meet with an accident or delay, Adams could have up to a thousand people in danger of being without provisions as nothing to eat could be had nearer than Key West or Havana, eight or ten days sail away. It would be unwise and even dangerous to wait for the arrival of *Supply*. He still hoped somehow to obtain provisions from the mainland. "If we had money, I feel quite sure it could be done, but cash is required, as nobody will buy a draft on the government. All transactions for provisions, etc., are attended with risk and difficulty." Adams then got to the point of his report. His officers and men were ready to land at the shortest notice, but he had received assurances from General Bragg that the Confederate authorities would respect the truce agreement made by Mallory, Chase, and the United States government. Bragg had assured him he intended to make no dispositions to attack Fort Pickens. Adams did not mention in his report the orders received by Captain Vogdes that day. What the army wrote to itself was of no concern to him. He did mention his need for additional navy officers, warning that if officers and men were landed to support the fort, the vessels offshore would not have sufficient officers to safely maintain and handle them. He was going to send this report by courier, he wrote. Lieutenant Gwathmey, of *Brooklyn,* would carry it overland with other dispatches to the Navy Department. If a messenger had not returned from the capital within ten days of Gwathmey's departure, Adams advised the secretary, he would assume that Gwathmey had been stopped along the way or that the Navy Department had decided to leave matters to his discretion as to going to Key West or Havana for provisions. One note Adams added to his report was that when *Fulton* had been run up on the ways at the navy yard for repairs, her signal book had been deposited at the navy yard and probably still remained there. Adams had no means of retrieving it nor determining its condition or present possession but he was assuming the Confederate authorities now had the navy's signal codes. He closed his report with the assurance that Lieutenant Gwathmey was well informed on the state of affairs ashore and afloat and could give any detailed information the secretary might require.[36]

Naval gunner Cornelius Cronin of *Sabine* wrote in his journal that the crew of the frigate had been saving its pay to fund a grand ball upon the return of the vessel to Portsmouth, New Hampshire, its home port. A respectable sum had been set aside and kept in the ship's safe by the paymaster. The crew met, Cronin wrote, and decided to place the money at the disposal of Captain Adams to be used to purchase provisions for the squadron. The men would make other arrangements to fund their grand ball upon their return to Portsmouth.[37]

From the mainland Bragg's adjutant, Captain Robert Wood, issued General Orders No. 4 which announced that the commanding general had learned with surprise and regret that some citizens were engaged in the business of furnishing supplies of coal, water, and

U.S.S. *Fulton*, the fastest steamer in the U.S. Navy, drawn up on the ways at the Pensacola Navy Yard for repairs, surrounded by an immense number of cannon balls (photograph by Southern Historical Collection, Samuel Henry Lockett Papers, Wilson Library, University of North Carolina at Chapel Hill).

provisions to the armed vessels of the United States now occupying threatening positions off the harbor. "That no misunderstanding may exist on this subject, it is announced to all concerned that this traffic is strictly forbidden, and all such supplies which may be captured in transit to such vessels, or to Fort Pickens, will be confiscated. The more effectively to enforce this prohibition, no boat or vessel will be allowed to visit Fort Pickens, or any United States naval vessel, without special sanction. Col. John H. Forney, acting inspector general, will organize an effective harbor police for the enforcement of this order." At this time, however, the commercial interests in the cities of the Deep South were not yet totally in step with the political interests there. On Wednesday, March 20, Captain Adams received a letter from the firm of A. & P. Horta of Mobile stating that filling the squadron's requisitions for stores and provisions might be done but would involve great hazard, based on General Bragg's order of Monday. If Captain Adams would pay for the squadron's needs in advance, Horta would agree to ship at the squadron's risk. Meantime, the firm had applied to Bragg's headquarters for permission to supply the Federal vessels off Santa Rosa Island. Adams was able to convince Horta to accept Federal treasury drafts at an extreme discount to pay for the goods but when the sailing sloop *Isabella* was laden with provisions and supplies by Horta and ready to sail for the offing at Pensacola, it was seized by city officials under the direction of the acting mayor at the request of General Bragg, and *Isabella's* cargo was confiscated. Meantime, Southern reinforcements continued to move in the direction of Pensacola. Samuel Cooper, who had formerly held the office of adjutant general of the United States Army, the senior member of the officer corps, was now serving in the same role as adjutant general of the Confederate States Army. Cooper wrote on Tuesday, March 19, from Montgomery to Bragg informing him the government had accepted the services of a battalion of Louisiana Zouaves consisting of between 400 and 500 men. One hundred and fifty of the Zouaves were to be sent to Pensacola immediately, with the remainder to follow in several days.[38]

At Washington Secretary of War Cameron told General Scott the president wanted accurate information regarding the condition of Anderson's command at Fort Sumter and wished a competent person sent there for that purpose. Gustavus Fox had been waiting in the city for permission to proceed to Charleston. Scott recommended he be sent. The president approved and Fox made the journey. At Charleston Gustavus Fox arrived in the evening and was escorted out to Fort Sumter where he held a confidential interview with Major Anderson. Returning to the mainland, he left immediately by rail for Washington.[39]

At the nation's capital, L. Q. Washington wrote Secretary Walker that he had received information indicating the Federal government intended to reinforce Fort Pickens and would do so soon. "I am aware there is an agreement to the contrary on the part of the government but I do not place any reliance on their promises," he wrote. "They will find some excuse for a violation of the stipulation." The newspaperman mentioned he was in communication with Martin Crawford, one of the Confederate commissioners at Washington, and had passed on to Crawford all he had learned. He understood Commissioner Forsythe would incorporate that information in his dispatch to Montgomery that evening. Also at Washington, Judge Campbell, acting as the intermediary between the Confederate commissioners and the Federal secretary of state, wrote to Seward complaining that he had been assured by Seward on March 15 that Fort Sumter would be evacuated within the next five days. Campbell had forwarded that information to Commissioner Crawford who had sent it on in good faith to the authorities at Montgomery and Charleston. Now, Campbell wrote, he had received a telegram from General Beauregard declaring not only had the fort not been evacuated but he had received information that Anderson's garrison was strengthening its position. Campbell demanded an explanation. After receiving Seward's reply, Campbell told the Confederate commissioners that Secretary Seward had assured him the failure to evacuate Fort Sumter within the five days he had indicated to them on March 23 was not the result of bad faith but "was attributable to causes consistent with the intentions of fulfilling the commitment," and, as for Fort Pickens, Seward assured him he would be given notice "of any design to alter the existing status there."[40]

On Thursday, March 21, Captain Vogdes wrote to the general-in-chief reminding Scott of his request for a decision on the subject of command at Santa Rosa Island. It was indispensable, he insisted, that a perfect understanding between the troops aboard the naval vessel and the force within Fort Pickens as to their relationship to each other be established before a landing became necessary. He could not see how this could be accomplished when his troops could only be landed when the fort was under attack. It could not be established at all unless Slemmer was allowed to give him orders and assign him to his place and role and, Vogdes insisted, he would never submit to being commanded by a junior officer.

Moreover, when he did enter the fort, it would be as its commander and that would most probably be when the enemy was already before the walls. Under these conditions, he would be totally ignorant of any preparations Slemmer had made for defense. He would not be held accountable, he declared, for the defense of Fort Pickens when he had not assumed the responsibility for the defense of the post until the last moment. He requested he be relieved at once and, if not, he entered his protest against being in any way held accountable for what might take place.[41]

In spite of the differences between their governments and the political positions they represented, some officers on both sides at Pensacola had maintained the friendly relations they had developed while serving together in the army and navy in the past. Confederate army officers came out from the mainland to dine and be entertained aboard Federal vessels offshore and United States Navy officers were given freedom of movement at Pensacola, although not at the navy yard nor at Fort Barrancas. No Southerners were welcome inside Fort Pickens. All this, of course, ended with Bragg's order of March 18.[42]

Captain Adams, writing to the secretary of the navy on Friday, March 22, reported he was sorely disappointed at the loss of stores and provisions on the schooner *Isabella*. He had read in a New York newspaper that *Supply* was still there on the 15th. *St. Louis*, he wrote, was entirely out of bread and other items of subsistence and the crew of his own vessel, *Sabine*, would be in similar condition in a week or ten days. Under these circumstances, he was ordering *Brooklyn* to Key West or Havana for supplies. He was reluctant to part with her because, with *Wyandotte* permanently stationed inside the harbor, *Brooklyn* was the only steam-powered vessel in the squadron. In case of an assault on Fort Pickens, *Brooklyn's* powerful battery and her ability to tow sailing vessels to different stations would be sorely missed. If *Wyandotte* were not serving so important a role inside the harbor entrance, he would rather send her, he wrote. Adams ordered Captain Vogdes to transfer his command from *Brooklyn* to *Sabine* and the steamer sailed for Key West that afternoon. Adams closed his report with the statement that he had been on station for six weeks and his last communication from the Navy Department had been dated February 16.[43]

On Saturday, March 12, William Howard Russell wrote to the editors of the *London Times* from Washington:

> It is presumed positively that the authorities in Pensacola and Charleston have refused to allow any further supplies to be sent to Fort Pickens, the United States fort in the Gulf of Mexico, or to Fort Sumter. Everywhere the Southern leaders are forcing on a solution with decision and energy, whilst the government appears to be helplessly drifting with the current, having neither bow nor stern, neither keel nor deck, neither rudder, compass, sails, nor steam. Mr. Seward had declined to receive or hold any intercourse with the three gentlemen called Southern Commissioners, who repaired to Washington accredited by the government and Congress of the seceding states, now sitting at Montgomery, so that there is no channel of mediation or means of adjustment left open. I hear, indeed, that the government is secretly preparing what force it can to strengthen the garrison at Pickens, and to reinforce Sumter at all hazard; but that its want of men, ships, and money compels it to temporize, lest the Southern authorities should forestall their designs by a vigorous attack on the enfeebled forts.[44]

On Sunday, March 24, Ward Hill Lamon met Governor Pickens at Charleston. Lamon was Abraham Lincoln's former law partner and his current body guard. Informing the governor that he acted in the role of authorized agent of the president, Lamon left the distinct impression with the governor that Major Anderson and his command would be transferred to another post within a matter of days. After this meeting General Beauregard wrote to Major Anderson that he had intended to demand the formal surrender of Fort Sumter but, since their countries were not at war and the issue would apparently be resolved shortly according to Lamon, Beauregard would not exact such a condition. He would be happy to provide the means of transportation for Anderson and his men, their baggage and personal and company property, if Anderson would inform him when and to where he wished to be sent. Ward Hill Lamon was Lincoln's long-time friend, his former law partner, and at this time, his confidential courier. Lamon did not elaborate in his later writing on his mission to Charleston as to what instructions Lincoln had given him nor did he indicate specifically what he said to Governor Pickens. However, he did leave the impression that Fort Sumter would be evacuated. Two days later, Beauregard wrote to Anderson referring to the "*high source* from which the rumors spoken of appeared to come." Lamon was acting far beyond his actual authority. In contrast to his actions at Charleston, when Lamon returned and reported to Lincoln that provisions on hand for Anderson's garrison would be exhausted in a matter of two weeks. Lincoln ordered that the preparations he had initiated to send supplies to Anderson were to move forward, stating he could not order the evacuation of Fort Sumter consistent with his understanding of his duties and the policies enunciated in his inaugural address.[45]

On the mainland at Pensacola Bay, Braxton Bragg was facing up to the difficulties he inherited when he assumed command of the Confederate forces there. On Wednesday, March 27, Bragg's troops numbered 1,100 men with 5,000 more on the way to join him. Most of these men were away from home for the first time in their lives and, since the assault on Fort Pickens did not seem imminent, many were more intent on relaxing and enjoying themselves than on performing the mundane chores of military living such as learning to march in formation and performing the labor involved in constructing batteries. Bragg complained in a letter to his wife Elise, "How I am to manage them I hardly know.... Night before last we were near a general row all around." A large number of men got "drunk and a free fight commenced and for a while things looked badly.... But by the free use of the bayonet and hand cuffs well applied by the Zouaves from New Orleans, they soon were quelled." Bragg declared martial law throughout his command and raided all the liquor shops. His provosts confiscated enough whiskey, he wrote, "to have kept the army drunk for two months." Bragg admitted to Elise that he was not prepared to launch the assault on Fort Pickens at that time. He lacked heavy guns, specialists, transportation, and money. "The department ... is crowding me with men and giving me nothing with them. They are useless without arms and ammunition." Bragg had asked for funds during his first days at Pensacola but had received none. "With our empty purse and an exhausted credit, it is pretty hard to feed men on a barren sand bank," he wrote to Elise. He had few trained troop commanders and no trained artillery officers. "According to my notions," he wrote, "things here are in the most deplorable condition.... Our troops are raw volunteers, without officers and without discipline, each man with the idea he can whip the world, and believing that nothing is necessary but to ... take Fort Pickens and all the navy." Unless the Federals attacked his positions, he confessed, "no fighting can occur here for a long time, as we are totally unprepared ... Fort Pickens cannot be taken without a regular siege, and we have no means to carry that on." Nonetheless, pressed by the authorities at Montgomery to develop of plan of attack, Bragg considered three possibilities. One involved a classical siege with

Aerial view of Confederate camps along the shore of Pensacola Bay, taken from the lighthouse tower (photograph by J.D. Edwards, U.S. Army Military History Institute).

regular approaches, digging trenches ever closer to the walls of the fort on its eastern side while siege guns, which he did not have, battered and weakened the walls from positions on the mainland. The second consisted of a flank attack from the east with several columns feinting against different portions of the walls to spread the defenders thin until the main column, using scaling ladders, could rush and climb over the walls. The third was a direct attack out of the darkness of night by a single column of men rushing the walls and carrying the fort by sheer numbers but at a very high cost in lives. Of the three, Bragg, an experienced artillery officer, naturally favored the assault after the walls had been battered and broken by the concentrated fire of heavy guns and mortars. He wrote to Adjutant General Cooper at Montgomery, "I entertain little doubt of being able to batter [the walls] down with 10-inch guns ... when an assaulting party from this side, aided by a false attack on the island, might carry the work with the bayonet. It will be difficult at this distance to determined when the breach is fully effected ... and should the enemy resist us by landing reinforcements, it will be a desperate struggle. A knowledge, however, that success or entire destruction is inevitable would serve to nerve our men for the work." Bragg favored the one option for which he did not have the heavy ordnance required and had no chance of obtaining soon, and the one option that would give the squadron offshore adequate time to land reinforcements and bring the battering positions on the mainland under fire from the powerful guns of the warships. Bragg's whole career in the United States Army, and his earned fame therein, had come from his service as an artillery officer. He naturally chose the option that made the greatest use of artillery. Had Tennent Lomax been asked to develop alternatives, he would have selected the same three because geography dictated those Bragg had chosen but Lomax surely would have arrived at a different first choice. In his response to Montgomery, Bragg described his deployment of men and equipment on Pensacola Bay and went into some detail on the problems he faced, concentrating primarily on the problems related to Fort McRee. His defense of the harbor was based, west to east, on Fort McRee on Foster's Bank at the eastern tip of Perdido Key, on Fort Barrancas on the mainland midway between Fort McRee and the navy yard, and on a series of sand batteries along the shore east and west of Fort Barrancas that had been constructed by his troops. Ordnance, provisions, and men could only be sent over to Fort McRee by boat, crossing the entrance to the bay directly under the guns of Fort Pickens or, were this not practical, by traveling west along the shore of the mainland to where the lagoon could be crossed and returning that same distance eastward on Perdido Key, a one-way trip of some fifteen miles. A force from the Federal squadron offshore could easily land on Perdido Key west of the fort and cut it off effectively from reinforcements and succor. Further, Fort McRee was built on a sand shoal on foundations that time and tide had weakened to the point where Bragg's engineers wondered whether the fort's walls would stand under the concussion of the firing of the fort's own guns. Owing to its exposed position and its structural weaknesses, Bragg had withdrawn those of its guns not necessary for its defense, placing some in sand batteries on the mainland and the remainder in a depot beyond Fort Barrancas, out of danger. Many of the guns of Fort McRee were not intended to bear on Fort Pickens, the fort on Foster's Bank having been designed to take under its fire hostile vessels approaching and entering the bay. Those guns could add no weight of shot to that being thrown against Fort Pickens while heavy fire from Fort Pickens and the Federal vessels offshore would probably silence Fort McRee within hours if not actually batter it down. There was no ditch nor any flank defense which left Fort McRee open to amphibious assault unless it was defended by a strong reserve which would have to be transported and maintained from the mainland. Bragg wrote to Montgomery that he would place little reliance in Fort McRee but would hold it and defend it as long as he could.[46]

From Washington, Secretary Welles telegraphed orders to Captain Samuel L. Breese, commanding the Brooklyn Navy Yard, for the sailing storeship U.S.S. *Release*, Lieutenant Commanding James L. Frailey, to proceed with all possible dispatch to the anchorage off Fort Pickens and there to report to the senior naval officer present. After discharging her cargo of stores and provisions, Frailey was to return his vessel to New York. *Release* would follow in the wake of *Supply* which had sailed from New York for the squadron off Pensacola on March 12.[47]

On his return from Charleston that day, Gustavus Fox met immediately with President Lincoln and convinced him that it was feasible, with a strong naval escort, to place troops and provisions into Fort Sumter. Major Anderson, he reported, now felt he could stretch his rations for about two weeks before he and his garrison would come up to the hunger line.[48]

On Thursday, March 28, Captain Samuel Mercer arrived in *Powhatan* at the Brooklyn Navy Yard from Vera Cruz for a complete re-work and overhaul of the side-wheel steamer. The large vessel, fully sloop-rigged, was worn out. Her engine was aged and unreliable and her hull was rotting. As was the practice when major vessels come in for a com-

5. "Too Much Dallying and Curtseying"   101

The side-wheel steamer U.S.S. *Powhatan*, one of the more powerful ships in the navy, was intended for Fort Sumter until Meigs and Porter absconded with it (Naval Historical Center).

plete retrofit, her guns had been taken ashore, her stores and munitions landed, her rigging dismantled, her masts and spars taken down, and her officers sent on leave. Her crew, some 300 sailors and marines, were sent to the receiving ship *North Carolina* for further transfer or discharge. On Monday, April 1, *Powhatan* was formally declared out of commission. The same day that *Powhatan* arrived at the navy yard, the *New York Times* printed the sensational news that the administration in Washington had disregarded the truce agreement in force at Pensacola and, two or three weeks earlier, had ordered the captain of *Brooklyn* to put ashore the company of artillerymen she carried to reinforce Fort Pickens. This brought General Scott hurrying to President Lincoln protesting that, since the news was out, his recent peremptory order to Vogdes to land his command immediately must be cancelled. If not, the old solider worried, the Confederate authorities might be provoked into attacking both Fort Pickens and Fort Sumter. After the interview with the president, Scott wrote to Secretary of War Cameron a long, wandering discourse suggesting that the evacuation of Forts Pickens and Sumter would "instantly soothe and give confidence to the eight remaining slave-holding states and render their cordial adherence to this Union perpetual."[49]

That evening the Lincoln's gave their first formal state dinner at the executive mansion. Members of the cabinet and their wives attended as did Vice President Hannibal Hamlin. William Howard Russell, the correspondent of the *London Times* was there. General Scott had been invited but declared himself unable to attend. After dining, Lincoln asked his cabinet to meet with him in an adjoining room. There he told his guests of General Scott's recommendation that the administration evacuate Forts Pickens and Sumter in order to soothe and give confidence to those slave-holding states which had not yet seceded. The president admitted he was surprised at General Scott's proposal. He had intended to do his best to retain Fort Sumter, he told the men with him, and he had never thought to abandon Fort Pickens. He and the assembled cabinet were under the impression that, in response to Scott's written order, Captain Vogdes's company would have landed and reinforced Fort Pickens which was already supported by a major portion of the Home Squadron offshore. No formal vote was taken but the members of the cabinet were unanimous in dissenting from Scott's proposal. Lincoln asked them to consider the events of the day and to plan to meet with him in the morning. Later in the evening, Ward Lamon returned to Washington from Charleston and met briefly with the president. Lamon told Lincoln that, in his opinion, it would be impossible to reinforce Fort Sumter and that Anderson and his men would be out of food by April 15. He did not mention his commitment to Governor Pickens that the fort would be given up in a few days. The president considered what Ward Lamon reported to him but he was still inclined to follow his own instincts in spite of the advice coming from most corners. The following morning, Friday, March 29, Abraham Lincoln weighed what he was hearing from his advisors against his own determination to do what he felt in his soul and he resolved to do what his oath and his duty required. He would do all in his power to hold both Fort Pickens and Fort Sumter. He would send provisions to Anderson and, if the secessionists forcibly resisted, then on them would rest the responsibility for initiating hostilities. This conclusion, although it conflicted with the military and political thinking taking place around him, Lincoln considered was politically necessary. He could not, consistent with his convictions and the policies he had enunciated in his inaugural address, order the evacuation of Fort Sumter and he felt it would be cruel on his part to permit its heroic garrison to be starved into surrender without making the attempt at relieving it. He met with his cabinet and asked each member for an opinion with regard to both forts. He stated that he wanted those opinions in writing. Secretary of War Cameron's views were not recorded. Secretary of the Treasury Chase, Secretary of the Navy Welles, and Postmaster General Blair were in favor of holding out and reinforcing both forts. Secretary of the Interior Smith and Attorney General Bates advised evacuating Fort Sumter and reinforcing Fort Pickens. Secretary of State Seward wrote his opinion that preparing an expedition to supply Fort Sumter would provoke an immediate attack at Charleston Harbor and inaugurate civil war. He would, instead, call in his protégé, Captain Montgomery Meigs, and, aided by his counsel instead of that of the aged general-in-chief, prepare for a war to begin at Pensacola and in Texas, far from the nation's capital city. Lastly, he would instruct Major Anderson to retire from Fort Sumter forthwith. Lincoln read the opinions and pondered the advice of the experienced politicians of his cabinet against his own instincts. He then directed Secretary Cameron to order an expedition which would move by sea, to be ready to sail as early as April 6, and to cooperate with Secretary Welles toward that objective. The navy's screw steamer *Pocahontas* at Norfolk, the screw sloop *Pawnee* at Washington, and the revenue service's side-wheel steamer *Harriet Lane* at New York were to be put under orders for sea with stores for one month. Three hundred sailors were to make ready to depart the receiving ship *North Carolina* at New York. Two hundred recruits would be prepared to depart the army's depot at Governor's Island in New York Harbor with provisions for twelve months. The quartermaster general of the army was to charter a large merchant steamer and three harbor tugs to accompany the expedition from New York. The commander-in-chief remembered the plan outlined by Gustavus Fox earlier in the week and decided to adopt it.[50]

The president and the cabinet had received no response to the order to Captain Vogdes sent by the steamers *Mohawk* and *Crusader* more than a week earlier. There was mention in the Southern newspapers that *Brooklyn* had departed the anchorage off Santa Rosa Island and gone to Key West. She had done so, of course, without landing Vogdes's command, having transferred it to *Sabine,* but this detail was not known at Washington and the inference drawn was that *Brooklyn* had landed the troops and reinforced the fort before leaving. Late in the day Seward told his son Frederick to send a messenger to find Captain Montgomery Meigs and bring him to the State Department. Seward and Meigs had been intimates for some time, corresponding since the early 1850s. Seward was impressed with the engineer's ability and initiative and Meigs relied on the senator for patronage. Meigs had asked Seward in 1857 to arrange an appointment-at-large to West Point for his son, John Rodgers Meigs, which Seward was pleased to do. Seward knew Meigs had only

Brigadier General Montgomery C. Meigs, U.S. Army, as an engineer captain was half of the Meigs-Porter plot to reinforce Fort Pickens (Library of Congress).

recently returned from his period of exile at Fort Jefferson on Dry Tortugas and that he was knowledgeable regarding Fort Pickens. The messenger found Meigs on his return from a visit to Great Falls where he had been reviewing construction work on the aqueduct project. When they met, Seward told Meigs that General Scott had advised the president to evacuate both Fort Sumter and Fort Pickens as political offerings to appease the seceded states and as an act of good faith to the remaining slave-holding states of the South. Seward voiced his lack of confidence in the abilities of the aged general-in-chief. After a discussion, Seward took Meigs to meet the president. As the two men walked across the lawn from the State Department to the executive mansion, Seward explained the situation facing the administration with regard to the two forts. The secretary wanted the president to talk with Meigs, a soldier who could assess military affairs from a professional viewpoint without injecting politics into the issue, and one capable of mounting a horse and taking to the field as neither the aged General Scott nor General Totten, the chief engineer, could any longer do. Meigs was ushered into the presence of Abraham Lincoln whom he had never met. The president talked with Seward and Meigs about the conditions at Charleston and Pensacola, stressing his determination to hold at least one, if not both, of the forts. He told Meigs that his senior military advisors were of the opinion that this could not be done. Meigs told the president he believed men could be found to volunteer to relieve Fort Sumter but he had heard that officers of higher rank thought it should not be attempted, that Charleston was not the place to start a war. Lincoln asked the captain if Fort Pickens could be held. Meigs answered it could be as long as the navy had done its duty and not lost the place already. To forestall this, Meigs urged that a warship be sent to enter Pensacola Harbor as soon as possible to prevent parties in small boats from crossing over from the mainland to Santa Rosa Island and mounting an assault on the fort before reinforcements could be landed from the vessels offshore. It would require a large contingent of sailors and marines from the squadron to defeat a concerted assault by a significant Confederate force, Meigs cautioned the president and secretary. Vogdes's company, lately ordered ashore, had only doubled the small number of regular troops originally garrisoning Fort Pickens. None of the three men were aware of the role *Wyandotte* had been playing inside the harbor, doing essentially what Meigs recommended a warship be sent to do. Meigs stated he had read in the newspapers that *Powhatan* was just back from service with the Home Squadron off Vera Cruz and might be available to make the effort he described. Meigs's positive response and manner impressed the president. He asked if the engineer would go to Florida and take command of Forts Pickens, Taylor, and Jefferson. Meigs deferred; he was but a captain and could not command more senior officers already there. Seward suggested the government promote Meigs. Meigs again deferred; there was no vacancy on the army list immediately above him into which he could be promoted. Seward suggested to Lincoln that Meigs develop an estimate of the means required for the safety of Fort Pickens by four o'clock in the afternoon of the following day. Lincoln, however, was not about to be rushed. He was not yet prepared to completely reject the opinions of Generals Scott and Totten. He told Meigs he would consider this conversation and let the captain know his decision in a day or so. Walking back to the State Department, Seward told Meigs he was pleased at the course the conversation had taken. Meigs recorded in his diary that evening, "Gen. Scott objected to relieving Forts Sumter and Pickens, thought it best to give them up and thus put a stop to all cry of coercion. For his own [Seward's] part, his policy had been all along to give up Sumter as too near Washington and leaving the temptation to [Jefferson] Davis to relieve it by an [attack] on Washington. That he wished to hold Pickens."[51]

On Saturday, March 30, Slemmer wrote to the adjutant general from Santa Rosa Island that matters still had not assumed a hostile attitude. Troops on the mainland were concentrating and seemed to be preparing for a movement should the present amicable agreement be interrupted. From what he could learn, there were nearly 1,000 men encamped along the shore of the bay and 5,000 more expected, "a marked difference existing between them and the volunteers who first had occupied these positions." His primary concern, he wrote, was that batteries too strong for his small garrison to overcome might be constructed east of the fort on Santa Rosa Island. With these batteries and those at Fort McRee, the sailing vessels offshore might be driven away and unable to land reinforcements in case of an attack on his position. With the steamer *Brooklyn* gone in quest of provisions and with the steamer *Wyandotte* permanently stationed inside the harbor, the sailing vessels remaining could only move where they might be needed if tide and wind allowed. His garrison would be unable to stand against a concentrated attack launched from the east by a large force landed there. He noted further that Lieutenant Gilman had been ordered back to Washington, this time to testify in the court-martial of Commodore Armstrong. This would again leave Slemmer as the sole officer within the fort so he intended to ask Captain Vogdes to order Lieutenant Langdon ashore to replace Gilman as he had done during Gilman's previous absence. Captain Adams brought the subject up that evening when he dined with General Bragg who assured the naval commander that the conditions of the truce would not be violated by Langdon's assignment as long as there was no attempt to actually reinforce the garrison of Fort Pickens.⁵²

At Washington President Lincoln summoned Gustavus Fox to the executive mansion and informed the former naval officer of the orders he had issued to the secretaries of war and the navy. Fox, Lincoln said, was to prepare to carry out his plan to relieve Fort Sumter. He was to proceed to New York and begin making the arrangements but, Lincoln cautioned him, he was to sign no binding commitments just at this time. Secretary Welles drew up preparatory orders to the commanding officers of the Norfolk, Washington, and Brooklyn navy yards. Welles thought that additional armament, boats, and manpower would help ensure the success of the expedition and so the secretary added *Powhatan* to the list of warships assigned to the task force. He was aware the steamer had just returned from a long cruise and was in the proves of being decommissioned in order to receive greatly needed repairs but the secretary felt she could be made available for the one brief service required of her off Charleston. Welles did not mention this reinforcement of the Fort Sumter task force to the president. Judge Campbell called on Secretary Seward later in the day to complain that Seward's promise that Fort Sumter would be evacuated in five days had been stretched to fifteen days. He showed the secretary a telegram from Governor Pickens stating that Ward Lamon had indicated during his visit to Charleston on March 23 that the fort would be evacuated a few days from then. Seward took the telegram and told the justice he would show it to the president and have a response that Campbell could pass on to the Confederate commissioners on Monday.⁵³

On Sunday, March 31, *Crusader*, Captain Strong, nineteen days out of New York, arrived off Santa Rosa Island bearing the written orders from General Scott to Captain Vogdes directing Vogdes to land his command. The same day *Brooklyn* returned from Key West with provisions, coal, and further copies of General Scott's order. Vogdes brought the documents to Captain Adams. Adams noted the date of the orders, March 12, and concluded they had been issued without a clear understanding of the current situation on Pensacola Bay. Adams was certain that permitting Vogdes to implement Scott's command would be seen by the Confederate authorities on the mainland as a hostile act in violation of the truce agreement which would precipitate a collision he felt would be against the wishes of the current administration. Both sides had been faithfully adhering to the terms of the agreement entered into between Mallory, Chase, and the Buchanan administration. Although none of the parties were any longer in place, Adams made up his mind to ignore the current instructions. They were issued by the War Department, not the Navy Department, and were addressed to Vogdes, not to himself. He refused Vogdes permission to land his command. Ashore, Bragg's returns for the final day of March reported his strength at 1,116, with more men on the way.⁵⁴

6

"Give the *Powhatan* to Captain Mercer"

At Washington early on Sunday, March 31, General Scott and his military secretary, Lieutenant Colonel Erasmus Keyes, discussed over breakfast the difficulties that would be encountered landing heavy guns with their carriages and munitions across the open beaches of the gulf shore of Santa Rosa Island, were the Lincoln administration to go forward with its stated plan to reinforce Fort Pickens. With Confederate batteries lining the shore of the mainland, it would be impossible to consider using the Fort Pickens wharf on the bay side of the island. Keyes agreed with the general that neither Fort Sumter nor Fort Pickens should be held and the garrisons at each location should be withdrawn as soon as possible. Picking up a map of Pensacola Bay, Scott told Keyes to take it to Secretary Seward and explain the difficulties involved in trying to land on the barren gulf shore of the island in order to reinforce the fort. When Keyes approached Seward, the secretary did not want to discuss any difficulties. He sent Keyes off to find Captain Montgomery Meigs and to bring the engineer back with him. When Keyes approached him, Meigs was at home preparing to depart with his family for St. John's Church, the day being Easter Sunday. At Seward's home the two officers were told to put on paper their estimates of what would be required to reinforce and hold Fort Pickens. The two were then to consult with General Scott and bring their plans to the executive mansion at three o'clock that afternoon. Working through the day at army headquarters, Keyes and Meigs developed separate plans and lists of requirements that, when compared, were surprisingly similar. They took too long at their work, however, and found they did not have time to go to General Scott's residence to review the plans with him. Instead, they hurried to keep their appointment at the executive mansion where they arrived at 2:30 P.M. Each of them read his plan for the president. Lincoln told them to go to General Scott and to tell him that the commander-in-chief wished the plans to be carried out, to tell Scott, "I wish this thing done and not to let it fail unless he can show that I have refused him something he asked for as necessary." Before departing Meigs mentioned to the president, as he had mentioned earlier to Secretary Seward, that his friend and next-door-neighbor, Navy Lieutenant David Dixon Porter, should be considered for command of the naval portion of the expedition. In 1852 Porter had shown great daring and courage when, commanding the mail steamer *Crescent City,* he had faced down Spanish authorities in the harbor of Havana, Cuba. Porter's vessel had been barred from the harbor for carrying as its purser a man wrongly accused of circulating rumors that thousands of political prisoners were incarcerated in the city's prisons. On his return voyage, Porter took *Crescent City* in through the difficult channel under the guns of Moro Castle in darkness and, at daylight, was anchored in the harbor defying the local authorities. Lincoln recalled reading of the incident and agreed to the inclusion of the naval officer for the role Meigs recommended. On the way to General Scott's home, Meigs and Keyes met Secretary Seward who went with them. Upon entering the general's sitting room, Seward announced, "General Scott, you have formally reported to the president your advice to evacuate Fort Pickens; notwithstanding this, I now come to bring you his order as commander-in-chief of the army and navy to reinforce it and hold it to the last extremity." Scott was an old man who harbored some strange and somewhat out of date political beliefs but he was first and foremost a disciplined soldier. "Sire," he replied, drawing himself painfully to his full height, "the great Frederick used to say, 'When the king commands, all things are possible.' It shall be done."

Lieutenant Colonel Erasmus Keyes, U.S. Army, was military secretary to General-in-Chief Winfield Scott when diverted to planning the Fort Pickens expedition (Military History Institute).

Scott took time to review the plans that Meigs and Keyes laid before him and then wrote out a note, handing it to Seward: "The immediate departure of a war steamer with instructions to enter Pensacola Harbor and use all means to prevent an attack from the mainland on Fort Pickens is of extreme importance. If the president, as commander-in-chief, will issue the order of which I enclose a draft, an important step towards the security of Fort Pickens will be taken." Scott, the nation's highest ranking army officer, could not order a naval vessel to sea. He asked Seward to ask the president to do so because Secretary of the Navy Welles was obviously not party to the plan.[1]

Seward and Meigs departed. The general-in-chief and his military secretary went in to dinner. The old soldier pondered the events of the day as they dined. He had sent Keyes out that morning with a map of Pensacola Bay to explain in detail to the secretary of state the difficulties that would be encountered in landing guns and munitions across the open beaches of Santa Rosa Island's gulf shore. He had heard nothing during the course of the day until Keyes returned late in the afternoon with Seward and Meigs bearing instructions from the commander-in-chief for the general to issue orders that were a contravention of his considered and stated judgment. Keyes had explained that Seward had refused to listen to what he had to say earlier in the day and had ordered him to find Meigs and spend the rest of the day preparing the plans the two officers had just laid before Scott. They had not had time to review the plans with the general-in-chief before their appointment with the president and, from the executive mansion, they had come directly to Scott's residence, Seward joining them along the way. Scott was understandably upset at being slighted and overruled. He sat at his table, slumped in his chair. Keyes, who had not eaten all day, later wrote he "brought to the table the appetite of a Siberian wolf in winter and the thirst of a Bedouin returned from a foray on the scorched sand of Arabia. The dinner was good and the wines were choice." As Scott fumed, Keyes got slightly drunk. He went to bed early and woke refreshed, he wrote in his diary, but his days as the military secretary to the general-in-chief of the United States Army were numbered.[2]

On Monday, April 1, Major Anderson requested permission from South Carolina authorities to send ashore the civilian laborers who had been working on completing Fort Sumter under the direction of the engineer in charge, Captain John G. Foster. Anderson wrote to the adjutant general, "Having been in daily expectation since the return of Colonel Lamon to Washington to receive orders to vacate this post, I have kept these men here as long as I could; but now, having completed the important work of cleaning up the area, &c., I am compelled in consequence of the small supply of provisions on hand, to discharge them." If the authorities on the mainland permitted him to send off the laborers, he added, he might be able to stretch the provisions for his command until the middle of the month. It was obvious from Anderson's wording that he considered his interview with Gustavus Fox regarding a relief expedition to be merely speculative and the communication from General Beauregard, based on Ward Lamon's statements to him, to be firm.[3]

From off Santa Rosa Island Captain Adams wrote to Secretary of the Navy Welles, "I have the honor to enclose a copy of a letter addressed to me by Captain Vogdes, U. S. Army, who is in command of some troops sent out in January last to reinforce the garrison of Fort Pickens. I have declined to land the men as Captain Vogdes requests, as it would be in direct violation of the orders of the navy department under which I am acting." General Scott's instructions to Vogdes, Adams wrote, were of old date and may have been issued without a full knowledge of the conditions existing on Pensacola Bay. Orders from the War Department, issued through the office of the general-in-chief held no authority for a naval officer. Adams wrote that no one acquainted with the feelings of the Southern troops under General Bragg on the mainland could doubt that landing Vogdes's command and reinforcing the fort would be considered not only a declaration of war but an absolute act of war. It would be a serious thing to bring on a collision which might be entirely against the wishes of the present administration. "While I can not take on myself under such insufficient authority as General Scott's order the fearful responsibility of such an act which seems to render civil war inevitable," Adams wrote, "I am ready at all times to carry out whatever orders I may receive from the honorable secretary of the navy." Adams also reported the return of *Brooklyn* from Key West with provisions and coal. Further, he advised, a number of the crew of his vessel, *Sabine,* were serving under expired enlistments and claimed their discharges on the ground that, being within the coastal waters of Florida, they were back within the jurisdiction of the United States. Adams had refused to release them. Ashore, volunteers from several states were arriving at Pensacola. The *Pensacola Gazette* reported, "The arrival of so many troops in our midst looks *squally*."[4]

At Washington General Scott informed the president he had received the letter from Captain Vogdes dated March 21 with the startling news that Vogdes's company had not been landed and had not reinforced Fort Pickens. Vogdes wrote that Captain Adams felt bound by the terms of a truce entered into under the Buchanan administration and refused him permission to land. Vogdes wrote, the conditions of the truce gave "every advantage to the seceders. They are not required to give any notice of its abrogation, and may attack the fort without a moment's notice." Lincoln was alarmed by what he learned was happening on Pensacola Bay and wondered what it would take to have his commands regarding the reinforcement of Fort Pickens carried out.[5]

However, the president suddenly had another and more pressing problem on his hands at the moment that took precedence even over the issue of Fort Pickens. Secretary of State Seward had just handed Lincoln a document titled *Some Thoughts for the President's Consideration*. At the end of its first month in office, Seward's document read, the Lincoln administration was without policy, either domestic or foreign. While admitting this condition was understandably caused by the press of issues involved in assuming office, responding to the pressure of patronage-seekers descending on the new executive, and the series of events taking place throughout the South, Seward warned that any further delay in adopting and prosecuting domestic and foreign policy would bring not only scandal to the administration but danger to the nation. With regard to domestic policy, Seward wrote, "we must change the question before the public from one upon slavery, or about slavery, for a question upon union or disunion." The occupation of Fort Sumter, he continued, was regarded as a slavery or party issue, and he considered it "fortunate that the last administration created the necessity." He would take advantage of that and evacuate Fort Sumter, placing the responsibility for this move upon the Buchanan administration. He would reinforce and defend all the forts in the Gulf of Mexico and have the navy recall its vessels from foreign stations in order to institute a blockade of the seceded states. As to foreign policy, he would demand explanations from Spain and France for their threatened intervention in Mexican affairs and would convene Congress and declare war upon the two powers if their explanations were not satisfactory. He would demand explanations from Great Britain and Russia for their interferences taking place in the hemisphere and he would send agents into Canada, Mexico, and Central America to rouse a vigorous continental spirit of independence against any European intervention. "But," Seward cautioned, "whatever policy we adopt, there must be an energetic prosecution of it. It must be somebody's business to pursue and direct incessantly. Either the president must do it himself, and be all the while active in it, or devolve it upon some member of his Cabinet. It is not my especial province, but I neither seek to evade or assume responsibility."[6] William H. Seward was making his move to assume within the administration of Abraham Lincoln the appropriate role he knew his experience and his ability justified. Were he not to be president, then in this manner he would become premier. After barely a month in office, Lincoln suddenly and abruptly faced the dismemberment of the government of the Union he was sworn to protect and preserve, He found that he had to react to foreign influences upon the national prestige of which he was barely aware. And he found himself at the helm of an administration that was unresponsive to the demands being made upon it by the executive newly come to office. Seward, "neither seeking to evade or assume responsibility," was humbly standing by ready to step in and take control of everything. Lincoln considered the document carefully. It was a startling indication of a lack of confidence in him and in his abilities on the part of the man he considered his mentor and guide in the unfamiliar world of national politics. He responded to Seward that same day. In a terse letter, he advised the secretary of state that his domestic policy had been clearly stated in his inaugural address when he said, "The power confided in me will be used to hold, occupy, and possess the property and places belonging to the government and to collect the duties and imposts." These words had undergone Seward's editing and had received his approval beforehand, the president reminded the secretary, and had to be viewed with Lincoln's order of that same day to General Scott to strengthen and hold the forts. With the exception of Seward's desire to give up Fort Sumter, this appeared to the president to be the same policy Seward's document was urging upon him. He could not conceive, Lincoln continued, how the reinforcement of Fort Sumter would be seen as a slavery or party issue while that of Fort Pickens would be seen as a national or patriotic issue. As to foreign policy, he wrote, even on that very day the administration had been preparing circulars and instructions to its ministers overseas, all in perfect harmony, without a suggestion that the administration had no policy. As to placing the responsibility for the energetic prosecution of both foreign and domestic policy in one person's hands, Lincoln agreed that it must be done and that he, as president, was the one to see to it. Abraham Lincoln was an unpolished and inexperienced politician in the early months of his administration but he was never incompetent. A very patient man, he would show the ability to work with the tools he was given in the form of the men in office around him. In this case, within one day Lincoln showed his ability to work with the former senator from New York and to indicate forcefully that there would be one president but no premier in this administration.[7]

From early morning Meigs and Keyes had worked at General Scott's office. They discussed several possible candidates and selected Colonel Harvey Brown to command the army's contingent of the Fort Pickens relief expedition. Brown was sixty-five, a graduate of West Point, class of 1818, and a man described as " a devoted soldier and staunch patriot." He had served in the Second Seminole War and the war with Mexico and was brevetted for gallantry in each. Brown was available for the assignment because he had been ordered to Washington to command the small force of regulars brought to the capital for security during the recent inauguration. Brown's force, as defined by the two officers planning the expedition, would consist of those companies of troops brought to the capital for the inauguration: Captain James Duane's company of sappers and miners from West Point; Captain William Barry's Company A, 2nd Artillery; Captain Henry Hunt's Company M, 2nd Artillery; Captain William John's Company C, 3rd Infantry; and Captain Henry Clitz's Company E, 3rd Infantry. The commands were to sail from New York with Brown on the first steamer for Fort Pickens. Other troops and supplies were to follow as soon as they could be assembled and embarked. Meigs would accompany the expedition as Brown's engineering officer. The remainder of Brown's military staff were to be Assistant Surgeon John Campbell, Assistant Quartermaster Rufus Ingalls, Assistant Commissary of Subsistence Henry F. Clarke, Assistant Adjutant General Brevet Captain George Hartstuff, and, as ordnance officer, First Lieutenant George Balch. Meigs and Keyes both insisted the objective and destination of Brown's expedition be communicated to no one to whom it was not already known. As a result, Colonel Brown's orders were signed by the general-in-chief and approved in writing by the president in order to keep the office of the adjutant general of the army out of the line of communication. This was a major departure from army procedures in that orders normally emanated from the office of the adjutant general but the secrecy called for by Meigs and Keyes demanded otherwise. To ensure that Brown received cooperation at every level, he was handed a special document drafted by Meigs:

> Executive Mansion, 1 April, 1861.
>
> All officers and men of the Army and Navy, to whom this order may be exhibited, will aid by every means in their power the expedition under the command of Colonel Harvey Brown, supplying him with men and materials, and cooperating with him as he may demand.
>
> Abraham Lincoln.[8]

Navy Lieutenant David Dixon Porter was at home at mid-day having a farewell dinner with his wife and children. Porter was a slight man, standing only five feet six inches tall. He was

Colonel Harvey Brown, U.S. Army, commanded the Federal side during the long standoff at Fort Pickens where "Bragg wouldn't fight, and Brown can't" (National Archives).

forty-eight and had been in the navy since 1829. In 1855, Porter had commanded the sailing storeship *Supply* on two voyages to the Middle East to purchase and carry back camels that Secretary of War Jefferson Davis wanted to try as pack animals for the army in the western deserts. Porter had held the rank of lieutenant for twenty years and there were still eight other officers ahead of him on the list awaiting promotion to lieutenant commander. He had recently been approached by the owners of the Pacific Mail Steamship Company with an attractive offer, a permanent and well-paid position as master of the largest and most modern American passenger steamship to be planned and built to date. Her keel had not yet been laid down and her construction would take from twelve to eighteen months before she would be ready to launch. Porter had accepted the offer and, interim, was planning to take a position commanding a steamer with the Treasury Department's survey of the California coast. He was scheduled to leave that evening for New York to take ship for California the following day. It was his farewell to his family that had him at the dinner table this noon. As neighbors, Porter and Meigs had often discussed the events taking place in the nation. They found in each other similar personalities. Both were rash, impatient, strong-willed, un-awed by the rank or station of those above them. Holding equivalent positions in the army and navy, both were frustrated by the slowness of a promotion system that was based entirely upon seniority rather than merit. Both had been friendly acquaintances of the current president of the Confederate States of America while Jefferson C. Davis was then in Washington as senator from Mississippi and later secretary of war. A carriage brought a messenger to Porter to come immediately to Seward's office at the State Department. Leaving his meal unfinished and his family wondering, Porter accompanied the messenger to find Seward reclining on a sofa in his office. Without changing his position, Seward asked Porter if Fort Pickens could be saved. It could, Porter assured him, and began verbally sketching out what he would recommend as the plan to do so. As he talked, Meigs walked into the room. Porter's plan involved sending a large steamer and six or seven companies of soldiers and, with a large number of guns and an abundant supply of ammunition, landing them on the gulf shore of Santa Rosa Island from where they could enter and reinforce the fort. With another steamer, Porter would force the way into the harbor and anchor under the guns of Fort Pickens, thereby preventing the Confederates from crossing over to the island from the mainland. Seward considered this, nodded, and told the officers to come with him to meet the president. When

The excitable, volatile Lieutenant David Dixon Porter, U.S. Navy, was constantly ready to head in any direction looking for action (Naval Historical Center).

the three arrived at the executive mansion, Lincoln was pacing between the window and his desk. The president had already sent Gustavus Fox to New York to prepare the expedition for the relief of Fort Sumter but had not yet given that mission his final approval. Lincoln was still thinking about the meeting he had held with Meigs and Keyes the day before regarding Fort Pickens. Seward asked Meigs and Porter to lay out their proposals for the president. The two men spoke confidently and quickly and were obviously in agreement with, and committed to, the idea. The president weighed the diffuse advice and the cautious council he had received from his senior military advisors against the fresh and active proposals he was receiving from these younger military and naval men and he found he felt better with this fresh and active advice. The president asked a few questions, nodded, thought for several minutes, and gave his assent. Porter raised the issue with Lincoln of the need for absolute secrecy. Washington was a Southern city, he told the president. The previous administration had given Southerners many patronage positions in the government's bureaucracy, especially in the War and Navy Departments, and many of these appointees remained and retained their offices. Some of the senior officers still on active duty were Southerners, many openly advocating secession and the seizure of the forts. Porter warned that, if word of the expedition were allowed to circulate, even at the level of the department secretaries, it would be impossible to prevent telegraph messages from flowing South with the result of immediate assaults most likely being launched against both forts. Lincoln agreed. He was about to set in motion the Fort Sumter expedition under Gustavus Fox in secrecy and he saw no reason to mention that effort to the two officers sitting with him. It did not strike the president that his secretary of state was privy to a plan that would exclude the secretaries of war and the navy from being informed of the disposition of forces normally under their exclusive control but Seward, Lincoln had already learned, routinely dabbled in the business of other departments of the government. He did ask Seward, "But, is this not a most irregular mode of proceeding?" Seward assured the president it was but the necessity of the case justified that. "You are commander-in-chief of the army and the navy," he told Lincoln, "and this is a case where it is necessary to issue direct orders without passing them through intermediaries." The president wondered, aloud, "But what will Uncle Gideon say?" Seward assured the president he would make it right with the secretary of the navy. Porter, following Meigs's suggestion, asked that orders be given that *Powhatan*, Captain Mercer's vessel, be designated to accompany the Fort Pickens expedition. Lincoln thumbed through some papers on his desk, one of which listed the vessels assigned to the Fort Sumter relief expedition. *Powhatan* was not on the list originally drawn up by Secretary Welles. The president concurred and Porter and Meigs went to a small room to draft the necessary orders for Lincoln's signature. As the two departed, Porter suggested that his friend, Captain Samuel Barron, be installed as head of the navy's Bureau of Detail, the office responsible for assigning officers to posts throughout the naval service. Lincoln, unfamiliar with the organization and operation of the Navy Department, agreed. When Porter and Meigs returned they carried four documents, drafted in rough form by Porter and copied as finals by Meigs. The first was addressed to Porter, directing him to proceed to New York with the least possible delay where he was to assume command of any naval vessel available. He was then to proceed immediately to Pensacola Harbor and, at any cost, enter the harbor and prevent an expedition from the mainland from reaching Fort Pickens. "This order, its object, and your destination will be communicated to no person whatsoever until you reach the harbor at Pensacola," the document read. The second was to Captain Samuel Mercer directing him to turn *Powhatan* over to "another officer who is duly informed and instructed in relation to the wishes of the government." The third was an open order which, referring to Porter, said, "All officers are commanded to afford him all such facilities as he may deem necessary for getting to sea as soon as possible." The final order, addressed to the secretary of the navy, was strange in concept in that it gave orders unrelated to the mission under which Porter was acting and it interfered with assignments and responsibilities of senior officers in the navy. It directed Commodore Pendergrast to remain at Vera Cruz with part of the Home Squadron, although he and it had departed that station weeks before. It ordered Captain Silas Stringham to Pensacola to assume command of the part of the Home Squadron there, and it appointed Captain Samuel Barron to head the Bureau of Detail. Lincoln signed the orders without reading them. Turning to Seward, he warned the secretary of state, "See that I don't burn my fingers." Porter and Meigs walked with Seward to the State Department where the secretary gave Meigs $20,000 of unaccountable State Department secret contingency funds to pay any expenses of the expedition In order to make arrangements for the troops and ordnance that were to be taken, Porter and Meigs went to General Scott's home. Porter was refused entrance by the crusty septuagenarian who was suffering from gout and sitting with his feet in a tub of ice water. "Tell Captain Meigs to walk in," Scott shouted. "I won't see that naval officer. He can't come in." Porter went home. Because of Scott's refusal, the orders for the army's role in the Fort Pickens expedition were prepared and issued without Porter's involvement or knowledge. Porter would not become aware of their contents until he arrived off Pensacola seventeen days later. This incident has to be compared to the example of Captain Adams off Pensacola who was refusing to act on orders issued by the general-in-chief of the United States Army because they didn't emanate from his own Navy Department. In this case, Scott had refused admission to his home, and to the subsequent planning session that took place, to the very navy officer slated to command the initial element of a joint army-navy operation the general-in-chief had contributed, if reluctantly, toward putting under way. The days of successful joint operations between officers of the army and the navy were not far off, if history were to be known at the time, but those days would require much frustration and loss before they came into being. Most significantly, they would require the passing from the scene of the old men holding senior command positions in both services in favor of younger men who had the ability to do something the old timers could not do which was to think beyond the limits of their branch of the service toward the goal of the common good. To many of the old men who had commanded in either branch of the armed forces and had done so with honor, this was simply beyond their abilities. At home, Porter told his wife Georgy to let their friends continue to think he was going to California as he had planned. He would take their seventeen-year-old son Essex on the expedition with him as his clerk. Porter bade farewell to their second son Carlisle, who was about to enter the United States Naval Academy at Annapolis, Maryland. Porter kissed Georgy and the younger children, entered a carriage with Essex, and left for the railroad depot. On the midnight train of cars to New York, Porter did not correct naval officers with whom he conversed who wished him well on going to California and taking service with the coast survey.[9]

Captain Andrew H. Foote, U.S. Navy, was never certain Porter and Meigs weren't Confederate spies intending to steal *Powhatan* and run her off to the rebels (National Archives).

Late in the day Secretary Seward informed the Confederate commissioners there might be an attempt to supply Fort Sumter with provisions. He assured the three men that Governor Pickens would receive prior notice were the attempt actually to be made. There was no suggestion in Seward's communication that reinforcement of the garrison was involved.[10]

Also late in the day the commandant of the Brooklyn Navy Yard received three telegrams that were somewhat similar in wording and meaning. One was from Abraham Lincoln ordering *Powhatan* fitted out for sea at the earliest possible moment. Written orders carried by a confidential messenger would go forward to the commandant the following day. The second telegram was from the secretary of the navy ordering him to revoke the detachment of the officers and men of *Powhatan* and hold her in readiness for sea service. The third telegram, also from the secretary of the navy, told Commodore Breese, "Fit out *Powhatan* to go to sea at the earliest possible moment." Commodore Breese, however, was on leave. Commanding in his stead at the Brooklyn Navy Yard was his executive officer, Captain Andrew H. Foote. Foote lost no time ordering *Powhatan* put back in service and recalling her officers and crew. Still, he wondered about the orders he held in his hands. Foote was fifty-five years old with thirty-nine years service in the navy. A native of Connecticut, he was a personal friend of Gideon Welles, the secretary of the navy. Foote had never known of an order to be issued directly to a naval officer by the president of the United States.[11]

Gideon Welles, Lincoln's secretary of the navy, was determined to conduct the affairs of his department without regard to meddling senior cabinet members (National Archives).

At Washington while having dinner at Willard's Hotel, Secretary of the Navy Gideon Welles was joined by the president's personal secretary, John J. Nicolay. Interrupting his meal, Welles opened an envelope Nicolay handed him and read the several documents it contained, one of which was, in his words, "of a singular character, being in the nature of instructions or orders from the Executive relative to naval matters of which I knew the president was not informed, and about which I had not been consulted. One of these papers relating to the government of the navy department was more singular and extraordinary than either of the others." The order Welles referred to was the directive from Lincoln ordering him to send Captain Stringham to Pensacola and to put Captain Barron in Stringham's place as the officer in charge of the Bureau of Detail. Copies of the orders to Porter, Meigs, and Breese were not in the envelope. Leaving his meal unfinished, Welles hurried to the executive mansion and met Lincoln who was alone in his office. Rising as the secretary came through the door, and reacting to the expression on Welles's face, Lincoln asked, "What have I done wrong?" Welles answered that he had been surprised to receive a package that evening containing documents that, among other things, contained the president's instructions respecting the Navy Department. Welles demanded an explanation, showing Lincoln the document ordering the officer reassignments within the department. Lincoln seemed surprised when he read the document which Welles handed him. He explained to the irate secretary that Seward and two officers had been with him earlier in the day on matters that Seward "had much at heart." He had let Seward and the officers prepare some orders that he had signed without reading, trusting the secretary of state. Lincoln did not mention any of the details of Seward's project but he did assure Welles he would never have signed the order the secretary held in his hands had he been aware of its content which had nothing to do with Seward's project. Welles asked who else was associated with Seward in this matter and Lincoln told him only that two officers had been with the secretary of state to act as clerks, to write the plans and orders down. Most of that had been done in another room, Lincoln explained. Welles asked who the officers were and Lincoln told him, "One was Captain Meigs; the other was a companion with whom he seemed intimate, a naval officer named Porter." Welles told Lincoln that he had no confidence in the fidelity of Captain Barron who, by this order, would be placed in a position of authority from which he could effectively take charge of the navy. Barron was the last man, Welles declared, he would trust to be responsible for officer assignments. Barron was an accomplished officer and a gentleman, Welles conceded, but one whose feelings, sympathies, and associations were notoriously with the secessionists. He was a prominent member of a clique of naval exclusives, most of whom were thought to be thoroughly tainted with the secession passion. Welles could not consent to have Barron in that position nor to give him the trust the president's order imposed. Lincoln repeated that the order did not contain his instructions even though his name was signed to it. He asked the secretary to give the order no more consideration than he thought proper, to treat it as cancelled if he wished.[12]

Confederate Navy Captain Duncan Ingraham was in charge at the Pensacola Navy Yard under Bragg's overall command of the Confederate forces on the bay. On Tuesday, April 2, he wrote to Captain Adams that he had never in his life been more shocked than when informed of Lieutenant Commanding Berryman's death. Berryman, since the occupation of the navy yard and the forts on the mainland in January, had been the sole officer on board *Wyandotte*. Maintaining station inside the harbor and working between the Confederate forces on the mainland and the United States forces on Santa Rosa Island and in the offing, Berryman had served without relief while keeping an eye on events taking place on the mainland. His vessel flew signals from her rigging to Slemmer within the fort and to Adams offshore. Otway Berryman had exhausted himself in the service of his nation and had made the ultimate sacrifice. Lieutenant Commander John Mullany immediately transferred from *Brooklyn* and took command of *Wyandotte*. Sectional differences and political distances were temporarily put aside among the naval officers who had served alongside each other for so many years with this, the death of the first of their now divided number. Ingraham wrote Adams that everything would be prepared for Berryman's interment the next day and suggested Adams provide an honor guard from the marines of the squadron since the Southern volunteers "are not in very good trim." Ingraham invited as many Federal officers as possible to attend the burial. He wrote Adams he had opened a grave at the navy yard cemetery and ended his letter, "We can supply a pine coffin. I only wish we had better."[13]

At New York Porter presented himself to Captain Foote at the Brooklyn Navy Yard at ten o'clock in the morning. The two were acquainted, having served together recently on a board commissioned to inspect navy yards along the east coast. Porter handed Foote the original of the message ordering *Powhatan* fitted out for sea. Foote had received the telegraphed version of the order the afternoon before and was expecting its confirmation but still it took Porter three hours to convince Foote he had no choice but to obey the presidential prohibition regarding communicating the contents of the order to any one. Foote did not think that applied to the secretary of the navy whom he wished to ask for advice in what was becoming a complex, irregular, and perplexing situation. Foote called Captain Samuel Mercer to his office and handed him the letter from the president which directed him to turn over command of *Powhatan*. Foote asked for Mercer's advice. Although disappointed at being relieved of command of one of the most powerful vessels in the navy, Mercer said he saw no alternative but for Foote to carry out the presidential directive. Mercer agreed with Foote that the whole process was highly irregular. He offered to remain aboard *Powhatan* as her skipper to oversee her re-commissioning, the recall of her officers and crew, and even to take her down the harbor as far as Staten Island upon her putting to sea in order to conceal Porter's role in the affair from the public. Foote was still not convinced Porter was not a rebel spy in disguise plotting with the officers of *Powhatan* to steal the ship and deliver her to the South. "You see, Porter," Foote argued, "there are many fellows whom I would have trusted to the death who have deserted the flag that I don't know whom to believe. How do I know you are not a traitor? Who ever heard of such orders emanating from the president? I should telegraph the secretary of the navy before I do anything and ask for instructions." Telegraph at his own peril, Porter warned Foote, adding that if he must telegraph someone, it should be the president or the secretary of state. "What would prevent you from having a confederate at the other end of the line to receive the message and answer it?" Foote asked. What would Foote say, Porter countered, if he were to tell the captain that several high-ranking officers of the United States Navy were about to resign and join the rebellion, naming Captain Samuel Barron as one of them. This was extremely strange on Porter's part since only the day before Porter had drafted an order for the signature of the president naming Barron to head the navy's Bureau of Detail which would have given the captain control over assignments of naval officers throughout the navy. "Good Lord deliver us!" Foote exclaimed. "I must telegraph Mr. Welles. I can't stand this strain any longer. It will kill me." Foote called his clerk to bring a telegraph blank. Porter quoted the prohibition against communicating the order, its object, and the destination of *Powhatan* to any person until after Porter reached Pensacola Harbor. Porter had no difficulty remembering the exact wording of the order; he had composed it himself. This left Foote noticeably upset. After considering for several minutes, he sent his orderly to the Irving House in New York where Porter was registered to collect the officer's trunks and bring them to Foote's residence at the navy yard. Porter would remain with him, he declared, and would be arrested "the very moment there is any treason about you." Further, Porter had come on a wild goose chase, Foote informed him. *Powhatan* had been stripped to the girt-line, her engines dismantled, her boilers taken apart to be repaired, and her worn boats sent off to be replaced. The vessel needed planking throughout, her magazines were too damp to keep powder in, and the yard crews were in the process dismantling her. Foote told Porter he had ordered *Powhatan* into dry dock that very morning. Porter was insistent. He convinced Foote to set his people to work putting things back together and he told Foote he would take the steamer as she was. If Foote complied, Porter felt he could get to sea in four days. Foote agreed, but with some hesitation. He gave the orders and told Porter to come to his home for lunch, adding he would put a marine sentry there with orders to keep an eye on Porter after Foote returned to his office. Porter countered by saying he would return with Foote to make sure the captain didn't telegraph the secretary of the navy. Foote and Porter spent the afternoon together and returned to the captain's quarters in the evening where they sat late into the night talking about adventures and events that had taken place during their years of service. At the navy yard the decommissioning work had been reversed. *Powhatan's* engines were put back together. Heavy cranes lifted her large guns back on deck. Double shifts of workers went into her with orders to continue working day and night. Few major repairs were attempted and *Powhatan* remained in shockingly poor condition for any service at sea.[14]

Gustavus Fox returned to Washington from New York where he had been preparing the Fort Sumter expedition. As directed by the president, he had not signed binding agreements to charter the ocean transport and the harbor tugs called for in his plan. Lincoln was still not completely committed to the Fort Sumter relief idea. Neither Fox nor Secretary Welles mentioned to the president that the secretary had ordered *Powhatan* brought back into commission and added to the Fort Sumter task force. That same evening Colonel Harvey Brown and Lieutenant Colonel Erasmus Keyes left Washington for New York to begin bringing together the army's contingent of the Fort Pickens expedition. Captain Meigs had business to close out at the capital having to do with his engineering projects. He would follow Brown and Keyes the next day. Neither party was in communication with the other regarding the two separate expeditions that were making ready.[15]

Confederate Secretary of State Robert Toombs wrote from Montgomery to the three commissioners at Washington regarding their interpretation of Seward's desire to forestall a conflict. "It is a matter of no importance to us what may induce the adoption of Mr. Seward's policy by his government. We are satisfied that it will redound to our advantage and, therefore, care little for Mr. Seward's calculations as to its future effect upon the Confederate States." Toombs was putting into words the policy the authorities of the new government were now following. They would delay taking any hostile action as long as they could in order to gain time to organize and bring together their resources but they had no intention of seeking a compromise with the United States government. This was a fact that William Seward completely missed in his efforts to calm and settle matters in order to allow time for feelings to cool and for moderate men to think through what their state governments were doing. Those states which had thus far seceded considered themselves sovereign entities and they had no desire to return to their former relationship with a central government headed by the Lincoln administration and dominated by Northern politicians. The *London Times* correspondent, William Howard Russell, expressed his reactions to an interview with the Confederate commissioners in an article to the editors of his paper. Russell wrote that, if the three men represented the feelings of their fellow citizens, the Union could never be restored. The commissioners saw themselves as ministers of a foreign power "treating with Yankeedom," Russell wrote, and their indignation was high at the refusal of the Federal government to negotiate with them on issues such as the adjustment of Federal claims for property, forts, stores, public works, debt, and land purchases. Even though a justice of the United States Supreme Court, John A. Campbell, was acting on their behalf as an intermediary, they were beginning to lose faith in Seward because of his continuing series of excuses and delays. Further, Russell wrote, the commissioners were hearing that preparations were being made at New York for sending reinforcements and provisions to Fort Sumter and that Fort Pickens had already been reinforced by sea.[16]

On Wednesday, April 3, Major Anderson at Fort Sumter wrote the adjutant general that the South Carolina authorities had again refused his request to send the civilian laborers ashore. This would have reduced the demands they made on his dwindling store of provisions. There was every indication, he wrote, that he would get no further support from the mainland. "I must, therefore, most respectfully and urgently, ask for instructions what I am to do as my provisions are exhausted," he wrote. "Our bread will last for four or five days."[17]

At New York, Lieutenant Colonel Keyes inspected several merchant steamers and chartered two of the sturdiest and fastest, the Collins Line transport *Atlantic* and the Vanderbilt liner *Illinois*. The following day he chartered the privately-owned steamer *Philadelphia*. Keyes was not restrained by the restrictions on moving forward with the Fort Pickens expedition that Fox was under with the Fort Sumter plan. Keyes was armed with an impressive order signed by the commander-in-chief that directed bluntly, "All requisitions made upon officers of the staff by your authority, and all orders given by you to any officer in the Army in my name, will be obeyed." Keyes made requisitions on the quartermaster, commissary, ordnance, and recruiting officers, the medical purveyor, and several engineering officers. He personally supervised the loading of *Atlantic*. Stevedores pushed, rolled, and hoisted into her holds 12,000 tons of heavy guns, munitions, and provisions. Seventy-three horses were herded up her gangplank and haltered along the rail of the forward deck.[18]

At Washington, Brigadier General Joseph Totten, the army's chief engineer, gave Secretary of War Cameron his professional analysis of the situations at Forts Sumter and Pickens. Fort Sumter, Totten explained, if reinforced with adequate men, provisions, and munitions, could hold out for only a short time. The fort was designed to ward off an approaching enemy fleet, not to withstand a siege by hostile forces on the mainland. Even if reinforced and supplied, Fort Sumter would eventually be obliged to surrender with great loss of life. The fort would be wrested from the government in spite of any preparations the government might take. As to Fort Pickens, were it provided with a garrison of eight hundred to a thousand men, fully supplied with everything necessary for the best defense, and ably commanded, its utmost term of resistance would be about three weeks — rather less than more. In any case, Totten advised, a quick surrender was inevitable. It was

Brigadier General Joseph Totten, chief engineer, U.S. Army. His best judgment was that Fort Pickens could stand for only three weeks (Military History Institute).

advice such as this, given by Joseph Totten, a man of seventy-three, and by Winfield Scott, a man of seventy-five, that drove the president outside the circles of ponderous military advisors toward younger and more enthusiastic men such as Gustavus Fox, David Porter, and Montgomery Meigs.[19]

The Confederate commissioners at Washington wired Secretary Toombs that there seemed to be great activity at the War and Navy Departments. *Minnesota* had been ordered from her home port at Boston to the mouth of the Mississippi River. *Powhatan,* at New York, had suddenly been ordered back in commission with orders to sail in the coming week. Four companies of soldiers presently at Washington had been ordered to New York for embarkation to an undisclosed destination, possibly Santo Domingo where an insurrection was taking place against Spanish domination of the island. *Pawnee,* at Washington, was ordered to make ready for sea by the coming Saturday. The source of this information, the commissioners wired, was the newspaperman L. Q. Washington. Toombs immediately wired the information to General Beauregard at Charleston.[20]

The officers sitting on the court-martial of Commodore Armstrong at Washington took time to recommend to the secretary of the navy that some appropriate mark of the department's approbation be bestowed on William Conway, "quartermaster of the navy on duty at the navy yard at Warrington, Fla., when the same was surrendered on the twelfth of January, 1861; who with manly pride and in a spirit of patriotic devotion refused to obey the order to haul down the national flag on the occasions of that surrender." Welles concurred and issued a laudatory order that was to be read publicly by the commanders of all naval stations and vessels in the presence of the offices and men of their commands. At this time there were no medals or other means of recognizing or commending meritorious or gallant performances by enlisted men in either the army or the navy.[21]

On Thursday, April 4, *Supply* dropped anchor off Santa Rosa Island, twenty-one days out of New York and five days after *Brooklyn* had returned with provisions and coal from Key West. Captain Adams reported the arrival of *Supply* to the secretary of the navy and added he would see to her immediate return to New York as soon as the needs of the vessels of his squadron were filled.[22]

Captain Montgomery Meigs arrived at New York at four in the morning. He met Lieutenant Colonel Keyes and, in his own words, "set everything going." Also at New York, Colonel Harvey Brown made contact with army headquarters to arrange for the troops and munitions that were to accompany him to Santa Rosa Island. From Washington Secretary Welles sent another telegram to the Brooklyn Navy Yard urging dispatch in preparing *Powhatan* but to Captain Foote's dismay the message contained no confirmation from the secretary regarding what her destination was to be nor who was to command her. At the yard *Powhatan's* officers were reporting back from their abbreviated leaves and the members of her crew were returning from the receiving ship *North Carolina*. Foote, having spent most of the night sitting up and talking with Porter, still had problems when he woke with the orders he had received from the commander-in-chief through irregular channels to fit out *Powhatan* for sea, and then from the secretary of the navy through normal channels to do the same thing. Foote was perplexed by the disparity and he needed direction but he was clearly prohibited from communicating with the Navy Department by the written order of the president. He worked and worried at his problem and then came up with a way to do what he felt he must do by responding to Welles's several demands for accelerated action to fit out *Powhatan*. He would keep the secretary informed of progress being made under the orders he had received from the Navy Department. "Captain Meigs had called on me with a letter showing his authority from the government to have certain preparations made and things placed on board of vessels to go to sea about which you are familiar; but as the orders did not come direct, I make this report; but as no time is to be lost, I am preparing what is called for and report my action." When the telegram was received at the Navy Department later in the day, no one called the attention of the secretary of the navy to Foote's cryptic reference to orders that "did not come direct."[23]

At Washington Lincoln finally decided to order the expedition to relieve Fort Sumter to go forward under the direction of Gustavus Fox. In an attempt to avoid a confrontation that could result in gunfire and bloodshed, Lincoln separated the re-supply of the fort from its reinforcement. Fox was instructed to try to send in provisions first. Only if the supply vessels drew fire from the batteries ringing the harbor would the troops aboard the transport and the crews of the warships be committed. Fox did not receive the order until late in the night. After a hurried meeting with Lincoln, he left by rail for New York. Fox was pleased when he learned Secretary Welles had added *Powhatan* to the Fort Sumter task force in order to provide her heavy guns, her trained crew, and her large boats. The president had forgotten, and Fox was unaware, that *Powhatan* was also assigned to another mission, one that was much further along in its planning and progress than the one under Gustavus Fox. Secretary of War Cameron wired Major Anderson at Fort Sumter that an attempt was going forward to provision his garrison. If the effort were resisted, then an attempt to reinforce him would be made. Anderson was told to try to hold out until the 11th or 12th if possible. And also at Washington the three still-unrecognized Confederate commissioners were by now no longer accepting any of Seward's promises. They were, however, gathering the many rumors they were hearing and telegraphing conflicting and confusing messages to Secretary Toombs at Montgomery. This day they wired advice for the Confederate government to strengthen the defenses at the mouth of the Mississippi River.[24]

On Friday, April 5, General Bragg wired Secretary Walker asking that, should the Federals break the truce agreement regarding the reinforcement of Fort Pickens, might he attack? Bragg asked for an immediate reply. Walker responded by asking Bragg to expand on his question, such as did the general feel he could prevent reinforcements being landed other than at the Fort Pickens wharf on the bay side of Santa Rosa Island? By attack, did he intend to open with his guns on the fort or on the vessels offshore also? If only the fort, would his operations be confined to battering the walls or did he contemplate sending troops over to Santa Rosa Island for a full assault? Walker wanted to know more from Bragg before he committed himself and the Confederate government to opening active hostilities with the Federal government. "Telegraph, and write also, fully," Walker ended his reply.[25]

At New York Gustavus Fox was hard at work along the waterfront. Orders had gone from the Navy Department for *Pocahontas, Pawnee,* and *Harriet Lane* to sail from their respective home ports and to rendezvous off the Charleston bar the morning of the following Thursday, April 11, and Gustavus Fox was counting on *Powhatan* to join the task force there. He signed the charter for the merchant steamer *Baltic* to carry the troops and their provisions and chartered, at what he considered exorbitant rates, the harbor tugs *Uncle Ben, Yankee,* and *Freeborn*. At the Brooklyn Navy Yard, and unaware of Fox's activity, Foote was still struggling with the confusing orders from Washington. He had no response to his

Confederate stand battery at Fort Barrancas (photograph by J.D. Edwards, Southern Historical Collection, Samuel Henry Lockett Papers, Wilson Library, University of North Carolina at Chapel Hill).

telegram the previous day. He attempted again to draw the attention of the Navy Department to the events taking place around him. "I am executing orders received from the government through the navy officer as well as through the army officer. Will write fully, if possible, today, certainly tomorrow. I hope *Powhatan* will sail this evening." At 2:00 P.M. the crew mustered and boarded *Powhatan*. The ship's officers assembled on the quarterdeck and the crew formed aft. Foote formally turned the vessel over to Captain Mercer, the national ensign was hoisted, and *Powhatan* was officially declared back in commission. All this time Foote had been muttering to himself at the strange ways things were being done. Nonetheless, he telegraphed the Navy Department that *Powhatan* was in commission and prepared for sea, and all in record time.[26]

From Washington, over Captain Stringham's signature, the Navy Department telegraphed the operational orders for the Fort Sumter naval task force under Captain Mercer in *Powhatan* to set to sea. The vessels were to support the relief expedition being mounted by the War Department which Gustavus Fox would command. Mercer was to put himself in contact with Fox and to cooperate fully with him. The object of the mission was to provision Fort Sumter and for this the War Department was furnishing the necessary chartered merchant vessels. Should the authorities at Charleston permit the landing of the provisions, no further service would be required of the naval vessels under Mercer's command and they would return to their home ports. Should the authorities at Charleston refuse permission or attempt to prevent any of the vessels from entering the harbor, Mercer was to open the way, overcoming all obstructions. Provisions and reinforcement would then be sent into the fort using the launches from the naval vessels towed by the chartered tugs. Mercer was to leave New York in *Powhatan* in time to arrive off the Charleston bar, ten miles east of the lighthouse, on the morning of the 11th, there to await the arrival of the other vessels, tugs, and ships of war of his task force. Captain Mercer, however, was not in command of *Powhatan* and the steamer was not about to sail for the Charleston bar. About then, after reading and approving Stringham's order to Mercer, Secretary Welles began to wonder about the cryptic telegrams the department had been receiving from Captain Foote. He wired Foote to delay the sailing of *Powhatan* pending further instructions. He needed time to figure out what was happening within his department. From New York, as soon as he learned that the telegram to delay the departure of *Powhatan* had been received at the navy yard, Meigs wired Seward, "*Powhatan* was ready to sail at 6 P.M.; telegram received by Captain Foote, commander of the navy yard, to detain. First, disobedience of order, came through Stringham; second, secretary of the navy. President's orders were to sail as soon as ready. This is fatal; what is to be done? Answer 110 Astor House." Porter flew into a rage when he learned of the delay, swearing he would do nothing more for this government. He would abandon the Fort Pickens expedition and go to California to spend his time surveying the coastline until his merchant steamer was launched and ready for him to take command. Meigs, the more stable of the temperamental two, tried to calm Porter. He declared they would have to find a way to have the secretary of the navy's order to Mercer ignored. They held signed orders from the commander-in-chief which surely took precedence over a telegraphic order from a cabinet officer. Porter sent a telegram across the city to Foote at the navy yard, "I am with Captain Meigs and we are telegraphing Mr. Seward. Meigs thinks Mr. Welles's telegram is bogus." Porter asked, would the secretary of the navy dare to countermand a written order of the president? The two of them, Porter wrote, thought that impossible. He would be at the navy yard at six the following morning. Porter ended his telegram, "Will you care for my boy overnight?"[27]

At Washington, some time after eleven that night, Seward, accompanied by his son Frederick, went to Welles's rooms at Willard's Hotel. He had received a telegram from Captain Meigs, he told the secretary of the navy, which stated that orders emanating from the Navy Department were in conflict with other orders and had become a source of obstruction and embarrassment to one of his enterprises. Seward asked that the Navy Department's orders be retracted. Welles was confused. What orders? he asked. How could an action by the Navy Department obstruct or embarrass an action by the State Department? Seward explained he supposed it had to do with *Powhatan* and Lieutenant Porter's command. There must be some mistake, Welles assured the secretary of state. Lieutenant Porter had no command and *Powhatan* was in New York where she was being made ready for sea as the flagship of the Fort Sumter relief expedition. No, Seward corrected Welles, Porter had been sent to New York under special orders

Captain Silas Stringham, U.S. Navy, a reliable, loyal officer who, like so many of his contemporaries as the war broke out, was a very old man (Library of Congress).

of the president, of which Welles had not been informed. Welles said he doubted the president would detach and send away a naval officer without informing the secretary of the navy. He would certainly not send the officer to take command of a commissioned vessel on the eve of its sailing on a most critical mission. Such irregular proceedings, Welles warned, would throw the departments of the government into confusion and were wholly inconsistent with correct and systematic administration. Seward suggested that, possibly, Captain Stringham might have some further facts. Welles remembered that Seward had been party to the issuance of orders that would have put Captain Barron in the position occupied by Stringham, who was an old friend of the secretary and an officer with known loyalties. Welles sent for the chief of the Bureau of Detail, who also roomed at Willard's. Stringham supported the secretary of the navy's contention: he knew nothing of an order to Porter having to do with *Powhatan*. The discussion became heated and Welles later admitted to some high excitement on his part. He insisted the two secretaries call upon the president even though the hour was approaching midnight. Welles was determined to get to the bottom of the issue and was, by now, furious at Seward's superior and condescending manner. Welles asked Captain Stringham to accompany him to the executive mansion. Seward brought along his son. On the way, Seward came to realize he had committed a serious breach of protocol. The secretary of the navy, whom Seward considered a relatively minor Connecticut politician placed in the cabinet in a role far beyond his abilities, appeared to be not only angry but acting like a person intent on running the Navy Department himself and hauling meddling cabinet colleagues before the president without regard to the hour of the day or night. Seward suggested he might have erred in interfering in Welles's department. Old as he was, he admitted, he had learned a lesson from this incident: he had better mind his own business and confine his labors to his own department in the future. Welles curtly agreed with him. In spite of the hour, Lincoln had not retired when the four men arrived. He was astonished by what Welles told him and by the telegram from New York that Seward handed him to read. He asked Welles if the secretary of the navy might not be in error with regard to the role *Powhatan* was to play in the Fort Sumter expedition. Welles insisted he was not. He left and walked to the Navy Department to bring back the documents he had reviewed with the president on the Fort Sumter expedition which clearly showed the later addition of *Powhatan* to the original list of vessels. Reading the record, Lincoln now remembered. He told Seward *Powhatan* must be restored to Captain Mercer. Lincoln confessed he never supposed he was interfering with the expedition to relieve Fort Sumter when he agreed to give *Powhatan* to Porter for the Fort Pickens expedition. Seward suggested it was probably too late to correct the mistake and, in his estimation, Fort Pickens was the more important of the two forts. Lincoln was becoming aware of the injury he had caused by permitting his secretary of state to lead him astray with orders he had signed without reading. He refused to discuss the matter further. The orders of the secretary of the navy regarding *Powhatan* must be carried out. The Fort Pickens expedition had time and could wait. No time could be lost by the Fort Sumter task force. Seward was ordered to send a telegram to New York immediately. When he again suggested it was too late at night to get a telegram through to the navy yard, Lincoln told him flatly *Powhatan* was to be restored to Captain Mercer. On no account, the president insisted, was the Fort Sumter expedition to be interfered with. Seward wrote out and gave the message to an aide, "Give the *Powhatan* to Captain Mercer.—Seward."[28]

7

"When the Arrow Has Fled from the Bow"

At New York, Porter had avoided going anywhere near *Powhatan*. During the night his luggage was delivered to the waterfront and put aboard the steamer identified as belonging to "American Minister, Vera Cruz." He arrived at the gate of the navy yard early on Saturday, April 6, and spent another three hours trying to convince Foote he was not a rebel in disguise attempting to steal *Powhatan* and run south with her. Foote was studying the telegram from the previous day containing the operational order for Mercer to command the task force, which included *Powhatan,* bound for Fort Sumter. Foote again insisted he had no choice but to wire the secretary of the navy for instructions. Porter again showed him the presidential order prohibiting such communication. Mercer joined the two men in Foote's office. Mercer temporarily considered trying to retain his command and following the orders of the secretary of the navy. Meigs arrived and managed to convince Foote and Mercer that no cabinet minister could countermand a written order of the commander-in-chief. Foote finally decided to let the other three argue the issue since, with *Powhatan* back in commission, she was no longer his responsibility but that of her commander, whomever they decided that should be. Mercer listened to the strong arguments and heated positions that Porter and Meigs made and eventually acquiesced. He would retain command until *Powhatan* was well down the bay. Porter would board in civilian clothing and remain out of sight in Mercer's stateroom. Past the Narrows, off Staten Island, Mercer would bring the steamer to, introduce Porter to the ship's officers, and have himself rowed ashore. Porter would then assume command and sail for Pensacola Bay. The three men left Foote's office, Mercer and Porter for *Powhatan* and Meigs to join Keyes in the work involved in loading the transports that would carry Colonel Brown's army contingent of ordnance, provisions, and men. The moment the three were gone, Foote telegraphed the secretary of the navy that *Powhatan* had sailed under the command of Lieutenant Porter in obedience to the written order of the commander-in-chief. At three that afternoon *Powhatan* did slip her moorings at the navy yard and but only to work out into the stream where she anchored and completed the final loading of her munitions. Half an hour later Foote received Seward's telegram, sent in the early hours of the morning from Washington at the president's insistence, ordering Porter to restore command of *Powhatan* to Captain Mercer. Foote was now in a quandary. During the morning's meetings, Porter and Meigs had managed to quash his objections by reminding him that the president's orders were explicit and peremptory. Now he stood with Seward's telegram in hand telling him the secretary of state, the official whose name had been flaunted by Porter and Meigs as the lead party behind the Fort Pickens expedition, was ordering the vessel back to Captain Mercer. Foote realized there was something terribly irregular happening at the Brooklyn Navy Yard under his charge. He dispatched Lieutenant Francis A. Roe, of the yard's ordnance department, bearing Seward's telegram with instructions to commandeer a fast tug and pursue *Powhatan* down the harbor. Meantime, *Powhatan* had completed loading and weighed anchor, drifting down with the stream and out toward the open sea. Off Tompkinsville, Staten Island, at the Narrows where the Lower Bay meets the Atlantic Ocean, Captain Mercer brought *Powhatan* to. He called the steamer's first lieutenant to his stateroom and had him introduce Porter to the other officers. Donning civilian dress, Mercer climbed into a small boat and was rowed ashore by sailors from the crew while Porter outlined for the steamer's officers the mission upon which they were about to embark. Just as the ship's boat returned and was being hoisted aboard, lookouts on *Powhatan* called out to Porter that a small steam tug was approaching and making signals she desired to communicate with the warship. Lieutenant Roe boarded and handed Seward's telegram to Porter who read the terse message that was signed only "Seward." Porter jotted a response to the secretary of state, "I received my orders from the president and shall proceed to execute them." Porter was placing his career and the relief of Fort Sumter in jeopardy by basing his response on the slim difference that his original order, signed by the president, could not be superseded by a subsequent order signed by the secretary of state whom Porter knew was intimately involved with the president in the Fort Pickens plan. He did, however, want to explain his conduct to Foote who might be held responsible for some of Porter's actions. "The telegram you sent me afforded me no comfort; on the contrary, burdened me. Still, the president says nothing and I must obey his orders; they were too explicit to be misunderstood. I got them from his own hand. He has not recalled them. Meigs is off and ahead of me. I could not go with him, and I recollect all Meigs's guns are aboard. This is an unpleasant position to be in, but I will work out of it. Am sustained by my sense of duty and will leave the rest to that kind Providence which has never deserted me in very trying circumstances. Will you please forward the enclosed dispatch to the secretary of state? Also, please detain all private letters that may be in the bag for five days." Porter handed the messages, one to Seward and one to Foote, to Roe and saw the officer over the side. As the propellers of the steam tug churned the water and the vessel headed back to New York, Porter gave the order for *Powhatan* to go ahead fast. When Roe handed Porter's message to Foote an hour later, the officer exclaimed, "He's clean daft!" Either Porter was sacrificing his naval career in order to carry out highly irregular orders or he had run off with *Powhatan* to join the rebels. Foote, at the time, was not clear which. Years later, talking to Porter, Foote told him, "You ought to have been tried and shot; no one but yourself would ever have been so impudent!"[1]

By what he described as incessant labor, Lieutenant Colonel Keyes oversaw the final loading of *Atlantic*. Colonel Brown was embarked with his sappers and miners, infantrymen, artillerymen, staff officers, and twenty-six civilian carpenters employed by Meigs, now the expedition's engineer. Captain A. A. Gray, commanding *Atlantic* under charter to the

Confederate formations in camp at Pensacola Bay (photograph by J.D. Edwards, Library of Congress).

War Department, was directed to take his instructions from Colonel Brown. In the early hours of the following day, *Atlantic* weighed anchor in the stream and put to sea. Keyes and his son, acting as his clerk, turned their attention to loading the steamers *Illinois* and *Philadelphia,* and three sailing ships chartered to carry the heaviest ordnance and gun carriages. In spite of Porter's insistence on the need for total secrecy, on Saturday, April 6, the day *Powhatan* sailed from New York, the newspaperman L. Q. Washington wrote to Secretary Walker that a formidable armada was reported preparing at New York. Every available ship at the Brooklyn Navy Yard had been ordered into service and L. Q. Washington indicated that the opinion of the best informed men at the nation's capital was that Pensacola was the point threatened. From Montgomery, Adjutant General Cooper wired Bragg that the Federal government was determined to reinforce Fort Pickens and troops were being embarked at the North for that purpose.[2]

From Pensacola Bragg responded to Secretary Walker's telegram asking for more information as to his thoughts on the attack on Fort Pickens, were the Federals to attempt to reinforce it. He could control the wharf at Fort Pickens with his batteries on the mainland, he wrote, since it was on the bay side of Santa Rosa Island and within range of his guns. He could readily prevent the landing of reinforcements and provisions there. The Federals, however, might land men and supplies to the east on the gulf shore of the island, well beyond the range of his guns. All the Federal ships offshore were beyond the range of his batteries except *Wyandotte* inside the harbor and she could easily be driven off or destroyed upon the opening of hostilities. "Any attack by us now must be secretly made by escalade. My batteries are not ready for breaching and we are entirely deficient in ammunition. No landing should be made on Santa Rosa Island with our present means. Will write." Bragg did write further. His request of the 3rd asking if he might attack was predicated on several occurrences which he could not explain in his telegram and which admitted of no delay. A strong easterly wind had been blowing for several days and Bragg expected the Federal vessels offshore to be driven away by the storm, leaving the approaches to Santa Rosa Island open for hours, even for days. Unfortunately, he wrote, this time the vessels seemed to be holding their positions, but with difficulty. Also, he noted, he had reason to believe the garrison of Fort Pickens was greatly demoralized "by influences which are operating in our favor." Under a repetition of these circumstances, he wanted to know, would he be free to act when another occasion might offer? "I am not prepared with my batteries for anything more than a feeble defense ... and that condition cannot be changed until I can get supplies. The only attack which I could hope to make now would be a sudden dash, distracting the enemy by a false attack, and scaling the walls in the opposite direction. The weakness of the garrison and the ardor or ignorance of my troops would be strong elements of success.... We have the force and labor necessary, but the skill to apply them is confined to a few." Bragg was still uncertain how far the War Department intended him to go. Jefferson Davis, mentioning the friendship between the two that went back to Bragg's regular battery firing in support of Davis's Mississippi volunteers at Buena Vista in the Mexican War, wrote in response to Bragg's letter to the secretary of war a personal note that Davis indicted was written freely and hurriedly by "your old comrade in arms, who hopes much and expects much, for you and from you." The Lincoln administration, Davis believed, was determined to hold both Fort Sumter and Fort Pickens. The case at Pensacola, the president wrote, was simply a military problem and Bragg's efforts should be directed at capturing Fort Pickens without fear of disturbing diplomatic efforts that might be under way elsewhere. Bragg would soon have sufficient force to occupy all points necessary to that end. It became clear to Bragg as he read Davis's note that he had a free hand with regard to an attack on Fort Pickens but Davis seemed to intimate, were Bragg to attack, he must capture the fort. Additional troops from the states of the Deep South were arriving at Pensacola in large numbers through the first week in April. "It is a matter of impossibility for me to keep you advised of the arrival of troops," Bragg complained to Secretary Walker. "They come in under such various orders and fail to report they are [here] for days sometimes before I hear of them." A correspondent for the *New York Tribune* described the influx of troops at Pensacola as unprecedented and astonishing. "Mississippi pours in her companies almost daily. Georgians from Augusta, Atlanta, and Columbus, Zouaves from New Orleans with females hailed *a la Fille du Regiment* at their head," Ellen Call Long wrote from Tallahassee. "The boys think it great fun and regard the trip as an excursion."[3]

At Washington President Lincoln handed a written message addressed to Governor Pickens at Charleston to Robert Chew, a clerk at the State Department. An attempt was about to be made to provision Fort Sumter, the message read, and in the absence of armed resistance by the Southern forces ringing Charleston Harbor, no attempt would be made by the Federal authorities to send military supplies or reinforcements into the fort without further notice. Chew left Washington that evening by rail. At the same time, demonstrating the lack of coordination and internal communication existing in the new administration, Secretary of War Simon Cameron ordered Captain Theodore Talbot of the adjutant general's staff also to proceed to Charleston. If the United States flag were still flying over Fort Sumter, Talbot was to seek an interview with Governor Pickens and read to him a message that paralleled in general that carried by Chew. At the same time, Secretary Seward assured the Confederate commissioners at Washington that the Federal moves toward Charleston Harbor were entirely defensive in nature.[4]

Unannounced and unexpected, a navy officer walked into Secretary Welles's office at the Navy Department on Saturday morning. Lieutenant Washington Gwathmey had left *Sabine* off Santa Rosa Island on Monday, April 1, five days earlier. He was weary and travel-stained from his journey by rail across the states of the South. Gwathmey removed a pouch from beneath his clothing and handed Welles a package that contained Captain Adams's letter of April 1 in which Adams informed the secretary of the navy that he had not landed Captain Vogdes's company and that Fort Pickens was still garrisoned only by Slemmer's small command. Welles was shocked to understand Adams was still observing a truce agreement left over from the Buchanan administration under which Federal forces had agreed not to reinforce Fort Pickens in return for Southern forces agreeing not to attack it; this in spite of several orders from the War Department to Vogdes to land his command. Welles later wrote, "We knew, however, of no written orders or truce of the character mentioned." The secretary did hold some suspicions about the fidelity of Captain Adams. The older sailor's sympathies were rumored to be with the secessionists. His home was in the South and some of his family were taking opposite sides in the coming conflict. Two sons would serve with the rebel forces; one would follow the Union. Welles was not sure where Adams's own loyalties were but the captain's actions had to be changed immediately. Welles hurried to the executive mansion and discussed Adams's letter with the president. Lincoln declared he knew nothing of a truce preventing the reinforcement of Fort Pickens and he was certain that a prior agreement made during the Buchanan administration held no force or substance on his own. His whole strategy regarding the forts had been to reinforce and hold Fort Pickens while trying to re-supply and reinforce Fort Sumter. He now faced the possibility that both forts might be taken and he could not let that happen Welles, Lincoln ordered, was to dispatch a special messenger overland to Adams with a specific and peremptory order to disregard any agreement or previous communication and to land Vogdes's company immediately. Lieutenant Gwathmey, Welles decided, was the ideal person to send, having just made the journey northward and being known to Adams. The lieutenant declined. Having carried Adams's dispatches from Pensacola at great risk and severe personal exhaustion, the Virginia native checked into a Washington hotel and rested for two days before sending his resignation to the Navy Department in order to take service with his home state. Unlike Secretary Toucey, Secretary Welles did not accept it. He ordered Gwathmey dismissed from the service and his name stricken from the navy roll. Searching for another officer to send, one he could trust, Welles found Navy Paymaster Henry Etting in his office at the Navy Department. Etting claimed to be too ill to make the arduous journey and tried to beg off. Welles told him to find a trustworthy substitute or prepare to go in spite of his physical condition. At the Washington railroad depot, Etting met Lieutenant John

Lieutenant John L. Worden, U.S. Navy, became the first prisoner of war in the Civil War. Later he commanded U.S.S. *Monitor* in the epic battle at Hampton Roads (U.S. Army Military History Institute).

L. Worden whom he took immediately to the Navy Department. Welles questioned Worden for some time to ascertain the New York native's loyalty. Worden was forty-three years of age and had been an officer in the Navy for eighteen years. He had only recently returned from duty as first lieutenant of the screw sloop U.S.S. *Savannah*. Welles sent Worden to his home on K Street to wait while he considered the government's next moves. He discussed Worden with the president. Deciding on the man, Welles sent for Worden about midnight. He handed the lieutenant an unsealed envelope directing Worden to commit its contents to memory and to destroy the document if he sensed it might be taken by Southern authorities. Not giving the officer time to change clothes or pack a bag, Welles put Worden on the next train south to commence a journey that would take him to Richmond, to Atlanta, to Montgomery, and finally to Pensacola. Welles's order to Adams that Worden carried read," The department regrets that you did not comply with the request of Captain Vogdes to carry into effect the orders of General Scott sent out by the *Crusader* under the orders of this department. You will immediately on the first favorable opportunity after receipt of this order afford every facility to Captain Vogdes by boats and other means to enable him to land the troops under his command, it being the wish and intention of the navy department to cooperate with the war department in that object."[5]

That evening in a meeting with Seward, Lincoln read the telegram the secretary had received from Porter, written as *Powhatan* cleared the Narrows and headed out into the Atlantic Ocean on her way to Pensacola. "Seward," he said, "if the Southerners get Sumter, we will be even with them by securing Pickens."[6]

On Sunday, April 7, aboard *Atlantic* with Colonel Brown and his command, Meigs wrote in his diary, "Well, Keyes and I have done our duty and set the ball in motion. Porter, the officer whom the whole navy by acclaim selected from the profession, is on his way to the harbor of Pensacola and into it he will go, God permitting, because man will not be able to prevent it." From New York, Keyes wrote to Seward that *Atlantic* was off with Meigs and Brown, well laden. Longshoremen were loading *Illinois* and she would be on her way before the sun went down. Keyes planned to take the following day to go through his and Meigs's notes to see what yet had to be done.[7]

From Pensacola Bragg wrote Secretary Walker that he would fire on any reinforcements to Fort Pickens unless the government at Montgomery ordered him not to do so. To President Davis Bragg wrote, in response to the executive's letter of the previous day, that subsequent information strengthened his opinion against launching an immediate attack. To try regular approaches against Fort Pickens with any but veteran troops would be difficult under the most favorable circumstances and in this case it would be impossible. The one plan which might succeed was that of an attack by escalade, a sudden rush from the darkness on the walls with scaling ladders. His troops were eager and would risk anything to avoid a prolonged siege. "Ignorant of the great degree of the danger, they would go at it with a will, and with ordinary luck would carry the point. Our greatest difficulty is the want of means to reach the island properly and secretly." Later that same day Secretary Walker expanded on his earlier correspondence with General Bragg regarding the proposed attack on Fort Pickens. He had not intended to order Bragg to land on the island, he wrote. The presumption at Montgomery, based on the conflicting reports from the commissioners at Washington, was that the Federals would attempt to reinforce the fort by landing troops at its wharf. Walker hoped Bragg could prevent that even though it might lead to a

Federal assault on Bragg's works. "The belief here is that they will not only attempt to reinforce the fort, but also to retake the navy yard." The secretary wired Mississippi's Governor John Pettus that more troops were needed at Pensacola. To Georgia's Governor Joseph Brown, he wired that news from Washington justified his asking for an artillery company from Augusta. Attorney General Judah Benjamin telegraphed Alabama's Governor Andrew Moore that news from Washington made it indispensable that more forces be moved to Pensacola.[8]

At Charleston, General Beauregard wrote to Major Anderson that no further communications having to do with supplies for the fort from the city would be permitted. Beauregard justified his declaration "in consequence of the delays and apparent vacillations of the United States government at Washington relative to the evacuation of Fort Sumter." Beauregard was reacting to reports he and Governor Pickens were receiving from the three commissioners at Washington regarding their frustrating correspondence with Seward and the multitude of conflicting and confusing rumors the commissioners were forwarding. Demonstrating this confusion, the commissioners telegraphed Secretary of State Toombs, "It may be Sumter and the Mississippi; it is almost certain it is Pickens and the Texas frontier."[9]

One of the larger Confederate sand batteries on Pensacola Bay, with the casual dress and attitude of the new Southern soldiers (photograph by J.D. Edwards, U.S. Army Military History Institute).

At Washington, Judge Campbell wrote to Seward complaining about the disparate reports in the press and throughout the city. Fort Pickens, he had heard, was to be reinforced in spite of the truce. Fort Sumter would be reinforced in spite of the understanding with Governor Pickens that he would be notified beforehand. Campbell stated the anxiety of his friends, the commissioners, and asked for an explanation. Seward's reply was terse, "Faith as to Sumter fully kept; wait and see."[10]

On Monday, April 8, Robert Chew met Governor Pickens and General Beauregard and read the message from President Lincoln. Standing beside Chew, as if vouching for his authenticity, was Captain Talbot who had been sent by Secretary Cameron with the same message. Beauregard wired Secretary Walker at Montgomery that provisions were to be sent into Fort Sumter peaceably, otherwise by force. Walker responded immediately that under no circumstances was Beauregard to permit provisions to be sent into the fort.[11]

At New York there was considerable maritime activity. The merchant steamer *Illinois* sailed for Santa Rosa Island carrying what *Atlantic* had not been able to take on board. The steam tug *Yankee* followed the *Uncle Ben,* which had sailed the day before, for the rendezvous off Charleston bar. The revenue cutter, *Harriet Lane*, Captain John Faunce, slipped her moorings at New York and steamed down the bay.[12]

From Barrancas Barracks General Bragg wrote to Captain Adams he had information from a reliable source that Major Tower, who was now quartered on one of the vessels in the gulf, was spending much time ashore in Fort Pickens, consulting with and advising the commanding officer there. Bragg wrote he regarded this as a reinforcement and felt it necessary to call it to Adams's attention. Bragg allowed, however, "It will give me great pleasure to learn I am misinformed." Bragg was immersed in the minutiae of protocol while the rest of the Confederate military establishment was wondering when he might get to thinking about making an assault on Fort Pickens. Both sides, North and South, were waiting and watching the events on Pensacola Bay. At this time, Bragg was showing his excellent organizational and administrative skills; he was showing none of the abilities he would have to develop in order to become a warrior.[13]

At Washington Secretary of State Seward delivered his response to the Confederate commissioners who had been awaiting it since March 4, more than a month. In regard to their request for recognition as ambassadors of a foreign government, and in response to their being accepted as representatives of a sovereign state, Seward read to them a letter he had composed and written on March 15 but kept in a desk drawer at the State Department. During all this time, through weeks of continuing to lead the commissioners on in their expectation of acknowledgment and eventually achieving effective recognition, Seward had already determined his response but had kept the letter containing that response from them. When delivered, the secretary's letter denied their request for recognition and their presumption of sovereignty.[14]

Off Cape Hatteras *Atlantic* ran into a heavy northeast gale that forced Captain Gray to heave to under steam power and head into the seas for thirty-six hours. When the storm abated, Meigs wrote in his diary that the steamer was now more than a hundred miles off course. The fierce storm was working its way all along the eastern coastline. *Atlantic* was so battered that the horses tethered to the steamer's railings suffered but none were lost. The screw sloop *Pawnee*, Captain Stephen Rowan, sailed from New York for the Charleston bar and met the fury of the storm the moment she left the shelter of the Narrows. The three

Confederate commissioners, furious at what they considered Seward's deceit, attempted to leave Washington to return to Montgomery but their departure was delayed by the heavy winds and rains that accompanied the storm.[15]

On Tuesday, April 9, Secretary Walker wrote from Montgomery to General Bragg that Captain William Boggs had left the Confederate capital carrying $40,000 for Bragg. The money was intended to be used "in the way he suggested as coming from you." Bragg responded that he would put the funds to use immediately but that great vigilance was being exercised on Santa Rosa Island. "They fear their own men," he wrote. He intended to take up the navigation buoys and lights from the main ship channel in order to make entry to the harbor more difficult, he added. Later in the day, he wired Walker that his ordnance supplies were still short for a continued resistance and he was in need of transportation to move his guns, shot, and troops. Sixteen hundred men had arrived the night before. Bragg wrote that he did not hesitate to put to use the special funds Boggs brought him by putting in place a plan to bribe on the men of the garrison on Santa Rosa Island. Information from the mainland had made Slemmer suspicious of letters passing between Fort Pickens and the village of Warrington on the mainland. On Wednesday, April 10, Slemmer ordered all correspondence and packages to or from the fort to pass through his hands. A roll of newspapers was intercepted and, on examining the roll, Slemmer found a letter addressed to Ordnance Sergeant Elias H. Broady. "Broady, you are without exception the dam'dest fool I have the pleasure of knowing. Bragg will give you a damn'd sight better berth than you now have, and besides, you will be on the right side. Don't be a jackass always. Look at Gardner — see his position. I have authority for offering you a commission. Answer me. When can I take you a cocktail? My regards to Flynn. Come over and see me. I can assure you that permission to visit your wife, and in a capacity she will be more than glad to find you in, will be granted. No humbug. Come over. Yours, B." Slemmer retained the letter and the following day another roll of newspapers was brought to him. Again, a letter to Broady was found. Opening by referring to Broady again as a jackass, the writer offered a lieutenant's commission in the Confederate forces and all back pay still owed Broady by the Federal government, two-fold. The writer, who again signed himself "B." was B. D. Williams, a civilian living in Warrington and known well to Sergeant Broady. Williams' proposal included offers to any man who would desert the Federal forces and join those on the mainland to make up all of all their back pay plus a $500 bonus for privates and a $1,000 bonus for non-commissioned officers along with a commission in the Confederate Army. Referring to the fort, Williams wrote Broady, "We *must* and *will have it.* Don't be a damned fool. Where and when can I see you? I will go over tonight, and take a cocktail if you say so." Slemmer had kept his men at the guns during that night with a close watch on Sergeant Broady. In the morning he decided to put the sergeant where he could not do harm. He was not sure Broady was about to act seditiously but he intended to keep him far from the opportunity to do so if that were the ordnance sergeant's intent. He sent Broady out to Captain Adams on *Sabine* with a letter explaining the circumstances. He did not wish to punish Broady because he did not know the extent to which the sergeant had committed himself but Slemmer did not think if wise to have Broady in the fort. Later in the day Private Owen McGarr, who had been on picket duty outside the fort the night before, came to Slemmer with $60 in currency and a story. Walking his post along the beach, a small boat had approached. He challenged the four occupants who told him not to shoot, they were friends. The men landed and asked McGarr about things in the fort, the number of men in the garrison, what the defenses consisted of, and whether the flank howitzers could be spiked. They asked McGarr when he would be back on picket duty again. He told them the following Monday night. The men asked how the garrison was for money. McGarr told them the men had not been paid for six months. One of the men put a roll of bills into McGarr's hands and told him to give it to the men in the fort. Their intent, Slemmer assumed, was to bribe some of the garrison into spiking the casemate howitzers along the eastern wall to prevent their being fired. A force from the mainland, having crossed over in boats under cover of night, could then storm the eastern wall with scaling ladders and be up and over the wall and in among the men of the small garrison in minutes. The principal point of danger for the attackers would be when they were crowded in the ditch at the base of the wall and working to get the scaling ladders in place. If the flank casemate guns were spiked, they could not be fired. Slemmer had to assume this would take place during the coming night. Also on that same day Slemmer received information "through private hands" that troops on the mainland were making preparations and outfitting boats to cross over to Santa Rosa Island that night. He sent a note to Captain Adams informing him of this and requesting that Vogdes's company and a force of sailors and marines be landed immediately. However, a severe storm descended on Pensacola Bay which prevented vessels putting out from the mainland in any direction. *Wyandotte* could not clear the channel to deliver Slemmer's note to Adams. The night passed without incident. When *Wyandotte* was able to steam through the channel and deliver Slemmer's note the following morning, Adams sent back a request for Slemmer to lay out for him in greater detail the information he claimed to have received. "So many unfounded rumors have been in circulation to this effect," Adams wrote, "that it is necessary to be cautious, and my orders are positive not to land reinforcements unless the fort is actually attacked or preparations are making to attack it." Slemmer did not intend to furnish the information Adams demanded. It was important to him to keep the source of his information secure for his own purpose and for the safety of the source. Once a day Slemmer was permitted to send a boat — occasionally *Wyandotte,* more often a rowboat — to the navy yard wharf to exchange communications, mail, and sometimes to receive fresh provisions. Slemmer's messenger, one of his corporals or sergeants, was carefully escorted from the wharf to Bragg's headquarters at Barrancas Barracks and then back to the boat. Richard Wilcox, a civilian watchman at the navy yard, had been retained in service by the Southern command from the day the yard was taken over. The Confederate authorities assumed Wilcox's allegiance to their cause and did not question it. They should have because Wilcox was a staunch Unionist. He managed, as often as he could, to be the escort for Slemmer's messenger between the wharf and Bragg's headquarters. Wilcox was Slemmer's source of information "through private hands." Mr. R. H. Watts later wrote a letter dated December 4, 1865 to then–Quartermaster General of the Union Army Montgomery C. Meigs regarding the information Wilcox had reported to Slemmer. Four steamers, scows, launches, and cutters were in readiness at Pensacola to convey troops over to Santa Rosa Island that evening. Seven hundred men had been detailed for the capture of *Wyandotte* when she came to the wharf under her flag of truce. Watts had received information from a loyal servant of B. D. Williams that Sergeant Broady had "sold the fort" which was to be assaulted that night. Watts's wife had sent a female servant to Wilcox's wife with this information which was passed to the corporal in charge of the boat. Slemmer's need for reinforcements for Fort Pickens had been superseded by the storm as had the plan

7. "When the Arrow Has Fled from the Bow"   135

Confederate troop encampment on Pensacola Bay. Note the leafy arbors constructed for shade from the sun (photograph by J.D. Edwards, U.S. Army Military History Institute).

for the Confederate assault on Santa Rosa Island. There is no evidence in the Confederate records of Bragg's plan for the attack on Santa Rosa Island this night but Slemmer's response and request for assistance was based on his understanding of the reports he received from the mainland. On this day Slemmer and his small garrison had managed to hold Fort Pickens for three months.[16]

A dispatch from New York copied in the *Charleston Courier* read, "Whatever else the opponents of Mr. Lincoln's administration may say or think, they are compelled to acknowledge that it possesses ... one great merit over its predecessors. It knows how to keep a secret. Extensive as have been the naval preparations at this port during the past week, all the prying and persistent ingenuity of the New York press has failed to discover to what specified end these preparations are made." Apparently security about the embarkations and sailings from New York had managed to keep some of these less than fully apparent to the Northern press. Under these circumstances, Gustavus Fox sailed from New York on Tuesday, April 9, in the merchant steamer *Baltic* with the reinforcements for Fort Sumter. From Norfolk *Pocahontas*, Captain John Gillis, steamed for the rendezvous off the Charleston bar. From Montgomery that same day, President Davis wired General Beauregard at Charleston that, if he was satisfied the messenger from President Lincoln with the announcement of the pending attempt to provision Fort Sumter was authentic, "you will at once demand the evacuation, and if that is refused, proceed ... to reduce it."[17]

Lieutenant Colonel Keyes wrote to Secretary Seward from New York that no other naval vessels could be ready for sea in the near future with the single exception of the sailing brig U.S.S. *Perry* which could add little to the Fort Pickens task force already steaming southward. The formidable steam frigates U.S.S. *Wabash* and U.S.S. *Roanoke* could not put to sea in less than three weeks and six weeks, respectively. "We must," he wrote, "rest content with what we have in the Gulf and on the way there." He had put on board *Illinois* an army battery of Napoleon guns and a naval battery of Dahlgren guns with ammunition. Between *Atlantic* and *Illinois* he had shipped better than six weeks forage for horses and four months complete rations for some 720 men. "Enough have gone to strike the first blow and hold for a while against all they can do, provided the naval vessels place themselves." Keyes ended his letter, "Curiosity to know what I am about has increased so much that I address this letter to you instead of to General Scott. I am known as his secretary, and my letters might be tampered with. Please show this to the general if it is worth showing." At sea, Colonel Brown, Captain Meigs, and those aboard *Atlantic* were being pounded by the raging storm. Meigs wrote to Seward that the steamer would touch at Key West and land a United States district attorney who would increase the authority of the Federal government there. To justify his and Porter's refusal to obey the telegram to turn *Powhatan* over to Captain Mercer, Meigs wrote, "Your dispatch arrived as I was on my way to the *Atlantic,* just before the hour at which she was to sail, and two or three hours after that appointed for the *Powhatan*. When the arrow has fled from the bow, it may glance aside, but who shall reclaim it before its flight is finished?"[18]

8

"Fort Pickens Now Stood Alone"

At Charleston, on Thursday, April 11, Brigadier General Beauregard wrote to Major Robert Anderson that the government of the Confederate States had heretofore forborne hostile demonstrations against Fort Sumter in the hope that the government of the United States would voluntarily vacate it. There had been reason at one time, Beauregard wrote, referring to the unofficial communications between the Confederate commissioners at Washington and Secretary Seward, to believe such would be the course of events. Under that impression his government had refrained from making any demands for the surrender of the fort. The Confederate States could no longer delay assuming possession of the fortification commanding the entrance to one of its principal harbors which was necessary for its defense and security. He was therefore ordered by his government to demand the evacuation of Fort Sumter. All proper facilities would be afforded for the removal of Anderson and his command, together with company arms and private property. Beauregard ended, "The flag which you have upheld so long and with such fortitude, under the most trying circumstances, may be saluted by you on taking it down." Anderson replied, "I have the honor to acknowledge the receipt of your communication demanding the evacuation of this fort, and to say, in reply thereto, that it is a demand with which I regret my sense of honor, and my obligation to my government, prevent my compliance." Anderson thanked Beauregard for the fair terms offered and for the high compliment paid him. The two men had known each other since Anderson had been Beauregard's artillery instructor at West Point. From Montgomery, Secretary Walker telegraphed General Bragg to inform him that General Beauregard had orders to demand the immediate surrender of Fort Sumter. If refused, Beauregard's batteries were to open fire.[1]

At 1:00 A.M. on Friday, April 12, four aides of General Beauregard came to Fort Sumter to ask Anderson to explain a statement he made the previous day, that he would "await the first shot, and if not battered to pieces, would be starved out in a few days." The aides, Colonel James Chestnut, Colonel Alexander Chisolm, Captain Stephen Lee, and Colonel Roger Pryor, discussed Anderson's response among themselves and then informed Anderson as they were leaving at about 3:00 A.M. that their batteries would open in one hour. At

4:30, a signal gun was fired and within twenty minutes Confederate batteries lining the shore of the mainland were in full play. Fort Sumter's guns did not reply until about 7:00 A.M. Firing continued on both sides throughout the day. Gustavus Fox arrived off Charleston Harbor in *Baltic* in the fierce gale, unaware because of the turbulence of the storm of the events taking place within the harbor. *Harriet Lane* had arrived earlier. *Pocahontas* and *Pawnee* had not yet appeared. None of the three tugs had shown: *Freeborn*'s owner reneged on his charter contract and did not permit her sailing from New York Harbor; *Uncle Ben* was driven into Wilmington Harbor by the storm and taken over by state authorities; *Yankee* did not arrive off Charleston until days later. *Pawnee* hove into view later in the day. Fox boarded her and discussed the wretched state of the weather with Captain Rowan. Fox wanted to attempt to send in provisions to Fort Sumter despite the weather. Rowan was against this, arguing his orders were to remain ten miles east of the lighthouse and await the arrival of the heavier-gunned *Powhatan*. He was not, he insisted, going to enter the harbor and inaugurate civil war on his own. Holding station off the bar and awaiting the tardy arrival of the remainder of the task force, Fox and Rowan met again on board *Pawnee*. Rowan was insistent he was not about to disobey specific orders governing when he should commit *Pawnee* to the effort to relieve Fort Sumter. Fox decided to go ahead without *Pawnee* and not to wait further for *Pocahontas* and *Powhatan*. For reasons known only to himself, Captain Rowan then gave Fox a letter he had received from Captain Mercer dated April 6 informing him that *Powhatan* had been detached from the Fort Sumter task force on orders "of a superior authority" for another destination. When Rowan produced the letter Fox was astounded and speechless. He returned to *Baltic* and, determined to do the best he could with the limited forces now at hand, he led the way toward the harbor entrance accompanied by *Harriet Lane*. As the steamers came in sight of Fort Sumter, the officers and crews were surprised to hear the firing of heavy guns and to see the pall of smoke that surrounded the bastion. Fox and his task force had arrived off Fort Sumter too late to accomplish any good. *Pocahontas* had been severely delayed by the fierce storm that was savaging the eastern seaboard and would arrive only after the events at Charleston Harbor had ended. *Powhatan* never would arrive; she was well down the coast and rounding the Florida peninsula under Porter's command bound for Pensacola and Fort Pickens. After thirty-four hours of intense bombardment, at about 2:30 in the afternoon of Saturday, April 13, Major Anderson lowered the national colors from Fort Sumter's shattered flagstaff and raised a white flag. Anderson's garrison had bravely stood in the face of a violent artillery assault but by now were out of provisions and even fabric from which to make cartridge bags for the big guns. Inexplicably, but symptomatic of the primitive relationship between the War and Navy Departments at the time, neither Anderson's garrison within the fort nor the sailors and merchantmen of Fox's task force were able to communicate because neither had been supplied with the proper codes for the other. On Sunday, April 14, in the last act Fort Sumter would play in the unfolding series of events taking place throughout the South, Major Anderson formed his command on the parade and, with colors flying and drums beating, marched out after firing a salute to the national colors. In so doing one of Anderson's men was killed by the explosion of some cartridges carelessly left below the muzzle of a gun. Two men were seriously injured, and four men were wounded slightly. One of the seriously wounded men died soon after being taken to a hospital in Charleston and the second was left behind for treatment as the remainder of Anderson's command was lightered out to *Baltic* for the voyage to New York. President Lincoln later wrote to Gustavus Fox how he sincerely regretted that the failure of the attempt to provision Fort Sumter might prove an annoyance to the former naval officer. The practicability of Fox's plan had not been brought to the test. By accident, for which Fox was in no way responsible and, possibly, for which the president was, the expedition was deprived of a major war vessel with her guns, boats, and men which Fox had deemed of great importance to the mission. For a future daring and dangerous enterprise of a similar character, Lincoln wrote, Fox would be the man he would select. He signed the letter, "Very truly, your friend, A. Lincoln." On August 1, the president created the position of assistant secretary of the navy, under Welles, to which Fox was appointed and were he served exceptionally well throughout the war that was to follow.[2]

Lieutenant John Worden arrived at the Pensacola railroad depot having destroyed the written orders he carried for Captain Adams as he passed through Atlanta on the assumption that he was being followed and might be taken into custody. At the Pensacola depot a Confederate officer, Lieutenant Charles LeBaron, asked Worden his business. Worden identified himself as an officer in the United States Navy with messages for Captain Adams. LeBaron took Worden to Bragg who questioned him briefly and wrote a pass authorizing Worden to go out to *Sabine*. Under the terms of the truce free passage of messengers carrying dispatches was provided for. Bragg asked Worden if he had dispatches for Adams. Worden replied that he had "only verbal communications of a pacific nature" from the Navy Department but nothing in writing. Worden asked Bragg whether he would be allowed to land on his return from *Sabine* and proceed back to Washington. Bragg assured him he would, provided neither he nor Adams did anything in violation of the terms of the truce. Worden boarded *Wyandotte* at the navy yard about 4:00 P.M. but was told by Lieutenant Commanding Mullany that, because of the strong winds and rough waters over the bar, he did not want to attempt to run out to the squadron offshore during the night. Mullany steamed across the bay and tied up at the Fort Pickens wharf. During the evening Slemmer came aboard *Wyandotte* where he and Worden had a few minutes of conversation. The two offices had met the previous summer when Worden arrived at Pensacola as first lieutenant of *Savannah*. That vessel's officers had invited the wives of the garrison's officers to tour their ship. Carry Slemmer asked so many questions and talked so much that Worden had been designated, in jest, to warn Slemmer that the next time his wife came on *Savannah*, the ship's officers would immediately put to sea with her on board and thus relieve him of a wife who must drive him half-distracted with all her chatter. Since Worden carried no orders for Slemmer, he said nothing regarding the information he was to deliver to Captain Adams. Worden assumed Slemmer knew why he had come but the army officer did nothing to indicate an interest or curiosity. Waiting for the waters of the gulf to subside so *Wyandotte* could pass over the bar to the squadron offshore, Lieutenant Mullany suggested he and Worden go ashore and take a tour of Fort Pickens. About 9:00 A.M. the following morning the two walked down the gangplank and strolled the ramparts for an hour. Neither saw Slemmer whom, they were informed, was sleeping. Worden did not want to disturb him as he had no reason to call on him other then to pay the proper visit of courtesy on going within the limits of Slemmer's command and the two had talked the previous evening. Lieutenant William Murdaugh was executive officer of *Sabine* when Worden came aboard the flagship later in the morning. After Worden spent some time with

Confederate sand battery on Pensacola Bay. This image presents a more uniform appearance of the men, possibly ready for a formal inspection (photograph by J.D. Edwards, U.S. Army Military History Institute).

Captain Adams in his cabin, Murdaugh was sent for and found Worden writing at a table. The document Worden handed Adams in Murdaugh's presence was an order for him to land the army company aboard *Brooklyn* and to reinforce it with as many marines and sailors as could be spared from the squadron as soon as practicable. At the bottom of the order was a certificate signed by Worden that, to the best of his knowledge and belief, the above was a verbatim copy of a dispatch which had been handed to Worden by the secretary of the navy to be delivered by hand to Captain Adams. On his way through the Southern states, Worden had reason to think the dispatch might be taken from him. Following specific orders of the secretary, he had opened the envelope, committed its contents to memory, and destroyed it. Murdaugh signed the document as a witness and then, on Adams's order, made preparations to have everything ready for hoisting out the boats of the squadron that afternoon in order to be prepared to land the reinforcements after nightfall. Adams told Vogdes of the orders he had just received from the Navy Department and promised Vogdes that all the marines and sailors he could spare from the vessels of the squadron, with their necessary officers, would be landed with Vogdes's artillerymen. The marines from *Sabine* and *St. Louis* transferred to *Brooklyn* to form a battalion of 115 men under Marine Corps Lieutenant John Cash of *Sabine*. The marines and Vogdes's eighty-six regular soldiers loaded into the squadron's boats and the entire force under the direct command of Lieutenant Albert Smith of *Brooklyn* pushed off as soon as darkness fell. Two hundred seamen from the squadron rowed with muffled oars up the channel and under the guns of Fort McRee, around the point of Santa Rosa Island, under the guns of Fort Barrancas, and landed at the wharf at Fort Pickens near its northeastern bastion about midnight. Captain Vogdes marched through the gate at the head of the column of reinforcements and finally officially assumed command of the post and the garrison from Slemmer. The Confederates on the mainland had postponed their attack on Santa Rosa Island and were completely unaware the reinforcement was taking place. Vogdes and his company had been aboard ship for seventy-two days, sixty-four of which had been spent off Santa Rosa Island because of Adams's stubborn determination to follow the orders from a navy secretary and an administration long since out of office and his further refusal to accept instructions issued by officers of the army. Slemmer, with his under-strength company of artillerymen and his detail of thirty reluctant seamen from the navy yard had managed to hold Fort Pickens for ninety-three days.[3]

Navy gunner Cornelius Cronin of *Sabine* wrote in his journal that the boat crews entered the fort with the reinforcements and manned extra guns in the casemates, awaiting the reaction from the forces on the mainland. After standing to the guns for two hours, Cronin continued, and with no hostile movement from the mainland detected, the sailors decided among themselves "the Southerners did not care to fight so early in the morning; after discussion, some hard tack, and pot of coffee for which we were grateful, we went to work with a will to mount the guns with such aids and appliances which we could control, and otherwise made preparations for whatever the future trend of events might develop."[4]

As soon as the transmittal and acceptance of Worden's message was completed, Adams indicated he wished to send correspondence back to the secretary of the navy. He told Worden to prepare to return to Washington immediately as his messenger. Worden landed at Pensacola at 5:00 p.m. and boarded the cars for Montgomery, hoping to report to Secretary Welles on Monday night and bring closure to his mission. From his headquarters at Barrancas Barracks, Bragg telegraphed Secretary Walker that reinforcements had been thrown into Fort Pickens the night before by boats from the outside. Bragg did not mention in his message anything having to do with the assault on the island he had planned to take place at the same time. He reported that the Federal reinforcement had not been detected from his side until it had been discovered by a reconnaissance boat the following morning. Bragg also telegraphed a description and warrant for the arrest of Worden. When the train of cars on which the Federal officer was riding came within five miles of Montgomery, several officers entered the car in which Worden was seated. One of the officers who had served with Worden in the navy identified him and the officers arrested Worden. When he learned of this and, later, after Worden had been brought before him, Secretary Walker telegraphed Bragg, "When you arrested Lieutenant Worden, what instructions, if any, did he show you? He is here under arrest, and it is important that you reply fully." Bragg, probably sensing he might be facing accusations of laxity, responded carefully by shifting the focus back to Montgomery. Worden had assured Bragg, he reported, that he carried "only verbal messages of a pacific nature." Bragg claimed that the reinforcement had been proceeded by signal guns fired from the fort and the squadron but he could not ascertain what had prompted the action, adding that Worden's messages might have had no connection with the landing. The reference to signal guns has to be erroneous on Bragg's part because the squadron offshore and the garrison within Fort Pickens would not have fired signal guns nor made any kind of detectable communication that might alert Bragg's force. Silence and secrecy were vital and were achieved on the part of the Federal forces by landing at night and by the use of muffled oars by the boatmen. Further, there is Bragg's statement that the landing was not detected until the following morning when it was discovered by a reconnaissance boat. This belies the reference by Bragg to signal guns. By this time, Worden had returned from Fort Pickens and had already landed at Pensacola when the reinforcement had taken place. Summarizing his own troop strength, Bragg reported that five thousand men were on the mainland and 2,000 more were coming. "You can now spare the supplies from Sumter which is now ours," he ended his telegram. On Monday, April 15, from Montgomery Worden wrote Confederate Secretary of War Leroy Walker that he unexpectedly found himself a prisoner and asked to be informed of the grounds on which he was being detained. He was granted permission to telegraph Secretary Welles at Washington that he had started his return from Pensacola but was now being held by the Confederate government. Worden gained the dubious honor of becoming the first prisoner of war in the American Civil War. He would remain incarcerated for almost seven months. During this time, his wife and several of his brother naval officers tried unsuccessfully to intercede with Secretary Welles to obtain his release. Unfortunately for Worden, his delivery from imprisonment was compounded by the decision of the Lincoln administration to avoid all acts which might imply recognition of the Confederacy which, of course, included any correspondence or communication having to do with prisoners held by either side. Finally, on Wednesday, November 13, Worden was released from captivity at Montgomery and sent under parole to Richmond. He was then ordered to Norfolk where he was exchanged on November 20 for Lieutenant William Sharp of the Confederate States Navy who had been captured at Hatteras Inlet by Federal forces on August 28. After a short rest to recover his health, Worden reported to the Brooklyn Navy Yard on December 3 where he took command of the new ironclad warship being constructed by John Ericcson, the U.S.S. *Monitor*. Worden commanded *Monitor* in her epic clash with C. S. S. *Virginia* at Hampton Roads, Virginia, on March 19, 1862.[5]

On the same day that Fort Pickens at Pensacola finally was reinforced, Fort Sumter at Charleston was surrendered to Confederate authorities. The firing on Fort Sumter would bring to the nation the much discussed and dreaded civil war that would tear its people apart for four full years. The reinforcement of Fort Pickens would result in that bastion, the harbor, and the bay remaining in Federal hands for all of that time. With the fall of Fort Sumter and the surrender of Anderson and his command, Fort Pickens now stood alone as the sole Federal facility with a Federal garrison flying the national flag in the seceded states of the South.

From within Fort Pickens Captain Vogdes wrote to Captain Adams that all were now safe ashore since the enemy did not deem it prudent to attack the strengthened fort. He asked Adams to land 250 more seamen with the proper contingent of officers and to furnish a list of requirements that included, as its first item, four barrels of whiskey but which also included shovels, picks, tarpaulins, and other items. Vogdes ordered out patrols to reconnoiter the beaches on both sides of the island to the east and, as soon as he was able to ascertain the island was clear of enemy forces, he wrote that he would signal Adams to begin landing men, supplies, and ordnance. He had reason to believe the authorities at the navy yard were in possession of the navy's signal book so he would therefore signal number 758, meaning "All clear," or number 282, meaning "Don't land." Later in the day Vogdes again wrote to Adams that he did not deem it improbable that the enemy might cross over and attempt to establish a force on the island even if an actual assault were not in the offing. He asked Captain Adams to move *Wyandotte* and *Brooklyn* to locations where the heavy guns of both steamers could take a landing force in flank were an attempt to be made to land. Such a move, even if firing by either steamer was not necessary, would have a positive moral effect on the men within Fort Pickens and would provide closer observation of the eastern reaches of the island by the ships' lookouts. The following morning at daybreak a small boat put our from the navy yard on the mainland and approached the wharf at Fort Pickens under a flag of truce. Captain Vogdes and Lieutenant Slemmer met the two men aboard who asked if Vogdes were now the commander of the post. When assured he was, Colonel Robert Wood introduced himself as General Bragg's adjutant. The other officer was Lieutenant John Ingraham, formerly of the United States Marine Corps. Wood told Vogdes he had been directed to inquire why the terms of the truce had been violated by throwing reinforcements into Fort Pickens. Vogdes answered he had never been party to any truce, he had been sent by his government to take command of the post, and he had entered the fort under orders from that government. Woods turned to Slemmer and said he was directed to inquire of the former commander of the post why the terms of the truce had been violated. Slemmer replied he obeyed the orders of his superiors. The official business now out of the way, the four men exchanged pleasantries for several minutes until Wood and Ingraham boarded the boat and pushed off for the navy yard. Later in the day

Confederate soldiers cooking in camp at Pensacola Bay (photograph by J.D. Edwards, Library of Congress).

Captain Adams wrote to Bragg to explain and to justify the landing which Adams still saw as a violation of the original truce agreement. Bragg responded the following day with a bitter letter, ""Your communication of the 13th instant, announcing the reinforcement of Fort Pickens, was received by me this evening. How you could suppose I was aware of the fact, and that it was done 'by order of the U. S. government,' I do not understand, when it was done under cover of darkness of night, and in violation of a sacred pact. I only wish I could construe the orders of your government as justification of the act." The following day, April 16, Captain Vogdes asked Captain Adams for 100 additional seamen to help ashore. There was evidence of activity among the Confederate forces on the mainland, he wrote. He did not anticipate an immediate assault but wanted the extra sailors for help in putting the fort in a proper state of defense. He also asked for any means Adams could provide for cooking. Were he able to cook for and feed more men, he wrote, he would have asked for 300 seamen.[6]

At Key West *Atlantic* dropped anchor after a dreadful voyage in heavy seas. Colonel Harvey Brown issued his General Orders No. 1 assuming command of the Department of Florida. *Atlantic* anchored three miles below Fort Taylor to prevent any communication between the vessel and the town other than that involved in landing the United States district attorney. *Brooklyn,* Meigs wrote to Seward in the report he dispatched from Key West, had sailed with provisions for the squadron off Pensacola Harbor and should have reached there by April 1. Meigs added in error, "There is little doubt that, as she carried orders for the troops to land, they landed immediately upon her arrival." The reinforcement of Fort Pickens, Meigs continued, "within one hundred miles of Montgomery, must have a great effect upon the rebellion." *Atlantic* sailed from Key West that evening and arrived at Fort Jefferson, Dry Tortugas, about 10:00 A.M. the following day. She remained at anchor only long enough to take on four mountain howitzers with prairie carriages, which would be useful in the loose sand of Santa Rosa Island, and twenty-one slaves owned by citizens of Key West who had been contracted out to the army by their owners. *Atlantic* sailed after dark into heavy seas, taking some damage to the horse stalls on her port bow.[7]

At 6:00 P.M. *Atlantic* hove into sight and dropped anchor off Santa Rosa Island. Colonel Brown and Captain Meigs had themselves rowed to the flagship where they met briefly with Captain Adams and then to the fort where they met with Vogdes, Slemmer, and Gilman. Colonel Brown announced his appointment as commander of the Department of Florida and informed the officers with him that he was assuming direct command of Fort Pickens and the army forces therein. After anticipating his own command there for seventy-seven days, Captain Vogdes had held that responsibility for only seventy-two hours when Colonel Brown relieved him. Brown gave orders to commence landing his troops on the open beaches of the gulf shore of the island which would prevent their coming under fire from the batteries on the mainland. By midnight Captain Duane's company of sappers and miners and Captain Clitz's Company E, 3rd Infantry, were ashore. The following morning the remainder of the reinforcements landed along with the horses which went overboard from *Atlantic* in slings and then were towed swimming three-quarters of a mile to the beach. Ordnance and cargo had to be lifted into boats to be rowed ashore where their loads were manhandled across the loose sand on the gulf beach and into the fort. During the night the troops on Santa Rosa Island noticed a commotion on the mainland that included lighting bonfires in the ditches of Fort Barrancas. Assuming this marked the long awaited attack by

Bragg, Colonel Brown had two red rockets fired from Fort Pickens, the signal of an impending assault, but none took place. The commotion ashore, Brown found out later, was a celebration of the news of the surrender of Fort Sumter, a fact as yet unknown to the garrison within Fort Pickens and the crews aboard the vessels offshore.[8]

At daybreak on Wednesday, April 17, Brown sent the greater portion of the seamen and marines back to the ships. In going through the fort with Vogdes and Slemmer and examining its condition, he was discouraged by the miserable state of its armament. He had been informed that Bragg had 7,000 men on the mainland and he could see that the guns in the forts and the sand batteries could take every face of Fort Pickens in reverse. Brown discovered he would be able to return the fire of the batteries on the mainland for only a short time due to the lack of prepared ammunition. The pending arrival of *Powhatan* and its entrance into the harbor, he was certain, would cause a collision for which he was totally unprepared. He desperately needed time to unload the ships and get his munitions and supplies ashore. He set the men to work mounting extra guns, making a road from the gulf beach to the fort, preparing quarters, and unloading *Atlantic*. Traverses were needed inside the fort for the protection of men and guns in case of bombardment but he could not commence work on these for want of tools and sandbags. He thought within days he would be prepared to make a respectable defense against fire from the forts and batteries and would inflict more injury than he would suffer, but he needed time. He wrote to Bragg first thing in the morning to announce his arrival and assumption of command. He informed Bragg he would, unless assailed, act only on the defensive and make only such dispositions of his forces as were necessary to protect them from any enemy, foreign or domestic. He further informed Bragg that no movement of troops under his command or of the vessels in the vicinity would have other than a defensive object unless he were compelled to act repelling aggression against the flag, persons, or property of the United States.[9]

Captain Adams reported the arrival of the forces under Brown to the secretary of the navy and went on to describe the condition of the vessels under his own command. *Sabine* and *St. Louis* were constantly short of fresh water. With their sources from the mainland cut off, they had no way of replenishing their supplies other than from the apparatus on *Brooklyn* which could fail at any time. Rainfall over the past several weeks had been scanty in spite of the heavy weather so that little water had been obtained in that manner. *Wyandotte*, he expected, could break down at any time. Her engines were worn and for the past hundred days her fires had been out for only twenty-four hours. Coal for the steamers would be needed soon. Owing to the fresh winds and rough seas, and the demand on the squadron's boats by the army, his vessels had been unable to take on needed provisions from *Supply*. He was having this done as fast as other circumstances allowed, he wrote, but he was also suffering a severe shortage of officers. Several including Walker of *Brooklyn* had been relieved for medical reasons. He had ordered Poor from *St. Louis* to *Brooklyn,* Gibson from *Supply* to *St. Louis,* Mullany from *Wyandotte* to *Supply,* and Williamson from *Brooklyn* to *Wyandotte*. On his own flagship, *Sabine,* with a crew of 375, he had four lieutenants, no gunner, no master, no sail maker, and no midshipmen. The other vessels of the squadron were in similar condition. At Washington, indicating a distant concern about Adams's supply situation, Secretary Welles ordered Lieutenant Commanding William Ronckendorff to proceed in the side-wheel steamer *Water Witch* from her home port at Philadelphia to the vicinity of Fort Pickens where he would report to the senior naval officer present. *Water*

Witch would then establish regular mail and provisioning trips between Havana, Key West, Dry Tortugas, and Fort Pickens. The government at Washington was able to communicate freely and frequently with the United States consul at Havana and the consulate there would thereafter serve as a message center for the forces in the gulf.[10]

Cornelius Cronin, working with the shore party from *Sabine*, wrote in his journal that *Illinois* had arrived with more troops and stores. "We continued to labor in unloading her, all hands worked day and night, wet through and sleeping on the beach in relief watches, yet there was not a groan or a murmur to be heard from anyone, a convincing proof of the patriotism of all." The troops coming ashore from *Illinois* were Captain Horace Brooks' Company H, and Captain Harvey Allen's Company K, both of the 2nd Artillery. A hundred unassigned recruits and sixteen stragglers from the commands that had arrived on *Atlantic* were also landed. Fort Pickens now held some 1,200 soldiers, nearly its full wartime compliment, and very close to its capacity for men and provisions.[11]

On Wednesday, April 17, *Powhatan* steamed into view with black smoke roiling from her stack and both side-wheels thumping. The men within Fort Pickens and the offices and crews of the vessels offshore watched as the steamer worked toward the offing. Porter had raised English colors at the flagstaff and had the gun ports painted over in an attempt to disguise her nationality and nature with the appearance of a British mail steamer. Slower than both *Atlantic* and *Illinois, Powhatan* had lost time to the more modern steamers on her way south through the severe storms that had churned the Atlantic for the past eleven days. Porter had not spoken to another commander since leaving New York on the 6th. He had not conversed with Brown nor Meigs since their own arrival on Santa Rosa Island and he was unaware of Brown's desire that a confrontation with the forces on the mainland be deferred until troops, munitions, ordnance, supplies, and provisions could be landed, sorted, stowed, and the fort brought into readiness for defense. Porter also was unaware that Brown felt confident he could defend Fort Pickens with the forces now at his command once he got settled in and organized and that he felt he did not need *Powhatan* in the harbor to prevent a crossing by Bragg's forces. Porter only knew of the conversation he had with the president in which he had put forward his own plan to take an armed steamer into Pensacola Harbor to prevent an enemy force from crossing from the mainland and landing on the island. It seemed irreconcilable to Porter that the Confederate forces with their obvious superiority in numbers had not done this by now and he was determined to lose no time with them in a race to prevent just that. *Powhatan's* decks were cleared for action, her engine was at full ahead, her port battery was loaded and standing by, the ten 9-inch guns run through the ports. The 11-inch pivot gun was primed and loaded and twelve howitzers were sited about the decks loaded with shrapnel. Porter was confident he could cross the bar and steam past Fort McRee and Fort Barrancas and the intervening sand batteries while raking the mainland positions with the steady and accurate fire of his trained naval gunners whom he had been drilling every day since *Powhatan* left New York. At best, he should be able to anchor inside the bay with minimal damage to his vessel and crew; at worst, a lucky shot from a battery ashore might damage the engine or hit his magazine which would blow *Powhatan* and her crew "to kingdom come." Porter was willing to run that risk in order to achieve his objective. That was what he had told the president he would do; that was what the president had ordered him to do. As *Powhatan* headed for the bar, *Wyandotte* closed with her and hoisted signals for *Powhatan* to come about and await instructions. Porter could make out Meigs standing on *Wyandotte's* quarterdeck waving a document in one hand. Porter had to order *Powhatan's* helmsman to veer off to avoid a collision as Lieutenant Williamson brought *Wyandotte* directly across his bow. For a time Porter considered ramming the smaller steamer but instead called for reduced steam and brought *Powhatan* about. "In twenty minutes more I should have been inside the harbor, or sunk," Porter wrote later. It was, he felt, "the greatest disappointment of my life." Meigs had himself rowed over the *Powhatan* and met the furious Porter, trying to calm the navy officer. while explaining that Colonel Brown wanted to put off a collision as long as possible so he could bring conditions within Fort Pickens closer to what his years of experience indicated the situation demanded. Brown wrote in a note to Meigs, "We want time; it is everything." Meigs agreed that a confrontation while the vessels offshore were unloading and landing stores and ordnance could be disastrous. Meigs in his own note to Porter initiating the delay stated that his familiarity with the views and intentions of the president justified him in making the request and added that this had the force of a presidential order itself. Once the unloading was completed in a few days, Porter could then make his entrance to the harbor. Porter

Confederate sand battery at Pensacola, showing the mix of clothing and the casual attitude of officers and men in the Southern army (photograph by J.D. Edwards, Southern Historical Collection, Samuel Henry Lockett Papers, Wilson Library, University of North Carolina at Chapel Hill).

wrote to Brown the following morning saying the orders of the president in relation to his entering the harbor were so imperative that they left no margin for a contingency. He did not allude to the fact that he himself was the author of the presidential order, not Abraham Lincoln. Porter asked Brown for an indication of how long it might take his forces ashore to reach the level of preparation he sought. Porter wrote that he could do little to prevent the enemy from coming over from the mainland in boats situated as he now was outside the main entrance channel. Were he not to enter within the next two nights, he would loose the advantage of darkness with the changes in the cycle of the moon. "Will you please make such suggestions as your good sense will dictate, and I will endeavor to follow them as near as I can." Brown was relieved that the impetuous Porter was, at least for the moment, agreeing to delay his entrance and therefore a certain confrontation with Bragg's forces on the mainland. Brown ordered guard boats to patrol inside the harbor entrance at night to add to the security of Fort Pickens.[12]

On Thursday, April 18, Meigs put his thoughts on paper to Colonel Brown, writing in his role of Brown's staff engineer. He suggested that the army commander visit Captain Adams and ask that one of the sailing vessels in the squadron be dispatched to Key West with orders for it to replace the steamer *Crusader* there which would then proceed to the offing at Pensacola. The steamer would be of more value off Santa Rosa Island where it could maneuver independently of tide, current, and wind, and could, if required, replace *Wyandotte* which was subject to breakdown from her long service without the opportunity for maintenance or repair. Meigs also suggested two companies of infantry be brought to Fort Pickens from Fort Taylor with such provisions as the three companies remaining there could spare. Let the civilian carpenters just landed on Santa Rosa Island be put to making wagon bodies now that the horses had been landed and were recovering from their long sea voyage, Meigs wrote. He would send mattresses from *Illinois* to the fort for the carpenters to make sure they were comfortably quartered and kept in good humor. Just now, Meigs wrote, carpenters were more valuable than soldiers.[13]

At New York Lieutenant Colonel Keyes was tying up loose ends. He was uncomfortable with his extended absence from his duties as military secretary to General-in-Chief Scott. He wrote to the adjutant general that *Philadelphia* was almost loaded. Some lumber, mules, beef cattle, and 150 barrels of gunpowder were all that had yet to be put on board. General Scott would understand the immense labor forced upon him by the president's orders, he hoped, and he asked the adjutant general to let the general-in-chief know how uneasy Keyes was at being in New York while Scott faced the many burdens, alone and without his assistance, of heading up the military efforts of a nation going to war. If the adjutant general thought Keyes should join Scott before completing the business he had been sent to New York to oversee, he would leave for Washington on Saturday. Otherwise he would start for Washington on Monday. Keyes had received no communication from the adjutant general nor the general-in-chief since leaving Washington. "The silence was ominous," he later wrote, "and indicted that I was laying up in store some kind of disapproval." Keyes had every right to suspect that he had earned the displeasure of the general-in-chief. He felt relief as he watched the merchant steamer *Philadelphia,* under Captain Kittridge, clear for Fort Pickens carrying the last of the cargo and munitions bound for Brown's forces on Santa Rosa Island but he was upset greatly at the letter he received from Scott that day complaining about Keyes having left his post without Scott's permission and accusing Keyes of acts of rudeness on his part. Scott advised, "I think it necessary to terminate our official connections without further correspondence or irritation."[14]

Unaware of this event, Colonel Brown wrote to Keyes at New York from Fort Pickens on Friday, April 19, addressing him as secretary to the general-in-chief, regarding his decision to delay Porter's entrance to Pensacola Bay. He had taken that action, while understanding the critically important desire of the government to have *Powhatan* inside the harbor for added protection, because of the conditions he found on taking command. *Atlantic* and *Illinois*, carrying vitally needed equipment, supplies, and reinforcements were lying within range of the batteries of Fort McRee. Time was everything, he explained to Keyes as he had to Meigs earlier, and to delay Porter's entrance for the chance to get as much landed from the transports as possible, he felt, was justified, and taking any act provoking hostilities was unwise. The same day Brown wrote to Porter in response to Porter's insistence that his entry must be within two days, saying he would not promise to be ready to provoke hostilities in a week and warning Porter that, if he did enter the harbor and bring on a confrontation before Brown could be prepared, the movement would be injurious to the interests of the nation. Meigs met with Porter and later assured Brown that he and the naval officer would await Brown's orders "in all obedience and fealty." While these discussions were taking place between the Federal commanders at the entrance to the bay, a flotilla

Fort Barrancas water battery, from Fort Barrancas (photograph by J.D. Edwards, Southern Historical Collection, Samuel Henry Lockett Papers, Wilson Library, University of North Caarolina at Chapel Hill).

from Pensacola of some twenty-five tugs, schooners, launches, and barges filled with soldiers came down the bay making either for a landing on Santa Rosa Island or for the navy yard wharf to further reinforce Bragg's command. Porter found relief from his frustration by ordering the 11-inch pivot gun on *Powhatan's* deck cast loose and a shell fired. The missile exploded directly over the flotilla which immediately turned back to Pensacola. A large crowd had gathered along the shore at the navy yard to watch and Porter ordered another shell fired in that direction, scattering the spectators. He signaled Brown that this would be an excellent opportunity to make his run into the harbor in the excitement and confusion but the army commander would not agree to it.[15]

From Montgomery Secretary Walker wired General Beauregard at Charleston to send to Pensacola the men who had planned and superintended the construction of the floating battery that had served with good effect against Fort Sumter. Heavy mortars were needed at Pensacola, he added, and he asked that Beauregard send as many as possible without delay.[16]

At Washington President Lincoln issued a proclamation of blockade. Vessels approaching any port in the seceded states were to be warned off and the warning endorsed in the vessel's register. Vessels found to have been so warned and endorsed, and again approaching a blockaded port would be seized and sent to the nearest Federal port for proceedings against the vessel and its cargo. Persons found guilty of molesting or boarding a vessel of United States registry would be held subject to the laws of piracy. A copy of the proclamation did not reach Captain Adams until May 12, thirty-three days later. Since the move of Slemmer and his command to Santa Rosa Island, there had been free and open access to Pensacola Harbor for any vessel willing to pass under the frowning embrasures of Fort Pickens. Commerce had moved to and from the port including the flow of men and munitions to Bragg's forces from the seceded states along the gulf coast. When Lieutenant Porter learned of the proclamation of blockade, but before receiving an actual copy of the document, he approached Captain Adams and insisted the navy immediately impose the blockade at Pensacola. Adams denied Porter's demand, telling him the army garrison was established within Fort Pickens to guard the public property there, the navy was established off Santa Rosa Island to support the army in its mission, and until he received direct orders to impose a blockade he was not going to authorize a single action beyond those required to fulfill the specific orders he had in hand.[17]

On Saturday, April 29, Meigs informed Brown that, with the arrival of the troops on *Illinois* and the two companies he had ordered up from Key West and counting the crews of the vessels offshore, Brown would command or have access to a total of 3,087 officers and men. With this large a force, the idea of an attack coming out of the night by escalade could be forgotten. Any attack on Fort Pickens now, most probably, would be preceded by a massive bombardment. With all the men on Santa Rosa Island concentrated within the walls of the fort, every shell that entered could cause massive death and destruction. Meigs recommended batteries be constructed outside the fort to permit mounting more guns, that two-thirds of the garrison be moved to an entrenched camp located well beyond the range of the guns on the mainland, and that a plank road be constructed across the dunes for communication and transportation between the camp, the batteries, and the fort. Only a working party and guard, detailed for twenty-four hour shifts of duty, should be kept in the fort to protect the provisions and munitions there and to man the guns were the enemy rash enough to mount an attack. Under these arrangements, Meigs suggested, the troops would be more healthy, cheerful, comfortable, and safe. The present crowded conditions at the fort would bring on disease if continued, he warned. Monday, April 22, brought favorable weather after a series of storms, gales, and heavy rains. Brown kept the men busy putting the fort in condition for defense and landing and storing provisions and munitions. He intended to discharge *Atlantic* to return to New York as soon as possible. With the troops ashore from *Illinois*, he had nine full companies of regulars with two more on the way from Key West. His command was more than sufficient to repel an assault, he felt, but to prevent a strong force from landing and making a lodgment to the east, he still required more force than he had. He was concerned that the squadron might be blown off station by severe weather as had happened several times prior to his arrival. He was content that the presence of his command on Santa Rosa Island did prevent the secessionists from weakening their forces on the mainland in order to divert large portions to other places where their presence could be unwelcome to Federal fortunes. He took Meigs's advice to throw up field works, one a mile and a half east of the fort to be manned by one company of artillery and two of infantry, and another about the same distance on the opposite shore, similarly manned. He was satisfied with progress being made within Fort Pickens on traverses built to minimize damage by bursting shells. He could not account, he wrote to Keyes, for the enemy not having taken possession of Fort Pickens prior to his arrival. The numbers that the command on the mainland could bring to bear would have rendered success certain. He could speculate that the Southern authorities had been reluctant to commence hostilities or had simply been unprepared for the actual opening of armed conflict. He thought their present attitude arose from a consciousness of his ability to destroy the navy yard and close the port while the only hope the Southern forces had was to do the Federal facility some partial injury by a long and fruitless bombardment.[18]

Adams reported the arrival of *Powhatan* to the secretary of the navy. Her boats and crew had since been usefully employed with those of the other vessels of the squadron in landing military supplies for Fort Pickens. He regretted to report that scurvy had broken out on *Sabine* and, in the opinion of the ship's surgeon, was likely to spread. The ship ought to be ordered to some place where fresh meat and vegetables could be available for the crew. With the steamers *Brooklyn, Powhatan,* and *Wyandotte* on the station, he considered that *Sabine's* presence could be dispensed with. Lieutenant Murdaugh had submitted his resignation, Adams wrote, which he had refused to accept or forward. Losing Murdaugh would reduce the number of lieutenants on the vessel to three, a number far too low to keep the ship and crew in order. It was Murdaugh's stated intention to follow his native state, Virginia, out of the Union now that the remaining states of the South had begun to secede. When Secretary Welles at Washington received Adams's letter and learned of Murdaugh's intent, he had the lieutenant's name stricken from the navy list and dismissed Murdaugh from the service. Captain Meigs, aboard *Atlantic,* wrote to Colonel Brown that, since Virginia had seceded and seized the Gosport Navy Yard, she would now possess major naval vessels of war and would soon have the officers to fight them. Brown should look to his lines of communication and the posts at Key West and Dry Tortugas against a Confederate naval expedition. Meigs advised sending *Sabine* and the sailing sloop *St. Louis*, both of which Meigs considered useless off Santa Rosa Island, to aid in the defense of Forts Taylor and Jefferson. The president's order of April 1, which Brown bore and which Adams had seen, gave Brown full and ample authority to call on Adams to make any necessary dispositions of his force. Satisfied that his work of overseeing the installation of Brown and his reinforcements in Fort Pickens was complete, Meigs sailed the next day on *Atlantic* for New York. At the same time, having served twenty years as a lieutenant in the United States Navy, David Dixon Porter was promoted due to seniority on the navy list to the rank of lieutenant commander.[19]

The events that had taken place at Charleston Harbor brought shock and surprise to many across the nation. Captain Henry J. Hunt, commanding Company M, 2nd Artillery, within Fort Pickens, answered a personal letter from his friend and West Point classmate, Braxton Bragg, commanding the Confederate forces on the mainland, on April 23:

> How strange it is! We have been united in our views of almost all subjects, public and private. We still have, I trust, a personal regard for each other, which will continue whatever course our sense of duty may dictate, yet in one short year after exchanging at your house assurances of friendship, here we are, face to face, with arms in our hands, with every prospect of a bloody collision. How strange![20]

At Washington on Wednesday, April 24, the court-martial of Commodore Armstrong came to a conclusion and found Armstrong guilty of neglect of duty, disobedience of orders, and conduct unbecoming an officer for the surrender of the navy yard at Pensacola. Armstrong was sentenced to be suspended from duty for five years with loss of pay and emoluments for the first half of that time. He was also to be reprimanded by the secretary of the navy in general orders that would be read on every naval vessel and at every naval station. The general order issued by the secretary of the navy that commended Quartermaster William Conway was appended to Armstrong's reprimand to be read aloud at the same time.[21]

On Friday, April 26, Colonel Brown wrote to Captain Adams that he thought it would be a good idea to establish a battery on Santa Rosa Island armed with 9-inch rifles from *Brooklyn* that would be manned and fought exclusively by the navy. "Their cooperation in this manner would be of the most essential importance, and the navy with the army in the defense of this fort would cause a generous emulation between the two services promotive of good feelings." Adams did not take to the idea at all. His men were exhausted from the labor involved in furnishing working parties to help in the fort and provide crews for the boats unloading supplies, provisions, and munitions. Wouldn't the same guns, he asked, do just as well in preventing the approach of Confederate forces from the east on Santa Rosa Island from where they now were on *Brooklyn?* At same time, however, Adams did formalize the procedure to be followed in the event of a Confederate attack during darkness. Two red rockets would be fired from the fort to be answered from the vessels offshore with the same. Boats, armed and manned by sailors and marines, would be launched and rowed to the beach. A detachment of soldiers would leave the fort and march along the beach on the gulf side displaying two red lanterns. The soldiers would form on the beach to provide cover for the landing of the sailors and marines who would join the soldiers in carrying out the orders of the army commander. On that Friday the *New Orleans Picayune* carried a contribution from its local correspondent regarding events at Pensacola. Soldiers were arriving every day by rail, he wrote, and by now General Bragg had under his command about 8,000 troops, more than General Scott had commanded in the valley of Mexico during the Mexican war. "A shark was caught yesterday morning with a pair of red breeches and a whole parcel of bowie knives in his belly—supposed to be the remains of a Zouave. I didn't see the shark. It will be remembered I reported the drowning of a Zouave the other day." A civilian presented himself to Brown's sentries on Sunday evening, April 28, declaring he was a Northern man and a reporter for a newspaper. At Brown's office in the fort, he was questioned. Thinking the fort's safety might be jeopardized if the man returned to the mainland after having seen what was taking place within the fort, Brown had him sent to Porter on *Powhatan*. Porter told his crew to keep an eye on the man. One of the sailors saw him tear a paper into small pieces which he dropped into the wooden spit-box. Porter had the fragments retrieved, cleaned, and pasted back together. The letter was addressed to J. C. Morris, Esq., and reported the writer's travels, ending with, "Hope to hear of the surrender of Fort Sumter today, next, Pickens, then Washington." A city constable came out to Colonel Brown from Pensacola bearing a warrant for the man's arrest. Brown ordered Porter to turn the man over. Porter protested this as an act of stupidity since the man had seen much of the fort's condition and what had been done to its defenses and since the man had time to observe the vessels of the squadron offshore but, as Porter was only holding the man at Brown's request, he complied and released the man to the marshal.[22]

On Tuesday, April 30, Captain Adams wrote a long letter to his old friend and shipmate, Captain Samuel Du Pont, who was then the head of the blockade strategy board at the Navy Department at Washington. Adams complained it was nearly three months since he had arrived off Santa Rosa Island. His orders were to remain on the defensive and to cooperate in the defense of Fort Pickens only if it were attacked. He wrote that *Brooklyn* had returned from Key West with provisions at the beginning of the month carrying copies of orders from General Scott for him to land the artillery company under Captain Vogdes. This he had refused to do, he explained to Du Pont, since it would have been a direct violation of the orders from the Navy Department under which he had been acting and, he insisted, he would accept no orders from General Scott. He wrote of the arrival of *Atlantic* and *Illinois* bearing Colonel Brown with his troops, provisions, and ordnance, and all the work that devolved upon the crews of the navy vessels in off-loading the steamers. The labor had been excessive in getting all this material ashore. The boat crews had to land through the surf on the open beach and the boats were sustaining damage. The crew of *Sabine*, he mentioned, were upset at the length of their cruise and the excessive amount of hard work now falling upon them. The enlistments of many had expired and several were demanding their discharges which he was not granting but he thought his vessel should be relieved. As for obtaining fresh provisions from the mainland, it was out of the question. Adams wrote he had heard of one merchant who had undertaken to bring fresh vegetables out to the vessels of the squadron from Mobile who had been taken and hanged by a mob although the merchant had permission from the governor of Alabama and the military command to do so. It was not possible to predict what General Bragg was contemplating, he continued. There were 7,000 or 8,000 men camped about the forts on the mainland and near the navy yard. Batteries lined the beach between the lighthouse and Fort McRee. Opinion was that, when everything was ready and in place, Bragg would demand the surrender of Fort Pickens and, in the event of a refusal, would bombard it as had been done at Fort Sumter. The main difference between Fort Sumter and Fort Pickens, Adams wrote, was here the distances were greater. The walls were thick enough to withstand a great deal of hammering and there were no houses or wooden buildings inside to catch fire and burn. More important, Colonel Brown, unlike Major Anderson, had unlimited provisions to ward off hunger which was what had forced the garrison at Fort Sumter to surrender. Himself, he wrote to Du Pont, was altogether without current orders from the Navy Department but Colonel Brown had shown him a copy of an order from the president that required him to assist the army. He wished the president could understand how the army interpreted that. It seemed to him they took the executive's instructions to mean the navy was to work for the army by day landing materials, watch over them by night, and be ready to land and fight for them when they made the signal. In a later letter to Du Pont, Adams wrote, "We have fallen on fearful times, and I have had my share of perplexity." He wished, he ended his letter, that he was already in his grave. On Wednesday, May 1, Captain Adams received a letter from the secretary of the navy informing him money was coming out for the squadron on *Water Witch* and *Minnesota*. Adams wrote back that, based on the rumored arrival of a vessel from Europe bearing a modern Armstrong gun for Bragg's forces, he was stopping every vessel bound for the port of Pensacola and was detaining any that were carrying munitions of war. He called the attention of the secretary to the condition of his ship's company. The men were very discontented with the length of their cruise. Scurvy was spreading. The men had not had fresh meat in more than three months. About seventy of the crew were beyond the terms of their enlistments or would become so in the course of the next month and, shortly thereafter, the entire crew would. The men wanted their discharges and they wanted to go home. He had offered extra pay as an inducement to stay but none were interested. If they were given the opportunity to go home now, Adams wrote, the nation would get the services of three-quarters of them back in a month. After they recovered their health and spirits, saw their families, and spent their money, they would be ready to ship out again. The crew of *Sabine* was a good crew, Adams insisted. It would be wise for the navy to get men as well-drilled as they were on ships that were just starting out on cruises. Since coming aboard in 1858, the crew had shore leave once for twenty-four hours. Ending his letter, Adams recommended that *Brooklyn* be ordered home for repairs. Her engines and boilers were in bad shape from long use and the necessity of keeping her fires up constantly.[23]

Colonel Brown's next regular report on Thursday, May 2, was addressed to the adjutant general at Washington, explaining that he had heretofore directed his reports to Lieutenant Colonel Keyes as the agent of the president because Keyes had superintended the fitting out of the expedition which, at the time, was a secret one. The need for secrecy having passed when he landed his force and assumed command, he would, according to army regulations, now be addressing future reports to the office of the adjutant general. To give some idea of the labors in which his command had been involved, he reported that every day except for one Sunday since his arrival on April 17, he had from 1,000 to 1,200 men constantly at work, 800 of whom were involved in making the necessary improvements to the fort. Still, he felt he needed another fortnight before he would feel fully prepared to resist the numerous batteries and heavy guns bearing on his position. The enemy, he reported, was equally busy, having large numbers of men at work on several batteries that were visible to him. He had no further apprehension of an attack by escalade as he felt certain he could whip the enemy in the open field and, in a very few days, with the assistance of Major Tower of the engineers, he should be so protected from bombardment he hoped to be able to hold the fort for a very long time. *Water Witch*, Lieutenant Ronckendorf, had arrived and anchored off Fort Pickens. After reporting to Captain Adams, Ronckendorf established

Confederate camps, just north of the brick wall of the navy yard at Pensacola (photograph by J.D. Edwards, U.S. Army Military History Institute).

a schedule for regular courier trips between Pensacola Bay, Dry Tortugas, Key West, and Havana.[24]

At New York, *Atlantic* made port and Captain Gray terminated his charter with the War Department. Captain Montgomery Meigs went ashore and took the first train of cars for Washington. Meigs reached Washington from New York on Friday, May 3, and hurried to the State Department to report to Secretary Seward who took him immediately to the executive mansion where he recounted his experiences to the president and the cabinet. He then called on General Scott who sent out word that he would not see Meigs. Scott, who had already dismissed Keyes, did not approve of junior officers who consulted with presidents and cabinet ministers over his head. Scott was losing his presence and his power and the administration was finding him more and more wrong or evasive. As an example of this, without Scott's knowledge or input, eleven days later Meigs was promoted to the rank of lieutenant colonel of infantry and the following day, May 15, he was appointed a brigadier general and named quartermaster general of the United States Army.[25]

On Saturday, May 4, the sailing storeship *Release,* Lieutenant Commanding Frailey, dropped anchor off Santa Rosa Island, thirty-seven days out of New York. On the same day, Lieutenant George Brown, formerly of *Powhatan,* now commanding the schooner *Oriental* which the army had chartered locally and loaned to the navy, overhauled two steamers flying the Confederate flag. Brown boarded both steamers but found nothing contraband of war and permitted the two vessels to proceed and enter Pensacola Harbor. The same day

Bragg had four old sailing vessels towed into the channel between Fort Barrancas and Fort Pickens where they were scuttled in an effort to block the entrance to the bay to the deep draft Federal vessels offshore. The entrance to the bay might be more effectively blocked, Bragg reported to Secretary Walker, but at heavy expense for the acquisition of the necessary additional vessels. Federal steamers capable of maneuvering around the four hulks now in place could still frustrate his planned movement of troops to Santa Rosa Island if it did not result in the capture or destruction of his whole attacking force. On Wednesday, May 8, Colonel Brown learned that the day before, Porter had stopped two other steamers bound from Mobile to Pensacola and had boarded them. Nothing contraband of war was found but both vessels were laden with provisions for Bragg's army. When Porter reported his action to Adams, the captain declared he did not have authority to take privately owned vessels. He ordered Porter to permit the steamers to return to Mobile. Colonel Brown called Adams's attention to the importance to the defense of Fort Pickens of excluding all such vessels from the harbor. Permitting entry would lead to injury to his command and permitting the two steamers with their cargoes intact to return to Mobile merely deferred their next attempt to gain access to the harbor. Articles meant for consumption by Bragg's army were as much contraband of war as were munitions. Brown had information that United States flag vessels had been seized and appropriated by Confederate authorities, that the Confederate government had issued letters of marque and was fitting out private vessels to serve as privateers to raid Northern commerce, and that Federal officers and men had been taken prisoner, Federal property stolen, and one of Adams's fellow officers — referring to Worden — was now a prisoner of war in Confederate hands. Under these circumstances, Brown asked, should not effective measures be taken to stop all vessels from entering the harbor and to seize those carrying materiel to aid or arm the enemy? He certainly thought so, he wrote. Adams replied he had given orders to his guard vessels to allow no provisions to enter Pensacola Harbor. In the absence of instructions from the Navy Department with regard to a blockade, he did not know how to proceed regarding foreign ships which were usually allowed a period of time to come and go, nor regarding coastal vessels which might have licenses from the United States government. It was just such doubt which caused him to send the two steamers Porter had stopped the day before back to Mobile. Should he learn of privateers, men-of-war, or letter of marque vessels being at sea under the secession flag, he would commence making captures immediately but would be embarrassed what to do with them since he had no officers he could spare to send them to a port for adjudication. Work on discharging cargo from *Philadelphia* would continue but slowly, he wrote to Brown, as the large boats of *Powhatan* had been in such bad condition when the steamer arrived and then had been so much injured as to require extensive repair, and those of *Brooklyn* would be employed for several more days in ballasting *Supply* with sand to offset the weight of the cargo transferred to the other vessels of the squadron prior to her return voyage to New York. Brown replied to Adams that he was not able to express an opinion on foreign vessels but he did suppose, since he had not yet heard the port was under blockade, it would be right to let them pass as long as they had on board no articles contraband of war. He was decidedly of the opinion that no United States vessel containing any article which might nourish or sustain the enemy should be permitted to enter and certainly no vessel from a seceded state. He regretted that Adams had not detained the two steamers the day before because they were, in his opinion, lawful prizes. As to Adams not having officers to spare to send seized vessels to a port for adjudication, Brown wondered, why send them anywhere? Why not just keep them off Santa Rosa Island with the squadron until matters clarified? He also asked, was not the unloading of *Philadelphia* and the transfer of provision and supplies into the fort of paramount importance when compared to ballasting *Supply*? Now that the seas were smooth and the enemy quiet, nothing should take boats from that work.[26]

From the Navy Department at Washington, Secretary Welles issued orders relieving Captain Adams from command off Santa Rosa Island and ordering him to proceed with *Sabine* to the sailing vessel's home port, the navy yard at Portsmouth, New Hampshire. These orders followed those that had only recently been issued to Captain William W. McKean to proceed in *Niagara* to the offing at Pensacola Bay and assume command as the senior naval officer on station. Secretary Welles had recently developed some confidence in Adams's loyalty but, after what he had witnesses over the past two months, he had serious doubts concerning the old mariner's basic ability.[27]

On Thursday, May 9, Brown's assistant surgeon discussed with Brown's adjutant the condition of the men of Company G, 1st Artillery, Slemmer's command. The company had been in Florida for three years and for the last four months had been confined within the limits of Fort Pickens. Prior to the arrival of the reinforcements, Slemmer and his men had been taxed to the utmost by the physical labor and the incessant watching against attacks by the enemy. They had been deprived of fresh fruits and vegetables during much of that time and a number of cases of scurvy had broken out, some in considerable severity, and, Surgeon Campbell warned, there was reason to fear the general prevalence of the disease

One of the larger sand batteries along Pensacola Bay (photograph by J.D. Edwards, U.S. Army Military History Institute).

throughout the company. The onset of the hot season on the Gulf of Mexico would only aggravate the illness. Supplies of antiscorbutics in the commissary were sufficient to prevent the development of the disease among the companies just arrived from the North but Campbell did not believe these would be adequate to relieve the cases that had already appeared among the men of Company G. He urged Colonel Brown to order the command north, or at least, to Key West where fruits and vegetables were available. On Monday, May 13, Slemmer and Gilman mustered the men of Company G on the parade at Fort Pickens in the afternoon. Slemmer called the men to attention and had First Sergeant Jamieson march them to the beach to board boats that would carry them out to *Philadelphia* for the voyage to Fort Hamilton in New York Harbor. Slemmer, Gilman, and Company G had been in Fort Pickens for 123 days. They marched away from a fort that once had been a vacant pile of masonry and unmounted guns and that now was an armed fortress and depot of ordnance and supply for the thousands of troops under Colonel Brown. Santa Rosa Island, Fort Pickens, and the great harbor at Pensacola would have long been in Confederate hands were it not for the stubborn officer and his small band of regular artillerymen who stood in the face of impossible odds alone until reinforced. Slemmer and his men had done their best to carry out their orders to protect the public property under their charge. Their best had been good enough.[28]

9

"A More Innocent War Was Never Carried On"

Probably in response to suggestions from the recently returned Captain Montgomery Meigs that the irregular command structure existing at the offing to Pensacola Bay now be clarified, President Lincoln wrote to Secretary Welles on Saturday, May 11, that Lieutenant Porter had been put in command of *Powhatan* and Captain Mercer detached therefrom by his special orders and neither of these officers was responsible for any apparent or real impropriety on their parts in connection with the assignments having to do with that vessel. Hereafter, Lincoln wrote, Porter was relieved from the special service he had been placed on and would now be under the direction of the Navy Department from whom he would receive orders and to whom he would report. Two days later Welles wrote to Porter informing him the president had notified the Navy Department that the special duty to which he had been assigned had been completed. *Powhatan*, under his command, would now constitute part of the Gulf Blockading Squadron and Porter would report accordingly to the senior naval officer there. Welles had delayed for three weeks after Porter's dramatic arrival off Pensacola to address the issue of Porter's further role and that of *Powhatan*. Welles was smarting under the president's and the secretary of state's interference with the Navy Department. He waited until he had in hand the president's written statement that Porter was relieved form his special duty, received at the Navy Department on May 11, before he addressed the wayward officer and his steamer.[1]

On Sunday, May 12, an official copy of the president's proclamation of blockade finally reached Captain Adams on *Sabine*. Adams immediately sent Bragg a copy of the proclamation "in order that the foreign ships lying there might be made fully aware of it." On the same day he ordered the ballasted *Supply* to sail for New York, touching at Dry Tortugas and at Key West to provision *St. Louis* and *Crusader* now stationed at these ports. On Tuesday, May 14, General Bragg responded to the copy of the blockade proclamation he had received from Captain Adams by calling it an act of aggressive war on the part of the Federal government. Adams was still on station, unaware of the orders on the way to him relieving him of command. The proclamation of blockade amounted, Bragg wrote, to a virtual recognition of the national existence of the Confederate States of America since a power could only blockade the ports of another sovereign nation, not its own ports. He notified Adams as the officer commanding off Santa Rosa Island to consider the harbor closed to all boats and vessels of the United States as he would henceforth allow none to enter except the dispatch boat under a flag of truce. Bragg could characteristically sputter about the legality of a sovereign power blockading its own ports and could close the harbor to all vessels of the United States, none of which were trying to make use of it. His posturing did nothing to the fact that there was a Federal fleet off the entrance channel effectively closing the port to commerce whether or not the blockade was legal.[2]

Among the Confederate forces on the mainland, sixteen-year-old Private Langdon Rumph of the 1st Alabama Infantry Regiment wrote to his father, Dr. James David Rumph, that he had the fever. "It would not be prudent for me to go to the hospital as they have Measles there." Ten days later he wrote, "We have had a good deal of sickness in our camp for the last few weeks. Dr. Billy Crossley has been very sick with chill and fever; nearly every man in the company that had any predisposition to them has had them. The Measles has surrounded our camp. We are looking for the younger boys to take them daily. If we should get them we will have a hard time with them, having no conveniences exposed to all kinds of weather." Sickness was taking a heavy toll among all the rural youths on the mainland who had not developed any immunity to communicable diseases. On August 14, Langdon's company commander, M. B. Locke, would have to write to Dr. Rumph, "It is with deep regret that I am compelled to inform you of the death of your son, Langdon, together with two other members of our Company, which occurred at the hospital ... Langdon, as I presume you are aware, has been [in] feeble health for four or five weeks, and had just gotten over a spell of Measles, when he was attacked, as his physician said with Typhoid Fever, but I think it was a relapse from Measles, and died in five or six days." Sickness was a constant threat to the Confederate formations on the mainland. Edward McMorries of the 1st Alabama wrote of the summer of 1861, "The hospital was full of sick from June to October. Every day several were carried down from the hospital to the 'dead house' for interment or shipment home.... To us, not yet accustomed to the horrors of war, the situation was distressing. Said a nervous comrade, 'A man can die and be buried here with the least ceremony and concern I ever saw.' Our regiment lost forty this year, mostly young men." Private C. L. Bonney was serving with the 10th Mississippi Volunteer Infantry. He wrote to his father describing life with Bragg's forces on the mainland. He and the men at Fort McRee were working twelve hours a day removing the carriages of guns that could not be brought to bear on Fort Pickens or the vessels in the gulf. They were stripping all combustible material from the fort: weatherboarding, window sashes, and doors. Nothing combustible was to be left within the fort were it to come under bombardment. "The casemate in which I sleep is 17 by 17," Bonney wrote, "and only 23 of us occupy it." In May he would write that he and his comrades had been rolling cannon balls to the batteries all day, piling them near the guns for instant use. Others were cutting wood for the hot shot furnace. "We hope this means action is not far off," he ended his letter.[3]

Colonel Brown reported to the adjutant general on Monday, May 13, on the progress being made unloading ships, storing provisions, and putting up interior works for the protection of the men and guns in the fort. His efforts had been hindered by a want of sandbags which were of such importance that he ordered an officer to Havana to purchase a supply. He had sent a requisition for 100,000 bags north with Gilman on his last visit to

Confederate sand battery along the shore of Pensacola Bay (photograph by J.D. Edwards, U.S. Army Military History Institute).

Washington but that had not been filled. He reported the construction of several outworks. Battery Scott was located between the fort and the shore of the gulf, facing across the channel toward Fort McRee. Battery Cameron, and to the east of it, Battery Lincoln, were on the shore of the bay, both facing the navy yard. Battery Totten was closer to the eastern walls of the fort, its heavy mortars able to take both the navy yard and Fort Barrancas under fire. Brown reported that he refused to accept communications from General Bragg addressed to him as "Commanding, Fort Pickens." He had informed the bearer that he was, by order of the president of the United States, commanding the Department of Florida and would accept no communications that did not recognize him as such. His sick list was increasing, attributable, he thought, to hard work in the hot sun, but none of the cases were serious. He had lost two men to death and two to desertion. "I have not received any orders or official communications," he concluded, "but see by the papers that affairs have materially changed since I received my instructions to act only on the defensive. Is it the intention of the government that the same orders should govern me, or may I, if occasion offer, take the offensive?" Brown was demonstrating from Santa Rosa Island the same hesitancy regarding the initiation of active hostilities as was Bragg on the mainland. He was ready to fight, he indicated, if someone in the government would tell him to.[4]

At Montgomery, Secretary of the Navy Mallory wrote to Charles Conrad, chairman of the Confederate Congress's naval committee, describing a situation that was typical of many taking place as the Confederate States of America seized and assumed responsibility for the on-going operation of what formerly had been properties and operations of the

United States government. The Pensacola Navy Yard had passed to the state of Florida and, under the authority of Colonel Chase, the mechanics, laborers, and other employees of the yard had been retained and continued in their places of employment and labor. These men, Mallory continued, had acted with fidelity and zeal in sustaining the interests of the Confederacy. They had lost not only the extensive back pay due them from the United States for the months prior to the surrender of the yard, for which they had not been paid and, further, had received nothing for their services since then and up to the 25th of March when the Confederate government had assumed control. "I can not doubt," Mallory wrote, "that justice, wisdom, and policy dictate that these men should be paid and I therefore submit the facts, and also an estimate of the amount due, $12,875.33."[5]

Having issued orders that relieved Captain Adams of command of the squadron off Santa Rosa Island, Secretary of the Navy Welles wrote to Commander Charles Poor, now commanding *Brooklyn*, addressing him as the senior naval officer off Fort Pickens and informing him that, in order to obviate the necessity for steamers engaged in the blockade having to leave their stations for the purpose of proceeding to Key West to take on coal, the Navy Department was purchasing a sailing vessel to send to the gulf. She would carry out a cargo of coal which would be distributed among the several steamers on the station and would thereafter be employed under Poor's direction transporting coal from Key West to the vessels of the squadron. Welles wrote again the same day telling Poor that Commodore William Mervine had been appointed to command the Gulf Blockading Squadron. Unavoidable delays had prevented Mervine from entering upon his duties. Commander Poor would, therefore, institute a rigid blockade of Pensacola Harbor and its vicinity in pursuance of the president's proclamation, a copy of which was enclosed for Poor's guidance. He was to allow no vessels to enter the harbor and, and after promulgating the notice that an effective blockade was now in place, was to allow fifteen days for foreign vessels to depart, with or without their cargoes. On all occasions, Poor was to afford protection to those who sought shelter under the American flag and to guard the persons and property of loyal citizens who sought his aid.[6]

New Orleans photographer J. D. Edwards had traveled to Pensacola Bay on business and then advertised that prints of the photographs he had been taking among the Confederate camps and fortifications were available for sale at $1 per copy. Edwards had spent about ten days with the Confederate forces on the mainland and had built a remarkable portfolio of images of people and places along the shore of Pensacola Bay. Thirty-nine views in all of camps, batteries, and even Federal vessels offshore were available. Most impressive were the photographs of Confederate soldiers, alone or in formation. Edwards' work represents one of the larger single collections of photography from the Confederate side of the American Civil War.[7]

On Monday, May 15, the much-traveled correspondent of the *London Times,* William Howard Russell, arrived off Santa Rosa Island aboard the sailing schooner *Diana* out of Mobile. When ordered to heave to, and then boarded by Lieutenant George Brown of *Oriental,* Russell noticed the skipper of *Diana* seemed uneasy. Russell learned that *Diana* had already been warned off from Pensacola Harbor by *Oriental* in the recent past and, on scrutinizing the schooner's papers, the fact was clearly endorsed therein. Brown ordered the skipper to bring *Diana* under *Powhatan's* quarter. Ushered aboard the warship, Russell was introduced to Porter who sent a query to Captain Adams asking for instructions. Porter, meantime, gave Russell a tour of *Powhatan*. Russell subsequently was taken over to *Sabine* and was introduced to Adams. Russell explained his wish to visit Fort Pickens and then the Confederate positions on the mainland. Adams did not think it a good idea to permit the English journalist to examine Fort Pickens first and then to proceed to the mainland where he could discuss what he had seen in the fort with the Confederate command. Major Vogdes, notified only the day before of his promotion from captain, happened to be aboard *Sabine* and offered to take a written request from Russell to Colonel Brown. Adams agreed that he would permit *Diana* to enter Pensacola Harbor and anchor at the Fort Barrancas wharf but left the matter of Russell landing at Fort Pickens to Colonel Brown. Adams told Russell of Bragg's reaction to the proclamation of blockade the pervious day and cautioned him that Bragg's batteries might fire on *Diana*. Russell took the time to interview Adams. A Pennsylvanian by birth, Adams had married a Louisiana woman and lived with her when not at sea on his plantation in that state. Adams told Russell he had just learned one of his sons had enlisted in the Confederate army and two others were serving with the naval forces of Virginia. "God knows," Russell quoted the old man saying, "when I open my broadside, I may be killing my own children." A passenger on *Diana* brought Adams a letter from a daughter informing him she had been elected a *vivandiére* to a New Orleans regiment with which, she wrote, she intended to "push on to Washington and get a lock of Old Abe's hair." The daughter's letter concluded with her wish that Adams would starve to death if he persisted in "this wicked blockade." Russell was given permission by Colonel Brown to visit Fort Pickens on his return from the mainland rather than prior to going there. Entering the harbor and proceeding to the navy yard on *Diana*, when abreast of Fort Barrancas Russell ordered "tablecloth No. 1 to be hoisted to the peak." As the schooner approached the navy yard, he could see musket barrels reflecting the blazing sunlight where regiments drilled on the mainland, clouds of dust raised over the dirt roads by marching columns, and black muzzles of guns peering from the white sand embrasures that stretched along the shore as far to the east as the navy yard. The Federal commander, Russell wrote, had made the same error here at Fort Pickens that Major Anderson had made at Fort Sumter, permitting state forces to erect fortifications and batteries at leisure that should have been blown out of existence at the very beginning. He was not sure the combined fire of the fort and batteries on Santa Rosa Island and the vessels of the fleet offshore could now silence the number of Confederate batteries that had been allowed to arise along the shore. Instead of opening fire on the schooner, Bragg gave permission for *Diana* to come alongside the navy yard wharf. An officer from Bragg's staff took Russell to headquarters where he was presented to a body of officers, most of whom were with the Zouave regiment from New Orleans. Russell joined them for dinner, commenting on the abundance of champagne, claret, beer, and ice. He learned President and Mrs. Davis had come from Montgomery with Secretary of the Navy Mallory and Senator Louis T. Wigfall of Texas and were dining with Bragg at that moment. After dinner, Russell was taken to meet Bragg whom he described as "a tall, elderly man in a blue frock coat with a gold star on his shoulder, trousers with a gold stripe, and gilt buttons." Bragg conducted a lengthy interview in which he explained from maps the positions of his works and the line of fire of his guns. "I know every inch of Fort Pickens," he told the journalist, "for I happened to be stationed there as soon as I left West Point, and I don't think there is a stone in it that I am not as well acquainted with as Harvey Brown." Bragg offered to provide a horse and guide in the morn-

Confederate sand battery on Pensacola Bay, with a connecting passage through to the adjacent battery (photograph by J.D. Edwards, U.S. Army Military History Institute).

ing for Russell to make an extensive tour of the Confederate fortifications. The journalist returned to *Diana* to spend the night. The following day, Thursday, May 16, after breakfast on *Diana* which consisted of "an ugly-looking but well-flavored fish from the waters outside us; fried ham and onions, biscuit, coffee, iced water, and Bordeaux," Russell was given a tour of the Confederate positions on the mainland by Lieutenant Towson Ellis, General Bragg's aide and brother-in-law. Russell visited ten of the thirteen sand batteries erected along the shore. Among the fifty or so pieces with which the batteries were armed, Russell counted only five that could be considered heavy siege guns. Altogether, taking into account the batteries he did not visit, Russell estimated there might be some eighty guns placed in an arc of 135 degrees stretching for three miles along the shore of the bay at an average distance of a mile and a third from Fort Pickens. He was not impressed by the soldiers assigned to the works. Russell had spent time in the Crimea among disciplined British and French regulars and he found the American volunteers lacking in many respects. They seemed to be "great long-bearded fellows in flannel shirts and slouched hats, uniformless in all save the brightly burnished arms and resolute purpose ... who were lying about and only contributing languidly to the effort." He was satisfied Bragg was correct in delaying to open fire on Fort Pickens and the fleet which, in his view, "would have knocked his works about his ears." The ordnance magazines he visited contained ammunition for not more than one day's ordinary firing and the shot was poorly cast with projecting flanges which would damage the soft metal of the gun barrels. He estimated Bragg's total force at between 8,000 and 10,000 men. After his tour, Bragg granted Russell permission to visit Fort Pickens on his way to Pensacola where he would take the railroad cars to Richmond. Bragg asked Russell's opinion of his positions and armaments since he would soon be "forced to try the mettle of our friends on the other side." Russell diplomatically intoned, "May God defend the right," taking neither side. Bragg accepted Russell's response and suggested the two men drink to that. When *Diana* put Russell ashore at the Fort Pickens wharf, Captain William Barry met him. Russell's initial reaction, he later wrote, was that he would not chose Fort Pickens if he were selecting a summer habitation. Like most other American works he had seen in his career, it was strong on its sea faces and weaker on its land face, the forts having been designed to bring the weight of their fire against hostile vessels and not against a land force attacking from the rear. The men of the garrison at Fort Pickens were United States regulars, not equal to the Southern volunteers in physique but infinitely superior in cleanliness and soldierly smartness, Russell wrote. Men were digging deep pits in the parade to serve as shell traps and the rear openings of the casemates were being protected by a covered way contrived by tilting up spare gun platforms and beams of wood and piling earth and sandbags for several feet of thickness. Russell's closing comment in his report to the editors was, "As it was approaching evening and I had seen everything in the fort, the hospital, casemates, magazines, bake houses, tasted the rations and drank the whiskey, I set out for the schooner accompanied by Colonel Brown and Captain Barry."[8]

Ashore in Pensacola, Father Louis-Hippolyte Gache, a Jesuit priest assigned to St. Michael's Catholic Church, wrote to his superiors passing along local speculation and gossip. New companies of troops were arriving every day and popular thinking was "the dance would not be long a-starting." Interim, the troops were working to strip the navy yard, sending all kinds of provisions and materials stored there to places of safety so that if Federal gunfire demolished the navy yard, only the buildings themselves would suffer. Father Gache repeated a rumor about planning taking place to block the channel between Fort Barrancas and Fort Pickens by towing the floating dry dock from the navy yard out to the same area where the hulks had been sunk and scuttling the huge structure there. This would probably be the signal for war, Father Gache wrote, since the Federal commander at Fort Pickens could not let it take place without opposition and would initiate a bombardment to which Bragg would have to rely. Every citizen of the city seemed to be aware of the current plan of attack, a bombardment of the fort followed by a raid on Santa Rosa Island. He was pleased, he wrote, with the soldiers to whom he ministered, many of them coming to confession and communion. He felt that more would take advantage of the sacraments were they not kept so busy and were it easier for them to get permission to leave the camps.[9]

Quartermaster General Meigs, only two weeks back at the nation's capital, wrote the secretary of war his thoughts on the situation at Pensacola Bay. The proper disposition of the garrison was to encamp it on the island at some point within communication of the fort and yet out of range of shot and shell from the rebel batteries on the mainland. Attempts by Federal vessels to enter the harbor under fire from the batteries of guns established on the mainland would be wasteful of life and force, Meigs thought. For the present the few thousand men on Santa Rosa Island were keeping up to 10,000 men idle on the mainland and thus doing useful and effective service in the cause of the country. Periodic activity would keep the Confederate command in fear of an attack and prevent their sending men to parts of the country where subsistence was less expensive and more readily available than at Pensacola.[10]

Secretary Walker wrote to General Bragg on Friday, May 17, asking if Bragg could spare a portion of his infantry for the Confederate army forming in Virginia. If so, Walker told Bragg to advise how many and to name the regiments he could send. Bragg responded he would need all the force he had if he were to attempt offensive operations against Fort Pickens but were he to restrain himself and remain on the defensive, he could send three regiments to Virginia, one from Alabama and two from Georgia. Bragg could not be aware of it but Walker's request was the beginning of the end of the role of the Confederate forces on Pensacola Bay. The Federal armies in the East were forming around the national capital at Washington. The Confederate armies in the East were forming around their newly re-located capital at Richmond, Virginia. Federal and Confederate armies in the West would soon gather at and around St. Louis, Missouri. The theaters of war would focus on the route to Richmond in the East and the Mississippi River Valley in the West. Pensacola was about to become a backwater but not in the immediate future. This was dramatically brought home to Bragg when he subsequently requisitioned more and heavier guns from the War Department at Richmond. He was advised the requisition had been returned by the ordnance bureau with the response that there would be no heavy guns for Pensacola. There was a greater need for ordnance by the forces forming in Virginia and all efforts were being made to supply that demand. Without saying so specifically, the adjutant general was telling Bragg that the army in close contact with the enemy would get priority. On Tuesday, May 28, Bragg wired President Davis that he could spare 2,500 men for the army in Virginia and start them on their way immediately, well armed. At the head of one of the regiments, this one reorganized and renumbered as the 3rd Alabama Infantry, Colonel Tennent Lomax led the first of the reinforcements to go from Bragg's army to the Confederate Army of the Potomac forming in Virginia under General Beauregard.[11]

On Wednesday morning, May 22, Colonel Brown was awakened and told the dry dock was being moved from its moorings at the navy yard. Brown had heard rumors, as had Father Gache at Pensacola, about the dock being used in some manner against Fort Pickens. Brown had heard specifically and erroneously that the dry dock had been fitted with heavy guns to serve as a floating battery. The huge black structure was being towed slowly that morning toward Battery Lincoln on Santa Rosa Island when it stopped broadside-to, less than a thousand yards away. Brown dispatched a messenger in a small boat to Bragg demanding an explanation of the move and putting the Confederate commander on notice that Brown intended to take offensive action whenever the interests and honor of his country required. Bragg returned Brown's letter. He replied he did not care for the tone of the letter and insisted on the propriety and courtesies of style and language that Bragg felt he had the right to expect in any future communication to his headquarters. By mid-day no hostile activity aboard the dry dock could been seen by Federal observers. Brown wrote to Bragg demanding to know the character of the massive structure now under his guns and the object for which it had been placed there. Any attempt to move or occupy the dock would be considered a hostile act and would be resisted by every means Brown possessed. Bragg responded that he was surprised at the reaction caused by the accidental positioning of the dry dock which had broken loose from its moorings and drifted to where it now lay, he claimed. He intended to move it as soon as means, wind, and tide would allow. Bragg actually had intended to block navigation into the harbor by Federal vessels at a location further down the channel but the dry dock had grounded where it sat. Brown called a council of war at his headquarters at Fort Pickens, inviting Porter to attend. When he arrived,

Porter found Brown and Captain Adams discussing the dry dock over supper. They were waiting for Bragg's answer to Brown's second letter. Porter was furious at what he witnessed. "Our senior commanders thought they had done their duty by inquiring of Bragg what he intended to do, and after seeing him carry out his intentions, sat quietly down to dinner. Colonel Brown filled more sandbags, and Bragg mounted extra guns. They were like two schoolboys daring each other to knock chips from their shoulders and playing a farce at war." During the night Confederate engineers partially scuttled the dry dock where it lay. Bragg was concerned he might not be able to move it further and leaving it at its present location it would work to some degree to block channel to the harbor. Later, Bragg's engineers tried to develop a method to pump most of the water from the dock and refloat it so they could tow it further down the bay to a position close under the guns of Fort McRee where the channel narrowed and where, with the dry dock completely submerged, it would effectively bar passage inward to any vessel of size.[12]

On Saturday, May 25, Captain William McKean arrived off Santa Rosa Island aboard *Niagara* as the naval officer in charge of establishing the blockade of the major gulf ports.

Confederate troop formation within Fort McRee. Note the wooden platforms within each casemate for a second tier of guns, the hot shot furnace in the upper left, and the powder magazine in the lower right (photograph by J.D. Edwards, U.S. Army Military History Institute).

McKean had twenty years service in the navy and was considered to be staunchly loyal. Before sailing from the home port of New York, McKean had purged the officers of *Niagara* by requiring each to sign a written oath of allegiance which caused several Southern officers to submit their resignations. McKean had been ordered to establish the blockade at New Orleans and Mobile and to use every vessel in the squadron that he could bring into service to do so. He ordered Poor in *Brooklyn* and Porter in *Powhatan* to the Mississippi passes below New Orleans, Poor to block Pass a L'Outre and Porter to block South West Pass. He would then station *Niagara* off Mobile. Colonel Brown immediately objected to these dispositions, arguing that McKean's placements would jeopardize the security of Fort Pickens. Without these vessels on station off Pensacola Bay, Brown insisted, he could not prevent an enemy force from crossing from the mainland and making a lodgment on Santa Rosa Island and then commencing regular approaches against the fort. The steamers should not be taken away without a more pressing necessity than just blockading two ports. Brown enclosed a copy of the authority he had from the president, dated April 1, calling on all officers of the army and navy to aid with every means in their power the expedition under his command in any way he might desire. McKean admitted, although his orders were of later date, they were of lesser authority than Brown's. He would do what he could to protect Fort Pickens, he promised, but he had other work to do. On Sunday, May 26, McKean replied to Brown's correspondence of the previous day with information that the screw steamer U.S.S. *Huntsville* would soon arrive off Santa Rosa Island. She was a fine vessel, McKean assured the colonel, mounting an 8-inch pivot gun and two 32-pounder carriage guns, and she had power enough to tow any of the sailing vessels of the squadron. The sailing sloop *St. Louis* with her battery of eighteen guns had been ordered up from Dry Tortugas and could be looked for hourly. McKean's opinion was that these two vessels would provide sufficient force to prevent a landing on Santa Rosa Island. It was vitally important, he wrote to Brown, that the blockade at Mobile be in place before shipments of arms and ordnance supplies thought to be on the way from Europe arrived and he was anxious to proceed to that place. In the event of an emergency, *Mohawk*, now blockading the far entrance to Santa Rosa Sound, could be sent to him and, since the distance was only fifty miles, he could return in a few hours time. Porter could hardly contain his relief when he received the orders sending him from the squadron. "There is a fascination about Pensacola Bay," he wrote, "that kept the commanding officers there day after day gazing at the harbor and fancying, perhaps, that they were acquiring experience in the art of war...."

Captain William W. McKean, U.S. Navy, who commanded the Gulf Blockading Squadron, was ready to fight whether Col. Harvey Brown was or not (Naval Historical Center).

Months passed away. Bragg built his fortifications and never molested Fort Pickens. Colonel Brown built up sandbags and never troubled Bragg. Neither of them committed an 'overt act.' A more innocent war was never carried on." Porter sailed in *Powhatan* to take station off Mobile until such time as McKean could replace him there when he would proceed further west to join Poor in *Brooklyn* blockading the Mississippi passes. *Powhatan* had been in sorry condition when Porter assumed command at the Brooklyn Navy Yard. The steamer had been ordered there in the first place because she desperately needed a complete overhaul and now, eight weeks later, she was in far worse shape. She could take on no more than 400 tons of coal because she leaked so badly when she had more aboard. Her wooden hull was rotted through and Porter had doubts whether she could retain her masts in a heavy storm. Her boilers were almost expended; they had been patched and re-patched until there was not a chance of patching them more. Two had burst holes while the engines were merely backing a little harder than usual. Without the emergency parts he had ordered through the United States consul at Havana, he felt he would have to let his fires go out and that would convert the powerful side-wheel steamer into a sailing vessel and prevent him from ensuring that nothing afloat got into or out of the Confederate ports. On Sunday, August 4, Porter reported that *Powhatan* was on her last legs. "I assume she is throughout decayed," he reported. Regardless, he took up station off Mobile in the side-wheeler.[13]

That day *Philadelphia* docked at Fort Hamilton in New York Harbor. Slemmer, Gilman, and the men of Company G, 1st Artillery, debarked. The men of the command were scheduled for a short period for rest and recruitment. The company, now commanded by Captain Truman Seymour who had been with the Fort Sumter garrison at its surrender, departed within weeks to join the army forming at Washington. The company's two original officers were headed for reassignment. Adam Slemmer initially superintended the recruitment and organization of the 16th United States Infantry Regiment at Fort Hamilton, having been promoted to major. He served later as inspector general of the Department of the Ohio and commanded a small expedition from Parkersburg, Virginia, to Rome Court House. He was taken ill with typhoid fever in November, 1861, and was listed as unfit for duty until the following May, being nursed back to health by Carrie at their home at Norristown, Pennsylvania. He rejoined the Union forces in the field with Major General William Rosecrans's Army of the Mississippi where he served during the siege and capture of Corinth, Mississippi. He suffered a severe wound in the leg from a musket ball at the battle of Stone's River and was relieved from active duty, thereafter presiding over a board examining sick and disabled officers at Cincinnati for the remainder of the war. Carrie Slemmer worked to obtain recognition for her husband's courageous holding of Fort Pickens to the extent of traveling to Washington and obtaining an interview with the president. Abraham Lincoln noted in his papers, "List of officers I wish to remember when I make appointments for Officers to the Regular Army: Major Doubleday, Major Anderson ... Lieut. Slemmer — his pretty wife says a Major, or First Captain." Slemmer was promoted to brevet brigadier general in 1867 and died of heart disease on October 7, 1868, at Fort Laramie, Dakota Territory. Slemmer was buried in Montgomery County, Pennsylvania, at his home in Norristown. Jeremiah Gilman was ordered to recruiting duty on his return to New York. He later commanded a battalion in Kentucky and was named inspector of artillery of the Department of the Ohio and Cumberland. He was brevetted for gallant and meritorious conduct at the battle of Shiloh, April 7, 1861, and fought, as did Slemmer, at

Stone's River where he was again brevetted for gallant and meritorious service. Gilman transferred to the commissary of subsistence department and served the remainder of his long career until his retirement in 1895. He died at Manhattan Beach, New York on August 25, 1909.[14]

By Monday, May 27, Colonel Brown had completed and armed Batteries Lincoln and Cameron, the former with two 10-inch siege mortars and one 8-inch sea coast howitzer, and the latter with two 10-inch columbiads. He planned to arm Battery Scott, located on the point of the island just south of the fort, with two 10-inch columbiads. He had completed a camp three-quarters of a mile east of the fort where two of the companies of regular infantry were stationed. On that Monday, the sailing schooner *J. N. Genin* arrived from New York with ordnance and provisions and recent newspapers. Brown wrote to the adjutant general that he was incensed by a report he read in the *New York Herald* quoting Quartermaster General Meigs saying that Fort Pickens was now secure from all possible attacks. If the quartermaster general had made that statement, Brown argued, he was notoriously incorrect because that might prevent further shipments of arms and munitions which would doubtless have been sent had the fort's actual condition been accurately reported. He repeated his concerns about Captain McKean's order removing the steamers from the island. "If ships are to be taken away by every commander who accidentally touches here, then a force

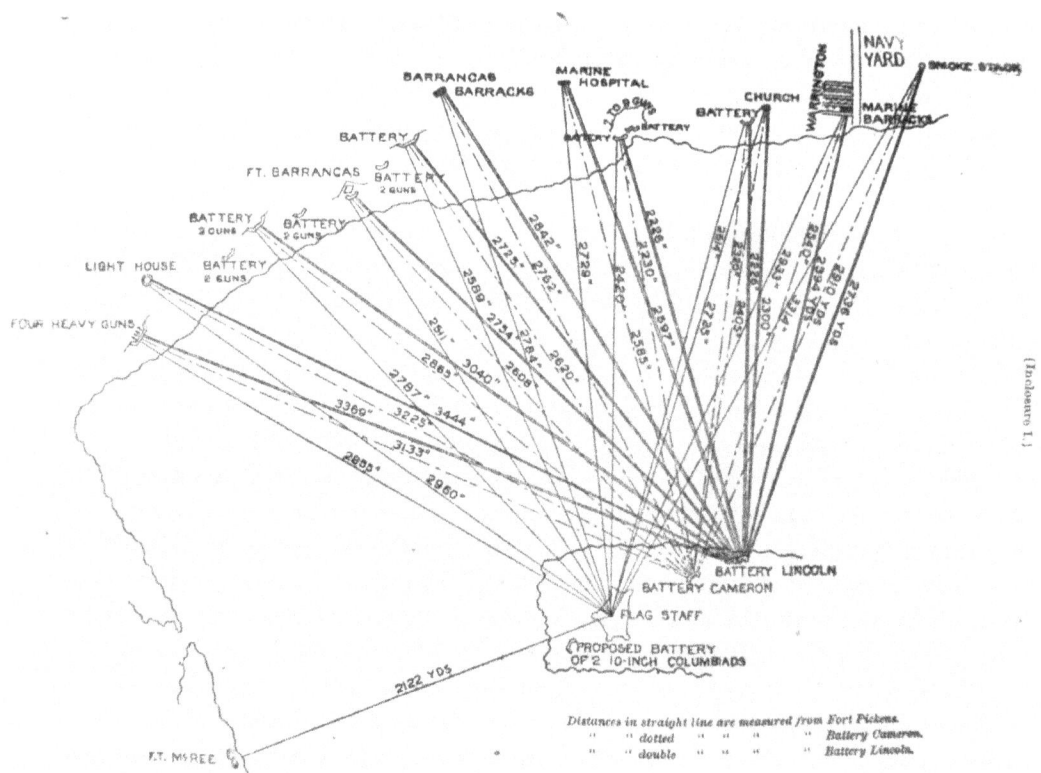

Pensacola Bay Artillery Ranges Plot. From *Official Records*, artillery ranges from Fort Pickens and the batteries on Santa Rosa Island to the forts and batteries on the mainland and Perdido Key (Official Records, U.S. War Department).

sufficiently large to hold the island should be sent but, under the existing conditions, I think the ships are preferable." He added that he had received no dispatches or instructions from the War Department at Washington since his departure from the capital city the first week in April. Brown wrote to McKean arguing that sailing vessels off Fort Pickens could not give adequate support on account of the difficulty of moving them in the shallow waters off the island, their inability to lie close inshore, and their projectiles consisting mainly of solid shot. Yet, in appreciation of the importance of establishing the blockade at Mobile and New Orleans, and intercepting vessels carrying arms from Europe, he would interpose no objection to the departure of *Niagara* after the arrival of *St. Louis*, provided *Mohawk* remained to guard the eastern entrance to Santa Rosa Sound. He also wanted *Wyandotte* and *Water Witch* to remain with *Huntsville* to blockade Pensacola Harbor and support the fort. He asked McKean to order Porter to return *Oriental*, the schooner Brown had chartered and loaned to the navy "which in so extraordinary a manner he took without my knowledge or consent." McKean, anxious to get on with the more important issue of putting in place an effective blockade of the two major ports of the Confederacy on the gulf, agreed to all Brown's conditions.[15]

At Washington Secretary of War Simon Cameron was overwhelmed with the details and complications involved in trying to raise, organize, house, supply, arm, and field two major armies, one within sight of the Capitol under Brigadier General Irwin McDowell, and another in the West at St. Louis under Major General John Charles Frémont. Cameron was an adept politician and manipulator but he was at a loss trying to perform as a departmental administrator and a cabinet secretary. He became suddenly aware of, and then responsive to, Colonel Harvey Brown's repeated complaints about reinforcements, support, and lack of communication. The situation at Fort Pickens was a distant and isolated event the former Pennsylvania senator could concentrate on. Writing to the adjutant general, Cameron ordered an expedition to further reinforce Fort Pickens. Steamers were to be purchased to take aboard a regiment of troops. Cameron directed Colonel James Ripley, chief of ordnance, to ensure a battery of English Whitworth guns, recently received by the government as a gift, was sent; all the 42-pounders that could be made ready in time; all the 30-pounders and 10-pounders at Governor's Island in New York Harbor; ammunition for all of them; lumber for forty or fifty gun platforms; thirty 9-inch naval guns; and all the ordnance stores, materials, and other items called for thus far by Colonel Brown which were to be readied at the earliest possible moment. One hundred thousand sandbags, a complete set of heavy wheels with slings, gins, and other equipment needed for moving heavy guns in the soft sand of Santa Rosa Island with their ropes, blocks, and cartridge bags were to go. As an afterthought, the secretary added all the sea coast mortars that could be got ready by the time the vessels sailed from New York or Boston. Fort Pickens appeared to be in danger for want of ordnance long since called for, the secretary wrote. Where the error was, the department did not intend to inquire. The important need was to deal with the questions at hand and to spare no exertion and no resource of the government to bring Fort Pickens out of its hazardous condition. Cameron wrote to Secretary Welles requesting those thirty 9-inch naval guns with carriages and implements and as many shells as could be supplied on short notice. He had learned the navy had the guns at Portsmouth Navy Yard and he would send a chartered steamer to get them if Welles would make them available. He intended to send out no less than ten large steamers, he wrote Welles, each armed with three or four guns. He would like to have some sailors under the command of capable navy officers on each of the steamers to work the guns if needed, and to assist in landing and setting them up when the expedition arrived at Santa Rosa Island. The steamers, their merchant officers, and civilian crews would be provided under charter using War Department funds. "In this," he closed, "the War Department will depend on the Navy, which is earnestly invited to secure the holding of Fort Pickens, whose military and political importance just now cannot be exaggerated." Cameron was leaping into the Fort Pickens situation with enthusiasm and was apparently unaware of the extensive efforts on the part of the Navy Department and his own War Department that were already taking place. In response to Secretary Cameron's request, Secretary Welles wrote to Captain Andrew Harwood, chief of the Navy's Bureau of Ordnance and Hydrography, to have the 9-inch guns from the old U.S.S. *Franklin's* battery furnished with carriages, equipment, and shells and to hold them at the Portsmouth Navy Yard ready to turn over to the War Department for immediate shipment to Fort Pickens. Colonel Brown reported to the adjutant general the merchant steamer *Suwanee* had arrived from Key West with Lieutenant Closson's Company F, 1st Artillery, and 12,000 gunny sacks which he would use for sandbags to complete his defensive works.[16]

On Saturday, June 1, Colonel Brown discovered he had mounted so many guns within Fort Pickens and the batteries outside that he did not have sufficient officers to fight them. He wrote to the adjutant general and asked for additional officers, mentioning that some of his command were probably due for promotion and some, he predicted accurately, might be ordered away. He would not consider himself at liberty to permit an officer to leave should he receive orders to do so, he wrote, unless another arrived. The safety of his command would be jeopardized otherwise. Three or four companies of regulars would be highly desirable as reinforcements, he added. Brown was either ignoring or unaware of the desperate straights the government was in trying to put together two massive field armies in the North. Trained and disciplined regulars, he continued, would be preferable to a large number of raw troops unless he were to receive enough to enable him to cross to the mainland and attack the Confederate fortifications there. Raw levies under decent officers would be useful for one bloody assault, relying on their enthusiasm and their ignorance. As it were, he could act only on the defensive with less than 5,000 new men, and the energies of his command would be exhausted in just feeding that number. Besides, he cautioned, the hot and sickly season was approaching and Northern levies would not be efficient for hard service in this climate. As it was, he was keeping an army of many thousands on the other side from operating elsewhere. If attacked, he would destroy the enemy, and if the government deemed it advisable to order him to attack, he would destroy the navy yard and inflict severe injury on Bragg's forces. However, he repeated, he had received no new instructions since he arrived at Fort Pickens and assumed command on April 16 and was still under orders to act only on the defensive. Off Santa Rosa Island the screw steamer U.S.S. *South Carolina*, Captain James Alden, dropped anchor and reported its arrival to the secretary of the navy. And Elise Bragg wrote to her husband she had heard fresh Federal troops had arrived at Fort Pickens to relieve Slemmer's men, the "scurvy patients, so there is no way of killing them that way."[17]

On Thursday, June 6, Captain Adams was still on station aboard *Sabine* and wondering about the confusing command relationship with Captain McKean who was his junior by twenty-seven years. Adams wrote to his friend, Captain Du Pont, that it seemed to him

Fort Pickens on Santa Rosa Island, seen from Fort Barrancas, with an unidentified U.S. Navy schooner (photograph by J.D. Edwards, Southern Historical Collection, Samuel Henry Lockett Papers, Wilson Library, University of North Carolina at Chapel Hill).

the heavy guns, mortars, military stores, and provisions would never cease arriving off Santa Rosa Island. The boat crews of his ships had to land them all because Captain McKean had come along and carried off *Brooklyn* and *Powhatan* for blockade duty at Mobile and the passes at the mouths of the Mississippi. Suddenly, however, the command situation had become even more muddied, it seemed to Adams, when Captain Mervine, commanding U.S.S. *Mississippi* at Key West, issued an announcement of his assumption of overall command of the Gulf Blockading Squadron. Mervine, at least, Adams wrote to Du Pont, was clearly Adams's senior, having entered the navy in 1809 and now had fifty-two years of service. On Saturday, June 16, Captain Adams received orders removing him from the confusing command situations that had developed in the Gulf of Mexico. *Sabine* sailed from the offing at Santa Rosa Island and after a stormy passage of eighteen days arrived at her home port at Portsmouth, New Hampshire, on July 4. Navy paymasters made right the loans from the ship's officers that had kept the vessel in provisions when regular funds ran out. The crew's savings were returned so that gunner Cronin and his mates were able to have their grand ball after all.[18]

From Fort Pickens Colonel Brown again wrote to the adjutant general reporting the arrival of *Star of the West, South Carolina,* and *Mississippi* with guns, howitzers, ammunition, hay and oats, twenty mules with carts, and other stores. He respectfully alluded to the fact he was still under orders to act only on the defensive unless attacked and he had received no further instructions from the War Department during the time he had been at this post and in command of the Department of Florida. The relationship between the seceded states and his country, he wrote, had changed since the date of his orders due to the bombardment and capitulation of Fort Sumter and the subsequent Confederate government's declaration of war, so that he no longer felt any obligation to confine himself to defensive measures should he, when ready, deem it to the advantage and honor of the United States for him to act offensively, believing such would be the wishes of the government. On Friday, June 14, Brown complained to the adjutant general he had been kept in such ignorance as to the future designs and intentions of the government respecting operations in his department, and whether anything beyond simply holding Fort Pickens was intended, that he had not felt at liberty to give his views on any topic other than holding where he was. There was, however, one subject he felt important enough to submit to the government. The weather on Pensacola Bay was now extremely hot and would become unhealthy to northern men exposed to the miasmas of the swamps. He would not throw a large body of troops into Fort Pickens until after the September gales were over and the severe weather had begun to abate. If the government intended offensive operations, the harbor had to be occupied by a naval force first. The rebel batteries on the mainland were numerous and so advantageously placed as to preclude entrance by major ships except at great cost and loss of life. He suggested, as an alternative, that steam-powered boats drawing no more than four and a half feet of water and carrying two or three rifled guns be used to gain entrance to the bay. There were two ways to do this. One was to enter through the main channel, hugging Santa Rosa Island under the cover of the heavy guns of Fort Pickens. The other was to come through the channel at the eastern end of Santa Rosa Island and arrive at the bay after traversing forty miles of Santa Rosa Sound along the northern shore of the island. The boats, whichever method they chose for entering, could lie out of range of the batteries on the mainland. Since the Confederates had no floating force of any significance in the bay, these boats could effectively cut off supplies and reinforcements to the Confederate forces by water and prevent the major threat to Fort Pickens, the crossing of an assault force in small boats in the dark of night to make a lodgment east the fort on Santa Rosa Island. Fort McRee, he added, was vulnerable, sitting as it did exposed on the eastern tip of Perdido Key. With 500 good troops more than he had now, and with the cooperation of the navy, he was confident he could reduce it in a few days time.[19]

On Tuesday, June 18, Colonel Brown wrote to Captain McKean that, on the day of the captain's arrival off Santa Rosa Island, he had sent a copy of the April 1 order of the president requiring all officers of the army and navy to whom the order was shown to aid the expedition by every means in their power. The expedition referred to, Brown reminded McKean, was the one which he commanded following his orders to reinforce and hold Fort Pickens. Brown complained he had made several requisitions upon McKean which had not been complied with. He was now respectfully asking whether McKean considered the order of the president of the United States to be binding on him and, if he did, whether it was up to Brown or to McKean to judge the necessity of the requested aid. From *Niagara* offshore McKean replied immediately by asking that he be informed what requisitions had been made and how they had been made, as he was ignorant of them. He assured Brown he did consider instructions from the president obligatory unless he should have received different orders of a later date from the Navy Department, it being inferred that the secretary of the navy would be cognizant of the earlier order of the president. He was not only willing, McKean added, but anxious to render all aid in his power to Brown and the garrison of Fort Pickens. He did suggest, however, that all future applications for aid be put in writing. McKean concluded by asking Brown what position *Niagara* could take to make it able to render the most efficient aid in case of an attack on the fort. The following day Brown replied that he was happy to learn the naval commander now considered the instructions of the president obligatory but he questioned whether orders of the secretary of the navy superseded those of the president unless expressly worded to that effect. Brown wrote that the order of the president had been signed in his presence and he happened to know the secretary of the navy was not cognizant of it. The requisitions which had not been complied with, Brown wrote, were those having to do with the withdrawal of the steamers *Brooklyn* and *Powhatan* against his solemn protest and the representations of his engineering officer, Major Tower. *Niagara* and *Water Witch* had sailed away the next day, *St. Louis* did not arrive for several days, *Wyandotte* was not there, *Mohawk* was guarding the eastern end of Santa Rosa Sound forty miles away, and Fort Pickens had been left with only the now-departed sailing frigate *Sabine* to guard the island and the steamer *Huntsville* to enforce the blockade of Pensacola Harbor. It was true, Brown admitted, that no landing had been attempted by the Confederate forces during this time but McKean's actions presented no evidence of concern at leaving the island unprotected. Further, while he had been on station, Captain Adams had placed at his disposal a boat with two crews for patrolling the harbor and the bay shore of Santa Rosa Island. On leaving for the North, Adams had withdrawn the boat crews. Brown claimed he had made repeated attempts through McKean's officers to have the crews replaced. Consequently he had not been able to continue the boat patrols which common prudence seemed to demand. He did not wish to appear unreasonable and he was not insensitive to the benefits his command had received thus far from the navy, he wrote. He was only asking for what he considered necessary and to which, under the instructions of the president of the United States and the commander-in-chief of the army and navy, he had a right. His command was a responsible one, he lectured McKean, not only of itself but in a national aspect since the honor of the nation now was vested in the preservation of Fort Pickens after the surrender of Fort Sumter. In compliance with McKean's request, he then put his applications in writing. Brown wanted McKean to place his vessels in a position to prevent a landing of the enemy on Santa Rosa Island, leaving the specific locations to McKean's judgment. McKean was to station a small steamer, as he was now doing, at the eastern end of the island to guard the entrance to Santa Rosa Sound there. He was to provide crews and facilities for unloading arriving vessels which, Brown admitted, had always been done to his entire satisfaction. Also, McKean was to send a quartermaster to live in the fort who was familiar with the signals to ensure that communication between the fort and the ships took place. Brown concluded, having harmoniously received the cooperation and assistance of the navy under Captain Adams, it would not be his fault if the same harmony did not continue. McKean, fuming at the tone and content of Brown's letter, wrote that, on his arrival off Santa Rosa Island, he had sent ashore Lieutenant John Guest, his executive officer on *Niagara,* to meet Brown and to point out that McKean's orders required him to proceed to put in place the blockade at Mobile and New Orleans. In the event of need, Guest had assured Brown, a steamer could be sent to McKean and he could return from Mobile in a matter of hours. Lieutenant Guest had informed McKean that Brown made no objection to this and, as a result, McKean had so proceeded. He corrected Brown's statement that he now considered the instructions of the president as obligatory by writing that he considered them no more obligatory now than he did at any time in the past, nor did he consider them in conflict with specific orders of the Navy Department that he immediately blockade Mobile and New Orleans. In response to Brown's written applications, he would keep a sufficient naval force available to prevent a landing by the enemy on Santa Rosa Island and he would send two crews to man the patrol boats left by Adams. He was fully sensitive, he concluded, to the importance attached by the government to the safety of Fort Pickens and repeated that he desired to render all aid he could without reducing the efficiency of the vessels he commanded. He regretted any differences of opinion or any misunderstanding between the two of them on the subject. Brown and McKean were both aware that their correspondence was official and, as such, would be copied and forwarded and reviewed by superiors who were not on the scene. The written record, no matter how minute or tiresome, had to be complete. In this, Brown was unwilling to concede the last word on the subject to the navy. He wrote to McKean that he would, without hesitation, ask for assistance whenever the wants of the service at Fort Pickens required under McKean's assurance it would cheerfully be tendered and, in return, any assistance he could give the navy would gladly be provided.[20]

A few days earlier a fugitive slave had made his way to Santa Rosa Island and was brought to Brown. The man had been employed by his master as a pilot in the harbor. He was familiar with currents, tides, shifting sand bars, and such. He told Brown that, of the hulks the Confederates had sink in the channel, one, a dredging boat, had drifted ashore and the other, a brig, had broken up. The half-sunk dry dock did not at all obstruct the channel, having settled a good twenty yards from it. The man reported a large floating battery had been build in pieces at Pensacola and brought to the navy yard where it was being assembled. Smallpox was raging among the forces on the mainland, he told Brown, and great sickness prevailed there, three or four men dying every day. Workers were removing material from the navy yard to Pensacola from where it was being shipped off by rail. Brown condensed all of this into his next report to the adjutant general in which he also asked for secret service funds to be spent at his discretion. His sick list, he wrote, was large, having upwards of ninety men on it, none serious. The men were suffering from hard work in the sun and surf, from having to sleep in damp casemates, and from having only impure water to drink. The island had gone more than six weeks without rain and one of the cisterns at the fort had leaked and lost its fresh water. What remained in the other cistern had to be used with great economy. Water for washing and cooking was being obtained by sinking wells in the sand. Since his arrival, he had lost three men to death, one of whom had been in an accident and the other two to disease. Referring to the twenty-one slaves brought from Dry Tortugas on *Atlantic,* Brown wrote that he would not return them to their masters, "as I will never be voluntarily instrumental in returning a poor wretch to slavery, but will hold them subject to orders." He asked for a powerful telescope. The garrison had several ordinary glasses but one of greater power would allow him to obtain valuable information by observing the movements of the enemy formations ashore.[21]

On Monday, September 2, Bragg's intent to block the channel to the harbor by moving and scuttling the dry dock at a more favorable location was completely frustrated by a boat expedition of twelve picked regulars from Fort Pickens under First Lieutenant Alexander Shipley which rowed out from the fort in darkness, boarded the huge wooden structure, set fires and explosives, and burned the dock to its waterline. The dock settled to the bottom where it had been anchored, leaving the channel into the bay unimpeded.[22]

Fort Pickens, casemate interiors, present day (photograph by the author).

On Sunday, June 23, Brown wrote to the adjutant general that the merchant steamer *Illinois* had returned with twenty-eight 9-inch Dahlgren guns, implements, and munitions. These were the guns asked for by Secretary of War Cameron and provided by Secretary Welles. The guns were the entire cargo *Illinois* carried and not one of the guns was wanted, Brown wrote, nor could they be used advantageously by the garrison at Fort Pickens. He would not touch the cargo but, having embarked Captain Hunt's company on board *Illinois* for the North as ordered, he would send the steamer to Dry Tortugas to be unloaded there. He asked that he be permitted, respectfully, to suggest the good of the service would be advanced by sending only those articles for which he had made requisition and which he wanted, not multitudes of articles which would only encumber the garrison. Captain Barry's company, he added, would embark for the North in about ten days on *Vanderbilt* which Brown had learned was on the way to him.[23]

On Thursday, July 4, Congress convened at Washington for the special session President Lincoln had called on April 15. The president sought advice and counsel on the issues suddenly facing the nation and the actions he had taken since the firing on Fort Sumter, many of which were irregular and done without congressional review or approval. He thought some kind of executive commentary would be in order regarding the situation at Fort Pickens as he had found it upon taking office. He informed Congress that an order had been sent at once for the landing of the troops under Captain Vogdes on *Brooklyn* off Santa Rosa Island. The first return from that message, received just one week before the surrender of Fort Sumter, was that Captain Adams, commanding the squadron as senior naval officer on station, had refused, acting under "some *quasi* armistice of the late administration," the existence of which the new administration, up to the time its order was dispatched, had only vague and uncertain rumors to call it to its attention. Subsequently Captain Vogdes's command had landed and had been reinforced several times over. Colonel Harvey Brown was now solidly in control of affairs on Santa Rosa Island.[24]

Captain Mervine, commanding the Gulf Blockading Squadron aboard the screw steamer *Mississippi,* wrote the secretary of the navy on Monday, July 8, that since his arrival off Santa Rosa Island on June 23, the crews of his flagship and *Niagara* had been employed from morning to night transferring army supplies from the transports offshore to the beach. The daily arrival of even more transports indicated there would be no cessation of this double duty for his officers and men. The demands of this effort excluded drilling in the exercises required to make the vessels efficient ships of war and converted them into mere appendages of the army. It appeared, Mervine continued, that the president had issued an order which authorized Colonel Brown to call upon the navy for aid, but at a time when Fort Pickens was in a defenseless condition. He could not believe the order was intended to be continued in force when the post was in a position to defy attack and was well supplied with men, scows, and large launches to the degree that, when manned by soldiers, the army could readily provide all the transportation the fort and its garrison needed. He would be pleased to hear form the secretary of the navy on the subject at the secretary's earliest convenience.[25]

10

"The Enemy Failed in All Objectives"

At Washington the adjutant general passed on to Colonel William B. Franklin on May 31 a request from the general-in-chief that Franklin ask the governor of New York to designate a regiment of three year volunteers from that state for a distant service which was not to be disclosed at this time. This request was in direct response to Secretary of War Cameron's sudden urge to take action in support of Colonel Brown and the security of Fort Pickens. Franklin was told in confidence that the destination was Fort Pickens. He was to oversee the inspection, mustering, and equipping of the regiment prior to its departure in order to ensure it was provided with everything necessary for its efficiency and comfort. The adjutant general wrote a confidential communication that was to be carried by hand to Colonel Brown informing him that a regiment of volunteers from New York was on the way to reinforce Fort Pickens which would then permit Brown to send Closson's company back to Key West. Further, the adjutant general ordered Brown to send Hunt's Company M, 2nd Artillery, with its battery of field guns, and Barry's Company A, 2nd Artillery, to Fort Hamilton, New York Harbor, for further assignment, and to detach Captain Clitz from his command, Company E, 3rd Infantry, and have him report to the War Department where he would be promoted to major and assigned to a new regiment. The adjutant general closed by saying he was forwarding ordnance supplies and provisions for 1,000 men for six months, a cargo of ice, and quartermaster's stores to Santa Rosa Island. The Federal adjutant general's orders to Brown to move regular army artillery companies and regular officers to the north, and Confederate Secretary Walker's earlier orders to Bragg, indicated that now both governments were beginning to concentrate their forces toward the more important theaters focused at Washington and Richmond in the East and St. Louis and the Mississippi Valley in the West.[1]

At New York Alderman William "Billy" Wilson, a Democrat, represented the city's 1st Ward. When President Lincoln issued the call for volunteers, Wilson opened a recruiting office at 618 Broadway on Thursday, April 25. Wilson advertised for volunteers to enlist in a regiment he intended to raise and by the end of the day he had signed 850 men into what would become the 6th Regiment, New York Volunteers, popularly known as Wilson's Zouave

Colonel William Wilson, U.S. Army, with the officers of his staff, commanded the 6th New York Infantry Regiment at Santa Rosa Island. They were known as "Wilson's Zouaves" (U.S. Army Military History Institute).

Battalion. Companies A, B, C, D, and E formed up and moved out to Staten Island into a camp of instruction at the Old Quarantine Grounds. Companies F, G, H, I, and K joined the regiment during the following month. Wilson would formally assume command of the regiment as its colonel on May 22.[2]

"Billy" Wilson was a character in New York politics who had "figured predominantly in almost every melee in our turbulent city Democracy, and is justly feared even by the strongest and boldest of the 'b'hoys.'" Wilson had made a name in his youth as a prize fighter and used those skills to get himself elected to, and then to lead the First Ward. He was usually able to call forth an unruly crowd of supporters who would resort to fists, bludgeons, knives, and even revolvers to help him retain his seat. During the 1856 aldermanic election, Wilson's followers had clashed all day long with the backers of another candidate, one McKean. Police reinforcements were called in from other wards and finally the reserve platoon from the police chief's office was required to quell the fighting between more than three hundred men, two of whom were shot in the fight, while "any quantity of eyes and noses were materially damaged." When President Lincoln called on the governors of the loyal states for 75,000 volunteers to put down the rebellion in the South on April 15, Wilson joined the wave of patriotic enthusiasm that swept the North. When the news was received that state militia units marching to the relief of Washington were attacked in Maryland, Wilson announced "that he would form a corps of 'roughs' to march through Baltimore." The volunteers were primarily local men who knew Wilson and in whom he had confidence. The men were organized into companies and elected their officers, captains and lieutenants, who were local political leaders well versed in New York City ward politics but totally inexperienced in anything having to do with military life.[3]

On Saturday. June 15, at New York all ten companies of the 6th Regiment assembled and were mustered into Federal service. The regiment packed up at the Old Quarantine Ground on Staten Island and marched to the steam ferry *Maryland* to cross over to Manhattan, officers and men at that time wearing the distinctive uniform Wilson had chosen for them, a gray shirt, gray pants, brown felt hat, and brogans, and carrying their recently issued .58 caliber rifled muskets. Many of the men also were armed with revolvers and with savage looking bowie knives. At the foot of 14th Street the regiment formed ranks and marched up 5th Avenue to No. 63 Chilton Place where a magnificent banner was presented to the officers of the regiment by the ladies of the regiment's relief committee. Forming platoon fronts, the 6th New York marched back down Broadway with its brass band at the head and a double line of cheering citizens along the sidewalks. At Pier No. 1 on North River, the volunteers, almost entirely from the city's 1st Ward, were lightered out to the merchant steamer *Vanderbilt* lying in the stream. During the parade down Broadway Colonel William "Billy" Wilson rode at the head of the regiment accompanied by the 6th New York's mascot, a goat also named "Billy." On Tuesday, June 25, *Vanderbilt* arrived off Santa Rosa Island and the 6th New York, under Colonel William Wilson, came ashore. Colonel Brown ordered the regiment of volunteers to a camp a mile to the east of the fort. The 6th New York's historian, a civilian raised in the city and used to the lower reaches of Manhattan, recorded his initial impressions of Santa Rosa Island:

> In the far south the tropical suns and rains assert their power, and these outlying sand ridges carry more or less of growth. So Santa Rosa Island, lying in the warm waters of the Gulf of Mexico, showed a good deal of scrub, and at its eastern end, some trees. Beside this, in its lagoons, the island possessed alligators, chameleons, lizards rather entertaining then otherwise, and a lively population of moccasin and rattle snakes. Add to this the fact that the water, being sea water filtered through the sand, was productive of intestinal troubles, and that the suns glared down alike on the white sand and blue water, and whichever of them a man looked upon his tired eyes wished he had looked upon the other, it is easy to see that the lives of the 6th were not altogether cast in pleasant places, and that a position in a good brigade in a marching army, engaged in operations, would have been far preferred to such a monstrosity as Santa Rosa Island in 1861.[4]

Similarly, a Southern cavalry officer on an scout locally added his impressions of Santa Rosa Island at that season, writing, "the suns rays were so fierce that the dry sandy soil glowed with scorching heat." Although considered strategically import by both sides, neither thought the place to be in any way hospitable.[5]

The day following the arrival of Wilson's regiment, Colonel Brown vented his anger and frustration in a letter to the adjutant general. Hunt's and Barry's companies of regulars had been taken from him and now he had a regiment of New York City volunteers on his hands. When, after repeated applications and entreaties for more regular officers, his strong presentations on the need for more regular companies, and his declaration that volunteers would only embarrass him and that none be sent, his applications, entreaties, and presentations had been ignored. "Nine of my officers, one-third of my whole number, and two artillery companies are taken from me, and a regiment of undrilled New York City volunteers entirely undisciplined, are sent to me. I can only attribute this to a want of confidence in my judgment, or of disbelief in, and disregard to, my urgent and repeated representations of the wants and necessities of this fort." He reported Battery Lincoln was completed and armed and Battery Scott had its final 10-inch columbiad mounted and serviceable. Not having officers and trained men to serve the guns, he had ordered one of the regular artillery companies from Dry Tortugas to Fort Pickens and had sent Companies B and E of the 6th New York there to take its place.[6]

Colonel Brown wrote again to the adjutant general on Wednesday, July 10, that volunteers and raw recruits might be useful to him as infantry but they were of no value at Fort Pickens other than as guards or for fatigue duty. An artillery soldier could not be improvised in a day, he decreed, thus the New York volunteers he had received were not of the slightest use in manning the guns and defending the forts. He repeated his request for regular artillery officers and at least four regular artillery companies. If these additional companies could not be sent, he asked that the officers absent from the companies presently under his command be sent instead, stating he had only thirteen officers, exactly half the number he needed. When the transports *Vanderbilt* and *State of Georgia* were unloaded, he continued, he would have shot and shell for four days bombardment. What course, he asked, should he then pursue? Should he remain on the defensive, or should he open with his batteries upon the enemy? The reasons for continuing to act on the defensive were, first, his instructions were to do so and, having called the attention of the War Department to this three or four times, no other instructions had been forthcoming; second, he was heavily outnumbered but the enemy was holding 8,000 men on the mainland to watch his 1,800; third, if Bragg attacked first and failed, his defeat would be disgraceful and fatal to his cause; fourth, the Federals gained more and lost less by delay than Bragg. Alternatively,

Fort Barrancas and water battery, present day (photograph by the author).

he continued, reasons for opening upon the enemy with his batteries were, first, the effect on morale which such a bombardment would have on the country; second, the great amount of ammunition the Confederates would consume in responding to a Federal bombardment which they could ill afford; third, the destruction and demoralization of the Confederate troops on the mainland who were but raw levies; and, finally, the prestige to be gained by the beleaguered garrison in turning on and attacking superior numbers. Brown then proceeded to talk himself out of any different course than the one he had assumed on his arrival on the island. Were he to resort to offensive operations, he wrote, first, he did not have the offices and men to carry them out effectively and vigorously; second, he could not follow up a successful bombardment with a crossing and an attack on the navy yard at this time, and Bragg would probably claim a victory over the Federal forces were the bombardment not followed by some exterior moves; fourth, there would be extensive damage to the navy yard that might not be wise in the view of the future operations desired by the government; and fifth, he was within eight days of the War Department by steamer and, if offensive operations were desired, he should have been so instructed by this time. Brown concluded that, having read in a newspaper that he was about to be relieved, he reluctantly had come to the conclusion it was his duty to continue to act on the defensive until the pleasure of the government was made known to him.[7]

Brown's frustration boiled over the following day, Thursday, July 11, on receipt of an order from the adjutant general taking more officers from him. A few weeks prior, he wrote to the adjutant general, Barry's and Hunt's companies had been ordered away and a regiment of raw, undisciplined recruits "from the purlieus of New York" had been sent to him. Now Captain Samuel Chalfin had received an order transferring him from command of Company F, 1st Artillery, and Captain Harvey Allen had been notified he had been dropped from the army list. He was left, Brown complained, in the most important post in the nation with an entirely inadequate command. If there was a designed purpose to sacrifice him, he could not be treated worse. It was true that there was no present threat as Bragg did not want to fight and he, Brown, could not, but an accident or an impudence of an individual on either side might at any moment bring on a battle he would have to fight under every possible disadvantage. Under the orders received from the adjutant general this day, he would be left with one officer at each of Batteries Lincoln and Cameron, two at Battery Scott, and, exclusive of staff officers, four line officers in Fort Pickens when he should have twenty-eight. Was that right, he asked? Was it fair to place an officer in such a situation when surrounded by an enemy ten times his number? Officers were promoted to the companies at Fort Pickens but none came. They were promoted from the companies at the fort and all went. If the remaining officers who were deserving of and overdue for promotion received what they had every right to expect and were ordered away, he expected to be left with no officers at all. However, he pledged, if worse came to worst, he had made up his mind never to surrender the fort and he would leave this letter as testimony of the reason why it was not gloriously victorious.[8]

In sharp contrast to his letter to the adjutant general, on Friday, July 12, Brown wrote to Quartermaster General Meigs that, by the time the letter reached him at Washington, Fort Pickens would be in complete readiness. He presumed no fort in the United States was ever better prepared for offensive or defensive operations if properly manned, which it was not by half. But he had received no orders, no instructions. His officers were taken from him and he was left helpless. "Where there is a will, there is a way, and I have the will, but am still under orders to act only on the defensive."[9]

Brown's complaints must have seemed justified to him, sitting as he was more than a week away from army headquarters and feeling ignored and forgotten. During his forty-three years service in the army, Brown had an active and successful career culminating in the approval of his selection for the Fort Pickens mission by the president himself. The importance of holding Fort Pickens had been accentuated by that personal order from the commander-in-chief of the army and the navy to all officers of both services to whom the order was shown to give instant and unquestioned obedience to his needs. This, of itself, made Brown, at this point in time, one of the more powerful officers in the military or naval services of the nation. But to Brown, from the moment he stepped ashore on Santa Rosa Island, it seemed that a heavy curtain had been drawn behind him closing him off from the rest of the nation. Now navy officers were opposing him or giving reluctant cooperation and the War Department seemed to have forgotten his name other than to send him orders taking away critically needed artillery officers and trained gunners. In his self-pity, Brown did not acknowledge that he was isolated from the major changes that were taking place in the nation and the immense pressures that were being brought to bear on the War Department and the administration to whom Fort Pickens and Pensacola Bay had become relatively a sideshow. After the surrender of Sumter and President Lincoln's call for volunteers from the loyal states of the North to put down the rebellion of the Southern states, the remaining slave-holding states of the South began their own processes of secession, Virginia in April, Arkansas and North Carolina in May, and Texas in June. Now eleven contiguous states stood united in rebellion against the Federal authority in Washington, determined to achieve sovereignty. A Confederate army was gathering and increasing in force daily in northern Virginia, a mere twenty-six miles from the national Capitol itself, and Brigadier General Irwin McDowell was forming a Federal army at Washington and in the camps and fortifications surrounding it, intending to take the field within a week. The Lincoln administration was newly formed, barely used to functioning together, and the War Department was riddled with resignations and desertions as senior officers and experienced clerical staff left to join the Confederacy. Brown seemed unaware of this and the War Department seemed too busy to tell him.

Among the forces gathering under General McDowell was Slemmer's former command, the reorganized Company G, 1st Artillery, now equipped with one 30-pounder cannon and two 20-pounder rifled guns and commanded by First Lieutenant John Edwards. On Wednesday, July 17, McDowell's divisions took to the roads marching in the direction of the Confederate forces under General Beauregard concentrated near the railroad junction at Manassas, Virginia, and formed along the banks of Bull Run. Company G went into action during some preliminary skirmishing at Blackburn's Ford and on Thursday, July 18, the command fired the opening shots across Bull Run in the first major battle of the war.[10]

Bull Run was a disaster. McDowell's poorly organized and barely disciplined Federals, almost entirely volunteers with mere months in uniform, went against Confederate forces of the same condition and quality on Sunday, July 21, and were defeated. The Federal regimens broke and fled. The long lines of tired, dirty, hungry, confused, and frustrated men did not stop until they reached the safety of the camps and forts around the capital.

The city and the government were saved from capture by the same disorder, thirst, fatigue, hunger, confusion, and frustration that existed among the victorious Confederates. President Lincoln called his cabinet into session as soon as the news of the disaster at Bull Run reached the city.[11]

On Monday, July 22, even while anticipating the sight of Confederate banners which might soon appear on the ridges of northern Virginia just across the Potomac River from his office at the Navy Department, Secretary Welles took time to reply to Captain Mervine's letter of July 8, writing that he had brought Mervine's concerns to the president's attention during an interview and had discussed the order given to Colonel Brown on April 1 that required compliance with Brown's wishes by all officers of the army and navy. The exigency which had been the cause for the order had passed, Welles wrote, and therefore any demand on the navy for labor or services that did not properly belong to it was no longer valid and Mervine was to consider himself and his command relieved therefrom. Welles added that Mervine had mentioned three negro slaves who had fled from the mainland to *Huntsville*. While it was not the policy of the government to invite or encourage this type of desertion from the enemy, for the present Mervine could let the men remain on *Huntsville* and employ them as usefully as possible.[12]

Off Pensacola Harbor on Saturday, August 3, lookouts at the mastheads of the vessels off Pensacola Bay called Captain Mervine's attention to workers making major modifications to a schooner lying at the navy yard on the mainland. Rumors had come out that the vessel, the steamer *William P. Judah*, was being fitted out as a privateer and, on completion of her work, would attempt to slip out of the harbor and sail in the gulf as a Confederate commerce raider. Mervine had learned she was to be armed with a powerful pivot gun and four broadside guns. He ordered a cutting out expedition for that night. The first and second cutters of his flagship, *Colorado*, and the first and second cutters of McKean's vessel, *Niagara*, were armed and manned under the direct command of Captain Theodorus Bailey of *Colorado*. The four boats rowed silently in darkness at midnight into the harbor undetected under the guns of Forts McRee and Barrancas to the far end of the navy yard wharf. Bailey ordered his cutter to close with the schooner, the other boats lying off a short distance. The small flotilla was challenged by a sentry on the shore who, without firing his musket, ran to the guard house at the end of the wharf. The alarm was sounded and guards turned out. Lights appeared in several gun emplacements ashore. Bailey deemed further demonstration on his part in the face of what appeared to be overwhelming force would be useless and ordered the cutters back to the ships. Mervine reported the incident to the secretary of the navy and mentioned his surprise at the absence of any discharge of ordnance by the Confederates. He surmised this to be due to their being taken unaware and having been unprepared. He considered the lack of gunfire fortunate, he wrote, because "in view of the boastful spirit of the rebels, had they fired, our retreat would doubtless have been magnified into an overwhelming defeat." The following day the Confederate command moved all vessels at the navy yard inside the wharf and mounted several guns in new locations at the yard. Captain Mervine had his officers continue to study what was taking place. He was not finished with that steamer.[13]

On August 22, Mervine reported to the secretary of the navy the schooner *Aid* had been intercepted and sunk by *Niagara* at the eastern entrance to Santa Rosa Sound. As long as the hulk remained in the water, it would obstruct egress and ingress at that pass which would allow Mervine to dispense with *Wyandotte* which had been stationed there. He ordered the screw steamer to New York for long overdue repairs. *Wyandotte* had been part of the Fort Pickens saga from the beginning. Later in the month, toward evening one day, the steamer *Judah* was reported moving toward the channel on a course to take her into the gulf. Prior to the attempt to cut out and destroy her earlier in the month, Mervine had informed Colonel Brown the vessel was armed and equipped to serve as a commerce raider. Brown had warned Bragg he would fire on the vessel if it attempted to leave Pensacola Bay. Volunteers of Company I, 6th New York, had been assigned to help the regular artillery gunners at Battery Cameron. As *Judah* approached the point of Santa Rosa Island, the battery's guns were brought to bear and one round was fired by Sergeant Jacob Theberath of the 6th New York. *Judah* quickly came about and returned to the navy yard.[14]

On Sunday, September 1, the organization and abstract from the field return of the Confederate forces at Pensacola under Bragg's command, aggregate present and absent, indicated 6,546 men present for duty.[15]

On Monday, September 9, Captain Mervine and Colonel Brown met and worked out a plan to attack Fort McRee the following night with a force of 300 soldiers, sailors, and marines. Mervine hand-picked the naval contingent and even had a special fuse developed with which to ignite a powder charge to blow in the fort's gate. Captain Bailey, of the cutting out attempt on *Judah,* was designated to command the naval contingent. Mervine had himself rowed ashore to Fort Pickens in order to work out the final details of the assault but, upon his arrival, Brown told him he had conferred with his officers and had decided not to make the attempt, its result being uncertain and the effects of a possible repulse disastrous.[16]

On that same Monday night, a boat from the mainland manned by nine Confederate marines rowed over to Santa Rosa Island where the men gave themselves up to the Federals. They all claimed to be Northern men stranded at New Orleans by the commencement of the war who had joined the Confederate Marine Corps either out of economic need or coercion. They had taken the first opportunity offered to escape to Santa Rosa Island in hopes of being sent on to their homes in the North. The marines gave Colonel Brown a detailed account of Bragg's strength and organization. The same day two citizens arrived on the island. They were contractors who had been supplying local sawmills with logs and had stayed in the country hoping to get the money due on their old contracts. For eighteen weeks they had been living in Milton, about thirty miles up the bay. They told Brown that there were other loyal men in the country but that voicing Union sentiments was quite dangerous. Brown agreed to keep the men at Fort Pickens until they could be sent north on one of the returning transports.[17]

Captain Mervine was chafing at the disappointment he felt after Colonel Brown called off the proposed joint attack on Fort McRee for what Mervine considered unacceptable reasoning. Mervine had not forgotten the schooner *Judah*. His officers had kept the steamer under observation at long range since its aborted attempt to slip out of the harbor on August 25. Mervine decided to launch an aggressive action on his own, this time relying only on naval forces entirely under his command. On Friday, September 13, four days after Brown had called off the assault on Fort McRee, he organized another cutting out expedition, this one commanded by Lieutenant John Russell of *Colorado.* Two sections of boats manned by sailors and marines would make the attempt, one led by Russell to attack the steamer directly, while another under Lieutenant John G. Sprotson and Midshipman Tecumseh Steece, also of *Colorado,* would go ashore and spike the guns at the southeastern end of the navy yard wharf that might interfere with the withdrawal of the other sections. The boats left *Colorado* about midnight and arrived off the navy yard at 3:30 A.M. They had counted on surprise which had worked in their favor during the earlier attempt but this time it was not to be. The crew of *Judah* was alert and waiting for something. The Southern sailors poured a volley of musketry into the approaching boats. Federal sailors and marines managed to fight their way aboard the steamer and drive its crew onto the wharf where it was joined by guards from the navy yard. Assistant Engineer White and coal heaver Patrick Driscoll, both of *Colorado,* set fires in several places in the cabin and the hold of the vessel. The raiders returned to their boats and rowed away as quickly as possible under heavy musket fire from the wharf. *Judah* burned to the water line and was cut adrift from the wharf. She drifted, settled, and then sank opposite Fort Barrancas. Meanwhile, Lieutenant Sprotson and gunner's mate John Horton, after an extensive search in the darkness ashore, finally were able to find the guns they were to spike. Midshipman Steece had taken the rest of his party to help the men attacking the steamer. A single sentry was guarding the guns. The man leveled his musket at Sprotson but was immediately shot in the head by Horton. The main gun, a 10-inch columbiad, was spiked and, taking the gun's tampion as a souvenir, the two returned to their boat. The small flotilla reassembled off the navy yard. On Russell's order, the crews fired six charges of canister from the boats' howitzers in the general direction of the navy yard and then made for their home vessels All returned at daylight with no interference as they passed Forts Barrancas and McRee. The raid was not without loss to the assaulting force. The first man to board *Judah* was John Smith, a marine who had lost the white cloth armband that was meant to distinguish him as one of the expedition members. Smith was bayoneted by another marine who mistook him in the darkness as one of *Judah's* crew in the darkness. Two sailors were killed by musket fire from the crosstrees above the deck as the boats approached the steamer, two more were mortally wounded, and nine were severely wounded. Four officers were slightly wounded. Southern losses were three dead.[18]

On Saturday, September 29, Captain William Mervine received orders that had been issued at the Navy Department on September 6, over three weeks earlier, to turn over command of the Gulf Blockading Squadron to Captain McKean and to report personally to New York for further assignment. Secretary Welles was becoming disenchanted with many of his senior naval officers who, to him, were too steeped in protocol and administration. He had not yet received the report on the cutting out expedition against *Judah* but it is questionable whether learning of that would have stayed his hand. He wanted more from the commander of the Gulf Blockading Squadron than the destruction of a small steamer in Pensacola Harbor. He wanted energy and initiative. Mervine was appointed president of the Navy Retiring Board at New York where he served for the remainder of the war. Welles ordered Captain William McKean to assume command of the Gulf Blockading Squadron.[19]

On Friday, October 1, Mr. Charles H. Moore, on behalf of the insurance underwriters of New York City, wrote to Secretary of War Cameron that reports of the cutting out expedition against *Judah* at Pensacola Harbor had mentioned that no guns had been fired from Fort Pickens. Moore wondered whether at any time the batteries of the fort might have destroyed *Judah* as she lay at the navy yard wharf. He referred to further reports that mechanics were finishing work on the reconstruction and re-fitting of *Fulton* which lay on the ways at the navy yard within range of the guns of the fort. Colonel Brown, Moore wrote, was referring to old orders to act only on the defensive and Moore begged to call the attention of the secretary to the inconsistency of the United States Navy acting offensively at Pensacola Bay while the United States Army was held strictly to the defensive on the same ground and at the same time. "Whether Colonel Brown already had sufficient liberty by his orders to use his discretion, or whether he needs some prompting to insure cooperation with the navy officers — often a difficult thing between Army and Navy — or whether another officer would be better at that place, we of course leave wholly to the government." He and his colleagues were deeply interested that no effort by either the army or the navy be omitted to prevent privateers from being built or fitted out to prey on the nation's commerce which they, his colleagues and himself, were insuring.[20]

The following day, unaware of Mr. Moore's letter to the secretary of war and probably stung by the successful cutting out expedition the navy had conducted, Colonel Brown proposed to Captain McKean on *Niagara* and to Captain Bailey on *Colorado* a combined bombardment of the navy yard and the rebel batteries on the mainland. Brown suggested opening fire on a day when the wind would seem fair for a general conflagration of the buildings at the navy yard. Bailey informed Brown he should plan to open fire as soon as possible since he in *Colorado* and McKean in *Niagara* had been ordered away on blockade duty. Brown indicated that no former time had been so favorable to initiate an attack as the present. From information he had just received, he told the navy officers, some of the best troops ashore had been sent to Virginia which meant that Bragg was thus weak in quantity as well as quality. Brown based much of his assumption on Bragg's not having responded to the firing of the dry dock and the burning of *Judah*. He invited McKean and Bailey to cooperate in whatever manner they thought might be advisable. Brown further proposed attacking and carrying Fort McRee by assault after having silenced its batteries by gunfire from Santa Rosa Island. McKean could then have the vessels of the squadron run into the harbor under the protection of the fire from the island. Provided the naval vessels were able to force the entrance to the harbor, Brown would furnish 300 men for the landing and assault on the navy yard and the land batteries. He was sure, at a minimum, that this combined force could take and hold the navy yard until reinforcements were sent from the North. He did allow in his correspondence with McKean that the idea of the vessels of the squadron entering the harbor under the protection of the fire from the forts and the vessels offshore had originated, not with himself, but with Captain Bailey. If the attempt were to be made, Brown urged, the sooner it was done, the better. This proposal, however, as was the case with Colonel Brown's other proposals for action, did not materialize.[21]

At Richmond on Sunday, October 5, Judah P. Benjamin was named to replace Leroy Pope Walker as secretary of war in the Confederate government. Benjamin wrote to Bragg, addressing the noble and self-sacrificing spirit displayed by Bragg and his gallant men who were now chafing at their lack of action on the sands of Pensacola Bay. Their sore trial was appreciated by the president and every member of the administration at Richmond, Benjamin wrote, all of whom were as anxious as Bragg himself to relieve him from a position to which the fortunes of war had condemned him But, Benjamin wrote, to remove him to some field of more active operations would have the most disastrous effect on the morale of the army under his command and, as for his officers, there was nothing that could be done under the present legislation. For Bragg himself, the president had suggested a partial relief to the tedium of his constant vigil at Pensacola by extending his command to embrace the entire coast of Alabama. Bragg would have an increased chance for actual combat in the event of a descent by the enemy anywhere along that shoreline, the new secretary assured him.[22]

Colonel Brown wrote to Bragg on Tuesday, October 8, that he noticed for the first time that morning a yellow flag indicating a hospital, flying over a large building directly across from his batteries. The building was the navy yard's former marine hospital now in service for the care of the large number of Confederate soldiers suffering from disease and fevers. Brown wrote that he further understood the wives and children of Confederate officers were in an adjoining building. Brown informed Bragg he did not make war on the sick, on women, or on their children. Since those buildings would be exposed to his fire should there be a bombardment, he was giving Bragg notice so the sick, the women, and the children could be removed in order that, should they remain and be fired upon, the responsibility would rest where it belonged. Bragg, however, had other matters on his mind that morning.[23]

Brigadier General Richard H. Anderson, C.S.A., earned Braxton Bragg's wrath while commanding at Pensacola but later was one of the Confederacy's better generals (Cook Collection, Valentine Richmond History Center).

Brigadier General Richard H. Anderson had arrived at Pensacola from Charleston on August 23. When General Beauregard was ordered from Charleston to take command of the Confederate forces at Manassas, Virginia, he had been replaced at Charleston by General Anderson. The new Confederate Secretary of War Judah Benjamin had then ordered Anderson to Pensacola. Shortly after his arrival, Bragg ordered Anderson to plan the long delayed assault on Santa Rosa Island. Anderson was to attack the camp of the 6th New York, overrun it, then attack and spike the guns of the batteries between the camp and Fort Pickens. He was not to assault the fort itself.[24]

Anderson was forty, a graduate of West Point, class of 1842. He had served on the frontier and in the war with Mexico, earning a brevet first lieutenancy for gallantry at San Augustin. On the secession of his native South Carolina, Anderson had resigned his commission in the United States Army and was appointed colonel of the 1st South Carolina Infantry Regiment which he commanded during the siege and surrender of Fort Sumter. Promoted to brigadier general, he succeeded General Beauregard at Charleston until he was ordered to Pensacola. On October 9, a Federal deserter reported to the Confederate commanders ashore that all but two of the vessels off Santa Rosa Island were away on blockade duty. Bragg ordered Anderson to launch the assault that night which would be moonless and extremely dark. Anderson organized his attack force into three strong battalions. The first, commanded by Colonel James Chalmers of the 9th Mississippi, consisted of 350 men from the 1st Alabama and detachments from the 9th and 10th Mississippi. The second, under Colonel J. Patton Anderson of the 1st Florida, was made up of 400 men from the 7th Alabama, the Louisiana Battalion, and the 1st Florida. The third, led by Colonel John Jackson of the 5th Georgia, was 260 men drawn from the 5th Georgia and the Georgia Battalion. An independent company under First Lieutenant James Hollonquist, ordnance corps, consisted of fifty-three men from the 5th Georgia and from Captain William Homer's artillery company who were lightly armed with pistols and knives and carrying materials for spiking guns and burning buildings. There was also a medical detachment of five surgeons and twenty men.[25]

Anderson mustered his battalions at the navy yard where they embarked for Pensacola on the steamer *Time* with Bragg at the wharf to see Anderson and the men off. Arriving at Pensacola about 10:00 P.M., the men transferred to scows and flats that were to be towed over to Santa Rosa Island by *Time* and another steamer, *Ewing*. Anderson discovered he did not have enough boats to get his battalions sorted out and organized as he wanted them so he requisitioned another steamer, *Neaffie*, to tow additional flats and scows. To distinguish friend from foe, Anderson had each man tie a strip of white cloth around his upper left arm.[26]

An existing section of the original brick wall of the Pensacola Navy Yard (photograph by the author).

10. "The Enemy Failed in All Objectives"

On Santa Rosa Island the camp of the 6th New York, named Camp Brown in an unsuccessful effort by Colonel Wilson to curry favor with the garrison commander, was located on the gulf shore a mile east of Fort Pickens. Its tents were arranged in parallel lines forming east and west streets. There were several wooden storage buildings to the rear of the tent lines and a wide parade in front. Boughs from trees and shrubs had been cut and formed into arbors and canopies to shade the tents and streets. Wilson was present in the camp as was his second in command, Lieutenant Colonel John Creighton. Five of the ten companies of the 6th New York had been shipped off by Colonel Brown to serve in the batteries on the island and to Key West and Dry Tortugas so, as a result, only Company C, Captain Richard Hazeltine; Company D, Captain Patrick Duffy; Company F, First Lieutenant Jacob Silloway; Company H, Captain Charles Henberer; and Company K, Captain Henry Hoelzle were present, fourteen officers and 220 men. Stretching from the bay shore to the gulf coast half a mile east of the camp was its outpost line of pickets and guards under the command of First Lieutenant Moore Hanham of Company H.[27]

Anderson's small flotilla of steamers and towed scows and flats departed Pensacola at midnight and crossed the bay under a dark, moonless sky, a distance of six miles. The force landed on Santa Rosa Island at two in the morning four miles east of Fort Pickens and three miles east of Camp Brown. The site was marked by three large ponds. At this point the island was half a mile wide. Three or four long ridges ran parallel to the gulf shore and low, swampy ground lay along the bay shore. Anderson gave his colonels their final orders. Chalmers was to advance westward along the bay beach. Patton Anderson would move westward along the gulf beach. Jackson would follow a few hundred yards to the rear of Chalmers in the center of the island, ready to deploy north or south when he heard firing. Hollonquist would bring his independent company in the rear of Jackson. The medical detachment as to find a sheltered location among the dunes and prepare to receive and treat wounded. Anderson gave specific instructions to the three colonels to restrain their men. There was to be no firing of weapons. Federal sentinels encountered were to be silently captured or bayoneted instead of being shot. Anderson intended to get his columns between Camp Brown and the batteries further west on the island before their presence was detected thus cutting off the 6th New York and putting themselves in position for an assault on the batteries. Anderson gave the command and the columns began a three mile march in darkness over loose sand that soon became, to the inexperienced soldiers making the march, fatiguing and confusing.[28]

Several hundred yards east of Camp Brown a detachment of Company H, 6th New York, manned the picket line. Private John Shaughnessy and another sentry, one O'Brien, had been standing in the darkness talking and passing time. About an hour before daylight, which would have been approximately 4:45 A.M., the two men parted and resumed walking their beats. O'Brien saw a man approach from the shadows. When challenged the man said he as an officer with the countersign. Since no countersign had been established, O'Brien told the man to approach closer and then raised his musket and fired, shooting the man dead. Immediately twenty or more muskets roared from the darkness, killing O'Brien. Shaughnessy raised his own musket and fired. A ball whistled through the hair of his head, stunning him. A blow from a musket butt came from the darkness and caught him in the chest, knocking him senseless. He was taken prisoner.[29]

On hearing the firing Lieutenant Hanham called in the pickets and formed the men in line of battle in the face of advancing the Confederate formation. Heavily outnumbered, he had the men fire and fall back toward the camp, losing several killed or wounded in the process. Within the camp itself, Colonel Wilson had the alarm sounded and brought the five companies into formation on the parade. Captain Hoelzle formed the main guard and marched from the camp in the direction of the sound of firing. He met Hanham's stragglers hurrying back along the bay beach. His men soon found themselves face to face with the oncoming Confederates. Hoelzle ordered a volley fired into the nearest formation from which his men received a return fire. Hoelzle was knocked down and walked over in the confusion but managed to get to his feet and shoot a Southerner who was aiming at him. He hurried back toward the camp, shouting for the men still with him to fall in on the end of the line of skirmishers forming under Captain Hazeltine on the parade. To the left, somewhat north of the camp, another skirmish line consisting of four men under Captain Duffy was cut off and had to hide in the dunes, away from the camp for the remainder of the day. Among Hazeltine's skirmishers, Corporal William Parsonage was shot three times through the body and bayoneted once but managed to kill one of his opponents before he too was killed. A Private McGrail, stationed on the bay shore, managed to fire three shots from his musket into Chalmer's column before he was killed. Lieutenant Hanham found Colonel Wilson and excitedly informed him that 2,000 men in two columns were marching on the camp and that, as far as he knew, all of the pickets and sentinels had been overrun or driven in. Wilson told his orderly to hurry to Fort Pickens and inform Colonel Brown of the situation. He ordered the lines of skirmishers forward and had the men of the five companies on the parade deploy to their left in the darkness, facing northward in the direction of the bay shore. Without warning Patton Anderson's battalion, advancing undetected along the gulf shore, crested a sand ridge and charged into the right flank of the line of the 6th New York. Jackson hurried his third Confederate column forward toward the sound of firing and arrived at the edge of Camp Brown at the same time as Anderson and ordered his men forward. Caught between the musketry of Chalmer's column coming down from the north and Anderson's and Jackson's columns coming in from the south and east, Wilson's untested and barely disciplined volunteers fled in the darkness in the direction of the protection of the nearest regulars, those manning Battery Totten on the gulf shore, and Battery Lincoln, on the bay shore, each about 1,500 yards east of Fort Pickens.[30]

Captains Henberer and Hazeltine managed to keep most of their commands together. They fell back a distance to the gulf shore and formed with their backs to the water's edge, numbering less than a hundred men. Private William Scott, standing in the first rank, watched the approaching Southerners until they were within ten yards of him before shooting and killing Captain Richard Bradford at the head of the column. This momentarily confused and halted the Confederate advance and gave time for the two companies of New York volunteers to move further westward in the darkness. Back at the camp, Colonel Wilson, with the assistance of Lieutenants Moore Hanham and Christian Kreall, managed to rally about sixty frightened and disorganized men. Wilson sent a messenger to find his second in command, Lieutenant Colonel Creighton, but the man returned without success. He told Wilson that stragglers had told him the lieutenant colonel and many men from the other companies had run to the protection of the batteries. On hearing this, the men with Wilson would not remain in ranks and fled westward. Chalmers', Anderson's, and Jackson's battalions gathered at the abandoned camp. Believing the enemy beaten and gone, the

Southern volunteers wandered about and some began plundering trunks and packs they found in the tents and storehouses. Hollonquist's independent company arrived and set to work burning the wooden structures and tents. The dried evergreen boughs Wilson's men had made into arbors for shade quickly flamed. In a short time, Camp Brown was ablaze.[31]

The officer of the day at Fort Pickens woke Colonel Brown at 3:30 A.M. and informed him that sentries had reported heavy musketry from the direction of Wilson's camp. Brown ordered the alarm sounded. The full garrison turned out under arms, ready to repel the long awaited rebel attack on the fort. Brown ordered First Lieutenant Loomis Langdon to mount and ride out from the fort to find Wilson and order him to close upon the enemy force and attack it. If compelled to fall back, Wilson was to do so slowly and maintain good order in his formation. Langdon rode eastward in the darkness following the plank road toward Camp Brown where he encountered scattered groups of Wilson's men hurrying in disorder toward the batteries. Riding on, he continued to seek out Wilson. Back at the fort, Brown ordered Major Lewis Arnold to see that all the guns on the ramparts and in the casemates were armed and manned. Assuming Wilson's volunteers would not be able to stop the advance of the Confederate columns, Brown ordered Major Vogdes to take two companies of regulars and find the New Yorkers. Vogdes ordered out Company E, 3rd Infantry, under Captain John Hildt, and his own former command, Company A, 1st Artillery, now under Captain Franck Taylor and serving as infantry. Vogdes marched the regulars east into the darkness, leading the way past Battery Cameron. Here he was reinforced by Company G, 6th New York, Captain James Dobie, who volunteered to accompany the regulars. Vogdes told Dobie to form on the right of his command and then proceed eastward along the bay beach. Dobie's company became separated in the darkness and was not seen again until the following day.[32]

Shortly thereafter Brown called First Lieutenant Chauncey Reese of the engineers and ordered him to mount and follow Vogdes with further instructions to pursue the enemy, keeping his left flank on the north, or bay, shore. About half a mile beyond Battery Lincoln, Reese ran into a column of about seventy men that he took in the darkness for Vogdes's command. Several musket shots from the formation in answer to his shouted query convinced him otherwise and he turned back. At Battery Lincoln, Reese found First Lieutenant Richard Duryea also looking for Vogdes with additional orders from Colonel Brown. Reese gave Duryea his own messages and returned to Fort Pickens to report what he had learned. Vogdes continued to lead his column eastward in the darkness and unknowingly passed between the columns of Confederates whose officers were trying to organize their men from the disorder and confusion that had taken over the attacking force during the capture and plunder of Camp Brown. Vogdes thought he saw a large force to the right of his column moving in the same direction. Ordering his command to face this possible danger, he rode forward to reconnoiter in the dark and was immediately taken prisoner. Captain Hildt, now the senior officer present, assumed command. A Southern officer approached Hildt and demanded the surrender of his whole force. In response, Hildt ordered a volley of musketry fired into the Confederate ranks. Seeing a slight ridge to his front, Hildt ran his command toward it and had the regulars take cover. A sharp skirmish took place with Hildt's men forced to give some ground. The Southern columns moved into the opening this caused and continued toward their point of debarkation. Falling back to the south, Hildt's men, firing and carrying their wounded with them, overran the Confederate hospital and took the five surgeons and eight of the attendants prisoner. About 5:00 A.M. Colonel Brown ordered Major Arnold to form two companies of regulars at Fort Pickens and proceed to support Vogdes, wherever out in the darkness his column might be. Arnold took Company H, 2nd Artillery, Captain James Robertson, and Company C, 3rd Infantry, First Lieutenant Alexander Shipley. About a mile and a half east of Fort Pickens this column came upon the scene of the recent fight between Hildt's command and the Confederate column. There was no sign of either formation.[33]

General Anderson had spent much of the early hours of the morning trying to regain control of his command. Once they had chased Wilson's volunteers away and pillaged and burned the camp of the 6th New York, the inexperienced Southerners wanted to stand and talk, walk around, brag about what they had one, how brave they had been, and generally head off in the direction of where they expected to embark for the return to Pensacola. Anderson understood by this time the Federal garrisons at Fort Pickens and the batteries would be fully alert and would be sending out companies of disciplined regulars into the steadily fading darkness to find and fight the attackers. Anderson himself was an experienced officer who had served in the regular United States Army prior to his resignation and that is exactly what he would do were he in the fort or in the batteries. Dawn would be breaking soon and his steamers would become easy targets for the gunners in the batteries and for the warships off the island. Deciding there was no longer any chance of mounting an assault on the batteries, Anderson gave the order for his three colonels to gather their men and retire.[34]

Anderson's battalions assembled and moved along the center of Santa Rosa Island toward their point of embarkation where the steamers and flats waited. What they did not realize was that the regulars under Major Arnold, the two companies commanded by Robertson and Shipley, were also moving in that same direction but along the bay shore and were outflanking them.[35]

Anderson was superintending the embarkation of the first troops to arrive on the beach when Captain William Lovell, skipper of *Neaffie*, informed him that a heavy hawser had become entangled in the steamer's propeller. Anderson ordered *Neaffie* and her tows to fasten to one side of the steamer *Ewing*. Thus encumbered, *Ewing* could not answer her helm. While desperate efforts were being made to free or cut loose the hawser, the flats and scows *Ewing* had in tow, now jammed with men, worked loose and began to drift off, requiring frantic efforts to get them back. While this was taking place, Anderson's whole command was crowded together on the beach or jammed on the decks and in the wells of the flats and scows. Few men were able to move to take any means to defend themselves.[36]

Lieutenant Reese reported back to Colonel Brown at Fort Pickens and was sent to join Major Arnold. Reese worked his way ahead in the lifting darkness to scout. He hurried back and told the major he had discovered a large force of Southerners that probably outnumbered Arnold's command ten to one. The Confederates, Reese reported, were embarking from the beach onto some steamers and flats. Arnold hurried Lieutenant Duryea with six soldiers forward to reconnoiter and report back. As Duryea left, Captain Hildt and Lieutenant Taylor arrived with their commands. Arnold now had four companies of regulars with him who were hidden from the nearby Confederates by a long sand ridge. He sent Lieutenant Langdon, who by now had reported to him, back to Fort Pickens to report to Colonel Brown and to request urgently a field piece be sent forward to him. Langdon returned to the fort and made his report only to find out all the horses that had been trained to haul field pieces in harness had been commandeered by officers for use as mounts. Attempts were made to fit mules into harness for this work but the affair ended before this could be accomplished.[37]

Arnold ordered Captain Robertson to move his company forward to where he could overlook the beach above the Confederates who were struggling to free the tangled hawser while others worked to get the scows and flats that had gone aground re-floated. Robertson moved his line of regulars to a low sand hill about 200 yards from the beach and had his men open a steady fire on the masses crammed helplessly on the beach, on the decks of the steamers, and in the wells of the scows and flats. Arnold had Lieutenant Shipley move his command up to support Robertson. This movement was delayed for almost an hour by Shipley's column having to make its way through a tangled swamp near the three ponds.[38]

Back at Fort Pickens Lieutenant Reese was told to find a boat and row out to the sailing frigate U.S.S. *Potomac* standing offshore where he was to ask Captain Levin Powell to have the frigate's marine detachment transfer over to the chartered army steamer *McClellan* and to direct the steamer's captain to move the steamer eastward along the gulf shore to where it could shell the Confederate vessels embarking troops on the far side of the island. It took Reese an hour to find a boat to take him out to *Potomac*. There Captain Powell insisted, since it would take his marines some time to prepare to make the move, that *McClellan* take his sailing vessel in tow and haul her down the shore to where he could bring his own heavier guns to bear. As forty-one marines and one officer had prepared to transfer from *Potomac* to *McClellan*, the towing hawser from the steamer parted and *Potomac*, her anchors now aweigh, began to drift free. By this time dawn was breaking. Officers on both vessels could see parties of soldiers on the beach, stragglers from Wilson's 6th New York. Taking a boat ashore, Reese learned that the enemy was leaving the island. *Potomac* anchored where she lay while *McClellan* steamed fifteen miles eastward along the gulf shore of the island to determine whether there were any signs of the Confederate landing force in that direction. *McClellan* returned to the anchorage about 2:00 P.M., having sighted nothing.[39]

The slaughter that might have taken place on the decks of *Neaffie* and *Ewing* and in the scows and flats was lighter than it might have been due to the distance between the firing lines of regulars and the vessels in the faint light of breaking dawn, and, in spite of their wretched condition, some of the Confederates were able to return fire toward the regulars behind the sand ridge. After what must have seemed an eternity, the fouled hawser was chopped away from *Neaffie's* propeller, the tows of *Ewing* were refloated and refastened, and both steamers churned the waters of the bay on their way back to Pensacola. As they drew off from shore, General Anderson received a painful wound from a Federal musket ball in his left elbow.[40]

Colonel Brown reported his losses from the battle as thirteen killed, twenty-seven wounded, and twenty-one missing or prisoners, including Major Vogdes. General Anderson reported his losses as eighteen killed, thirty-nine wounded, and thirty missing or prisoners. Due to the confused and rapid retirement of the Confederate raiding force from Santa Rosa Island, many of its wounded and all of his dead were left behind. Bragg maliciously and falsely reported to the adjutant general at Richmond that eleven of the thirteen bodies returned to him by the Federals afterwards had been shot through the head although they also had disabling wounds elsewhere in the body, indicating they had been deliberately murdered.⁴¹

Colonel Brown claimed in his report the enemy failed in all objectives other than to burn some tents of the 6th New York and pillage some officers' trunks. The attackers never came within 500 yards of the batteries they intended to assault and spike nor did they approach within a mile of Fort Pickens. General Bragg claimed the attack had chastised the enemy, driving him from his camps, burning his tents and stores, and spiking his guns. The attacking force had returned in good order after having inflicted a large loss on the Federals due to having surprised them. Finally Bragg ended his report by asking if he could exchange his West Point classmate, Major Vogdes, now a prisoner in his hands.⁴²

The battle of Santa Rosa Island, which took place nine months to the day after Slemmer moved his command from the mainland and occupied Fort Pickens, had little effect on the nation or the other events taking place to the north. Bragg's attack was a waste of lives and energy. There was no possibility that Anderson could inflict any significant damage on the Federal facilities on the island with an attacking force that numbered a little more than a thousand men. There was no possibility of reaching the walls of Fort Pickens because of the intervening troops and guns at the batteries east of the fort, and it was Fort Pickens that blocked the entrance to Pensacola Harbor, not the supporting batteries. The one creditable result of the battle for the Confederacy was the emergence of the three battalion commanders, Anderson, Chalmers, and Jackson, who would soon prove their merit on the field at Shiloh, in Tennessee, six months later, as would many of the formations that came together and trained as part of the Confederate forces at Pensacola. Bragg had commanded there for seven months and had outnumbered the garrison on Santa Rosa Island every day of that time. Why he chose to attack the reinforced and fortified positions Brown had established when he did is open to speculation.

On the Federal side Wilson's New York volunteers had broken and run while the disciplined regulars stood and fought. The entire strategy for defending Fort Pickens from the first day Slemmer brought his command over was to prevent a Confederate force from crossing over from the mainland and mounting an attack from the east. At times major portions of the United States Navy's Home Squadron had been stationed off the island to prevent this. Anderson's forces had managed to cross and mount the attack without being detected by either the army or the navy until the attack was well under way. Once the attack was taking place, the vessels stationed offshore were able to play no role in repulsing it. From the day Brown and the reinforcements arrived from the North, Fort Pickens and Santa Rosa Island were safe in Federal hands because Braxton Bragg did not intend to make an attack and did not attempt to land on the island until after it was fortified and reinforced beyond his ability to transport sufficient troops over to the island.

Through the months they faced each other across Pensacola Bay, Brown and Bragg demonstrated the characteristics that had served both men well during their careers in the peacetime United States Army. They demonstrated they were accomplished bureaucrats, but not warriors.

11

"A Signal Gun Fired at 10:00 A.M."

Three days after the battle of Santa Rosa Island on October 12, Brown wrote a personal letter to Quartermaster General Meigs complaining that he would have taken a better account of the enemy had so many of the regular companies not been taken from him over the preceding months. Had he sat and grieved over what he considered the great wrongs done to him instead of exerting every nerve and taking responsibilities few others would have taken in sending away companies of Wilson's 6th New York and replacing them with regular companies, he asked Meigs, what would be his condition now? He would have been whipped and the fort at this time beleaguered by the Southerners. All the batteries would have been lost for he would not have been able to send a man to sustain the batteries and repel the raiders. Wilson's Zouaves, he was sorry to say, had run away disgracefully and taken shelter under his guns. To the adjutant general Brown wrote, bordering on insubordination, that since all his letters, all his suggestions, and all his requests from the day he had been placed in command of the post had met with so mortifying and undeserved neglect, he now reported only out of sense of duty. The fort, with its outlying batteries, was now as ready for service as it probably would be at any time. He would have opened with his batteries upon the enemy earlier were he not confined by positive orders to defensive operations only, which orders he had tried in vain to have rescinded. He felt he could only patiently wait the course of events while the strength of his command was diminished by disease and transfers. He respectfully requested that he be relieved by an officer in whom the government could have confidence. This brought a response from Adjutant General Lorenzo Thomas that the general-in-chief directed him to say that all of Brown's communications from the time of his assuming command at Fort Pickens had been read to him and such as required had been passed on to the proper bureaus of the War Department. His operations had been approved and his zeal and energy were appreciated. The usual punctuality in acknowledging his letters had been unavoidably departed from because of the pressures of other matters which demanded immediate attention and left no time for anything else. The nation was, after all, embarked on a struggle for its life with victorious Confederate formations just across the Potomac River from the Capitol. As to his own case,

Brown should understand that the circumstances which prevented offensive operations on his part had changed with his ability to assume them, as did the existence of active and open warfare. More regular officers and troops would gladly have been sent if they were available but the need for them elsewhere could hardly be appreciated except by the authorities on whom the urgent requisitions were being made from all quarters. At some posts in the nation there was not one officer to a company. His recent request to be relieved, he was told, could not be granted because there was no one to relieve him in whom the general-in-chief could confide trust for so responsible a command. Colonel Thomas was patiently but firmly letting Brown know that he should have understood all of this. The adjutant general added that a vessel had left New York for Santa Rosa Island in September laden with ice and beef cattle and another was preparing to sail with more cattle, stores, and vegetables. The subject of pay for his command had been brought to the attention of the paymaster general.[1]

The New York volunteers, Brown continued in his letter to Meigs, had not behaved well during the battle. He had spared the regiment the stigma of cowardice because he felt the material in the rank and file was good and in the hands of even reasonably intelligent officers might be made efficient. However, as a body and with only certain exceptions, Brown wrote, the officers of the volunteer regiment were in every respect unfit and incapable of performing their duties. He suggested the few efficient officers be transferred to other regiments and the enlisted men be reassigned to the regular companies at Fort Pickens. Within a month, he assured Meigs, the regiment would be made efficient to where he would, with confidence, lead it into battle which, at this time, he would be very sorry to have to do. Brown, an experienced regular army officer, surely understood that his suggestions on the disposition of the volunteer officers and enlisted men of the 6th New York was impossible and without any basis in law.[2]

Bragg wrote a letter to President Davis that was intended to remain outside official channels complaining of the series of little annoyances committed by the Federals and not responded to by him but which had reflected negatively on his officers and men, impairing their confidence and weakening his own influence over them. He had determined to launch the assault to restore the commanding position his forces held on Pensacola Bay, he wrote the president. He described the attack as a daring, almost desperate descent on the Federal outposts. His available transports were only a small river steamer and some flats with no gunboats for support. Fortune had favored the attempt but, Bragg characteristically indicated, there had been some bumbling by others which caused his losses to be larger then they should have been. However, he wrote, the effect upon his formations was almost electrical. Low morale had been replaced. The sick list fell over 250 in two days. All was now cheerful and pleasant. Colonel Brown, Bragg claimed, had intimated in an interview with one of Bragg's staff officers sent out to Santa Rosa Island to collect the Confederate dead that, in case of a bombardment, he would at once destroy the navy yard. Bragg had responded with a message telling Brown that his Federal prisoners were now confined there.[3]

In the month following the battle on Santa Rosa Island both commanders tried to make the best of what had taken place in their correspondence. Brown tried to make a meaningful victory out of what amounted to merely a raid by the enemy that came and went without his inflicting much more damage on the attacking force than what had been achieved by the several disconnected columns of regulars floundering about in the dark. His excuses for not crushing the assaulting force were hollow. Less than half his regulars had been committed to searching for, finding, and fighting the Confederate force. Of significance, his constant arguing that the fort could not be defended without the help of naval steamers off the gulf shore of the island was exposed as meaningless. The two vessels that were present were never involved. It was questionable whether an armed steamer inside the harbor would have prevented Anderson's men from crossing and landing; the vessel would have had to station herself within range of the Confederate batteries on the mainland in order to do so and could have easily been driven off or severely damaged. Communications between the army and navy commands during the battle were so primitive that Anderson had come and gone before Brown was able to send Lieutenant Reese off to find a boat to take him out to the vessels offshore to ask for help. Why the agreed-upon rocket signal was never used is unclear. Harvey Brown had never intended to fight. He was a career soldier in an army most of which had not smelled gun smoke since it captured Chapultapec, the final fortress guarding Mexico City, in 1847. His attention while in command at Fort Pickens had been directed toward keeping the record straight, observing the forms and procedures, asking for more, and proposing to be ready to fight at some time in the ever receding future. He complained, he vented his frustrations, he sandbagged the fort and built batteries, and he found excuses for doing nothing more by hiding behind shopworn orders to remain on the defensive. One of his first actions upon landing on Santa Rosa Island had been to send Bragg a written statement declaring he would not attack the Southern forces. Brown did what successful officers in his army up to this time were used to doing: he fussed, he protested, he argued, he countered, but he had no intention of fighting. He showed a remarkable ability for overlooking what was happening in the rest of the nation. He was distant from the War Department at Washington but he still received mail from vessels supplying him, from *Water Witch* plying between Santa Rosa Island and the American consulate at Havana, from merchant vessels that called at Key West. Even the Southern authorities ashore allowed some communication to take place between the mainland, the island, and the vessels offshore. As he complained to the adjutant general of neglect, he had to know the Lincoln administration was desperately trying to build a series of armies to defend the capital, to hold the western reaches of Virginia, and to keep Missouri and the border states within the Union. The members of the administration of President Abraham Lincoln had long before realized that the war coming onto the land would be beyond the ability of the regular army. It was going to be a civil war, one that would be fought by the very volunteer soldiers Brown had such low opinion of under their amateur officers, and it would be costly, inefficient, filled with mistakes, and directed by politicians. Brown, at sixty-five years of age, was out of step with the times. At least, doing what he did do, he had been able to hold Fort Pickens and control the channel into Pensacola Harbor and prevent the use of the magnificent anchorage by the Confederacy as a blockade runner's haven and a base for commerce raiders, while keeping large numbers of Confederate soldiers idle on the mainland.

Bragg likewise tried to make a victory out of a raid that had managed to burn some tents, scatter some barely disciplined volunteers, accomplish little more than get some men on both sides killed or wounded, and present him with his West Point classmate, Major Israel Vogdes, as a prisoner of war in his hands. His references to the blundering that caused his losses to be heavier than they could have been were a gratuitous slur on the men who crossed over to Santa Rosa Island and took part in the fighting. Bragg made no reference to what could have happened had he sent an attacking force to Santa Rosa Island before the arrival of Colonel Brown and his reinforcements when the place was defended by Slemmer and fifty artillerymen. Not unlike Harvey Brown, Braxton Bragg had not wanted to fight. He too, until recently, had been an officer in the same army as Brown, an army that was experienced with little more than how to organize, maneuver, draw rations, obey orders, and await promotions based upon seniority. Had Bragg wanted to give battle and accomplish something worth the blood and effort it was bound to cost, he would have sent over a much larger force which he well could have done. He could have ordered Anderson to move directly on Fort Pickens, leaving Wilson's volunteers and the batteries for a later mopping up action. There was no reason to believe that a surprise assault by escalade out of the darkness of the night would not have had an even chance of success in spite of Brown's reinforced command, most of which was not within the walls of Fort Pickens when the attack was launched. Bragg's men were volunteers, poorly disciplined and led, but fully capable of one grand assault. They could and would fight, as they would demonstrate in April of the coming year in the woods and fields around Shiloh Meeting House on the bank of the Tennessee River. As it was, Bragg's limited attack with a smaller than adequate force indicated that all he had in mind was a raid, a pin prick, a slap. What he could not have realized was that there was a benefit unknown to himself or his government at the time. He was organizing, disciplining, and building the core of what would become the Confederate Army of Tennessee.

On Tuesday, October 9, the morning of the night Anderson would attack the island, Colonel Brown had sent dispatches by the steamer *McClellan* to Captain McKean off Mobile proposing a joint attack on the enemy, to which McKean acceded. Two days after the battle on Santa Rosa Island McKean arrived off Pensacola Bay with the steamers *Niagara* and *Colorado*. The commanders conferred and developed a plan of attack which was to be put into execution the morning of the 16th. Brown now was anxious to retaliate for the attack Bragg had sprung on him and McKean was generally ready for a fight. However, on the 12th, the Confederates sent their new ram, C. S. S. *Manassas*, down the Mississippi River to Head of Passes escorted by two armed steamers. *Manassas* rammed and ran aground the Federal steamers *Richmond* and *Vincennes* and for a time the Federal blockade of the mouth of the Mississippi River was broken. *Richmond* had three planks stove in and *Vincennes* was damaged so severely and taking water so rapidly that her crew had to throw overboard all her guns but four. McKean returned immediately to the mouth of the Mississippi, sailing in *Niagara* and leaving *Colorado* off Fort Pickens. Before sailing, McKean sent a message to Brown deferring the attack until he could return with a sufficient naval force.[4]

A little over a month after the battle on Santa Rosa Island, on Monday, November 11, a slave escaping from the mainland arrived at Fort Pickens to tell Brown that Bragg had intended to again attack Santa Rosa Island the night before with some 4,000 men but had been deterred by the dense fog that had risen after sunset. If the man were correct, Brown wrote to McKean who was still off the mouth of the Mississippi River in *Niagara*, Bragg could attempt the attack on any of the following nights. He urged McKean to keep *Colorado* stationed off the island. There was no confirmation of Bragg's plan in any of the Confederate records.[5]

On the following Saturday, November 16, Brown wrote to McKean that there was not a doubt in his mind that the Confederates on the mainland were sending their most efficient and best trained troops from there to the armies in Virginia. One regiment had left the previous Monday, he had learned, and he had reason to believe the best of Bragg's remaining regiments, the Louisiana Regulars, would soon follow. The present seemed to him an auspicious time to make a combined attack on Bragg's batteries. As McKean had held out hopes that cooperation between their forces had only been suspended by the emergency in October, Brown asked whether affairs at the mouth of the Mississippi River might soon be such as to enable them to renew the attempt.[6]

McKean was again in favor of the idea and made preparations to take part. Before sailing from the mouth of the great river McKean took time to write a personal letter to the petty officers and crew of *Mississippi* acknowledging the request they had made that they and their vessel be permitted to participate in the pending attack on Pensacola Bay. McKean praised the petty officers and crew for their offer which, he told them, convinced him "the spirit of patriotism and gallantry which had so distinguished the character of American sailors during the War of 1812 had not degenerated." *Richmond,* however, would be the vessel to accompany *Niagara* because her lighter draft would allow her to lie in close enough to use her whole broadside in action. Were *Mississippi* to take part, due to her deeper draft she would be able to bring only her forward pivot gun to bear. That, in connection with their fine performance in the recent action with the Confederate ram *Manassas*, should assure the petty officers and crew of *Mississippi* that duty alone had influenced him in ordering the change. He promised, when the opportunity occurred which would enable him to grant their desire to distinguish themselves and their vessel, it would give him great pleasure to do so. *Niagara* and *Richmond* then weighed anchor and steamed together for Santa Rosa Island. The steamers arrived on Thursday, November 21. Both vessels were of relatively deep draft. *Niagara,* drawing twenty-four feet, could not cross the bar and enter the bay. *Richmond,* drawing slightly less than twenty feet, could barely do so. Captain McKean and Colonel Brown agreed, therefore, that the steamers would attack Fort McRee and its adjacent sand batteries from out in the gulf, lying in as close to shore as they could. To help with this McKean did what he could to lighten *Niagara,* taking down and sending ashore her topgallant masts and rigging and landing all her spare parts. He loaded the vessel's howitzers into boats and lowered them to be towed alongside. With all unnecessary ordnance, coal, and provisions sent ashore, McKean was able to reduce *Niagara*'s draft to twenty-one feet. During the night he sent out crews in launches to take soundings for both steamers, indicating their proposed positions with buoys marking four fathoms or more.[7]

On Friday, November 22, a signal gun fired at 10:00 A.M. from Fort Pickens initiated the action. The two steamers approached and took their stations with Fort McRee bearing due north at a range of two miles. Both vessels anchored with springs on their cables to allow them to draw themselves broadside-to, and opened fire. Finding the shells from *Niagara's* guns falling short, McKean again sent out crews in launches to sound the depths closer in. A buoy was set marking twenty-three feet of water near the edge of the shoal, one and three-quarters of a mile from the fort. About noon McKean had *Niagara* raise anchor and stand in to the buoy. Anchoring again with springs on her cables, *Niagara* commenced firing with telling effect, her shells falling directly onto the sand batteries along the shore and into the fort. The exposed guns mounted *en barbette* at Fort McRee were silenced almost immediately. Captain Francis Ellison, commanding *Richmond,* was able with her lighter draft to move his vessel closer to shore and well enough to the rear of Fort McRee and the sand batteries that no Southern guns could be brought to bear on her. She fired throughout the day with no return until into the afternoon when a battery of heavy guns opened from the sand hills on the mainland across the lagoon. *Richmond* changed position several times as large shells began to fall nearby until she was struck on her starboard side, forward of the mizzen chains, four feet above the water line. The ball sheared off two planks and started serious leaking. She was again struck in the fore rigging by a ball that killed the captain of her number two gun and wounded several crew members in a shower of splinters. Ellison examined the results of the hit and reported his vessel was leaking seriously from the damage. She was taking on about one foot of water an hour. She could barely be kept afloat with all her pumps working but any accident or bad fortune might prove hazardous to the vessel. McKean signaled from *Niagara* for *Richmond* to drop back from the line of fire. Ellison brought the steamer around, fired his full starboard battery, and moved to the south, anchoring at 6:00 P.M. in twenty-seven feet of water several miles from Fort McRee and well out of range of the fort's batteries. During the day *Niagara* took two hits from the guns ashore, one aft of the fore chains and one a little forward of the main chains, both causing minor damage and no injury to the crew. By 3:15 in the afternoon the return fire from the sand batteries had ceased and the fire from the casemate guns within Fort McRee had gradually slackened and then ceased about 5:00 P.M.[8]

At Fort Pickens Colonel Brown had opened at 10:00 A.M. with the guns of the fort and its outlying batteries. The Confederate line on the mainland stretched from the navy yard westward to Fort McRee, in an arc reaching four miles and containing the two forts and fourteen sand batteries. The distance from the flag pole at Fort Pickens to the guns ashore ranged between 2,100 yards and 1,900 yards. Brown directed his gun captains to maintain a rate of fire of one shot from each gun that could be brought to bear every fifteen to twenty minutes which they did until it was too dark for the crews to see. He had Batteries Lincoln, Cameron, and Totten concentrate on the batteries adjacent to the navy yard and the yard itself, those of Battery Scott on Fort McRee and the sand batteries near the lighthouse, and those within Fort Pickens on all targets within their scope and range. Brown claimed to have reduced the return fire from Fort Barrancas perceptively, entirely silencing the batteries near the navy yard and two of the sand batteries there. He was disappointed in not being able to set the buildings at the navy yard afire against which he had been using hot shot.[9]

General Bragg reported that the affair began with the fire from Fort Pickens being joined shortly thereafter by that of the two large steamers, *Niagara* and *Richmond*, which he incorrectly identified as *Hartford*. The point of concentration for the Federal fire seemed to be Fort McRee, Bragg thought. Knowing the poor condition of that structure, he had to rely on the confidence he had in its commander, Colonel John Villepigue, and his garrison of Georgians and Mississippians. The fort was structurally unsound, close to collapsing from weakened foundations that had been washed and eroded by wave action over the years. Its casemates had been designed for double tiers of ordnance, the upper guns mounted above the lower on wooden platforms. Three times during the day's bombardment this woodwork had caught fire and showered the fort's open magazine with flame and sparks that threatened an explosion and the destruction of the entire works. Bragg commented in his after-action report how Villepigue's coolness and self-possession under fire inspired his men with confidence and enabled his command to hold a position which seemed to others utterly untenable. Over the course of the day Bragg reported two men mortally wounded, two severely wounded, and five slightly wounded in addition to six men who had been smothered when a poorly constructed magazine collapsed on them within Fort McRee. Toward evening dark clouds, wind, and rain obscured the bay and brought an end to the firing which Bragg overstated as ranking as the heaviest bombardment in the world. Houses in Pensacola, eight miles up the bay, had trembled and were shaken and the surface of the bay was covered with floating bodies of fish dead from concussion. Bragg praised his troops for the regularity and accuracy of their fire which he said would have been creditable even with veterans. The firing of the Federals, he reported, although terrific in sound and fury, proved to have been only slightly destructive in its effect except in the case of the damage done to Fort McRee. During the night, Bragg's commanders gathered at his headquarters at Fort Barrancas. They advised him that Fort McRee, having been exposed front, flank, and rear to heavy fire from the vessels offshore and the batteries on Santa Rosa Island, with half its armament disabled and its magazine exposed, might not be able to return enemy fire in the morning. They proposed to abandon the

Colonel John Villepigue, C.S.A., gallantly defended the crumbling Fort McRee, holding the garrison together by personal example even after suffering a severe wound (courtesy of the Civil War Library and Museum, Philadelphia, Pennsylvania).

fort and blow it up, moving its garrison to the sand batteries between the lighthouse and the navy yard. Reflecting on the effect this might have on the morale of the rest of his troops, Bragg decided to hold the fort to the last. He dispatched an engineer and a large working party to the reliable Villepigue who, late in the day, had received a painful wound in this arm. The repairs necessary to maintain minimum structural integrity to the fort were made through the hours of the night. A storm closed over the bay and added to the time available to the Confederate forces working to bring Fort McRee back into shape. The storm brought a fall of tide which caused *Niagara* to touch bottom several times. Captain McKean weighed anchor and stood out to deeper water for the night as silence settled over Pensacola Bay.[10]

In the morning, Saturday, November 23, Captain McKean stood in with *Niagara* in the face of strong winds from the north and west and anchored approximately on his position of the previous day where he opened fire which the batteries ashore immediately returned. Finding his shot falling short, he ceased firing. The buoys which had marked his position the day before had blown away in the storm so McKean sent launches to again sound the depths and, following the launches, moved *Niagara* closer in, anchoring in twenty-three feet of water. His shells were still falling short yet he found it impossible to approach closer, the steamer touching bottom as he tried; the strong winds of the storm had lowered the water level offshore. He shifted weight to one side, careening the vessel to try to gain more elevation for his guns, and he increased the powder charges, but still could not get his shells to fall into the fort. During this time fire from the sand batteries on shore was falling close about him. Unable to contribute the weight of his shot to the affray, he weighed anchor and stood out into the gulf, joining *Richmond* which, later in the day, McKean ordered to Key West for repairs to the damage she had sustained at the mouth of the Mississippi and off Fort McRee.[11]

Colonel Brown opened fire from Fort Pickens at the same time as the day before, ordering his gunners to be less rapid and therefore more efficient with their fire. About 3:00 P.M., his observers saw flames from several houses at Warrington and the steeple of the Catholic church there. The fires spread rapidly, eventually consuming at least two-thirds of the structures in the village. At the same time fires broke out in Woolsey on the far side of the navy yard. Soon buildings within the navy yard itself were burning and all three conflagrations continued far into the night. With the constant battering of shot and shell against the brick walls and slate roofs of the buildings at the navy yard, Brown was satisfied great damage was being done there. The bombardment from Santa Rosa Island continued until 2:00 A.M. the following morning. Brown reported his loss as one man killed and five wounded, one of these seriously. In closing his report to the adjutant general, Brown complimented the companies of Captains Dobie and Bailey of the 6th New York for faithfully and efficiently assisting at Batteries Lincoln and Cameron and those of Captains Henberer and Duffy which rendered assistance within the fort itself. This was strange commentary from the commander who only days before had barely spared the New York volunteer regiment the condemnation of cowardice.[12]

Bragg claimed credit for disabling *Richmond* as it did not return to the bombardment on the second day and he claimed to have driven off *Niagara*. Toward evening he wrote in his report to the adjutant general that the Federals, finding the Confederate batteries on the mainland were still firing and Fort McRee was still standing, maliciously turned their shell and hot shot on the hospital and the empty dwellings of non-combatants in Warrington and Woolsey with the result that major portions of both villages and some wooden structures in the navy yard had burned. Bragg had assumed the second day's bombardment was the prelude to an amphibious attack on Fort McRee and the navy yard and ordered all troops not needed to serve the guns in the batteries to rendezvous in the shelter of the brick wall between the navy yard and Woolsey. A shot from Fort Pickens penetrated the wall and wounded three men and the gathering there was quickly dispersed. Bragg was mistaken. There was no follow-up assault on Fort McRee or the navy yard.[13]

On Sunday, November 24, three days after the bombardment, General Bragg reported to the adjutant general that the enemy vessels offshore were keeping a respectful distance and the Federal garrison within Fort Pickens was observing an ominous silence. His command stood ready for further challenge at all points. A week after the shelling Bragg sent a packet of letters under a flag of truce to the Confederate prisoners captured during Anderson's attack and still being held on Santa Rosa Island. The officer accompanying the flag reported back to Bragg that Fort Pickens appeared not to have been seriously injured. Bragg claimed, in a subsequent report to the adjutant general, that this was deliberate on his part since his fire was not directed at the fort, which rightly belonged to the Confederate States of America, but only at those within it. That same day a company of Confederate marines left Bragg's force for Virginia under orders from Secretary of the Navy Mallory. This was the third detachment of troops from Bragg to the forces gathering at Richmond. That same day a small boat from one of Federal the vessels off Santa Rosa Island attempted to enter Pensacola Bay. There had been an unwritten understanding that such small craft could move between the vessels offshore, Santa Rosa Island, the navy yard, and Pensacola. The boat was fired upon as it worked past Fort McRee forcing its crew to abandon the boat, jumping overboard and swimming to the island. Brown reported this to the adjutant general as a major breach of protocol on Bragg's part.[14]

A week later on Monday, December 1, Headquarters of the Army at Washington issued General Orders No. 169 in which the new general-in-chef, Major General George B. McClellan, who had replaced the aged, 75-year-old Winfield Scott on November 1, announced to the entire army the instance of skill and good conduct on the part of the beleaguered garrison at Fort Pickens in the harbor at Pensacola under the command of Colonel Harvey Brown. The order described the repulse of the landing force under Anderson and the two-day bombardment of the enemy's mainland positions by the guns of Fort Pickens and the naval squadron offshore. It was with pride and gratification that the general-in-chief found in the official reports the most honorable mention of each and every officer as well as the enlisted men on those occasions. McClellan's order made much of a distant and relatively minor affair but at these times the fortunes of war made it vitally necessary that Federal arms take an opportunity to claim any amount of success anywhere in the nation. Events elsewhere were not going that well for the Federal forces. The battle of Santa Rosa Island could be shown as a notable victory for Federal arms.[15]

Toward the end of November Colonel Brown reported the arrival of the 75th New York Volunteer Infantry Regiment, Colonel John R. Dodge, which was now encamped on Santa Rosa Island and engaged in drilling. Brown was sorry to report the 6th New York, as far as its officers were concerned, was in a complete state of disorganization, especially regarding its colonel and two or three officers espousing his side against the balance of the officers of the regiment. Criminations, recriminations, charges, and counter-charges had become a daily occurrence to the point where Brown issued a peremptory order to stop them. He notified the officers of the regiment he would hear no further complaints until those forwarded to the War Department had been acted upon. Charges had been sent to him, he wrote to the adjutant general, against almost every officer in the regiment. He brought to the attention of the War Department the worrisome fact that, next to him, Colonel Wilson was the senior army officer in rank on the station. Were Brown rendered unserviceable, command at Fort Pickens and its entire garrison would devolve on Wilson and that, under any circumstance, could be of the most vital consequence in the remote and isolated condition of the post. He requested an officer of more rank than he be sent to Santa Rosa Island. He stated that, while he was willing to devote his whole being to the army, he could not endure another summer in the enervating climate of Florida. He had spent upwards of fifteen years there and he required the bracing influences of a northern climate. He repeated his request that he be relieved.[16]

Until the end of the calendar year, things remained quiet on Pensacola Bay.

12

"Fort Pickens Stands to This Day"

At 4:30 in the afternoon of Thursday, January 1, 1862, the steamer *Time* came down from Pensacola to the navy yard wharf where she commenced to take on a cargo of coal. In retaliation for the gunfire Fort McRee had opened on his own small craft on November 29, Colonel Brown ordered three salvoes fired at *Time*. When batteries ashore responded, Brown ordered their fire returned. He thought the affair would end with that but forty-five minutes later the entire line of batteries on the mainland from the navy yard to Fort McRee opened on Fort Pickens. Brown ordered all his batteries to return the fire. A full bombardment from both sides ensued which continued until after dark. Brown's batteries ceased firing first. The Confederate guns continued intermittently until 2:00 A.M. the following morning. About 9:00 in the evening a bright blaze appeared from within the navy yard and in an hour the whole area of the bay was lit by several large buildings burning fiercely. Brown later acknowledged in his report to the adjutant general that his guns had been firing hot shot, carcasses, and rock fire with the intent of setting fires within the Confederate camps and the navy yard.[1]

Brown assumed from the wild and uncoordinated fire of the Southern batteries that Bragg was not present and that some less experienced officer was in command on the mainland. He reported two of his men slightly wounded in the affair and he immediately ordered Colonel Dodge to march the 75th New York a good two miles from Fort Pickens both to get the new men out of range of the Confederate fire and to guard against a possible assault the bombardment might be intended to cover. Brown noted in his report that the 75th New York was a fine regiment and would, no doubt, do good service given the chance. Colonel Brown was showing a major change in attitude from his original opinion toward volunteer regiments which was based more on the qualities of the two commanders serving under him, Colonel John Dodge and Colonel Billy Wilson.[2]

Braxton Bragg, in fact, was not present on the mainland during the bombardment. He had been called to Mobile where he was advised by telegraph that firing had broken out between his batteries and those of the Federal forces on Santa Rosa Island and that the firing had been returned by order of General Anderson who commanded in Bragg's absence. Bragg reported no casualties other than the loss of a valuable storehouse at the navy yard which had burned. He regretted to report, he wrote to the adjutant general, that the testimony of many officers of rank represented that Anderson had been so intoxicated as to be entirely unfit for duty and that his personal conduct had been reprehensible. Anderson's performance was being investigated and, Bragg wrote, an arrest would probably result therefrom. Not the least of Bragg's concerns was the large and criminal waste permitted by Anderson of munitions necessary for the future defense of his position. As had Harvey Brown on Santa Rosa Island, Braxton Bragg asked for a second in command who could be trusted with the army at Pensacola should he be absent or unable to serve. As it now was, in Bragg's absence Anderson was next in rank and would assume command.[3]

Bragg's condemnation of Anderson must to be taken with caution. Anderson was not subsequently brought up on charges for the bombardment of Santa Rosa Island as Bragg had indicated would be done. Anderson did admit that he and his wife were receiving visitors on New Years Eve when they heard firing from the batteries along the shore and at the navy yard and that the charge of intemperance was one he could not defend himself against. He promised to abstain thereafter and did not drink again during the war. Brigadier General William R. Boggs wrote that the charges were a "vile libel on a gallant officer and an honorable gentleman." Anderson's subsequent conduct during the war more than bears out Boggs's description of him. Historian Douglas Southall Freeman wrote that "Whispers that he was overfond of a social glass seem to have no foundation."[4]

At the beginning of January Brigadier General Samuel Jones was commanding a Georgia brigade with the Confederate forces in northern Virginia when he received orders to report to Pensacola and relieve General Anderson of command after Bragg relocated his own headquarters to Mobile. Bragg thought highly of Samuel Jones and described him as an officer with high character and one with experience as an artillerist in whom there was every reason to hope for success in his new command which, Bragg typically added, was generally in fine order although somewhat disorganized after the short tenure of its former commander, Anderson. At the end of the first week in February Secretary Benjamin at Richmond directed Bragg to have Jones rush four regiments from Pensacola to Corinth, Mississippi, to reinforce the force General Albert Sidney Johnston was organizing against the threat of Federals approaching from Kentucky and Tennessee.[5]

On Saturday, February 22, under orders from General-in-Chief McClellan, Colonel Harvey Brown turned command of the Department of Florida over to recently promoted Brigadier General Lewis Arnold at Fort Pickens. Brown proceeded to New York City where he was given command of the defenses of the harbor and the city. Brown had declined an offered temporary promotion to brigadier general of volunteers on September 28, preferring to retain his permanent commission in the regular United States Army. He was subsequently brevetted to the rank of brigadier general in the regular army to date from November 23, the date of the initial bombardment of the Confederate positions on the mainland. Brown later commanded the Federal troops rushed to New York City from General Grant's armies in Virginia to suppress the draft riots in mid–July, 1863, for which he was brevetted a major general in the United States Army in 1866. Brown retired from active service in August, 1863, and died at his home in Rahway, New Jersey, on March 31, 1874. He is buried at Hazel Wood Cemetery there. Arnold, formerly in command at Fort Jefferson on Dry Tortugas, was forty-five, a graduate of West Point, class of 1837. He had served in the Seminole Wars in Florida, along the Canadian frontier, and in the Mexican War where he suffered had two wounds and won two brevets.[6]

Toward the end of February General Bragg informed General Jones that the Confederacy was being forced to concentrate its resources to face the pressure from the Federal armies in Tennessee. Jones was ordered to abandon Pensacola. All ordnance and munitions there were to be shipped to Mobile, provisions and supplies were to go to Montgomery. Jones was to have these actions made secretly, removing his heavy guns at night and masking their former positions afterwards. He was to retain sufficient troops who were to be kept out of sight of the enemy until the very end but he was to send all possible reinforcements to General Johnston at Corinth, Mississippi. He was to leave nothing behind that the Federals might use, burning everything he could not carry off. He was to destroy all public and private vessels and machinery, to disable sawmills around the bay, and to burn their lumber stocks. The railroad from Pensacola to its junction with the line from Mobile to Montgomery at Pollard, Alabama, was to be taken up and the rails carried off to safety. Bragg commenced the reinforcement of Johnston's forces with a movement of 10,000 of his own men from Mobile to Corinth by means of the Mobile & Ohio Railroad. An officer writing at the time described Bragg's troops as the finest and best disciplined body of troops the Confederacy had. In spite of his many personal weaknesses, Braxton Bragg was an outstanding organizer and disciplinarian.[7]

On Saturday, March 4, Bragg expanded his orders to Jones, explaining that the situation in Tennessee had beome so serious that he was on the way there himself and was transferring command of the Department of Alabama and West Florida to Jones who would command from Pensacola as he completed the abandonment of the works and the destruction of public property there. Late that week Pensacola citizen Lucius Merritt wrote to his wife Lizzie at Montgomery that the 17th Alabama was leaving for Tennessee. The following day Colonel Thomas Jones of the 27th Mississippi was given command of the troops remaining at Pensacola by General Jones who had also been ordered to Tennessee. Colonel Jones had identical orders to burn or destroy everything he could not take or ship off that might be of use to the Federals. Colonel Jones sent the 9th Mississippi Regiment, the Mississippi Battalion, the Florida Battalion, and the 4th Alabama Battalion off to the army at Corinth. He and the remainder of his force would follow when he completed the work of abandonment and destruction.[8]

By the first day of April, more than a month after Bragg had ordered him to hurry the abandonment of Pensacola, Colonel Jones was still shipping guns, munitions, supplies, and provisions. As the Confederate military presence drew down, stragglers and wanderers began to accumulate in the town. Jones issued a proclamation directed in part at "certain lounging, worthless people, white as well as black, who frequent the neighborhood of Pensacola, and have no observable occupation; their intentions may be honest, but the colonel commanding does not believe the fact, and as he has no use for their presence, they are warned to leave, or the consequences will be on their own heads – the gallows is erected in Pensacola and will be in constant use after the 3rd day of April, 1862 – the town is under complete martial law."[9]

On Sunday, April 6, on the banks of the Tennessee River, Federal forces under Brigadier General Ulysses Grant were suddenly attacked by Confederate forces under General Albert Sidney Johnston who had moved from his base at Corinth. Braxton Bragg's Second Corps came in on the Confederate right as desperate fighting surged around Shiloh Meeting House. Bragg's corps consisted of many of the regiments he had organized and trained at Pensacola and brought with him to Tennessee. The battle raged all through the day and night and into the following day. On the death of Johnston, General Beauregard assumed command and, at the close of the second day, ordered the Southern forces to fall back to Corinth. Bragg wrote to his wife describing his significant role in the fighting and telling her the behavior of his troops from Pensacola and Mobile was beyond praise. In typical Bragg fashion, he had less than complimentary comments regarding several other Confederate units and their leaders.[10]

At the same time a Federal squadron under the command of Admiral David Farragut was standing off the mouth of the Mississippi River ready to launch the attack on New Orleans. A squadron of small mortar boats under Commander David Porter had begun lobbing shells into Fort Jackson and Fort St. Phillip, the outer defenses of the city. On Thursday, April 24, Farragut issued orders for his steamers to run upriver past the concentrated fire of the forts and batteries lining the riverbank. Farragut arrived off the levee on Friday and on Saturday, April 26, he accepted the surrender of the largest city in the South. He then turned his attention toward Mobile.[11]

During the first week in May, Porter moved his mortar boat squadron to Mobile Bay and commended taking soundings and placing marker buoys in preparation for the arrival of Farragut's squadron. This caused great excitement and confusion among the authorities in the city. A severe storm coming up, Porter ordered his boats to take shelter off Ship Island, sixty miles to the east in the gulf, while he rode out the storm in his flag ship, the former revenue service steamer *Harriet Lane* which had taken the place of the worn-out *Powhatan*. Eastward at Pensacola, Colonel Jones reacted to the information that Farragut was expected daily off Mobile and made his final arrangements for evacuation. He ordered a regiment of unarmed volunteers that had arrived at Pensacola back to Mobile. Beginning on Thursday, May 8, Jones oversaw the removal of the final columbiads from their carriages and their replacement with black painted logs. He had already sent off gunpowder, shot and shell, quantities of copper, lead, brass, and iron. Gutters, lightning rods, window sash weights, bells, and piping all had been taken down and shipped off with cordage, blocks, chains, and other loose items from the navy yard. Jones ordered the 8th Mississippi Regiment to depart for Mobile. Three companies of cavalry arrived from Montgomery and Jones added these to the two mounted companies he had retained. The infantry quietly withdrew and marched from the camps, taking the road for Oakfield, six miles north of Pensacola on the line of the railroad. Jones assigned the cavalry to posts between Fort McRee and the navy yard. At 11:30 P.M. in the midst of the raging storm Jones had two blue lights raised at the marine hospital. At once every combustible item from Fort McRee to the navy yard went up in flames and several minutes later the fires from burning public property rose over the town of Pensacola up the shore.[12]

Federal batteries on Santa Rosa Island opened a furious bombardment but the work of destruction continued. Jones's cavalry destroyed the tents still standing in the abandoned camps, everything that would burn in Fort McRee and Fort Barrancas, the marine hospital, the officers quarters at the navy yard, the hull of *Fulton* still lying on the ways, the remaining stocks of coal at the navy yard, and all the machinery for drawing vessels up on the ways. Jones had men place loaded artillery shells in the coal piles to explode as the fuel

Fort Barrancas ditch and drawbridge, where a party of men were chased off some time before midnight January 8, 1861 (photograph by J.D. Edwards, Southern Historical Collection, Samuel Henry Lockett Papers, Wilson Library, University of North Carolina at Chapel Hill).

burned in order to prevent Federals from approaching and extinguishing the flames and this was done in the fireplaces of the houses at the navy yard. The long boom of the shear crane at the navy yard was cut in two and the spars and masts of *Fulton* which were lying alongside the steamer were burned. At Pensacola, obeying orders not to destroy private property, Jones limited the burning to a large oil factory, the quartermaster's warehouses, some large boats, and three steam vessels. The steamer *Turel* which had been commandeered for use as an army transport was sent up the Escambia River with orders to fell trees into the river and place every other possible obstruction in the river as she passed. The casemates and galleries at Fort McRee were filled with old lumber and loaded shells and set afire and the galleries and implement rooms at Fort Barrancas were similarly dealt with. Jones considered the work of destruction as complete as could be done without actually blowing up the buildings and their walls with gunpowder. Jones and the cavalry then joined the rest of the force at Oakfield, leaving the 29th Alabama and five companies of Florida volunteers behind to guard the crews taking up the iron from the railroad. The Federal bombardment of the burning sites on the mainland continued through the night until dawn of the following day.[13]

About 2:00 A.M. off Mobile, the masthead lookout on *Harriet Lane* reported a bright light in the east in the direction of Pensacola. Porter ordered the steamer there at full speed in spite of the raging storm. Bows awash part of the time, Porter conned the steamer through the channel between Fort Pickens and Fort McRee and into the harbor on the same course he had planned to follow on April 17 of the previous year. The shelling from Fort Pickens ceased when *Harriet Lane* steamed past. Earlier in the day, however, First Lieutenant Richard Jackson, General Arnold's aide and adjutant, had taken a detail of soldiers on board the navy schooner *Maria Wood* and sailed up the bay to Pensacola. Landing at the town wharf Jackson demanded the surrender of the town. Acting Mayor Dr. John Brosnahan offered to surrender what he had which, he told Jackson, was not much. The population of Pensacola that had not fled or left with the last of the Confederate troops earlier in the day consisted of twenty-seven persons.[14]

As *Maria Wood* was returning to Fort Pickens she passed *Harriet Lane* heading up the bay. Signal flags from Porter's vessel went unanswered so Porter ordered a shot fired across *Maria Woods's* stern. Jackson ordered the schooner to come about and followed the steamer back to Pensacola. There Porter demanded the surrender of the town only to learn from Dr. Brosnahan this had already been tendered to Lieutenant Jackson. Chagrined, Porter demanded a promise from the acting mayor that Federal forces arriving at Pensacola would not be molested. Returning to Fort Pickens, Porter converted *Harriet Lane* hastily into a troop carrier and by 3:00 P.M. had moved 400 soldiers, two field pieces, horses, and carts from Santa Rosa Island over to the navy yard. General Arnold reported that, with Porter's help, he had taken military possession of Fort Barrancas, Fort McRee, Barrancas Barracks, and the navy yard that afternoon. In the evening a flag raising ceremony was conducted by Federal troops in the Plaza Ferdinand at Pensacola. Transportation of military supplies into the town from the wharf had to be by hand-propelled railroad flatcars since the Confederates had taken the locomotives with them. Confederate Secretary of the Navy Mallory's luxurious home at 286 Palafox Street was commandeered as living quarters and regimental headquarters by Colonel Billy Wilson of the 6th New York.[15]

On Monday, May 12, Company G, Captain Dobie, and Company I, Captain Bailey, of the 6th New York crossed over from Santa Rosa Island and raised the national flag at the navy yard, sixteen months to the day from when Quartermaster William Conway had courageously refused to strike it.[16]

Fort Pickens remained in Federal hands throughout the years of the American Civil War. The great anchorage and the refurbished navy yard were never again taken by the Confederacy and were never able to serve as a base for blockade runners and commerce raiders although, as events unfolded, the South never developed the capacity after its early months to mount any such efforts. Fort Pickens remained an active army post through the years after the Civil War as did Fort Barrancas and Barrancas Barracks. Between 1875 and 1876 Fort McRee was dismantled because of deteriorating foundations brought on by action of tide and wind since it was first built.[17]

On June 23, 1899, a fire broke out in the casemate just west of the main gate of Fort Pickens at 12:45 A.M. Details of soldiers worked to extinguish the blaze but were not able to contain it. Flames reached the northwest bastion where 8,000 pounds of gunpowder were stored. The magazine exploded at 5:20 A.M. in a roar that was felt and heard for miles. The northwest bastion was entirely destroyed and one soldier was killed by flying debris. The gap in the wall was never repaired. In 1914, the United States Navy established the Pensacola Naval Aviating Training Station on the land the navy yard had occupied. Generations of navy and marine aviators trained at Pensacola in aircraft that began as flimsy wooden and fabric kites and eventually reached well to the supersonic and the superb. Fort Pickens was placed under the jurisdiction of the Florida Board of Parks and Historic Memorials in 1949 and then transferred to the National Park Service as part of the Gulf Islands National Seashore.[18]

After all these years, Fort Pickens stands to this day.

Notes

Chapter 1

1. Virginia Parks and Judith A. Bense, *Underground Pensacola*, Publication Number 1, Pensacola Archeological Society, Pensacola, FL, 1989, 17 [Parks, *Underground*]; Virginia Parks, *Pensacola: Spaniards to Space Age*, Pensacola Historical Society, Pensacola, FL, 1986, 1–5 [Parks, *Pensacola,*]; Panzacola, later Pensacola, comes from *pa shi okla* which means "bread people" in the closely related Chocktaw tongue, according to the Pensacola Historical Society; Lelia Abercrombie, "Early Churches in Pensacola," *The Florida Historical Quarterly*, Pensacola Quadricentennial Issue, Vol. XXXVII, Numbers 3 and 4, The Florida Historical Society, Jacksonville, FL, January, 1959, 447 [Abercrombie]; William B. Griffin, "Spanish Pensacola, 1700–1763," *The Florida Historical Quarterly*, Pensacola Quadricentennial Issue, Volume XXXVII, Nos. 3 and 4, The Florida Historical Society, Jacksonville, FL, 1959, 242n [Griffin]; Charles W. Arnade, "Tristan de Luna and the Ochuse (Pensacola Bay), 1559," *The Florida Historical Quarterly*, Pensacola Quadricentennial Issue, Volume XXXVII, Numbers 3 and 4, The Florida Historical Society, Jacksonville, FL, 1959, 213 [Arnade]; Judith A. Bense, "The Colonial Archeological Record in Pensacola, Florida," paper presented in the Symposium: Colonial Pensacola: A First Syntheses, (Forts of Pensacola), Society for Historical Archeology Conference, Washington, DC, 1995, 2 [Bense]; Alfred Thayer Mahan, *The Navy in the Civil War, Vol. III, The Gulf and Inland Waters*, Charles Scribner's Sons, New York, NY, 1883, 3 [Mahan]; Albert Manucy, "The Founding of Pensacola—Reasons and Reality," *The Florida Historical Quarterly*, Pensacola Quadricentennial Issue, Volume XXXVII, Numbers 3 and 4, The Florida Historical Society, Jacksonville, FL, 1959, 229 [Manucy].

2. Edwin C. Bearss, *Historical Structure Report, Fort Pickens, Historical Data Section, 1821–1895,* U.S. Department of the Interior, National Park Service, Denver Service Center, Denver, CO, 1983, 18 [Bearss, *Structure*]; John A. Eisterhold, "Lumber and Trade in Pensacola and West Florida, 1800–1860," *The Florida Historical Quarterly,* Volume LI, No. 3, The Florida Historical Society, Gainesville, FL, 1973, 267 [Eisterhold]; Henry Clay Armstrong, *History of Escambia County, Florida,* The Record Company, Printers, St. Augustine, FL, 1930, 91 [Armstrong]; George A. Pearce, *Pensacola during the Civil War, A Thorn in the Side of the Confederacy,* University Press of Florida, Gainesville, FL, 2000, 2 [Pearce, *Pensacola*]; Cecil Johnson, "Pensacola in the British Period: Summary and Significance," *The Florida Historical Quarterly,* Pensacola Quadricentennial Issue, Volume XXXVII, Nos. 3 and 4, The Florida Historical Society, Jacksonville, FL, 1959, 271 [Cecil Johnson]; Ernest F. Dibble, *William H. Chase—Gulf Coast Fort Builder,* The Gulf Coast Collection, Wilmington, DE, n. d., n. p. [Dibble, *Chase*]; National Archives, Office of the Chief Engineer, Record Group 77, Joseph G. Totten, Lieutenant Colonel, to Major James Kearney, Mobile, January 1822, mss letter, *Letters and Reports of Colonel Joseph G. Totten, 1803–64,* 10 Volumes, Volume 1, No. 2, E148, Washington, DC [Totten]; United States Congress, 27th Congress, 2nd Session, *Senate Executive Document No. 98,* "Report from the Secretary of the Navy, in compliance with a resolution of the Senate, in relation to the necessity and practicability of establishing a navy-yard, naval depot, and station upon the Gulf of Mexico," Washington, DC, January 31, 1842 [*Ex Doc 98*].

3. Thomas M. Garner, *The Pensacola Lighthouse,* Pensacola Historical Society, Pensacola, FL, 1994, 8 [Garner].

4. Ernest F. Dibble, "Ante-Bellum Pensacola and the Military Presence," The Pensacola Series Commemorating the American Revolution Bicentennial, Volume 3, *Pensacola News Journal,* Pensacola, FL, 1974, 3, 13 [Dibble, *Pensacola*]. Although located at the village of Warrington, eight miles southwest on the shore of the mainland from the town of Pensacola, the navy yard was officially designated the Pensacola Navy Yard: Henry Walke, *Naval Scenes and Reminiscences of the Civil War...,* F. R. Reed & Co., New York, NY, 1877, 9n [Walke]; Dibble, *Pensacola,* 13; George F. Pearce, *The U. S. Navy in Pensacola: From Sailing Ships to Naval Aviation, (1825–1930),* University Presses of Florida, Pensacola, FL, 1980, 16 [Pearce, *Navy*]. Woolsey's actual rank was that of naval captain, the highest commissioned rank in the United States Navy at the time; naval captains in com-

mand of squadrons afloat or of major installations ashore bore the honorary rank of commodore. Virgil Carrington Jones, *The Civil War at Sea, The Blockaders*, Vol. 1, Holt, Reinhart, Winston, New York, NY, 1960, 47 [Jones]; William C. Davis, ed., *Shadows of the Storm, Volume 2 of the Image of War, 1861–1865*, Doubleday & Company, Inc., Garden City, NY, 1981, 168 [Davis, *Image*]; Mary Dawkins, "Warrington and Woolsey, Where Are They?" *Pensacola, Magazine*, Pensacola, FL, 1995, 29 [Dawkins]; United States Government, Navy Department, *Official Records of the Union and Confederate Navies in the War of the Rebellion*, Series I, Volume 4, Government Printing Office, Washington, DC, 1896, 25–27 [*ORN I, 4*]; United States Congress, 26th Congress, 2nd Session, *House of Representatives Report No. 87*, "Naval Forces of the United States — Where Ships Are Now Stationed," Washington, DC, February 21, 1861, 65 [*House Report 87*]; Herbert H. Doherty, "Ante-Bellum Pensacola, 1821–1860," *The Florida Historical Quarterly*, Pensacola Quadricentennial Issue, Vol. XXXVII, Nos. 3 and 4, The Florida Historical Society, Jacksonville, FL, January, 1959, 351 [Doherty]; L. R. Hammersly & Co., publ., *A Naval Encyclopedia...*, Philadelphia, PA, 1881, 601, [Hammersly]; Herman Hattaway and Archer Jones, *How the North Won: A Military History of the Civil War*, University of Illinois Press, Champagne-Urbana, IL, 1983, 127 [Hattaway].

5. United States Congress, *American State Papers, Class V, (Military Affairs)*, Vol. 3, No. 287, Brigadier General S. Bernard to Major General A. Macomb, "Fortification of the Harbor of Pensacola, Sept. 19, 1825 [ASP, *Military*].

6. James C. Coleman, *A Castle Built on Sand*, Pensacola Historical Society, Pensacola, FL, 1988, viii [Coleman, *Castle*,]; United States Government, War Department, *War of the Rebellion, A Compilation of the Official Records of the Union and Confederate Armies*, Government Printing Office, Washington, DC, Series 1, Volume 1, 1880, 421 [*ORA I, 1*]; United States Government, Department of the Interior, National Park Service, Gulf Islands National Seashore, site pamphlets, *Fort Barrancas*, n. loc., n. d. [Sites].

7. James C. and Irene S. Coleman, *Guardians of the Gulf, Pensacola Fortifications, 1698–1980*, Pensacola Historical Society, Pensacola, FL, 1982, 60 [Coleman, *Guardians*]; *ORA I, 1*, 421.

8. Coleman, *Guardians*, 60; *ORA I, 1*, 421.

9. Dibble, *Pensacola*, 37–39; Dibble, *Chase*, 8; John Shipley Tilley, *Lincoln Takes Command*, The University of North Carolina Press, Chapel Hill, NC, 1941, 37n [Tilley]; Charles H. Hildreth, "Railroads Out of Pensacola, 1833–1883," *The Florida Historical Quarterly*, Pensacola Quadricentennial Issue, Nos. 3 and 4, The Florida Historical Society, Jacksonville, FL, January, 1959, 408 [Hildreth]; Warren G. Fouraker, *The Administration of Robert Raymond Reid*, master's thesis, Florida State University, Tallahassee, FL, 1949, 12 [Fouraker]; Virginia Parks, Alan Rick, and Norman Simons, "Pensacola in the Civil War," *Pensacola Historical Society Quarterly*, Vol. 2, Spring, 1978, the Pensacola Historical Society, Pensacola, FL, 30 [Parks, *Civil War*]; Thomas Muir, Jr., and David P. Ogden, *The Fort Pickens Story*, Pensacola Historical Society, Pensacola, FL, 1989, 5 [Muir]; Coleman, *Guardians*, 3, 55, 60, 69; *ORA I, 1*, 349.

10. Dibble, *Pensacola*, 35.

11. Parks, *Civil War*, 3; Donald R. Hadd, *Secession Movement in Florida, 1850–1861*, master's thesis, Florida State University, Tallahassee, FL, 1960, 1, 2 [Hadd]; Marjory Stoneman Douglas, *Florida, The Long Frontier*, Harper & Row, Publishers, New York, NY, 1967, 172 [Douglas]; Everett B. Long, with Barbara Long, *The Civil War, Day by Day, An Almanac, 1861–1865*, Doubleday Company, New York, NY. 1971, [Long, *Almanac*]; James Bulger Mool, *Florida in Federal Politics: Statehood to Secession*, master's thesis, Duke University, Durham, NC, 1940, 10, 12 [Mool].

12. John E. Johns, *Florida During the Civil War*, University of Florida Press, Gainesville, FL, 1963, 12 [Johns]; Benson J. Lossing, *Pictoral History of the Civil War in the United States of America*, George W. Childs, Publishers, Philadelphia, PA, 1866, 60 [Lossing]; Edwin L. Williams, Jr., *Florida in the Union, 1845–1861*, doctoral thesis, University of North Carolina, Chapel Hill, NC, 1951, 559 [Williams].

13. National Archives, *Abstracts of Service Records of Naval Officers, 1798–1893*, National Archives Microfilm Publications, James Armstrong, Washington, DC, 1960 [Armstrong, *File*]; Dudley W. Knox, *A History of the United States Navy*, G. Putnam's Sons, New York, NY, 1936, 186 [Knox]; Johns, 48; Richard S. West, Jr., *Gideon Welles, Lincoln's Navy Department*, The Bobbs-Merrill Company, New York, NY, 1943, 109 [West, *Welles*]; *ORN I, 4*, 16, 48–60; John O. Johnson, "William Conway, A Forgotten Camden Hero," *War Papers Read Before the Commandery of the State of Maine, Military Order of the Loyal Legion of the United States*, Lefavor-Rower Company, Portland, ME, 1908, 1–5 [John Johnson]; David P. Ogden, *Scapegoat: Captain James Armstrong and the Surrender of the Pensacola Navy Yard in 1861*, master's thesis, University of Central Florida, Orlando, FL, 1992, 16 [Ogden]; Jeremiah H. Gilman, "With Slemmer in Pensacola Harbor," *Battles and Leaders of the Civil War*, Robert Underwood Johnson and Clarence Clough Buel, eds., Volume 1, Thomas Yoseloff, Inc., New York, NY, 1956, 27 [Gilman]; Edward W. Callahan, ed., *List of Officers of the Navy of the United States and the Marine Corps from 1775 to 1900...*, Haskin House Publishers, Ltd., New York, NY, 1969, 189 [Callahan]; Hammersly, 601; Pearce, *Pensacola*, 27.

14. Henry Erben, "Surrender of the Navy Yard at Pensacola, Florida, January 12, 1861," *Personal Recollections of the War of the Rebellion, Address Delivered Before the Commandery of the State of New York, Military Order of the Loyal Legion of the United States*, G. Putnam's Sons, New York, NY, 1897, 213–214 [Erben]; K. Jack Bauer and Stephen S. Roberts, *Register of Ships of the United States Navy, 1775–1900, Major Combatants*, Greenwood Press, New York, NY, 1991, 60 [Bauer]; Charles J. Meyer, Jr., "U.S.S. *Fulton* (AS-11)," 50th Anniversary, *Silent Partner of the Silent Service*, Turner Publishing Company, Paducah, KY, 1991, 10 [Meyer]; *House Report 87*, 632; George E. Belknap, *The Home Squadron in the Winter of 1860–61*, Papers of the Military Historical Society of Massachusetts, Volume XII, Naval Actions and History, 1799–1898, Griffith-Stillings Press, Boston, MA, 1902, 79 [Belknap]; Patricia Faust, ed., *Historical Times Illustrated Encyclopedia of the Civil War*, Harper & Row, Publishers, New

York, NY, 1986, 796 [Faust]; Samuel Eliot Morison, *The Oxford History of the American People*, Oxford University Press, New York, NY, 1965, 662 [Morison]; National Archives, Office of the Quartermaster General, Record Group 92, Consolidated Correspondence File, R. H. Watts to Montgomery C. Meigs, mss letter, December 6, 1865, Washington, DC [Watts].

15. *ORN I, 4*, 6–7, 34; *House Report 87*, 63.

16. Gilman, 26. Major John H. Winder, a native of Maryland, later resigned his commission in the United States Army and entered service with the Confederacy; he eventually became commissary-general of prisoners responsible for all prisoners of war held by Confederate forces east of the Mississippi River. William B. Hesseltine, *Civil War Prisons*, Frederick Ungar Publishing Co., New York, NY, 1930, 168 [Hesseltine]; National Archives, Office of the Adjutant General, Record Group 94, Regular Army Muster Rolls, Entry 53, Muster Rolls of Captain John H. Winder's Co. G of the First Regiment of Artillery, from 31 December, 1860, to 28 February, 1861 [Co. G Muster Roll];National Archives, Office of the Adjutant General, Record Group 94, Letters Received by the Appointment, Commission, and Personnel Branch of the Adjutant-General's Office, 1863–1870, Adam J. Slemmer, Roll 218, 1865, S1224-S1280, Washington, DC [Slemmer, *File*]; George W. Cullum, *Biographical Register of the Officers and Graduates of the U. S. Military Academy at West Point...*, Houghton Mifflin and Company, Boston, MA, 1891, 415 [Cullum]; William Watson Davis, *The Civil War and Reconstruction in Florida*, Columbia University Press, New York, NY, 1913, 74 [Davis, *War*]; Edwin C. Bearss, "Fort Pickens and the Secession Crisis, January–February, 1861,: *Gulf Coast Historical Review*, History Department of the University of South Alabama, Mobile, AL, Spring, 1995, 14 [Bearss, *Pensacola*]; Moses Auge, *Lives of the Eminent Dead and Biographical Notices of Prominent Living Citizens of Montgomery County, Pa.*, self-published, Norristown, PA, 1897, 225 [Auge]; Arch Frederick Blakely, *General John H. Winder, C. S. A.*, The University of Florida Press, Gainesville, FL, 1990, 6 [Blakely]; National Archives, Office of the Adjutant General, Record Group 94, Register of Letters Received by the Office of the Adjutant General, Main Series, 1812–1889, John H. Winder, Roll 62, Washington, DC [Winder, *File*]; Mary Reed Bobbitt, ed., *With Dearest Love To All, The Life and Letters of Lady Jebb*, Henry Regnery Company, Chicago, IL, 1966, 25 [Bobbitt]; National Archives, Textural Records Branch, Service Records, Jeremiah H. Gilman, Washington, DC, [Gilman, *Service Record*]; Cullum, 656; Jones, 27; Walke, 8; *Harper's Weekly*, Vol. V, Nos. 191,192.

17. *ORA I, 1*, 3, 5, 70, 129, 252; John G. Nicolay and John Hays, eds., *Abraham Lincoln*, The Century Co., New York, NY, 1894, 57 [Nicolay]; Samuel Wylie Crawford, *The Genesis of the Civil War, The Story of Sumter, 1860–1861*, Charles L. Webster Co., New York, NY, 1887, 106 [Crawford]. South Carolina Governor Francis W. Pickens was the grandson of Brigadier General Andrew Pickens for whom Fort Pickens at Pensacola Bay was named; Johns, 26; Mary Elizabeth Dickison, *Dickison and His Men*, facsimile reproduction of the 1890 edition, University of Florida Press, Gainesville, FL, 1962, ix [Dickison, *Men*]; *St. Augustine Examiner*, December 29, 1860; *Fernandina East Floridian*, November 13, 1860; George C. Bittle, "Florida Prepares for War," *Florida Historical Quarterly, Volume LI, Number 2*, The Florida Historical Society, Gainesville, FL, 1972, 144 [Bittle]; Sydney J. Weinberg, *Slavery and Secession in Florida, 1845–1861*, master's thesis, University of Florida, Tallahassee, FL, 1940, [Weinberg].

18. Margaret Leech, *Reveille in Washington, 1860–1861*, Harper & Brothers, Publishers, New York, NY, 1941, 4 [Leech]; Nicolay, *Lincoln*, 336; Kenneth M. Stampp, *And the War Came, The North and the Secession Crisis, 1860–1861*, Louisiana State University Press, Baton Rouge, LA, 1950, 19 [Stampp, *War*]; Frederick Bancroft, *The Life of William H. Seward*, Vol. 2, Harper Brothers Publishers, New York, NY, 1900, 3 [Bancroft]; Edward Everett Hale, Jr., *William H. Seward*, George W. Jacobs & Company, Philadelphia, PA, 1910, 267 [Hale]; Gilman, 5; Ivan Musicant, *Divided Waters, The Naval History of the Civil War*, Harper Collins Publishers, Inc., New York, NY, 1995, 2 [Musicant]; Philip Gerald Auchampaugh, *James Buchanan and His Cabinet on the Eve of Secession*, privately printed, Lancaster, PA, 1926, 85 [Auchampaugh]; William M. Fowler, Jr., *Under Two Flags, The American Navy in the Civil War*, W. W. Norman & Company, New York, NY, 1990, 33 [Fowler].

19. Russell Frank Weigley, *Quartermaster General of the Union Army, A Biography of M. C. Meigs*, Columbia University Press, New York, NY, 1959, 126 [Weigley]; Leech, 3; Nicolay, *Lincoln* 249; Faust, 662; Mark Mayo Boatner, *The Civil War Dictionary*, David McKay Company, New York, NY, 1959, 778 [Boatner]; Crawford, 168, 174; James Buchanan, *Mr. Buchanan's Administration on the Eve of the Rebellion*, D. Appleton and Company, New York, NY, 1866, 175 [Buchanan]; Philip Schriver Klein, *President Buchanan, A Biography*, The Pennsylvania State University Press, University Park, PA, 1962, 355 [Klein]; Joseph T. S. Durkin, *Stephen Mallory, Confederate Navy Chief*, The University of North Carolina Press, Chapel Hill, NC, 1954, 168 [Durkin]; *ORA I, 1*, 9, 128.

20. *ORA I, 1*, 334; *ORN* I, 4, 5; Dwight Lowell Drummond, *The Secessionist Movement, 1860–1861*, The Macmillan Company, New York, NY, 1931, 175 [Drummond, *Secession*]; *ORN I, 4*, 6.

21. *ORA I, 1*, 29, 349; Arthur William Thompson, *David Yulee: A Study in Nineteenth Century American Thought and Enterprise*, Columbia University Press, New York, NY, 1954, 139 [Thompson]; Evelyn T. Meredith, *The Secession Movement in Florida, 1850–1861*, master's thesis, Duke University, Durham, NC, 1941, 97 [Meredith].

Chapter 2

1. *ORN, I, 4*, 143; *ORA I, 1*, 318–322; Gilman, 2; William Thomas Cash, *The Story of Florida*, Vol. 1, The American Society, Inc., New York, NY, 1938, 428 [Cash]; David C. Childress, "Mount Vernon Barracks: The Blue, The Gray, and The Red," *The Alabama Review*, University of Alabama Press, Auburn, AL, 42 (April, 1989), 125–135 [Childress].

2. Bobbitt, 33.

3. *ORA, I, 1*, 350, 364.

4. William L. Haskin, *The History of the First Regiment of Artillery...*, B. Thurston and Company, Portland, ME, 1879, 48 [Haskin]; *ORN I, 4*, 35; *ORA I*, 334; Avery Craven and Frank E. Vandiver, *The American Tragedy, the Civil War in Retrospect*, A Series of Lectures at Hampden-Sydney College, Hampden-Sydney, VA, April, 1959, 48 [Craven]; Watts; *ORA I, 1*, 334. All communications to and from army headquarters were directed to and emanated from the office of the adjutant general.

5. *ORN I, 4*, 24, 33.

6. Gary R. Rice, "Pre-Dawn Strike at Santa Rosa Island," *America's Civil War*, A Primedia Publication, Leesburg, VA, January, 1998, 55 [Rice]; Charlton W. Tebeau, *A History of Florida*, University of Miami Press, Coral Gables, FL, 1971, 201 [Tebeau]; *ORA I, 1*, 334; Bill Kaczor, "Puzzles of the Past, Fort Pickens Could Have Been the Start of the Civil War," *Tampa Tribune*, August 3, 1984 [Kaczor]. In 1867, R. L. Sweetman wrote to then Lieutenant Colonel Slemmer telling him the party that approached Fort Barrancas on the night of January 8, 1861, consisted only of himself and a Mr. Williams who were making a reconnaissance of the fort which they expected to find unoccupied [Bobbitt, 42.]

7. *ORA, I, 1*, 443.

8. Parks, *Civil War*, 3; Tebeau, 201; *ORA I, 1*, 444; Charles L. Lufkin, "War Council in Pensacola, January 17, 1861," *Gulf Coast Historical Review*, Volume I, Number 3, University of South Alabama, Mobile, AL, 1993, 49 [Lufkin]; Dorothy Dodd, ed., "Edmund Ruffin's Account of the Florida Secession Convention, 1861," *The Florida Historical Quarterly*, Volume IX, Number 2, The Florida Historical Society, Tallahassee, FL, October, 1933, 74, [Dodd].

9. *ORA I, 1*, 253; Crawford, 183; Johns, 19; Robert Hendrickson, *Sumter, the First Day of the Civil War*, Rowan and Littlefield, Publishers, New York, NY, 1990, 123 [Hendrickson]. Citadel Cadet George Edward Haynesworth is credited with firing the first shot of the American Civil War at 7:14 A.M. on the morning of Wednesday, January 9, 1861. Haynesworth's shot was fired some seven hours or more after the challenge by Corporal David H. Boyd to the party of men approaching the gate and drawbridge at Fort Barrancas on Pensacola Bay shortly before midnight on January 8. This can be considered the first confrontation between opposing forces in the war that was to follow.

10. Davis, *War*, 78; Walke, 2; *ORA I, 1*, 335. Armstrong and Slemmer did not hold equivalent rank although each was in complete command of the forces and functions under him. Armstrong, a navy captain, held rank equal to that of an army colonel and the highest commissioned rank in the navy. Slemmer, an army first lieutenant, held the second lowest commissioned rank in the army. Neither could exercise command or control over the other or over members of the other's command.

11. *ORA I, 1*, 335; *ORN I, 4*, 31, 35; Johns, 27. Gilman reported on the confrontation between Slemmer and Armstrong, "On that occasion, Lieutenant Slemmer spoke as he had never heard one man speak to another. Treason and bad faith were manifest, and Lieutenant Slemmer hesitated not to upbraid them in unbecoming terms. That the world may never know more than this, the Old Commodore trembled before the patriotic impulse of the young lieutenant," Auge, 227; Bobbitt, 37; Auge, 277; *Harper's Weekly*, February 23, 1861, New York, NY.

12. Hendrickson, 3.

13. Lufkin, 51.

14. *ORN I, 4*, 9; *ORA I, 1*, 444.

15. Long, *Almanac*, 23.

16. Johns, 20; Dickison, *Men*, x; *ORA I, 1*, 345; Frederick H. Dyer, *A Compendium of the War of the Rebellion*, Vol. 3, Thomas Yoseloff, New York, NY, 1959, 1659 [Dyer].

17. *House Report 87*, 23; *ORA I, 1*, 334; Gilman, 22; Coleman, *Guardians*, 40; *ORN I, 4*, 11, 331; Walke, 3; Haskin, 490–496.

18. *ORN I, 4*, 10; *ORA I, 1*, 334.

Chapter 3

1. Occie Clubbs, *Stephen Russell Mallory, The Elder*, master's thesis, University of Florida, Gainesville, FL, 1936, 193, [Clubbs]; Coleman, *Guardians*, 40; Musicant, 492; Cash, 428.

2. Walke, 3; Haskin, 490, 491, 496; *ORN I, 4*, 13, 48; *ORA I, 1*, 336; *House Report 87*, 47; Bobbitt, 37.

3. *ORN I, 4*, 40; *House Report 87*, 79; Erben, 215–216; Walke, 5; John Johnson, 5.

4. Pearce, *Pensacola*, 18; *Pensacola Journal*, Pensacola, FL, August 12, 1908; *Montgomery Weekly Advertiser*, Montgomery, AL, January 28, 1861; Johns, 38; Julian C. Yonge, "Pensacola in the War for Southern Independence," *The Florida Historical Quarterly*, Vol. XXXCII, Nos. 3 and 4, The Florida Historical Society, Jacksonville, FL, 1959, 357 [Yonge]; Lufkin, 51.

5. Johns, 51; Richard S. West, Jr., *Mr. Lincoln's Navy*, Longmans, Green and Company, New York, NY, 1957, 9 [West, *Navy*]; Erasmus D. Keyes, *Fifty Years' Observations of Men and Events, Civil and Military*, Charles Scribners's Sons, New York, NY, 1884, 127n, 351 [Keyes]; Lufkin, 53; *ORN I, 4*, 29.

6. Doherty, 345; Erben, 218; Johns, 29; *ORN I 4*, 27, 45; *House Report 87*, 40, 57; Thomas J. Scharf, *History of the Confederate Navy from Its Organization to the Surrender of the Last Vessel*, Rogers Sherwood, New York NY, 1887, 601 [Scharf]; Lufkin, 51, 57, 60.

7. *ORN I, 4*, 15; *ORA I, 1*, 336.

8. *ORN I, 4*, 16, 60; *Pensacola Observer*, Pensacola, FL, January 15, 1861, reported in *Harper's Weekly Journal of Civilization*, New York, NY, February 9, 1861 [*Harper's Weekly*]; John Johns, 6,30; Walke, 12; Johns, 30; David M. Sullivan, *The United States Marine Corps in the Civil War—The First Year*, White Mane Publishing Company, Inc., Shippensburg, PA, 1997 [Sullivan]; J. Michael Miller, "Marine's Telling of 1861 Florida Navy Yard Fall Given," *Fortitude*, v. 20, no. 4, Spring, 1991, 8–9 [Miller].

9. Haskin, 76; Gilman, 28.

10. *ORN I, 4*, 29.

11. *ORN I, 4*, 15.

12. *ORN I, 4*, 32; Tebeau, 202; *House Report 87*, 35; Watts, n. p.

13. *ORN I, 4*, 58.

14. Erben, 219. Apparently there was no problem with the army meeting its obligations with cash as was the case with the navy. Each department was on a separate appropriation within the Federal budget; *ORA I, 1*, 337; Gilman, 29.

15. *ORA I, 1,* 337; Gilman, 29; Haskin, 493; Erben, 219. Abert was in error about Fort Sumter having been given up to South Carolina authorities. Slemmer and Gilman had no way of knowing whether or not their regimental brothers-in-arms were still holding out in Charleston Harbor.

16. Johns, 31; *ORA I, 1,* 52, 54.

17. *ORA I,* 52, 4. 7. The three companies that joined Lomax that day were the Conecuh Guards, Captain Samuel H. Wimberley; the Greenville Guards, Captain T. G. Pou; and the Alabama Zouaves from Tuskegee, Captain E. M. Law; *ORN I, 4,* 27, 58; Vann C. Wood and Elisabeth Muhlenfeld, eds., *The Private Mary Chestnut, The Unpublished Civil War Diaries,* Oxford University Press, New York, NY, 1984 [Wood]. The thirteen gun salute was to honor the thirteen Southern states that Southerners hoped would eventually make up their new nation.

18. *ORN I, 4,* 62.

19. *ORN I, 4,* 46.

20. *ORA I, 1,* 337; Haskin, 493.

21. Johns, 20; Dickison, *Men,* x; *ORA* I, 1, 353, 354; Frederick H. Dyer, *A Compendium of the War of the Rebellion,* Vol. 3, Thomas Yoseloff, New York, NY, 1959, 1698 [Dyer]; *ORN* I, 4, 17. The message is annotated, "This letter did not reach its destination, the officer to whom it was entrusted having failed to deliver it." The message incorrectly named Lieutenant John N. Maffitt as commanding *Crusader* which was actually under the command of Lieutenant Tunis A. M. Craven.

22. Haskin, 494.

23. *ORA I, 1,* 342.

24. *ORA I, 1,* 337.

25. *ORA I, 1,* 337; Lufkin, 55.

26. *ORN I, 4,* 64; Walke, 14; *ORA I, 1,* 338; Haskin, 496.

Chapter 4

1. Crawford, 174; Buchanan, 180; *Charlotte Observer,* Charlotte, NC, June 18, 1926; *Harper's Weekly,* New York, NY, November 18, 1865; John G. Nicolay, *The Outbreak of the Rebellion,* Charles Scribner's Sons, New York, NY, 1881, 35 [Nicolay, *Rebellion*]; *ORN* I, 52, 8; Dorothy Dodd, "The Secession Movement in Florida, 1850–1861," *The Florida Historical Quarterly,* Vol. XII, No. 1, Tallahassee, FL, July, 1933, 63 [Dodd, *Secession*].

2. Ernest F. Dibble, "War Averters: Seward, Mallory, and Fort Pickens," *Florida Historical Quarterly,* Vol. XLIX, No. 3, The Florida Historical Society, Jacksonville, FL, 1971, n. p. [Dibble, *Averters*]; *ORA I, 1,* 445; Bearss, *Pensacola,* 24n; John L. Moore, ed., "Guide to U.S. Elections," *Congressional Quarterly,* 3rd edition, Washington, DC, 1994 [Moore]. In the 36th Congress the senators from the states of the Deep South were Stephen R. Mallory and David L. Yulee, Florida; Judah P. Benjamin and John Slidell, Louisiana; Louis T. Wigfall and John Hemphill, Texas; Alfred Iverson and Robert A. Toombs, Georgia; Jefferson Davis and Albert G. Brown, Mississippi; and Clement C. Clay and Benjamin Fitzpatrick, Alabama; all of which by now had passed ordinances of secession.

3. *ORA I, 1,* 338.

4. Lufkin, 56, 57; *Montgomery Weekly Mail,* February 1, 1861; *National Intelligencer,* January 21, 1861; Jeffrey D. Stocker, ed., *From Huntsville to Appomattox,* The University of Tennessee Press, Knoxville, TN, 1996, 12n [Stocker]; John Appleyard and Norman Haines, M. D., *Pensacola and the War Between the States,* John Appleyard Agency, Pensacola, FL, 1993, 13 [Appleyard].

5. *ORA I, 1,* 339.

6. *ORA I, 1,* 339, 346; Haskin, 498; Gilman, 32.

7. Cornelius Cronin, *Recollections of Service in the U.S. Navy,* privately published, New York, NY, 1894, n. p. [Cronin]; Grady McWhiney, *Braxton Bragg and Confederate Defeat, Vol. I—Field Command,"* Columbia University Press, New York, NY, 1969, 159 [McWhiney]; Gilman, 32; Haskin, 497–498; *ORA I,* 52, 11.

8. Morison, 609.

9. *ORN I, 4,* 66–67; Charles B. Boynton, *The History of the Navy during the Rebellion,* D. Appleton Company, New York, NY, 1867, 244 [Boynton]; *ORA I, 1,* 351–353; Faust, 790; Keyes, 377.

10. *House Report 87,* 8; *ORA I,* 52, 13. Slidell being Louisiana's Senator John Slidell who retained is seat in the Congress for the time.

11. *ORA I, 1,* 330, 346; Haskin, 496–497; State of Florida, Board of State Institutions, *Soldiers of Florida in the Seminole, Indian, Civil, and Spanish-American Wars,* Democrat Book and Job Print, Shorewood Pound, Proprietors, Live Oak, FL, 1903, 37 [Soldiers].

12. *ORA I,* 52, 15.

13. *ORA I, 1,* 340.

14. Nicolay, *Lincoln,* 166.

15. *ORN I, 4,* 16–18, 76. .

16. *ORN I, 4,* 214; *ORA I, 1,* 356; Haskin, 500.

17. *ORA I, 1,* 445.

18. Haskin, 500; *ORN I, 4,* 212; *ORA* I, 1, 354–355; Buchanan, 215–216; W. A. Swanberg, *The Story of Fort Sumter,* Charles Scribner's Sons, New York, NY, 1957, 225 [Swanberg].

19. *ORA I, 1,* 355.

20. *ORN I, 4,* 19, 214; *ORA I, 1,* 344; Douglas, 168.

21. *ORA I, 1,* 344; Chester D. Hearn, *Admiral David Dixon Porter,* Naval Institute Press, Annapolis, MD, 1996, 46 [Hearn]; Haskin, 501; Davis, *War,* 103. "Bucking" was a common Army punishment at the time which consisted of tying a man's wrists together, forcing the man's knees up between his elbows, and inserting a rod under the knees and over the elbows; it was as painful as it was humiliating. "Bucking" was usually accompanied by gagging the man's mouth with a cloth.

22. Haskin, 499, 501.

23. Nicolay, *Lincoln,* 196.

24. Erben, 220; *ORN I, 4,* 78; Walke, 10. Walke was man enough to overlook the court-martial and its sentence. He remained on duty in the United States Navy, serving with distinction in the Civil War commanding vessels on the western rivers and pursuing Confederate raiders in European waters. He was promoted to rear admiral in 1870, retired in 1871, and died in Brooklyn, New York, in 1896 [Faust].

25. *ORA I, 1,* 334.

26. McWhiney, 151; Don Carlos Seitz, *Braxton Bragg, General of the Confederacy,* The State Company, Columbia, SC, 1924, 3 [Seitz]; Boatner, 78, 244.

27. *ORA I, 1*, 358. Slemmer had served for the year prior to his admission to West Point as the druggist's helper in the pharmacy operated by his brother, Dr. Henry T. Slemmer. Slemmer had an interest in medicine and during his years at Fort Moultrie had read on the subject. During the months Company G was stranded in Fort Pickens, Slemmer served both as its commander and its physician [Auge, 224–229]; Gideon Welles, "Facts Relating to the Reinforcement of Fort Pickens in the Spring of 1861," *The Galaxy,* January, 1871, to July, 1871, AMS Press, New York, NY, 97 [Welles, *Galaxy I*].

28. John Niven, *Gideon Welles, Lincoln's Secretary of the Navy,* Oxford University Press, New York, NY, 1973, 7, 327 [Niven]; Erben, 249; Robert Means Thompson and Richard Wainwright, eds., *Confidential Correspondence of Gustavus Vasa Fox, Assistant Secretary of the Navy, 1861–1865,* Volume 1, printed for the Naval History Society by De Vinne Press, New York, NY, 1918, 3 [Thompson].

29. *ORN I, 4*, 80; Haskin, 502.
30. *ORN I, 4*, 86; Cronin, n. p.
31. Haskin, 142; Cronin, n. p.; *ORN I, 4*, 85.
32. Daniel P. Smith, *Company K, First Alabama Regiment, or Three Years in the Confederate Service,* published by the Survivors, Prattville, AL, 1885, 3 [Smith, *Alabama*].
33. *ORA I, 1*, 359.
34. Douglas, 168; *ORA I, 1*, 254.
35. Weigley, 52, 75, 79–87; Sherrod E. East, "The Banishment of Captain Meigs," *Records of the Columbia Historical Society of Washington, DC,* Vol. 40–41, Maud Burr Morris, ed., Washington, DC, 1949, 99, 130 [East].
36. Haskin, 502.
37. *ORN I, 4*, 215.
38. *ORA I, 1*, 258; Bancroft, 92.
39. *ORN I, 4*, 84, 85; Jesse Early Bowden, Gordon Norman Simons, and Sarah L. Johnson, *Pensacola, Florida's First Place City,* The Donning Company, Norfolk, VA, 1989, 65 [Bowden]; Cronin, n. p.
40. *ORA I, 1*, 516.
41. *ORA I, 1*, 364; *ORN I, 4*, 85, 88.
42. Weigley, 129.
43. *ORA I, 1*, 447.
44. Haskin, 502; *ORN I, 4*, 88, 216; West, *Navy,* 13.
45. Dickison, *Men,* x.
46. *ORA I, 1*, 259; *Soldiers,* 324; *ORN I, 4*, 215.
47. Rush Rhees Library, University of Rochester, Montgomery C. Meigs mss. letter to William H. Seward, March 1, 1861, Rochester, NY [Rhees].
48. Nicolay, *Lincoln,* 315; Stampp, *War,* 502.

Chapter 5

1. Buchanan, 169.
2. Nicolay, *Lincoln,* 315; Stampp, *War,* 502; The *New Orleans Bee,* January 3, 1861, in Dwight Lowell Dummond, ed., *Southern Editorials on Secession,* The Century Co., New York, NY, 1931, 395 [Dummond, *Editorials*].
3. Library of Congress, Abraham Lincoln, *First Inaugural Address, Monday, March 4, 1861,* Washington, DC, n. p.
4. Bern Anderson, *By Sea and River, The Naval History of the Civil War,* Alfred A. Knopf, New York, NY, 1961, 16 [Anderson, *History*].
5. Faust, 439; Allan Nevins, *The War for the Union,* Vol. 1, Charles Scribner's Sons, New York, NY, 1959, 32 [Nevins, *Union*]; Richard L. Current, *Lincoln and the First Shot,* J. Lippincott Company, Philadelphia, PA, 1963, 32 [Current]; Charles W. Ramsdell, "Lincoln and Fort Sumter," *The Journal of Southern History,* Southern Historical Association, Department of History, University of Georgia, Albany, GA, Vol. III, No. 3, August, 1937, 270 [Ramsdell].
6. Anderson, *History,* 3; West, *Welles,* 94.
7. Current, 466; Gideon Welles, "Fort Sumter, Facts in Relation to the Expedition Ordered by the Administration of President Lincoln for the Relief of the Garrison of Fort Sumter," *The Galaxy,* AMS Press, Inc., New York, NY, November, 1870, 613 [Welles, *Galaxy 2*]; Thomas Kirkland Lathrop, *William Henry Seward,* Houghton Mifflin Company, Boston, MA, 1896 [Lathrop]; Nicolay, *Lincoln,* 376, William Ernest Smith, *The Francis Preston Blair Family in Politics,* Vol. 2, The McMillan Company, New York, NY, 1933 [Smith, *Blair*]; Montgomery C. Meigs, "General Montgomery C. Meigs on the Conduct of the Civil War," *The American Historical Review,* Volume XXVI, October, 1920, The McMillan Company, New York NY, 1921, 300 [Meigs, *Conduct*]; Avery O. Craven, *Civil War in the Making, 1815–1860,* Louisiana State University Press, Baton Rouge, LA, 1959, 46 [Craven, *Making*].
8. Welles, *Galaxy 2*, 620; Smith, *Blair,* 6.
9. *ORA I,* 263; David Scott Turk, *Give My Regards to the Ladies, The Life of Littleton Quinton Washington,* Heritage Books, Inc., Bowie, MD, 2001, 1 [Turk].
10. Nicolay, *Lincoln,* 397; *ORA I, 1*, 779; Davis, *Image,* 80; Tebeau, 204. Fort Sumter was designed for a wartime garrison of 650. Anderson's command numbered seventy-five officers and men.
11. Welles, *Galaxy 2*, 616; Niven, 324. The Navy Department's detailing officer would equate to the head of the present day Bureau of Naval Personnel.
12. Howard K. Beale, ed., *The Diary of Gideon Welles, Secretary of the Navy under Lincoln and Johnson,* W. W. Norton Co., New York, NY, 1960, 3 [Beale]; Lossing, 308n.
13. *The Southern Messenger,* editorial, March 6, 1861, Greenville, AL; *ORA I, 1*, 448.
14. Frederick Seward, *Seward at Washington, as Senator and Secretary of State, 1846–1861,* Derby and Miller, New York, NY, 1991, 536 [Seward]; Niven, 325; Beale, 6.
15. *ORN I, 4*, 89, 93.
16. Smith, *Blair,* 6.
17. *ORA I, 1*, 449.
18. Nevins, *Union,* 42, 55; Nicolay, *Lincoln,* 9; Stanley Erwin Bradley, *Simon Cameron, Lincoln's War Secretary,* The University of Pennsylvania Press, Philadelphia, PA, 1966, 175 [Bradley].
19. McWhiney, 160; *ORN I, 4*, 217.
20. Nicolay, *Lincoln,* 400–410; Welles, *Galaxy 2*, 620.
21. 1 Seitz, 3, 31; *ORA I, 1*, 449; Faust, 75, 790; Bruce Catton, *U. S. Grant and the American Military Tradition,* Little, Brown and Company, Publishers, Boston, MA, 1954, 92 [Catton]; Army and Navy Journal, "Recollections of Cadet Life," n. auth., *Army and Navy Journal,*

Vol. XXXIV (June 14, 1902), New York, NY, 1027 [Army and Navy]; Jones M. Withers to C. C. Clay, February 13, 1862, Clement C. Clay Papers, Duke University, Durham NC; James L. Pugh to Braxton Bragg, March 16, 1862, William P. Palmer Collection of Braxton Bragg Papers, Western Reserve Historical Society, Cleveland, OH [Pugh]. McWhiney, 28, 33; Thomas Lawrence Connelly, *Autumn of Glory, The Army of Tennessee, 1862, 1865,* Louisiana State University Press, Baton Rouge, PA, 1971, 70 [Connelly, *Glory*]; Judith Hallock, *Braxton Bragg and Confederate Defeat,* Vol. II, The University of Alabama Press, Tuscaloosa, AL, 1991, 4 [Hallock]; *Richmond Examiner,* March 23, 1861.The reference to Benny Havens' is to the notorious drinking establishment frequented by some West Point cadets in the nearby village of Highland Falls.
22. ORA I, 1, 273.
23. ORA I, 1, 393.
24. ORA I, 1, 362.
25. ORA I, 1, 360; Beale, 28; Parks, *Civil War,* 4; Nicolay, *Lincoln,* 394; Welles, *Galaxy 2,* 618.
26. ORA I, 1, 362.
27. ORN I, 4, 93.
28. Smith, *Blair,* 11.
29. ORA I, 1, 275, 449.
30. ORN I, 4, 95.
31. West, *Welles,* 98; ORA I, 1, 96; Niven, 325; Nicolay, *Lincoln,* 51. The United States Revenue Service was the predecessor of the United States Coast Guard. It's first steam vessel, the cutter *Harriet Lane,* was commissioned during the administration of President James Buchanan, a bachelor, and christened in the name of his niece and official hostess; Lathrop, 259; John Johnson, 230; Welles, *Galaxy 2,* 623; Thomas M. Anderson, *The Political Conspiracies Preceding the Rebellion or the True Stories of Sumter and Pickens,* G. P. Putnam's Sons, New York, NY, 1882, 50 [Anderson].
32. ORN I, 4, 96, 99.
33. ORA, I, 1, 450; ORN I, 4, 217.
34. ORA I, 1, 31-360.
35. William H. Russell, *My Diary North and South,* Harper Brothers, Publishers, New York, NY, 1861, 6 [Russell]. Russell meant to give Florida as the location of Fort Pickens. He was not welcome for long by either side. Diarist Mary Chestnut describes Russell as "a typical English writer with three P's: Pen, Paper, and Prejudices," Faust, 449.
36. ORN I, 4, 91; Scharf, 606n.
37. Cronin, n. p.
38. ORA I, 1, 451. Zouave militia units were formed throughout the nation in the years before the war, dressing in uniforms resembling French colonial Algerian units with baggy red trousers and blue jackets; they became proficient in a complex drill process and were somewhat popular early in the war on both sides, Faust 850.
39. ORA I, 1, 209-211; Welles, *Galaxy 2,* 618; ORN I, 4, 98; ORA I, 1, 452.
40. ORA I, 1, 52, 27; Welles, *Galaxy 2,* 606n, 623.
41. ORA I, 1, 363.
42. Scharf, 606n.
43. ORN I, 4, 100.
44. Ru7ssell, 12.
45. ORA I, 1, 222-223; Welles, *Galaxy6 2,* 619; Ward Hill Lamon, *Recollections of Abraham Lincoln, 1847–1865,* A. C. McLurg and Company, Chicago, IL, 1895, 68-79 [Lamon]; James G. Randall, "Ward Hill Lamon,," *Dictionary of American Biography,* Dumas Malone, ed., Vol. X, 562–563, Charles Scribner's Sons, New York, NY, 1933 [Russell].
46. McWhiney, 161-165.
47. ORN I, 4, 88.
48. West, *Welles,* 101.
49. Richard S. West, Jr., *The Second Admiral, A Life of David Dixon Porter, 1813–1891,* Coward-McCann, Inc., New York, NY, 1937, 83 [West, *Porter*]; Musicant, 15; *House Report 87,* 2; Current, 75; Nicolay, *Lincoln,* 295; *New York Times,* March 28, 1861; James Russell Soley, *Admiral Porter,* D. Appleton and Company, New York, NY, 1903, 98 [Soley]; Crawford, 406.
50. Leech, 51; Niven, 326; Current, 76; Welles, *Galaxy 2,* 619.
51. Current, 83; Nicolay, *Lincoln,* 434-35; Seward, 533; Dibble, *Avengers,* n. p.; Weigley, 137; Meigs, *Conduct,* 229-301.
52. ORA I, 1, 365; Haskin, 502; Boynton, 301; ORN I, 4, 125.
53. Niven, 327; Welles, *Galaxy 2,* 620; Swanberg, 257.
54. Parks, *Civil War,* 4; Tilley, 48; ORN I, 4, 125; ORA I, 1, 365; Clement A. Evans, ed., *Confederate Military History, Military History of Florida,* by J. J. Dickison, Confederate Publishing Company, Atlanta, GA, 1899, 24 [Dickison, *History*].

Chapter 6

1. Keyes, 378–380; West, *Porter,* 58; ORA I, 1, 230.
2. Keyes, 383.
3. ORA I, 1, 230.
4. *Pensacola Gazette,* April 2, 1861, Pensacola, FL; Horace L. Davis, Jr., "Pensacola Newspapers, 1821– 1900," *The Florida Historical Quarterly,* Vol. XXXVII, Nos. 3 and 4, The Florida Historical Society, Jacksonville, FL, January, 1959, 432, [Davis, *Papers*];ORN I, 4, 104, 109; Johns, 54.
5. ORA I, 1, 383.
6. Current, 84; Lathrop, 276; John G. Nicolay and John Hays, eds., *Abraham Lincoln, A History,"* Volume Three, The Century Co., New York, NY, 1890,447 [Nicolay, *Lincoln 1890*].
7. Nicolay, *Lincoln,* 30; Nicolay, *Lincoln 1890,* 447.
8. Boatner, 90; ORA I, 1, 365-367.
9. Musicant, 15; Hearn, 37; West, *Porter,* 31; Paul Lewis, *Yankee Admiral, A Biography of David Dixon Porter,* David McKay Company, New York, NY, 1968, 88 [Lewis]; West, *Porter,* 78; Hearn, 38; David Dixon Porter, *Incidents and Anecdotes of the Civil War,* D. Appleton and Company, New York, NY, 1885, 14 [Porter, *Incidents*]; Welles, *Galaxy 1,* 105; Welles, *Galaxy 2,* 642; Hearn, 40; Soley, 100, 105; Porter, *Incidents,* 16, 17; West, *Porter,* 79–83.
10. Beale, 26.
11. Welles, *Galaxy 2,* 620; Faust, 265.
12. Welles, *Galaxy 2,* 623–624.
13. ORN I, 4, 104; ORA I, 1, 102.
14. David Dixon Porter, *The Naval History of the Civil War,* The Sherman Publishing Company, New York, NY,

1886, 102 [Porter, *History*]; Porter, *Incidents*, 17; *ORA I, 1,* 253; Faust, 265. A vessel's girt-line was the first line to be installed when the vessel's masts are rigged, and the last line to be taken down when the vessel is de-rigged.
   15. Soley, 99; *American Historical,* 301.
   16. Nevins, *Union,* 51; Russell, 34.
   17. *ORA I, 1,* 232.
   18. Weigley, 144; Keyes, 387.
   19. *ORA I, 1,* 232.
   20. *ORA I, 1,* 286.
   21. John Johnson, 7.
   22. *ORN* I, 4, 105.
   23. *American Historical,* 301; *ORA I, 1,* 372; Soley, 98; Porter. *History,* 102; Soley, 108; West, *Welles,* 102.
   24. Lewis, 99; John M. Taylor, *William Henry Seward, Lincoln's Right Hand,* Harper Collins Publishers, New York, NY, 1991, 156 [Taylor]; Niven, 338; *ORA I, 1,* 235; Swanberg, 270.
   25. *ORA I, 1,* 465.
   26. Soley, 98–99; Porter, *History,* 97; Musicant, 19; Nicolay, *Lincoln,* 4.
   27. *ORA I, 1,* 240; Boynton, 263; Beale, 23; West, *Welles,* 102; *ORN I, 4,* 111; Weigley, 144.
   28. Niven, 334; Beale, 23; Welles, *Galaxy 2,* 629, 635.

Chapter 7

   1. Musicant, 20; Weigley, 144; Porter, *History,* 102; Tilley, 70; Niven, 335–338; *ORN I, 4,* 112; Hearn, 45; *ORN I, 4,* 112; Soley, 112; Porter, *Incidents,* 22. Meigs, aboard the chartered merchant transport *Atlantic,* had left the city wharf at noon of the day but was still anchored in the stream and waiting as additional munitions and provisions were loaded from lighters and barges. Porter had no way of knowing Meigs and *Atlantic* were actually behind *Powhatan*.
   2. Keyes, 391; Jones, 66; *ORA* I, 1, 372, 456; Davis, *War,* 107.
   3. *ORA I, 1,* 456, 461; Ellen Call Long, *Florida Breezes, or Florida, New and Old,* Asmead Bros., Booksellers, Stationers, Printers and Binders, Jacksonville, FL, 1883, 308 [Ellen Long]; *The New York Tribune,* April 11, 1861; Johns, 47. Bragg's references to an attack by escalade meant an attack using scaling ladders to bring the assaulting troops to the top of the walls of the fort; McWhiney, 167.
   4. Taylor, 157; *ORA I, 1,* 245,
   5. Welles, *Galaxy 2,* 96; West, *Welles,* 103; Nicolay, *Lincoln,* 297; Faust, 102; William N. Still, Jr., *Ironclad Captains The Commanding Officers of the USS Monitor,* Marine and Estuarine Management Division, National Oceanic and Atmospheric Administration, United States Department of Commerce, Washington, DC, 1988, 4 [Still]; *ORN I, 4,* 111.
   6. Porter, *Incidents,* 22.
   7. *American Historical,* 302; Keyes, 392.
   8. McWhiney, 169; *ORA I, 1,* 458; *ORA I, 52,* 38.
   9. *ORA I, 1,* 248; Swanberg, 270.
   10. Taylor, 157.
   11. West, *Navy,* 20; *ORA I, 1,* 289.
   12. *ORA* I, 1, 394; Porter, *History,* 97.
   13. *ORN I, 4,* 113.
   14. Glyndon G. Van Deusen, *William Henry Seward,* Oxford University Press, New York, NY, 1967, 286 [Van Deusen]; Current, 114.
   15. *ORA I, 1,* 372, 394; Porter, *History,* 97; Jones, 68.
   16. *ORA I, 1,* 387–389, 459; Lossing, 366, 370n; Watts, n. p.; Davis, *Papers,* 432. Ordnance Sergeant John Flynn was among the Fort Pickens garrison; Gardner is not otherwise identified. Wilcox later tried to escape to the North. He reached Norfolk, Virginia, before he was taken and conscripted into Confederate service, in which he served until Norfolk was taken by Federal forces in May, 1861.
   17. Swanberg, 265; *Charleston Courier,* Charleston, SC, April 11, 1861; *ORA I, 1,* 11; *ORN I, 4,* 581; Taylor, 157.
   18. Keyes, 394; *ORA I, 1,* 368–369.

Chapter 8

   1. *ORA I, 1,* 13; Faust, 51; *ORA I, 52,* 42; Nicolay, *Lincoln,* 13.
   2. *ORA I, 1,* 18, 29, 66; Porter, *History,* 98; Porter, *History,* 98; Abner Doubleday, *Reminiscences of Forts Sumter and Moultrie in 1860–61,* Harper Brothers, Publishers, New York, NY, 1876, 149–150 [Doubleday]; Crawford, 420; *ORN I, 4,* 154; Long, *Almanac,* 58.
   3. Still, 5; *ORA I, 1,* 376, 463; Scharf, 606n; Bobbitt, 24; James P. Jones, "Lincoln's Courier: John L. Worden's Mission to Fort Pickens," *The Florida Historical Quarterly,* Volume XLI, Number 2, The Florida Historical Society, Jacksonville, FL, October, 1961, 149 [James Jones]; Johns, 45; Cronin, n. p.
   4. Cronin, n. p.
   5. *ORA I, 1,* 461; *ORN I, 4,* 118; Welles, *Galaxy 1,* 100; James Jones, 150; Seitz, 37; Lossing, 368; *Register of Officers of the Confederate States Navy, 1861–1865,* United States Government Printing Office, Washington, DC, 1931, 176 [*Register*]; James Jones, 150.
   6. *ORN I, 4,* 116, 117, 118. Vogdes's request for seamen put a severe demand on the remaining crews of Adams's vessels. The authorized compliment of *Brooklyn* was 381 officers and men; *Sabine* 375; *St. Louis,* 118; and *Wyandotte* 71. Seldom were active vessels at their authorized strength so fulfilling Vogdes's request would take more than a third of the ships' authorized compliments.
   7. *ORA I, 1,* 331, 374–375, 378, 395; *ORA I, 52,* 51.
   8. Weigley, 150; *ORA I, 1,* 396.
   9. *ORA I, 1,* 378–380.
   10. *ORN I, 4,* 118, 141.
   11. Cronin, n. p.; *ORA* I, 1, 479; Nicolay, *Lincoln,* 17.
   12. Porter, *History,* 103; Porter, *Incidents,* 23; *ORN I, 4,* 119; 144; West, *Porter,* 90; Musicant, 27; *ORA I, 1,* 382.
   13. *ORA I, 1,* 382.
   14. Keyes, 399; 404. Keyes was replaced as Scott's military secretary by Captain George W. Cullum. Keyes moved to the staff of Governor Edwin Morgan of New York. He later commanded brigades, divisions, and eventually the IV Corps of the Army of the Potomac.
   15. *ORA I, 1,* 380, 385; *ORN I, 4,* 124; Hearn, 49.
   16. *ORA I, 1,* 464; Scharf, 610.
   17. Hearn, 49.
   18. Weigley, 152; *ORA I,1,* 390.

19. *ORN I, 4,* 143; Scharf, 606n; *ORA I, 1,* 391, 396; Weigley, 154; Soley, 125.
20. Henry J. Hunt to Braxton Bragg, April 23, 1861, copy in Henry J. Hunt Papers, United States Army Military History Institute, Carlisle, PA, quoted from Edward M. Coffman, *The Old Army, A Portrait of the American Army in Peacetime, 1784–1898,* Oxford University Press, New York, NY, 1986, 96 [Coffman].
21. *ORA I, 4,* 55.
22. ORA I, 1, 403; *ORN I, 4,* 146; *New Orleans Picayune,* April 26, 1861, from Frank Moore, *The Rebellion Record,* Vol. 1, G. P. Putnam, New York, NY, 1861, R143 [Moore]; Hearn, 49; West, *Porter,* 91.
23. Faust, 230; West, *Porter,* 91; *ORN I, 4,* 400.
24. *ORA I, 1,* 400; *ORN I, 4,* 154.
25. Weigley,. 66, 154; Faust, 485.
26. Tebeau, 206; Caroline Mays Brevard, *A History of Florida, From the Treaty of 1783 to Our Own Times,* The Florida State Historical Society, Deland, FL, 1925, 59n [Brevard]; *ORA I, 1,* 408–409, 466; Scott Rye, *Ships of the Civil War,* Longmeadow Press, Stamford, CT, 1995, 19 [Rye].
27. *ORN I, 4,* 163.
28. *ORA I, 1,* 410; Haskin, 134.

Chapter 9

1. *ORA* I, 1, 40; *ORN* I, 4, 166.
2. Musicant, 60; *ORN* l, 4, 166; *ORA* I, 1, 413.
3. Langdon L. Rumph to Dr. James David Rumph, in *Letters From Pensacola: The Civil War Years,* Norman W. Haines, Jr., M. D., ed., The Civil War Soldiers Museum, Pensacola, FL, 1991, 21, 35 [Rumph]; Edward Young McMorries, *History of the First Regiment, Alabama Volunteer Infantry, C. S. A.,* The Browning Printing Company, Montgomery, AL, 1904, 25 [McMorries]; P. K. Younge Library, University of Florida, Gainesville, FL, *C. L. Bonney Letters, April–September, 1861,* mss letter to his father May 15, 1861 [Bonney].
4. Morris, n. p.; *ORA* I, 1, 407.
5. *ORN* I, 4, 61.
6. *ORN* I, 4, 167.
7. Davis, *Image,* 344.
8. The *vivandiére* came from a European tradition of a woman unofficially attached to a regiment performing camp and nursing duties, if not acting as an our-right camp follower, and wearing a version of the regimental uniform. The idea was popular in the opening months of the American Civil War but very short-lived; Faust, 789; Russell, 115–119. Russell, who was forty-one at the time, described Bragg as elderly; Bragg was forty-four. The appearance of age came from Bragg's chronic physical problems; Faust, 649; McWhiney 179, 486; Russell, 118–124; Martin Crawford, ed., *William Howard Russell's Civil War, Private Diary and Letters, 1861–1862,* The University of Georgia Press, Athens, GA, 1992, 52–58 [Crawford].
9. Cornelius M. Buckley, S. J., ed. and trans., *A Frenchman, A Chaplain, A Rebel, The War Letters of Pere Louis-Hippolyte Gache, S. J.,* Loyola University Press, Chicago, IL, 1981, 27 [Gache].
10. Meigs makes a reversal from his original position explained to President Lincoln on April 1 in which he had advocated Porter's entry to the harbor at Pensacola. Since then, Meigs had been on the scene and had become aware of the batteries now lining the shore of the mainland.
11. *ORA* I, 1, 419, 468, 472; Robert Johnson, 194; Malcolm C. McMullen, *The Alabama Confederate Reader,* University of Alabama Press, Tuscaloosa, AL, 1963, 209 [McMullen]. Colonel Tennent Lomax was killed at the head of his regiment during the Battle of Seven Pines, east of Richmond, on June 1, 1862, National Archives, Textural Records Branch, Service Records, Tennent Lomax, Washington, DC.
12. *ORA* I, 1, 415–420; Hearn, 49; West, *Porter,* 93; Scharf, 613.
13. Soley, 125; *ORA* I, 1, 418; Hearn, 51; Faust, 462; West, *Porter,* 574; *ORN* I, 16, 571, 614.
14. Haskin, 134: Slemmer, *File;* Gilman, *File;* Bobbitt, 46; Auge, 231; Vivian F. Taylor, *Tombstone Inscriptions in Montgomery County, Pa.,* New Norris Township, Historical Society of Montgomery County, PA, 1958, 50 [Taylor, *Tombstone*];
15. *ORA* I, 1, 416, 419; *New York Herald,* May 4, 1861.
16. *ORA* I, 1, 424.
17. *ORA* I, 1, 428; *ORN* I, 4, 200; Seitz, 43.
18. *ORA* I, 1, 429; Cronin, n. p.
19. *ORA* I, 1, 429, 431.
20. *ORA* I, 52, 180–181.
21. *ORA* I, 1, 432.
22. Morris, 51.
23. *ORA* I, 1, 432.
24. Tilley, 90.
25. *ORN* I, 16, 574.

Chapter 10

1. *ORA* I, 1, 427.
2. National Archives, Textural Records Branch, Service Records, William Wilson, Washington, DC; Gouveneur Morris, *The History of a Volunteer Regiment,* Veteran Volunteer Publishing Company, New York, NY, 1891, 21 [Morris]. There was no Company J in the Sixth New York; there was never a Company, Battery, or Squadron J in the United States Army.
3. *Harper's Weekly,* New York, NY, May 11, May 18, 1861; *New York Herald,* New York, NY, November 5, 1856.
4. Morris, 31, 45.
5. Bele Estvan, *War Pictures from the South,* D. Appleton Company, New York, NY, 1863, 14 [Estvan].
6. *ORA* I, 1, 434; Morris, 41.
7. *ORA* I, 1, 435.
8. *ORA* I, 1, 437, 439.
9. *ORA* I, 1, 438.
10. Robert Johnson, 194; Haskin, 145–146.
11. Robert Johnson, 194; Haskin, 146.
12. *ORN* I, 4, 593.
13. Edwin C. Bearss, "Civil War Operations In and Around Pensacola," *The Florida Historical Society Quarterly,* Vol. XXVI, No. 2, Jacksonville, FL, 1957, 144 [Bearss, *Pensacola*]; *ORN* I, 16, 610.
14. *ORN* I, 16, 644; Morris, 47.
15. *ORA* I, 6, 725.

16. *ORN* I, 16, 662.
17. *ORA* I, 6, 666; Ralph W. Donnelly, *The Confederate States Marine Corps, The Rebel Leathernecks,* White Mane Publishing Company, Inc., Shippensburg, PA, 1989, 21[Donnelly].
18. Scharf, 613; Knox, 196; Mahan, 5.
19. *ORN* I, 16, 685; Faust, 489.
20. *ORN* I, 16, 667.
21. *ORN* I, 16, 694,735.
22. *ORA* I, 52, 168.
23. *ORA* I, 6, 670.
24. Rice, 56.
25. McWhiney, 192; *ORA* I, 6, 460.
26. *ORA* I, 6, 460; Rice, 56; McWhiney, 193; J. L. Larkin, "Battle of Santa Rosa Island," *The Florida Historical Quarterly,* Vol. XXXVII, Nos. 3 and 4, The Florida Historical Society, Jacksonville, FL, January 1959, 372 [Larkin].
27. Morris, 57; Lossing, 111n.
28. *ORA* I, 6, 439; Parks, *Civil War,* 17; Lossing, 111; Morris, 133.
29. Morris, 113.
30. Morris, 59; *ORA* I, 6, 448.
31. Morris, 59.
32. *ORA* I, 6, 469; Larkin, 374.
33. *ORA* I, 5, 451; Larkin, 375.
34. *ORA* I, 6, 462.
35. *ORA* I, 6, 449; Parks, *Civil War,* 17; Brevard, 61. In an army primarily officered by graduates of West Point, Robertson and Shipley stand out as examples of men who enlisted in the ranks as privates and subsequently earned commissions. Robertson was brevetted a second lieutenant in the 2nd Artillery in 1848. Shipley was brevetted a second lieutenant in the 5th Infantry in 1857; Bearss, *Civil War,* 152n.
36. *ORA* I, 6, 462.
37. *ORA* I, 6, 445.
38. *ORA* I, 6, 453.
39. Brevard, 61; *ORA* I, 6, 454.
40. *ORA* I, 6, 459.
41. *ORA* I, 6, 442, 443, 462; Larkin, 376.
42. *ORA* I, 6, 388, 442.

Chapter 11

1. *ORA* I, 6, 667, 673.
2. *ORA* I, 6, 442.
3. Seitz, 58.
4. *ORA* I, 6, 668–669.
5. *ORN* I, 16, 766.
6. *ORN* I, 16, 768.
7. *ORN* I, 16, 770; Porter, *History,* 93.
8. *ORN* I6, 775; Mahan, 8.
9. *ORA* I, 6, 469; *ORN* I, 16, 779.
10. *ORN* I, 16, 775; *ORA* I, 6, 488.
11. *ORN* I, 16, 775.
12. *ORA* I, 6, 491; *ORN* I, 16, 780.
13. *ORA* I, 6, 491.
14. *ORA* I, 6, 491.
15. *ORA* I, 6, 457.
16. *ORA* I, 6, 457.

Chapter 12

1. *ORA* I, 6, 457. Hot shot consisted of cannon balls heated to a red glow; a carcass was a cast iron projectile filled with flammable composition, the flame of which issued through several openings and which was intended to strike and ignite combustible targets; rock fire was a phosphoric compound fitted into a shell casing and intended to burst into flame upon bursting.
2. *ORA* I, 6, 495.
3. *ORA* I, 6, 497.
4. James Cantey Elliott, *Lieutenant General Richard Herron Anderson, Lee's Noble Solider,* Morningside Press, Dayton, OH, 1985, 36–37, [Elliott]; Douglas Southall Freeman, *Lee's Lieutenants, A Study in Command,* Charles Scribner's Sons, New York, NY, 1943, 158 [Freeman].
5. Seitz, 79; Faust, 404; *ORA* I, 6, 824.
6. Boatner, 27, 90.
7. Seitz, 87; Bowden, 69.
8. Seitz, 89; Merritt L. Nickinson, comp., "Kiss the Children for Father," *Pensacola Historical Society Quarterly,* Vol. 8, Nos. 2 and 3, The Pensacola Historical Society, Pensacola, FL, 1975, 8 [Nickinson]; *ORA* I, 6, 848.
9. Tebeau, 210; Gloria Jahoda, *Florida, A Bicentennial History,* W. W. Norton Company, Inc., New York, NY, 1976, 73 [Jahoda]; Thomas Lawrence Connelly, *Army of the Heartland, The Army of Tennessee, 1861–1862,* Louisiana State University Press, Baton Rouge, LA, 1967, 140 [Connelly, *Heartland*].
10. Seitz, 113.
11. Long, *Almanac,* 203.
12. West, *Porter,* 146; *ORA* I, 6, 660.
13. Parks, *Civil War,* 19; Scharf, 616; *ORA* I, 6, 660–662.
14. West, *Porter,* 147; Parks, *Underground,* 57.
15. Parks, *Civil War,* 19; Scharf, 616; *ORA* I, 6, 616.
16. *ORA* I, 6, 659; Morris, 74.
17. Coleman, *Guardians,* 53.
18. Coleman, *Guardians,* 53.

Bibliography

Archival Sources

Duke University. Jones M. Withers to C.C. Clay, February 13, 1862, Clement C. Clay Papers, Durham, NC.

Library of Congress. Abraham Lincoln, *First Inaugural Address, Monday, March 4, 1861.* Washington, DC.

National Archives. *Abstracts of Service Records of Naval Officers, 1798–1893,* National Archives Microfilm Publications, James Armstrong. Washington, DC, 1960.

_____. Office of the Adjutant General. Record Group 94, Letters Received by the Appointment, Commission, and Personnel Branch of the Adjutant-General's Office, 1863–1870, Adam J. Slemmer, Roll 218, 1865, S1224-S1280. Washington, DC.

_____. Record Group 94, Regular Army Muster Rolls, Entry 53, Muster Rolls of Captain John H. Winder's Co. G of the First Regiment of Artillery, from 31 December 1860 to 28 February 1861.

_____. Record Group 94, Register of Letters Received by the Office of the Adjutant General, Main Series, 1812–1889, John H. Winder, Roll 62. Washington, DC.

_____. Office of the Chief Engineer, Record Group 77, Joseph G. Totten, Lieutenant Colonel, to Major James Kearney, Mobile, January 1822, mss letter, *Letters and Reports of Colonel Joseph G. Totten, 1803–64,* 10 Volumes, Volume 1, No. 2, E148. Washington, DC.

_____. Office of the Quartermaster General, Record Group 92, Consolidated Correspondence File, R. H. Watts to Montgomery C. Meigs, mss letter, December 6, 1865.

_____. Textural Records Branch, Service Records, Jeremiah H. Gilman. Washington, DC.

_____. Textural Records Branch, Service Records, Tennent Lomax. Washington, DC.

_____. Textural Records Branch, Service Records, William Wilson. Washington, DC.

P.K. Younge Library, University of Florida, Gainesville. *C.L. Bonney Letters, April–September, 1861,* mss letter to his father, May 15, 1861.

Rush Rhees Library, University of Rochester. Montgomery C. Meigs mss. letter to William H. Seward, March 1, 1861, Rochester, NY.

United States Army Military History Institute. Henry J. Hunt to Braxton Bragg, April 23, 1861, copy in Henry J. Hunt Papers.

United States Congress. *American State Papers, Class V, (Military Affairs),* Vol. 3, No. 287, Brigadier General S. Bernard to Major General A. Macomb, "Fortification of the Harbor of Pensacola," Sept. 19, 1825.

_____. 26th Congress, 2nd Session. *House of Representatives Report No. 87,* "Naval Forces of the United States—Where Ships Are Now Stationed," Washington, DC, February 21, 1861.

_____. 27th Congress, 2nd Session. *Senate Executive Document No. 98,* "Report from the Secretary of the Navy, in compliance with a resolution of the Senate, in relation to the necessity and practicability of establishing a navy-yard, naval depot, and station upon the Gulf of Mexico," Washington, DC, January 31, 1842.

Western Reserve Historical Society. William P. Palmer Collection of Braxton Bragg Papers, James L. Pugh to Braxton Bragg, March 16, 1862. Cleveland, OH.

Newspapers

Charleston Courier, Charleston, SC.
Charlotte Observer, Charlotte, NC.
Fernandina East Floridian, Fernandina, FL.
Harper's Weekly, New York, NY.
Harper's Weekly Journal of Civilization, New York, NY.
Montgomery Weekly Advertiser, Montgomery, AL.
Montgomery Weekly Mail, Montgomery, AL.
National Intelligencer, Washington, DC.
New Orleans Bee, New Orleans, LA.
New Orleans Picayune, New Orleans, LA.
New York Herald, New York, NY.
New York Times, New York, NY.
New York Tribune, New York, NY.
Pensacola Gazette, Pensacola, FL.

Pensacola Journal, Pensacola, FL.
Pensacola Observer, Pensacola, FL.
Richmond Examiner, Richmond, VA.
St. Augustine Examiner, St. Augustine, FL.
Southern Messenger, Greenville, AL.
Tampa Tribune, Tampa, FL.

Periodicals and Papers

Abercrombie, Lelia. "Early Churches in Pensacola." *The Florida Historical Quarterly,* Pensacola Quadricentennial Issue, Vol. XXXVII, Numbers 3 and 4, 1959. Jacksonville, FL: Florida Historical Society.

Arnade, Charles W. "Tristan de Luna and the Ochuse (Pensacola Bay), 1559." *The Florida Historical Quarterly,* Pensacola Quadricentennial Issue, Vol. XXXVII, Numbers 3 and 4, 1959. Jacksonville, FL: Florida Historical Society.

Bearss, Edwin C. "Civil War Operations In and Around Pensacola." *The Florida Historical Society Quarterly,* Vol. XXVI, No. 2, 1957. Jacksonville, FL: Florida Historical Society.

———. "Fort Pickens and the Secession Crisis, January–February, 1861." *Gulf Coast Historical Review,* Spring 1995. Mobile, AL: History Department of the University of South Alabama.

Bense, Judith A. "The Colonial Archeological Record in Pensacola, Florida," paper presented in the Symposium: *Colonial Pensacola: A First Syntheses, (Forts of Pensacola).* Washington, DC: Society for Historical Archeology Conference, 1995.

Bittle, George C. "Florida Prepares for War." *Florida Historical Quarterly,* Volume LI, Number 2, 1972. Gainesville, FL: Florida Historical Society.

Childress, David C. "Mount Vernon Barracks: The Blue, The Gray, and The Red." *The Alabama Review,* 42, April, 1989. Auburn, AL: University of Alabama Press.

Davis, Horace L., Jr. "Pensacola Newspapers, 1821–1900." *The Florida Historical Quarterly,* Vol. XXXVII, Nos. 3 and 4, January, 1959. Jacksonville, FL: Florida Historical Society.

Dawkins, Mary, "Warrington and Woolsey, Where Are They?" *Pensacola, Magazine,* 1995. Pensacola, FL.

Dibble, Ernest F. "Ante-Bellum Pensacola and the Military Presence." The Pensacola Series Commemorating the American Revolution Bicentennial, Volume 3, 1974. Pensacola, FL: *Pensacola News Journal.*

———. "War Averters: Seward, Mallory, and Fort Pickens." *Florida Historical Quarterly,* Vol. XLIX, No. 3, 1971. Jacksonville, FL: Florida Historical Society.

Dodd, Dorothy, ed., "Edmund Ruffin's Account of the Florida Secession Convention, 1861." *The Florida Historical Quarterly,* Volume IX, Number 2, October 1933. Tallahassee, FL: Florida Historical Society.

———. "The Secession Movement in Florida, 1850–1861." *The Florida Historical Quarterly,* Vol. XII, No. 1, July, 1933. Tallahassee, FL.

Doherty, Herbert H. "Ante-Bellum Pensacola, 1821–1860." *The Florida Historical Quarterly,* Pensacola Quadricentennial Issue, Vol. XXXVII, Nos. 3 and 4, January, 1959. Jacksonville, FL: Florida Historical Society.

East, Sherrod E. "The Banishment of Captain Meigs." *Records of the Columbia Historical Society of Washington, DC,* Vol. 40–41, Maud Burr Morris, ed., 1949. Washington, DC.

Eisterhold, John A. "Lumber and Trade in Pensacola and West Florida, 1800–1860." *The Florida Historical Quarterly,* Volume LI, No. 3, 1973. Gainesville, FL: Florida Historical Society.

Griffin, William B." Spanish Pensacola, 1700–1763." *The Florida Historical Quarterly,* Pensacola Quadricentennial Issue, Vol. XXXVII, Numbers 3 and 4, 1959. Jacksonville, FL: Florida Historical Society.

Hildreth, Charles H. "Railroads Out of Pensacola, 1833–1883." *The Florida Historical Quarterly,* Pensacola Quadricentennial Issue, Nos. 3 and 4, January, 1959. Jacksonville, FL: Florida Historical Society.

Johnson, Cecil. "Pensacola in the British Period: Summary and Significance." *The Florida Historical Quarterly,* Pensacola Quadricentennial Issue, Volume XXXVII, Nos. 3 and 4, 1959. Jacksonville, FL: Florida Historical Society.

Johnson, John O. "William Conway, A Forgotten Camden Hero." *War Papers Read Before the Commandery of the State of Maine, Military Order of the Loyal Legion of the United States.* Portland, ME: Lefavor-Rower, 1908.

Jones, James P. "Lincoln's Courier: John L. Worden's Mission to Fort Pickens." *The Florida Historical Quarterly,* Volume XLI, Number 2, October 1961. Jacksonville, FL: Florida Historical Society.

Kaczor, Bill. "Puzzles of the Past, Fort Pickens Could Have Been the Start of the Civil War." *Tampa Tribune,* August 3, 1984.

Larkin, J. L. "Battle of Santa Rosa Island." *The Florida Historical Quarterly,* Vol. XXXVII, Nos. 3 and 4, January 1959. Jacksonville, FL: Florida Historical Society.

Lufkin, Charles L. "War Council in Pensacola, January 17, 1861." *Gulf Coast Historical Review,* Volume I, Number 9, 1993. Mobile, AL: University of South Alabama.

Manucy, Albert. "The Founding of Pensacola — Reasons and Reality." *The Florida Historical Quarterly,* Pensacola Quadricentennial Issue, Volume XXXVII, Numbers 3 and 4, 1959. Jacksonville, FL: Florida Historical Society.

Meigs, Montgomery C. "General Montgomery C. Meigs on the Conduct of the Civil War." *The American Historical Review,* Volume XXVI, October 1920. New York: McMillan.

Miller, J. Michael. "Marine's Telling of 1861 Florida Navy Yard Fall Given." *Fortitude,* v. 20, no. 4, Spring, 1991.

Moore, John L., ed. "Guide to U.S. Elections," *Congressional Quarterly,* 3rd edition, 1994. Washington, DC.

Nickinson, Merritt L., comp. "Kiss the Children for Father." *Pensacola Historical Society Quarterly,* Vol. 8, Nos. 2 and 3, 1975. Pensacola, FL: Pensacola Historical Society.

Parks, Virginia, Alan Rick, and Norman Simons.

"Pensacola in the Civil War," *Pensacola Historical Society Quarterly*, Vol. 2, Spring 1978. Pensacola, FL: Pensacola Historical Society.

Ramsdell, Charles W. "Lincoln and Fort Sumter." *The Journal of Southern History*, Vol. III, No. 3, August 1937. Albany, GA: Southern Historical Association, Department of History, University of Georgia.

Randall, James G. "Ward Hill Lamon." *Dictionary of American Biography*, Dumas Malone, ed., Vol. X, 562–563, 1933. New York: Charles Scribner's Sons.

"Recollections of Cadet Life," n. auth. New York, NY: *Army and Navy Journal*, Vol. XXXIV (June 14, 1902).

Rice, Gary R. "Pre-Dawn Strike at Santa Rosa Island. *America's Civil War*, January 1998. Leesburg, VA: Primedia.

Welles, Gideon. "Facts Relating to the Reinforcement of Fort Pickens in the Spring of 1861." *The Galaxy*, January 1871 to July 1871. New York: AMS.

_____. "Fort Sumter, Facts in Relation to the Expedition Ordered by the Administration of President Lincoln for the Relief of the Garrison of Fort Sumter." *The Galaxy*, November 1870. New York: AMS Press.

Yonge, Julian C. "Pensacola in the War for Southern Independence." *The Florida Historical Quarterly*, Vol. XXXCII, Nos. 3 and 4, 1959. Jacksonville, FL: Florida Historical Society.

Original Sources

Beale, Howard K., ed. *The Diary of Gideon Welles, Secretary of the Navy under Lincoln and Johnson*. New York: W.W. Norton, 1960.

Bobbitt, Mary Reed, ed. *With Dearest Love to All, The Life and Letters of Lady Jebb*. Chicago: Henry Regnery, 1966.

Buchanan, James. *Mr. Buchanan's Administration on the Eve of the Rebellio*. New York: D. Appleton, 1866.

Buckley, Cornelius M., S.J., ed. and trans. *A Frenchman, A Chaplain, A Rebel, The War Letters of Pere Louis-Hippolyte Gache, S. J.* Chicago: Loyola University, 1981.

Crawford, Martin, ed. *William Howard Russell's Civil War, Private Diary and Letters, 1861–1862*. Athens, GA: University of Georgia, 1992.

Cronin, Cornelius. *Recollections of Service in the U.S. Navy*. New York: privately published, 1894.

Dickison, Mary Elizabeth. *Dickison and His Men*, facsimile reproduction of the 1890 edition. Gainesville, FL: University of Florida, 1962.

Doubleday, Abner. *Reminiscences of Forts Sumter and Moultrie in 1860–61*. New York: Harper Brothers, 1876.

Erben, Henry. "Surrender of the Navy Yard at Pensacola, Florida, January 12, 1861," in *Personal Recollections of the War of the Rebellion, Addressed Delivered Before the Commandery of the State of New York, Military Order of the Loyal Legion of the United States*. New York: G. Putnam's Sons, 1897.

Estvan, Bele. *War Pictures from the South*. New York: D. Appleton, 1863.

Gilman, Jeremiah H. "With Slemmer in Pensacola Harbor," in *Battles and Leaders of the Civil War*, Robert Underwood Johnson and Clarence Clough Buel, eds., Volume 1. New York: Thomas Yoseloff, 1956.

Haynes, Norman W., M.D., ed. Langdon L. Rumph to Dr. James David Rumph, in *Letters From Pensacola: The Civil War Years*. Pensacola, FL: Civil War Soldiers Museum, 1991.

Hunt, Henry J., to Braxton Bragg. April 23, 1861, copy in Henry J. Hunt Papers, United States Army Military History Institute, Carlisle, PA, quoted from Edward M. Coffman, *The Old Army, A Portrait of the American Army in Peacetime, 1784–1898*. New York: Oxford University, 1956.

Keyes, Erasmus D. *Fifty Years' Observations of Men and Events, Civil and Military*. New York: Charles Scribners's Sons, 1884.

Lamon, Ward Hill. *Recollections of Abraham Lincoln, 1847–1865*. Chicago: A.C. McLurg, 1895.

Long, Ellen Call. *Florida Breezes, or Florida, New and Old*. Jacksonville, FL: Asmead Bros., 1883.

McMorries, Edward Young. *History of the First Regiment, Alabama Volunteer Infantry, C. S. A.* Montgomery, AL: Browning, 1904.

Moore, Frank. *The Rebellion Record*. New York: G.P. Putnam, 1861.

Morris. Gouveneur. *The History of a Volunteer Regiment*. New York: Veteran Volunteer, 1891.

Nicolay, John G. *The Outbreak of the Rebellion*. New York: Charles Scribner's Sons, 1881.

_____, and John Hays, eds. *Abraham Lincoln, A History*. New York: Century, 1890.

_____, and John Hays, eds. *Abraham Lincoln*. New York: Century, 1894.

Porter, David Dixon. *Incidents and Anecdotes of the Civil War*. New York: D. Appleton, 1885.

_____. *The Naval History of the Civil War*. New York: Sherman, 1886.

Rumph, Langdon L., to Dr. James David Rumph. In *Letters from Pensacola: The Civil War Years*. Norman W. Haines, Jr., M.C., ed. Pensacola, FL: Civil War Soldiers Museum, 1991.

Russell, William H. *My Diary North and South*. New York: Harper Brothers, 1861.

Smith, Daniel P. *Company K, First Alabama Regiment, or Three Years in the Confederate Service*. Prattville, AL: Survivors, 1885.

Stocker, Jeffrey D., ed., *From Huntsville to Appomattox*. Knoxville, TN: University of Tennessee, 1996.

Thompson, Robert Means, and Richard Wainwright, eds. *Confidential Correspondence of Gustavus Vasa Fox, Assistant Secretary of the Navy, 1861–1865*, Volume 1. New York: De Vinne for the Naval History Society, 1918.

United States Government Printing Office. *Register of Officers of the Confederate States Navy, 1861–1865*. Washington, DC, 1931.

_____, Navy Department. *Official Records of the Union and Confederate Navies in the War of the Rebellion*, Series I, Volume 4. Washington, DC: Government Printing Office, 1896.

_____, War Department, *War of the Rebellion, A Compilation of the Official Records of the Union and Con-

federate Armies, 3 Series, 128 Volumes. Washington, DC: Government Printing Office, 1881–1901.
Walke, Henry. *Naval Scenes and Reminiscences of the Civil War....* New York: F.R. Reed, 1877.
Wood, Vann C., and Elisabeth Muhlenfeld, eds. *The Private Mary Chestnut, The Unpublished Civil War Diaries.* New York: Oxford University, 1984.

Secondary Sources

Anderson, Bern. *By Sea and River, The Naval History of the Civil War.* New York: Alfred A. Knopf, 1961.
Anderson, Thomas M. *The Political Conspiracies Preceding the Rebellion or the True Stories of Sumter and Pickens.* New York: G.P. Putnam's Sons, 1882.
Appleyard, John, and Norman Haines, M.D. *Pensacola and the War Between the States.* Pensacola, FL: John Appleyard, 1993.
Armstrong, Henry Clay. *History of Escambia County, Florida.* St. Augustine, FL: Record, 1930.
Auchampaugh, Philip Gerald. *James Buchanan and His Cabinet on the Eve of Secession.* Lancaster, PA: private, 1926.
Auge, Moses. *Lives of the Eminent Dead and Biographical Notices of Prominent Living Citizens of Montgomery County, Pa.* Norristown, PA: self-published, 1897.
Bancroft, Frederick. *The Life of William H. Seward,* Vol. 2. New York: Harper Brothers, 1900.
Bauer, K. Jack, and Stephen S. Roberts. *Register of Ships of the United States Navy, 1775–1900, Major Combatants.* New York: Greenwood, 1991.
Bearss, Edwin C. *Historical Structure Report, Fort Pickens, Historical Data Section, 1821–1895.* Denver, CO: U.S. Department of the Interior, National Park Service, Denver Service Center, 1983.
Belknap, George E. *The Home Squadron in the Winter of 1860–61: Papers of the Military Historical Society of Massachusetts, Volume XII, Naval Actions and History, 1799–1898.* Boston: Griffith-Stillings, 1902.
Bense, Judith A. *The Colonial Archeological Record in Pensacola, Florida.* Paper presented in the Symposium: Colonial Pensacola: A First Syntheses (Forts of Pensacola), Society for Historical Archeology Conference, Washington, DC, 1995.
Blakely, Arch Frederick. *General John H. Winder, C.S.A.* Gainesville, FL: University of Florida, 1990.
Boatner, Mark Mayo. *The Civil War Dictionary.* New York: David McKay, 1959.
Bowden, Jesse Early, Gordon Norman Simons, and Sarah L. Johnson. *Pensacola, Florida's First Place City.* Norfolk, VA: Donning, 1989.
Boynton, Charles B. *The History of the Navy during the Rebellion.* New York: D. Appleton, 1867.
Bradley, Stanley Erwin. *Simon Cameron, Lincoln's War Secretary.* Philadelphia, PA: University of Pennsylvania, 1966.
Brevard, Caroline Mays. *A History of Florida, From the Treaty of 1783 to Our Own Times.* Deland, FL: Florida State Historical Society, 1925.
Callahan, Edward W., ed. *List of Officers of the Navy of the United States and the Marine Corps from 1775 to 1900....* New York: Haskin House, 1969.

Cash, William Thomas. *The Story of Florida,* Vol. 1. New York: American Society, 1938.
Catton, Bruce. *U.S. Grant and the American Military Tradition.* Boston: Little, Brown, 1954.
Clubbs, Occie. *Stephen Russell Mallory, The Elder,* master's thesis. Gainesville, FL: University of Florida, 1936.
Coffman, Edward M. *The Old Army, A Portrait of the American Army in Peacetime, 1784–1898.* New York: Oxford University, 1986.
Coleman, James C. *A Castle Built on Sand.* Pensacola, FL: Pensacola Historical Society, 1988.
_____, and Irene S. Coleman, *Guardians on the Gulf, Pensacola Fortifications, 1698–1980,* Pensacola Historical Society, Pensacola, FL, 1982.
Connelly, Thomas Lawrence. *Army of the Heartland, The Army of Tennessee, 1861–1862.* Baton Rouge, LA: Louisiana State University, 1967.
_____, *Autumn of Glory, The Army of Tennessee, 1862, 1865.* Baton Rouge, LA: Louisiana State University, 1971.
Craven, Avery O. *Civil War in the Making, 1815–1860.* Baton Rouge, LA: Louisiana State University, 1959.
_____, and Frank E. Vandiver. *The American Tragedy, the Civil War in Retrospect: A Series of Lectures at Hampden-Sydney College.* Hampden-Sydney, VA, April 1959.
Crawford, Samuel Wylie. *The Genesis of the Civil War, The Story of Sumter, 1860–1861.* New York: Charles L. Webster, 1887.
Cullum, George W. *Biographical Register of the Officers and Graduates of the U.S. Military Academy at West Point....* Boston: Houghton Mifflin, 1891.
Currant, Richard L. *Lincoln and the First Shot.* Philadelphia: J. Lippincott, 1963.
Davis, William C., ed. *Shadows of the Storm, Volume 2 of the Image of War, 1861–1865.* Garden City, NY: Doubleday, 1981.
Davis, William Watson. *The Civil War and Reconstruction in Florida.* New York: Columbia University, 1913.
Dibble, Ernest F. *William H. Chase—Gulf Coast Fort Builder.* Wilmington, DE: Gulf Coast Collection, n.d.
Donnelly. Ralph W. *The Confederate States Marine Corps, The Rebel Leathernecks.* Shippensburg, PA: White Mane, 1989.
Douglas, Marjory Stoneman. *Florida, The Long Frontier.* New York: Harper & Row, 1967.
Drummond, Dwight Lowell. *The Secessionist Movement, 1860–1861.* New York: Macmillan, 1931.
_____, and Dwight Lowell, eds. *Southern Editorials on Secession.* New York: Century, 1931.
Durkin, Joseph T. S. *Stephen Mallory, Confederate Navy Chief.* Chapel Hill, NC: University of North Carolina, 1954.
Dyer, Frederick H. *A Compendium of the War of the Rebellion,* Vol. 3. New York: Thomas Yoseloff, 1959.
Elliott, James Cantey. *Lieutenant General Richard Herron Anderson, Lee's Noble Solider.* Dayton, OH: Morningside, 1985.
Evans, Clement A., ed. *Confederate Military History,*

Military History of Florida, by J. J. Dickison. Atlanta, GA: Confederate, 1899.

Faust, Patricia, ed. *Historical Times Illustrated Encyclopedia of the Civil War.* New York: Harper & Row, 1986.

Fouraker, Warren G. *The Administration of Robert Raymond Reid,* master's thesis. Tallahassee, FL: Florida State University, 1949.

Fowler, William M., Jr. *Under Two Flags, The American Navy in the Civil War.* New York: W.W. Norman, 1990.

Freeman, Douglas Southall., *Lee's Lieutenants, A Study in Command.* New York: Charles Scribner's Sons, 1943.

Garner, Thomas M. *The Pensacola Lighthouse.* Pensacola, FL: Pensacola Historical Society, 1994.

Hadd, Donald R. *Secession Movement in Florida, 1850–1861,* master's thesis. Tallahassee, FL: Florida State University, 1960.

Hale, Edward Everett, Jr. *William H. Seward.* Philadelphia: George W. Jacobs, 1910.

Hallock, Judith. *Braxton Bragg and Confederate Defeat,* Vol. II. Tuscaloosa, AL: University of Alabama Press, 1991.

Haskin, William L. *The History of the First Regiment of Artillery....* Portland, ME: B. Thurston, 1879.

Hattaway, Herman, and Archer Jones. *How the North Won: A Military History of the Civil War.* Champagne-Urbana, IL: University of Illinois, 1983.

Hearn, Chester D. *Admiral David Dixon Porter.* Annapolis, MD: Naval Institute, 1996.

Hendrickson, Robert. *Sumter, the First Day of the Civil War.* New York: Rowan and Littlefield, 1990.

Hesseltine, William B. *Civil War Prisons.* New York: Frederick Ungar, 1930.

Jahoda, Gloria. *Florida, A Bicentennial History.* New York: W.W. Norton, 1976.

Johns, John E. *Florida During the Civil War.* Gainesville, FL: University of Florida, 1963.

Jones, Virgil Carrington. *The Civil War at Sea, The Blockaders,* Vol. 1. New York: Holt, Reinhart, Winston, 1960.

Klein, Philip Schriver. *President Buchanan, A Biography.* University Park, PA: Pennsylvania State University, 1962.

Knox, Dudley W. *A History of the United States Navy.* New York: G. Putnam's Sons, 1936.

Lathrop, Thomas Kirkland. *William Henry Seward.* Boston: Houghton Mifflin, 1896.

Leech, Margaret. *Reveille in Washington, 1860–1861.* New York: Harper & Brothers, 1941.

Lewis, Paul. *Yankee Admiral, A Biography of David Dixon Porter.* New York: David McKay, 1968.

Long, Everett B., with Barbara Long. *The Civil War, Day by Day, An Almanac, 1861–1865.* New York: Doubleday, 1971.

Lossing, Benson J. *Pictoral History of the Civil War in the United States of America.* Philadelphia: George W. Childs, 1866.

Mahan, Alfred Thayer. *The Navy in the Civil War, Vol. III, The Gulf and Inland Waters.* New York: Charles Scribner's Sons, 1883.

McMullen, Malcolm C. *The Alabama Confederate Reader.* Tuscaloosa, AL: University of Alabama, 1963.

McWhiney, Grady. *Braxton Bragg and Confederate Defeat, Vol. I — Field Command.* New York: Columbia University, 1969.

Meredith, Evelyn T. *The Secession Movement in Florida, 1850–1861,* master's thesis. Durham, NC: Duke University, 1941.

Meyer, Charles J., Jr. *U.S.S. Fulton (AS-11), 50th Anniversary, Silent Partner of the Silent Service,* Paducah, KY: Turner, 1991.

Mool, James Bulger. *Florida in Federal Politics: Statehood to Secession,* master's thesis. Durham, NC: Duke University, 1940.

Moore, Frank. *The Rebellion Record.* New York: G.P. Putnam, 1861.

Morison, Samuel Eliot. *The Oxford History of the American People.* New York: Oxford University, 1965.

Muir, Thomas, Jr., and David P. Ogden. *The Fort Pickens Story.* Pensacola, FL: Pensacola Historical Society, 1989.

Musicant, Ivan. *Divided Waters, The Naval History of the Civil War.* New York: HarperCollins, 1995.

A Naval Encyclopedia.... Philadelphia, PA: L.&R. Hammersly, 1881.

Nevins, Allan. *The War for the Union,* Vol. 1. New York: Charles Scribner's Sons, 1959.

Niven, John. *Gideon Welles, Lincoln's Secretary of the Navy.* New York: Oxford University, 1973.

Ogden, David P. *Scapegoat: Captain James Armstrong and the Surrender of the Pensacola Navy Yard in 1861,* master's thesis. Orlando, FL: University of Central Florida, 1992.

Parks, Virginia. *Pensacola: Spaniards to Space Age.* Pensacola, FL: Pensacola Historical Society, 1986.

_____, and Judith A. Bense, *Underground Pensacola,* Publication Number 1. Pensacola, FL: Pensacola Archeological Society, 1989.

Pearce, George F. *Pensacola during the Civil War, A Thorn in the Side of the Confederacy.* Gainesville, FL: University Press of Florida, 2000.

_____. *The U.S. Navy in Pensacola: From Sailing Ships to Naval Aviation, (1825–1930).* Pensacola, FL: University Presses of Florida, 1980.

Rye, Scott. *Ships of the Civil War.* Stamford, CT: Longmeadow, 1995.

Scharf, Thomas J. *History of the Confederate Navy from Its Organization to the Surrender of the Last Vessel.* New York: Rogers Sherwood, 1887.

Seitz, Don Carlos. *Braxton Bragg, General of the Confederacy.* Columbia, SC: State, 1924.

Seward, Frederick. *Seward at Washington, as Senator and Secretary of State, 1846–1861.* New York: Derby and Miller, 1991.

Smith, William Ernest. *The Francis Preston Blair Family in Politics,* Vol. 2. New York: McMillan, 1933.

Soley, James Russell. *Admiral Porter.* New York: D. Appleton, 1903.

Stampp, Kenneth M. *And the War Came, The North and the Secession Crisis, 1860–1861.* Baton Rouge, LA: Louisiana State University, 1950.

State of Florida, Board of State Institutions. *Soldiers of Florida in the Seminole, Indian, Civil, and Spanish-American Wars*. Live Oak, FL: Democrat Book and Job Print, 1903.

Still, William N., Jr. *Ironclad Captains: The Commanding Officers of the USS Monitor*. Washington, DC: Marine and Estuarine Management Division, National Oceanic and Atmospheric Administration, United States Department of Commerce, 1988.

Sullivan, David M. *The United States Marine Corps in the Civil War—The First Year*. Shippensburg, PA: White Mane, 1997.

Swanberg, W.A. *The Story of Fort Sumter*. New York: Charles Scribner's Sons, 1957.

Taylor, John M. *William Henry Seward, Lincoln's Right Hand*. New York: HarperCollins, 1991.

Taylor, Vivian F. *Tombstone Inscriptions in Montgomery County, Pa., New Norris Township*. Historical Society of Montgomery County, PA, 1958.

Tebeau, Charlton W. *A History of Florida*. Coral Gables, FL: University of Miami, 1971.

Thompson, Arthur William. *David Yulee: A Study in Nineteenth Century American Thought and Enterprise*. New York: Columbia University, 1954.

Tilley, John Shipley. *Lincoln Takes Command*. Chapel Hill, NC: University of North Carolina, 1941.

Turk, David Scott. *Give My Regards to the Ladies: The Life of Littleton Quinton Washington*. Bowie, MD: Heritage, 2001.

United States Government, Department of the Interior, National Park Service. Gulf Islands National Seashore, site pamphlets, *Fort Barrancas*, n. loc., n.d.

Van Deusen, Glyndon G. *William Henry Seward*. New York: Oxford University, 1967.

Walker, Irvine C. *The Life of Lt. Gen. R.H. Anderson, of the Confederate States Army*. Charleston, SC: Art, 1917.

Weigley, Russell Frank. *Quartermaster General of the Union Army, A Biography of M.C. Meigs*. New York: Columbia University, 1959.

Weinberg, Sydney J. *Slavery and Secession in Florida, 1845–1861*, master's thesis. Tallahassee, FL: University of Florida, 1940.

West, Richard S., Jr. *Gideon Welles, Lincoln's Navy Department*. New York: Bobbs-Merrill, 1943.

_____. *Mr. Lincoln's Navy*. New York: Longmans, Green, 1957.

_____. *The Second Admiral, A Life of David Dixon Porter, 1813–1891*. New York: Coward-McCann, 1937.

Williams, Edwin L., Jr. *Florida in the Union, 1845–1861*, doctoral thesis. Chapel Hill, NC: University of North Carolina, 1951.

Index

Abert, Charles H. 52
Abert, S. Thayer 42
Adams, Henry A. 29, 67, 68, 69, 70, 71, 73, 74, 75, 76, 84, 89, 91, 92, 93, 95, 97, 104, 105, 108, 109, 114, 116, 120, 129, 132, 133, 134, 139, 140, 141, 142, 143, 144, 145, 148, 150, 152, 153, 155, 156, 159, 160, 162, 163, 167, 172, 175, 176, 177
vessel *Aid* 185
Alabama & Florida Railroad 9, 11
Alabama River 4
Alabama State 14, 19, 20, 26, 29, 30, 37, 38, 40, 42, 43, 52, 54, 59, 64, 65, 84, 90, 93
Alabama State Troops: 1st Infantry Regiment 71, 160; 2nd Infantry Regiment 29, 37, 38, 40, 52, 59; 3rd Infantry Regiment 166; 4th Infantry Battalion 208; 7th Infantry Regiment 190; 29th Infantry Regiment 210
Alden, James 172
Allen, Harvey 146
Anderson, J. Patton 190, 191, 192, 196
Anderson, Richard H. 189, 190, 191, 192, 194, 195, 196, 199, 200, 204, 205, 207
Anderson, Robert 15, 26, 27, 32, 51, 62, 68, 81, 83, 85, 87, 96, 97, 98, 100, 102, 108, 119, 121, 137, 142, 154, 163
Annapolis, Maryland 114
Apalachicola, Florida 24
vessel *Arabia* 93
Arkansas State 19, 184
Armstrong, James 11, 12, 13, 18, 23, 24, 27, 28, 31, 34, 36, 37, 38, 39, 43, 44, 45, 52, 58, 65, 82, 104, 120, 152
Armstrong, Mrs. 38
Arnold, Lewis G. 30, 44, 46, 52, 56, 57, 193, 194, 195, 207, 211
Astor House, New York City, New York 123

Atlanta, Georgia 130
vessel *Atlantic* 119, 126, 127, 130, 132, 136, 139, 144, 145, 146, 149, 151, 152, 155
Atlantic Ocean 126, 130
Augusta, Georgia 43, 131

Bahia Santa Maria de Filipina 3
Bailey, Theodorus 185, 186, 188, 204, 211
Bainbridge, William 4
Balch, George 59, 110
vessel *Baltic* 121, 135, 138, 139
Baltimore, Maryland 9
Bancroft, Frederick 73
Bank of Mobile 92
Bank of Pensacola, Florida 9
Barnwell, Robert W. 50
barrancas 3
Barrancas Barracks 10, 14, 15, 20, 23, 24, 28, 31, 40, 41, 48, 64, 71, 86, 132, 134, 141, 211
Barron, Samuel 55, 60, 113, 115, 116, 117, 124
Barry, William 110, 165, 177, 183
Bates, Edward 102
Baton Rouge, Louisiana 66, 71, 83
Battery Cameron 161, 170, 183, 186, 193, 202, 204
Battery Lincoln 161, 166, 170, 182, 183, 192, 193, 202, 204
Battery Scott 161, 170, 182, 183, 202
Battery Totten 161, 192, 202
Bay State Woolen Company 68
Beauregard, Pierre G.T. 77, 82, 87, 90, 96, 98, 108, 120, 131, 132, 135, 137, 150, 166, 184, 189, 209
Belknap, Lieutenant 94
Benjamin, Judah P. 188, 189, 207
Bernard, Simon 6, 7
Berryman, Otway H. 13, 27, 28, 29, 31, 34, 36, 42, 45, 48, 49, 52, 53, 56, 63, 68, 76, 88, 116
Biddle, James 4
Bigler, William 61
Bishop, Ethan, 2
Black, Jeremiah 16, 58

Blackburn's Ford, Virginia 184
Blair, Montgomery 88, 89, 90, 91, 102
blockade 150, 155, 159, 162, 168, 170
Boggs, William 133, 207
Bonaparte, Napoleon 55
Bonney, C.L. 160
Booth, John C. 92
Boston, Massachusetts 12, 30, 44, 120
Boyd, David A. 66
Bradford, Richard 192
Brannan, John 45, 46, 56, 62
Bragg, Braxton 66, 71, 77, 83, 85, 86, 87, 89, 90, 94, 95, 96, 98, 100, 104, 105, 108, 116, 121, 127, 128, 131, 132, 133, 134, 135, 139, 141, 142, 144, 145, 146, 150, 152, 153, 155, 159, 160, 161, 165, 166, 169, 182, 186, 188, 189, 195, 196, 198, 199, 200, 201, 202, 203, 204, 205, 206, 207, 208, 209
Bragg, Elise 98, 172
Breese, Samuel L. 100, 115
Broady, Elias 133
U.S.S. *Brooklyn* 18, 55, 56, 58, 60, 61, 62, 66, 67, 68, 69, 70, 73, 74, 75, 84, 85, 86, 89, 91, 92, 93, 94, 97, 101, 103, 104, 105, 108, 116, 120, 140, 143, 144, 145, 151, 153, 154, 155, 162, 175, 177
Brooklyn Navy Yard 70, 77, 83, 88, 100, 105, 115, 116, 120, 121, 124, 126, 127, 142, 169
Brooks, Horace 146
Brosnahan, John 211
Brown, George 155, 162
Brown, Harvey 79, 110, 111, 118, 120, 125, 126, 127, 136, 144, 145, 146, 147, 148, 149, 150, 151, 152, 153, 154, 155, 158, 160, 161, 163, 165, 166, 167, 168, 169, 170, 171, 173, 174, 175, 176, 177, 178, 179, 181, 183, 184, 185, 186, 188, 189, 192, 193, 194, 195, 196, 197, 198, 199, 200, 202, 204, 205, 206, 207

229

Index

Brown, Joseph 19, 131
Buchanan, James 16, 18, 26, 30, 50, 54, 58, 59, 61, 68, 69, 71, 72, 78, 84, 89, 90, 91, 105, 109, 129, 130
Buena Vista, Mexico 66, 128
Bull Run, Virginia 184
Burrows, Captain 38, 39

Caldwell, James 66
Calhoun, John C. 81
California State 110, 114, 123
Cameron, Simon 81, 83, 85, 87, 96, 101, 102, 119, 121, 128, 132, 165, 170, 172, 177, 179
Camp Brown 191, 192, 193
Campbell, John 110, 157, 158
Campbell, John A. 91, 96, 105, 118, 132
Campbell, Richard 38
Canada 109
Caribbean Sea 5
Carlisle, James M. 58
Carlisle Barracks, Pennsylvania 79
Cash, John 93, 140
Cass, Lewis 16, 60
Catton, Bruce 86
Central America 109
Chalfin, Samuel 183
Chalmers, James 190, 191, 192, 196
Chapultepec, Mexico 199
Charleston Courier 135
Charleston, South Carolina 15, 23, 26, 42, 58, 62, 68, 73, 77, 80, 82, 83, 87, 88, 89, 90, 93, 96, 97, 98, 100, 102, 103, 105, 120, 122, 123, 128, 131, 137, 138, 142, 189
Chase, Salmon P. 90, 102
Chase, William H. 9, 10, 11, 26, 30, 37, 38, 40, 42, 43, 45, 46, 47, 48, 49, 50, 51, 52, 54, 56, 58, 59, 60, 61, 64, 66, 70, 71, 72, 76, 94, 105
Chestnut, James 137
Chew, Robert 128, 132
Chisolm, Alexander 137
Chocktawhatchee Bay 3
Cincinnati, Ohio 169
Clarke, Henry F. 110
Clay, Clement C. 82
Clay, Henry 81
Clitz, Henry 110, 144, 179
Closson, Henry W. 172, 179
Cobb, Howell 17
U.S.S. *Colorado* 185, 187, 188, 200
Columbia, South Carolina 50
Confederate Army of Tennessee 200
Confederate Department of Alabama and West Florida 208
Confederate States Army 82, 96
Confederate States Congress 75, 82, 97
Confederate States Constitution 76
Confederate States Government 51, 64, 69, 71, 73, 77, 82, 85, 101, 111, 118, 121, 122, 137, 159, 205

Confederate States Navy 75, 86
Confederate States War Department 64, 84, 128
Connecticut State 115
Conrad, Charles 161
Conway, William 39, 44, 120, 152, 211
Coombs, Robert 86
Cooper, James 43
Cooper, Samuel 96, 99, 127
Corinth, Mississippi 169, 207, 208, 209
Craven, Tunis A.M. 13, 88
Crawford, Martin J. 81, 82, 84, 91, 96
Creighton, John 191, 192
vessel *Crescent City* 107
Crimea 93, 164
Cronin, Cornelius 94, 141, 146, 173
Crossley, Billy 160
U.S.S. *Crusader* 12, 20, 44, 45, 88, 90, 103, 105, 130, 148, 159, 168, 169
Cuba 4, 13, 34
U.S.S. *Cumberland* 70

Daniels, Lieutenant 43
Davis, Jefferson 51, 66, 71, 73, 75, 91, 104, 111, 127, 130, 135, 163, 198
Davis, Varina 163
de Arriola, Andrés 3
Deas, George 83, 89, 92
de Luna, Tristan 3
Democratic Party 59
vessel *Diana* 162, 164, 165
Dimmick, Justin 55, 56
Dixon, Robert 43, 211
Dodge, John R. 205, 206
Doyle, James 29
Driscoll, Patrick 187
Dry Tortugas, Florida 31, 44, 46, 54, 56, 57, 61, 71, 72, 80, 103, 144, 146, 151, 155, 159, 168, 177, 182, 191, 207
Duane, James 110, 144
Duffy, Patrick 191, 192, 204
Du Pont, Samuel 153, 154
Duryea, Richard 193, 194

Eddy, Asher B. 13, 59
Edwards, J.D. 162
Edwards, John 184
Ellis, Towson 164
Ellison, Francis 201, 202
vessel *Empire City* 88, 90
England 93
Erben, Henry 35, 36, 37, 38, 41
Ericcson, John 142
Escambia River 3, 4, 210
Etting, Henry 129
vessel *Ewing* 190, 194, 195
executive mansion 72, 112, 115, 155

Farragut, David 209
Farrand, Ebenezer 12, 13, 23, 24, 27, 28, 29, 31, 35, 36, 37, 38, 39, 40, 44, 46, 47, 52, 53, 56, 76, 78, 86, 89, 92

Faunce, John 132
Fell, William H. 12
Fernandina East Floridian 15
Finnegan, Joseph 19, 25
Fitzpatrick, Benjamin 59
Florida Board of Parks and Historical Memorials 212
Florida State 10, 11, 14, 21, 26, 48, 50, 54, 55, 65, 76, 84, 90; 1st Infantry Regiment 190; secession 13, 19, 30; state forces 15, 26, 29, 37, 40, 42, 64
Floyd, John B. 15, 16, 18, 19, 71, 72, 75, 85
Flynn, John 133
Follansbee, Joshua 84
Foote, Andrew H. 88, 115, 116, 117, 118, 120, 121, 123, 125, 126
Forney, John H. 77, 95
Forsythe, John 81, 84, 96
Fort Adams, Rhode Island 14
Fort Advanced Redoubt, Florida 9, 10
Fort Barrancas, Florida 8, 9, 10, 23, 25, 28, 31, 33, 35, 40, 54, 72, 73, 97, 100, 144, 155, 161, 163, 185, 187, 202, 203, 209, 210, 211
Fort Barrancas Water Battery, Florida 8
Fort Gaines, Alabama 20
Fort Hamilton, New York 79, 158, 169, 179
Fort Jackson, Louisiana 90, 209
Fort Jefferson, Florida 30, 44, 45, 46, 54, 56, 57, 61, 71, 72, 80, 91, 103, 104, 144, 151, 207
Fort Laramie, Dakota Territory 169
Fort Marion, Florida 20
Fort McHenry, Maryland 9
Fort McRee, Florida 7, 9, 10, 31, 35, 36, 40, 48, 54, 60, 72, 76, 100, 104, 141, 147, 153, 160, 167, 185, 186, 188, 201, 202, 203, 204, 205, 206, 209, 210, 211
Fort Monroe, Virginia 15, 55, 58, 60, 62, 80, 92
Fort Morgan, Alabama 20, 90
Fort Moultrie, South Carolina 14, 15, 18, 26
Fort Niagara, New York 9
Fort Pickens, Florida 7, 8, 9, 10, 18, 24, 27, 28, 29, 31, 33, 34, 35, 36, 41, 42, 43, 45, 46, 48, 49, 51, 52, 53, 54, 55, 57, 58, 59, 60, 62, 64, 66, 67, 69, 70, 72, 73, 74, 75, 76, 77, 78, 80, 81, 83, 84, 86, 87, 88, 91, 92, 93, 94, 95, 96, 97, 98, 100, 101, 102, 103, 104, 105, 106, 107, 108, 109, 110, 112, 113, 114, 119, 121, 123, 126, 127, 129, 130, 131, 132, 133, 139, 141, 142, 145, 146, 147, 153, 155, 163, 164, 165, 168, 169, 170, 171, 174, 176, 177, 179, 183, 184, 189, 191, 192, 194, 196, 199, 200, 202, 204, 206, 210, 211, 212; truce 61

Fort Pulaski, Georgia 20
Fort St. Philip, Louisiana 90, 209
Fort San Carlos de Austria, Florida 3, 4, 6
Fort Sumter, South Carolina 15, 18, 26, 30, 42, 50, 59, 60, 62, 68, 69, 73, 75, 77, 80, 81, 82, 83, 84, 85, 86, 87,119, 121, 124, 128, 130, 131, 132, 137, 138, 139, 142, 150, 169, 177, 184
Fort Taylor, Florida 45, 46, 56, 57, 62, 80, 91, 104, 144, 145, 148, 151, 153, 163, 173
forts on Pensacola Bay 6, 18, 19, 20, 26, 30, 31
Foster, John G. 108
Foster's Bank 8, 35, 40, 100
Fox, Gustavus V. 68, 88, 89, 90, 100, 102, 105, 108, 112, 113, 118, 120, 121, 122, 135, 138, 139
Frailey, James L. 100, 155
France 109
U.S.S. *Franklin* 172
Franklin, William B. 179
Frederick, the Great, of Prussia 107
vessel *Freeborn* 121, 138
Freeman, Douglas Southall 207
Frémont, John Charles 170
U.S.S. *Fulton* 12, 40, 43, 86, 92, 94, 188, 209, 210

Gache, Louis-Hippolyte 165, 166
vessel *Galveston* 57
Garden Key, Florida 57
Gardner 133
Georgetown, District of Columbia 71, 75
Georgia State 19, 20, 30, 65, 84, 90, 96, 128; 5th Infantry Regiment 190; Georgia Battalion 190
Gibraltar 82
Gibson, Alexander 74, 145
Gillis, John 135
Gilman, Jeremiah 14, 15, 20, 23, 27, 28, 29, 31, 33, 39, 41, 43, 44, 45, 46, 47, 48, 49, 52, 54, 56, 58, 59, 63, 64, 66, 69, 70, 72, 73, 75, 76, 77, 104, 144, 158, 160, 169
Gilman, Mary 14, 28, 31, 40, 48
Glynn, James 19, 61, 62, 69
Gonzales, Samuel Z. 12
Gosport Navy Yard 151
Gosport, Virginia 5
Governor's Island, New York 102, 171
Grant, Ulysses S. 87, 207, 208
Gray, A.A. 126, 132, 155
Great Britain 109
Great Falls, Virginia 103
Greenville, Alabama 83
Gregory, Francis H. 82
Gulf Islands National Seashore 212
Gulf of Mexico 1, 5, 30, 44, 70, 73, 75, 91, 97, 109, 158
Gwathmey, Washington 94, 128, 129

Hamlin, Hannibal 101
Hampton Roads, Virginia 70, 80
Hanham, Moore 191, 192
U.S.S. *Harriet Lane* 90, 102, 132, 138, 209, 210, 211
Harrisburg, Pennsylvania 85
U.S.S. *Hartford* 202
Hartstuff, George 110
Harwood, Andrew 172
Havana, Cuba 74, 75, 94, 107, 146, 155, 160, 169, 199
Havens, Benny 86
Hawkins, George S. 30
Hayne, Isaac W. 50
Hazeltine, Richard 191, 192
Head of Passes, Mississippi River 200
Henberer, Charles 191, 192, 204
Heuer, Sharon 2
Hildt, John 193, 194
Hoelzle, Henry 191, 192
Hollonquist, James 190, 191, 193
Holt, Joseph 16, 19, 50, 61, 65, 68, 73, 75, 81, 83, 92, 105
Hong Kong, China 12
Hoodless, John 92
Hopkins, James A. 50
Horta, A. & P. 95
Horton, John 187
Hunt, Edwin B. 46
Hunt, Henry J. 110, 152, 177, 179, 183
Hunter, Robert M.T. 61, 82, 86
U.S.S. *Huntsville* 168, 170, 175, 185

vessel *Illinois* 119, 127, 130, 132, 136, 146, 148, 149, 151, 177
Ingalls, Rufus 110
Ingraham, Duncan 116
Ingraham, John 143
Irving House, New York City 117
Irwin, John 13, 31, 40, 43, 45, 48
vessel *Isabella* 95, 96, 97
Ivey, James 39

Jackson, Andrew 4
Jackson, John 190, 191, 192, 196
Jackson, Richard 211
Jackson, Mississippi 30
Jamieson, Alexander 33, 63, 66, 158
vessel *J.N. Genin* 170
John, William 110
Johnston, Albert Sydney 207, 208
Jones, Samuel 207, 208
Jones, Thomas 208, 209, 210
vessel *Joseph Whitney* 30, 44, 54, 57
Juárez, Benito 12

Kearney, James 4
Kelly, William H.J. 52, 135
Key West, Florida 4, 15, 30, 44, 45, 155, 158, 159, 162, 191, 199, 204
Keyes, Erasmus 106, 107, 108, 110, 111, 114, 116, 119, 120, 126, 130, 136, 148, 149, 154, 155
King, Horatio 16

King, W.A. 36
Kittridge, Captain 148
Knapp, C.P. 13, 84, 89, 98
Kreall, Christian 192

Lamon, Ward 97, 98, 101, 102, 105, 108
Langdon, Loomis 56, 69, 70, 104, 105, 193, 194
Lavallette, Elie A.F. 58
Lawrence, Massachusetts 68
Lawton, Eldridge 43
Lay, George W. 18, 65
Le Baron, Charles 139
Lee, Stephen 137
Lincoln, Abraham 1, 11, 16, 26, 50, 59, 69, 72, 75, 79, 80, 81, 82, 83, 84, 85, 86, 87, 88, 89, 90, 91, 93, 97, 98, 100, 101, 102, 103, 105, 106, 107, 109, 110, 111, 112, 113, 115, 116, 118, 121, 128, 129, 130, 135, 139, 148, 150, 155, 159, 169, 184, 185, 199
Locke, M.B. 160
Lomax, Tennent 29, 37, 38, 39, 40, 42, 43, 51, 52, 54, 57, 100, 166
London Times 93, 97, 101, 118, 162
Long, Ellen Call 128
Looker, Thomas 91
Louisiana State 65, 66, 84, 90
Louisiana *Zouaves* 96, 98, 128, 152, 163
Lovell, William 194

U.S.S. *Macedonian* 19, 60, 61, 62, 69, 70, 74
Macomb, Alexander 6
Mallory, Stephen R. 19, 30, 50, 51, 56, 59, 60, 61, 75, 83, 86, 94, 105, 161, 163, 205, 211
C.S.S. *Manassas* 200, 201
Manassas, Virginia 184, 189
Manhattan Beach, New York 170
U.S.S. *Maria Wood* 211
vessel *Marie Norton* 64
Marks, Samuel B. 38, 39, 42, 52
vessel *Maryland* 180
Maxwell, Augustus E. 51
vessel *McClellan* 195, 200
McClellan, George B. 205, 207
McDowell, Irwin 170, 184
McGarr, Owen 133, 134
McGowan, John 26
McGrail, soldier 192
McKean, William W. 157, 167, 170, 173, 174, 175, 176, 185, 187, 188, 200, 201, 202, 203, 204
McMorries, Edward 160
McRee, William 8
McWhiney, Grady 86, 87
Meigs, John R. 103
Meigs, Montgomery C. 54, 57, 62, 71, 72, 75, 77, 78, 79, 102, 103, 104, 106, 107, 110, 111, 112, 113, 114, 115, 118, 120, 121, 122, 125, 126, 130, 132, 134, 136, 144,

146, 147, 148, 151, 152, 155, 159, 165, 170, 183, 197, 198
Mercer, Samuel 63, 100, 113, 116, 122, 123, 125, 126, 136, 138, 159
Merritt, Lucius 208
Mervine, William 162, 172, 177, 185, 186, 187
Mexico 109
Mexico City 199
Milton, Florida 186
U.S.S. *Minnesota* 120, 154
Miruelo, Don Diego 3
Missouri State 199
U.S.S. *Mississippi* 173, 178, 201
Mississippi River 4, 120, 121, 131, 209
Mississippi River Valley 166, 179, 204
Mississippi State 19, 30, 43, 48, 64, 65, 84, 90, 111, 128, 160
Mississippi State Troops: 9th Infantry Regiment 190, 208; 10th Infantry Regiment 190; 27th Infantry Regiment 208; 8th Mississippi Regiment 209
Mobile, Alabama 1, 4, 11, 20, 24, 43, 44, 45, 86, 95, 153, 155, 162, 169, 176, 200, 208
Mobile & Ohio Railroad 208
Mobile Bay 4, 209
U.S.S. *Mohawk* 88, 90, 93, 103, 168, 171, 175
U.S.S. *Monitor* 142
Montgomery, Alabama 11, 12, 19, 43, 44, 58, 59, 64, 69, 70, 71, 75, 76, 77, 82, 83, 85, 86, 87, 89, 90, 91, 92, 96, 97, 98, 99, 100, 118, 121, 127, 130, 132, 137, 141, 144, 161, 168, 208
Moore, Andrew B. 26, 29, 42, 43, 51, 52, 54, 57, 59, 72, 82, 130
Moore, Charles H. 187
Moore, Thomas O. 66
Moro Castle, Havana, Cuba 107
Morris, J.C. 153
Morris Island, South Carolina 26
Mullany, John 116, 139, 145
Murdaugh, William 93, 139, 140, 151

National Intelligencer 84
National Park Service 212
vessel *Neaffie* 190, 194, 195
Nelson, Samuel 91
New Orleans Bee 80
New Orleans, Louisiana 1, 4, 9, 57, 64, 71, 90, 98, 176, 209
New Orleans Picayune 152
New York City, New York 17, 26, 48, 63, 65, 74, 75, 77, 90, 94, 97, 105, 110, 112, 113, 114, 118, 119, 120, 121, 123, 125, 132, 148, 152, 159, 207
New York Herald 14, 170
New York State 179
New York Times 101
New York Tribune 128
New York Volunteers, 6th Infantry Regiment 180, 181, 182, 189, 191, 192, 194, 195, 196, 197, 205, 211; Company A 180; Company B 180, 182; Company C 180, 191; Company D 180, 191; Company E 180, 182; Company F 180, 191; Company G 180, 193, 211; Company H 180, 191; Company I 180, 186, 211; Company K 180, 191
New York Volunteers, 75th Infantry Regiment 205, 206
U.S.S. *Niagara* 157, 167, 168, 171, 175, 178, 185, 188, 200, 201, 202, 203, 204
Nicolay, John J. 115
Norfolk Navy Yard 105
Norfolk, Virginia 5, 55, 102
Norristown, Pennsylvania 169
U.S.S. *North Carolina* 83, 101, 102, 120
North Carolina State 184

Oakfield, Florida 209, 210
O'Brien, soldier 191
O'Donnell, Frederick 66
O'Hara, Theodore 76
Old Point Comfort, Virginia 55
Old Quarantine Grounds, Staten Island, New York 180
vessel *Oregon* 48
vessel *Oriental* 155, 162, 170
Orr, James L. 50

Pacific Mail Steamship Company 111
Palafox Street, Pensacola, Florida 40, 45, 211
Panzacola Indians 3
Parkersburg, Virginia 169
Parsonage, William 192
Pass a L'Outre, Mississippi River 168
Paulding, Hiram 82
U.S.S. *Pawnee* 68, 90, 102, 120, 132, 138
Pearson, sailing master 35
Pendergrast, Garrett J. 29, 54, 63, 65, 70, 113
U.S.S. *Pensacola* 6
Pensacola Bay 1, 4, 5, 6, 7, 9, 14, 21, 23, 24, 29, 30, 33, 41, 43, 51, 53, 54, 55, 57, 58, 60, 61, 62, 69, 71, 72, 73, 80, 85, 86, 88, 92, 93, 98, 100, 104, 105, 106, 107, 109, 113, 117, 125, 134, 150, 155, 168, 174, 184, 185, 196, 198, 205
Pensacola, Florida 1, 2, 3, 9, 10, 11, 19, 20, 23, 25, 26, 27, 29, 37, 38, 39, 43, 44, 45, 47, 48, 51, 54, 56, 58, 59, 60, 61, 62, 64, 65, 71, 74, 75, 77, 82, 83, 84, 85, 86, 87, 88, 89, 90, 92, 95, 96, 97, 100, 101, 102, 103, 113, 114, 115, 127, 128, 130, 139, 141, 150, 155, 176, 190, 191, 194, 195, 203, 205, 208, 210, 212

Pensacola Gazette 108
Pensacola Historical Society 2
Pensacola Lighthouse 4, 54, 153, 202
Pensacola Naval Aviation Training Station 211
Pensacola Navy Yard 5, 6, 11, 12, 13, 20, 27, 29, 37, 38, 39, 40, 44, 45, 48, 49, 50, 52, 54, 58, 59, 64, 71, 72, 73, 78, 83, 88, 89, 94, 100, 116, 150, 161, 185, 188, 190, 206, 209, 211; dry dock 6, 13, 20; 25, 165, 166, 167, 176, 206; seamen detachment 27, 29, 30, 33, 35, 44, 45, 63, 65, 67, 77, 86
Perdido Key 3, 7, 100, 174
U.S.S. *Perry* 136
Perry, Edward A. 26
Perry, Madison S. 11, 26, 30, 50, 51, 54, 75, 83
Pettus, John 131
vessel *Philadelphia* 119, 127, 148, 155, 156, 158, 169
Philadelphia, Pennsylvania 145
Pickens, Andrew 7
Pickens, Francis W. 15, 26, 50, 77, 97, 98, 102, 105, 114, 128, 131, 132
Pierce, Franklin 71
Pittsburgh, Pennsylvania 31, 40
Plaza Ferdinand, Pensacola, Florida 211
U.S.S. *Pocahontas* 70, 102, 135, 138
Pollard, Alabama 11, 208
Poor, Charles H. 69, 73, 145, 162, 168, 169
Porter, Carlisle 114
Porter, David Dixon 77, 106, 107, 111, 112, 113, 114, 115, 116, 117, 118, 120, 123, 125, 126, 127, 130, 136, 146, 148, 150, 152, 153, 155, 159, 162, 166, 167, 168, 169, 170, 209, 210, 211
Porter, Essex 114
Porter, Georgy 114
Porter, John 40
Portsmouth, New Hampshire 19, 62, 94, 157, 171, 172, 173
U.S.S. *Potomac* 195
Powderhorn, Texas 64
Powell, Levin M. 38, 40, 195
U.S.S. *Powhatan* 63, 70, 77, 78, 100, 101, 103, 105, 113, 115, 116, 117, 118, 120, 121, 122, 123, 124, 126, 127, 130, 136, 138, 145, 146, 149, 150, 151, 153, 155, 159, 162, 163, 168, 169, 175, 209
Price, Paymaster 94
Pryor, Roger 137
Pugh, James L. 86

Rahway, New Jersey 207
Randolph, John 42
Randolph, Victor M. 38, 42, 43, 45, 52, 59, 76, 86
Reese, Chauncey B. 71, 193, 194, 195

U.S.S. *Release* 100, 155
Renshaw, Francis T. 12, 13, 23, 27, 28, 29, 36, 39, 44, 56, 78
Republican party 26, 59, 79, 80, 91
U.S.S. *Richmond* 200, 201, 202, 204
Richmond, Virginia 55, 130, 166, 179
Ripley, James 171
U.S.S. *Roanoke* 136
Robertson, James 194, 195
Robertson, John 55, 58
Roe, Francis A. 126
Roman, Andrew B. 81, 84
Rome Court House, 169
Ronckendorff, William 145, 154
Rosecrans, William 169
Rowan, Stephen 132, 138
Rumph, James David 160
Rumph, Langdon 160
Russell, John 186
Russell, William Howard 93, 97, 101, 118, 162, 163, 164, 165
Russia 109

U.S.S. *Sabine* 29, 54, 60, 67, 69, 70, 73, 91, 93, 97, 103, 108, 128, 133, 139, 140, 141, 145, 146, 151, 153, 157, 163, 172, 172
Saint, Daniel 23, 24, 40
St. Augustine Examiner 15
St. Augustine, Florida 20
St. John, Power & Co. 92
U.S.S. *St. Louis* 54, 60, 69, 70, 73, 97, 140, 145, 151, 159, 168, 170
St. Louis, Missouri 166, 179
Santa Rosa Island 1, 3, 6, 7, 12, 27, 31, 33, 35, 38, 40, 41, 44, 48, 53, 55, 58, 61, 63, 66, 68, 69, 71, 73, 74, 76, 77, 88, 89, 93, 95, 96, 103, 104, 105, 106, 108, 112, 116, 120, 121, 127, 128, 133, 134, 135, 140, 141, 144, 146, 149, 150, 151, 160, 161, 162, 165, 168, 171, 172, 174, 176, 178, 181, 184, 185, 186, 188, 189, 191, 194, 196, 197, 199, 200, 205, 209, 211
Santo Domingo 120
Saunders, John S. 44, 45, 61, 62, 65, 74
U.S.S. *Savannah* 130, 139
Savannah, Georgia 20, 24
Scott, William 192
Scott, Winfield 17, 18, 22, 23, 26, 31, 44, 45, 68, 73, 79, 81, 83, 87, 88, 89, 93, 94, 96, 101, 102, 104, 105, 106, 107, 108, 109, 114, 120, 130, 136, 148, 149, 152, 155, 179, 205
Second Seminole War 55, 66 114, 110, 208
Seibels, John 42, 43, 54, 57
U.S.S. *Seminole* 6
Seward, Frederick 103, 123
Seward, William H. 16, 71, 77, 79, 80, 82, 83, 84, 85, 86, 87, 90, 91, 96, 102, 103, 104, 105, 106, 107, 108, 109, 110, 112, 113, 114, 116, 118, 121, 123, 126, 128, 130, 131, 132, 135, 136, 137, 144, 155
Seymour, Truman 169
Sharp, William 142
Shaughnessy, John 191
Shiloh, Tennessee 169, 196, 200, 208, 209
Ship Island, Mississippi 209
Shipley, Alexander 176, 194, 195
Silloway, Jacob 191
Slack, William B. 13
Slemmer, Adam 13, 15, 18, 20, 23, 24, 25, 27, 29, 30, 31, 32, 33, 34, 35, 38, 39, 41, 42, 43, 44, 46, 47, 48, 49, 51, 52, 53, 54, 55, 58, 59, 60, 61, 63, 64, 65, 67, 70, 71, 76, 77, 82, 83, 87, 88, 89, 92, 96, 104, 129, 133, 134, 135, 139, 140, 141, 143, 145, 150, 157, 158, 169, 184, 196, 200
Slemmer, Albert "Bertie" 14, 31, 48
Slemmer, Caroline 14, 22, 28, 31, 40, 48, 139, 169
Slidell, John 56, 59, 60, 61
Smith, Albert 140
Smith, Caleb B. 102
Smith, John 187
Snead, Abner 56
U.S.S. *South Carolina* 172, 173
South Carolina State 11, 14, 16, 18, 23, 30, 42, 50, 51, 65, 77, 81, 93, 108, 119
Southern Atlantic Ocean 5
Southern Messenger 83
Southwest Pass, Mississippi River 168
Spain 109
Sprotson, John G. 187
Stanton, Edwin M. 17, 58, 126
vessel *Star of the West* 18, 22, 26, 83, 90, 173
vessel *State of Georgia* 182
Staten Island, New York 125, 126, 180
Steece, Tecumseh 187
Steward, Charles 82, 170
Storer, George W. 58
Straights of Florida 4
Stringham, Silas H. 82, 83, 84, 113, 115, 122, 123, 124
Strong, James 88, 105
U.S.S. *Supply* 12, 13, 27, 31, 34, 36, 37, 38, 39, 41, 42, 43, 45, 48, 63, 65, 74, 75, 94, 97, 100, 111, 120, 145, 155, 156, 159

Talbot, Theodore 128, 132
Tallahassee, Florida 11, 12, 19, 30, 75, 76, 128
Taney, Roger B. 79, 81
Tartar's Point, Pensacola Bay 4
Taylor, Franck 193
Taylor, Zachary 66
Tennessee River 208
Texas Department 74
Texas State 19, 88, 102, 131, 184

Theberath, Jacob 186
Thomas, Lorenzo 55, 197, 198
Thomas, Philip F. 16
Thompson, Jacob M. 16
vessel *Time* 190, 206
Tombigbee River 4
Toombs, Robert 19, 118, 120, 121, 131
vessel *Tortugas* 71
Totten, Joseph G. 4, 8, 75, 83, 84, 103, 104, 119, 120
Toucey, Isaac 17, 18, 29, 31, 39, 44, 45, 52, 54, 55, 56, 58, 59, 61, 65, 73, 74, 78, 81, 129
Tower, Zealous B. 22, 23, 74, 132, 175
Townsend, Edward D. 88, 93
vessel *Turel* 210
Travers, Patrick 64
Twiggs, David E. 74, 88
Tyler, John 54, 58, 79

vessel *Uncle Ben* 121, 132, 138
United States Army 4, 6, 18, 23, 42, 55, 74, 77, 83, 96, 99, 188
United States Army Adjutant General 15, 31, 56, 62, 87, 104, 111, 119, 148, 154, 160, 170, 173, 176, 179, 197
United States Army Corps of Engineers 4, 9, 22, 72
United States Army Department of Florida 144, 161, 173
United States Army Department of the Ohio 169
United States Army Department of the Ohio and Cumberland 169
United States Arsenal, Apalachicola, Florida 20
United States Arsenal, Baton Rouge, Louisiana 92
United States Arsenal, Charleston, South Carolina 15
United States Arsenal, Mount Vernon, Alabama 20, 83
United States Artillery 193; 1st Regiment, Company B 45; 1st Regiment, Company E 15, 55, 183; 1st Regiment, Company F 172; 1st Regiment, Company G 13, 23, 27, 31, 33, 51, 55, 59, 64, 65, 66, 77, 86, 157, 158, 169, 184; 1st Regiment, Company H 15, 55; 2nd Regiment, Company A 110, 179, 194; 2nd Regiment, Company C 30; 2nd Regiment, Company H 9, 146, 194; 2nd Regiment, Company K 146; 2nd Regiment, Company M 110, 152
United States Capitol 71, 75, 79
United States Central Post Office 71
United States Congress 16, 18, 19, 50, 78, 80, 109, 177
United States Congress House Select Committee 78
United States Constitution 16, 18, 28, 41, 47, 80

United States Government 50, 54, 82, 85, 92, 93, 94, 118, 127, 137, 144
United States Infantry: 3rd Regiment, Company A 193; 3rd Regiment, Company C 110, 194; 3rd Regiment, Company E 110, 144, 179; 16th Regiment 169
United States Marine Corps 5, 13, 25, 37, 38, 44, 94, 143
United States Military Academy 9, 10, 13, 14, 22, 44, 55, 66, 71, 79, 86, 103, 110, 137, 189, 207
United States Naval Academy 114
United States Navy 4, 12, 13, 40, 44, 49, 55, 70, 75, 77, 83, 97, 117, 172, 188; East Indies Squadron 11; Gulf Blockading Squadron 159, 162, 173, 178, 187; Home Squadron 12, 29, 31, 34, 43, 52, 54, 65, 69, 70, 77, 102, 104, 113, 196; West Indies Squadron 5
United States Navy Department 18, 23, 24, 27, 35, 38, 50, 56, 74, 82, 83, 93, 94, 97, 105, 114, 120, 121, 122, 123, 128, 129, 138, 139, 140, 153, 154, 155, 159, 162, 174, 176, 185, 187
United States Navy Detailing Department 82, 112, 113, 115, 117, 124
United States Ordnance Department 44
United States Senate 60
United States State Department 91, 103, 104, 112, 113, 123, 128, 155
United States Treasury 92, 111
United States War Department 15, 18, 19, 22, 23, 24, 27, 32, 33, 34, 44, 45, 49, 53, 55, 61, 65, 67, 70, 81, 83, 85, 87, 93, 105, 108, 112, 120, 122, 127, 129, 138, 170, 172, 182, 183, 197, 199, 205
Usabel, Gaizka 2

vessel *Vanderbilt* 177, 181, 182

Vera Cruz, Mexico 3, 12, 29, 31, 34, 38, 39, 52, 54, 63, 65, 68, 70, 74, 77, 100, 104, 113, 125
Villepigue, John 202
U.S.S. *Vincennes* 200
C.S.S. *Virginia* 142
Virginia State 61, 65, 184, 199
Vogdes, Israel 55, 56, 62, 66, 67, 69, 70, 71, 74, 75, 81, 84, 85, 86, 87, 88, 89, 92, 93, 94, 96, 97, 101, 102, 103, 104, 105, 108, 109, 129, 130, 140, 142, 143, 144, 145, 163, 177, 178, 193, 195, 196, 199

U.S.S. *Wabash* 136
Walke, Henry 12, 13, 27, 28, 29, 31, 33, 36, 38, 42, 45, 48, 65, 74
Walker, Leroy Pope 77, 82, 85, 90, 96, 121, 127, 128, 130, 132, 133, 137, 141, 142, 150, 155, 165, 166, 179, 188
Walker, William 55, 61, 67, 68, 69, 73, 84, 89, 145
Walsh, Boatswain's Mate 41
War of 1812 18, 82
War with Mexico 10, 66, 110, 128, 189, 208
Ward, James H. 83, 84, 88
Warrington, Lewis 4, 5, 9, 20
Warrington, Florida 2, 5, 13, 15, 28, 31, 35, 36, 38, 40, 58, 65, 120, 133, 204
Washburne, Elihu 79
Washington, District of Columbia 19, 44, 45, 50, 51, 52, 53, 54, 55, 56, 57, 58, 59, 61, 63, 65, 68, 69, 70, 71, 72, 75, 77, 78, 79, 82, 83, 85, 88, 89, 93, 96, 97, 100, 101, 102, 103, 104, 105, 106, 109, 111, 112, 115, 118, 119, 128, 131, 141, 148, 153, 166, 179
Washington, Littleton Quinton Dennis 82, 87, 90, 96, 120, 127
Washington Navy Yard 105

U.S.S. *Water Witch* 145, 146, 154, 170, 175, 199
Watson, Josiah 13, 37, 38, 39, 44
Watts, R. H. 23, 24, 40, 134
Webster, Daniel 81
Wells, Gideon 81, 82, 83, 84, 88, 93, 100, 102, 105, 107, 108, 113, 115, 116, 117, 118, 120, 121, 123, 124, 128, 129, 139, 141, 142, 145, 151, 156, 159, 162, 171, 177, 185, 187
White, Assistant Engineer 187
Whithers, Jones M. 86
Wigfall, Louis T. 26, 87, 163
Wilcox, Richard 134
Willard's Hotel, Washington, District of Columbia 115, 124
vessel *William P. Judah* 185, 186, 187, 188
Williams, B.D. 133
Williamson, Lieutenant 145, 147
Wilson, William "Billy" 179, 180, 181, 191, 192, 193, 194, 200, 205, 206, 211
Wilson's Zouave Volunteer Battalion 180
Winder, John H. 13, 22, 59
Wisconsin State Historical Society 2
Wittemore, James 56
Wood, Robert 94, 143
Wood, Roger C. 88
Woods, Charles R. 26
Woolsey, Florida 2, 5, 9, 14, 28, 31, 38, 204
Woolsey, Melanchthon 5
Worden, John L. 130, 139, 140, 141, 142, 155
U.S.S. *Wyandotte* 13, 20, 25, 27, 28, 29, 31, 34, 35, 37, 40, 42, 43, 45, 48, 49, 52, 53, 54, 56, 58, 63, 68, 69, 70, 73, 74, 76, 97, 104, 116, 127, 134, 139, 143, 145, 146, 147, 151, 170, 175, 186

vessel *Yankee* 121, 132, 138
Yulee, David L. 19, 25, 30, 50, 51

www.ingramcontent.com/pod-product-compliance
Ingram Content Group UK Ltd.
Pitfield, Milton Keynes, MK11 3LW, UK
UKHW050532150426
5217IPUK00026B/1902